Oracle Business Intelligence Enterprise Edition 12c

Second Edition

Build your organization's Business Intelligence system

Adrian Ward

Christian Screen

Haroun Khan

BIRMINGHAM - MUMBAI

Oracle Business Intelligence Enterprise Edition 12c

Second Edition

Copyright © 2017 Packt Publishing

All rights reserved. No part of this book may be reproduced, stored in a retrieval system, or transmitted in any form or by any means, without the prior written permission of the publisher, except in the case of brief quotations embedded in critical articles or reviews.

Every effort has been made in the preparation of this book to ensure the accuracy of the information presented. However, the information contained in this book is sold without warranty, either express or implied. Neither the authors, nor Packt Publishing, and its dealers and distributors will be held liable for any damages caused or alleged to be caused directly or indirectly by this book.

Packt Publishing has endeavored to provide trademark information about all of the companies and products mentioned in this book by the appropriate use of capitals. However, Packt Publishing cannot guarantee the accuracy of this information.

First published: July 2012
Second edition: April 2017

Production reference: 1140417

Published by Packt Publishing Ltd.
Livery Place
35 Livery Street
Birmingham
B3 2PB, UK.
ISBN 978-1-78646-471-2

www.packtpub.com

Credits

Authors

Adrian Ward

Christian Screen

Haroun Khan

Reviewer

Bill Anderson

Commissioning Editor

Veena Pagare

Acquisition Editor

Tushar Gupta

Content Development Editor

Amrita Noronha

Technical Editor

Akash Patel

Nilesh Sawakhande

Copy Editor

Safis Editing

Project Coordinator

Shweta H Birwatkar

Proofreader

Safis Editing

Indexer

Aishwarya Gangawane

Graphics

Tania Dutta

Production Coordinator

Arvindkumar Gupta

About the Authors

Adrian Ward is an Oracle ACE Associate who started working in Siebel Analytics back in 2001 and quickly realized the potential in the technology. He formed the UK's first independent consultancy focusing purely on OBIEE (nee Siebel Analytics) and Oracle BI Applications. He has led many large successful OBIEE implementations in a wide range of business sectors, from investment banking to military operations. His deep technical OBIEE and BI Applications knowledge has been applied on dozens of projects throughout the globe, including HR, Sales, Service, Pharma, and Custom Analytics, which is enabling hundreds of thousands of users in their day-to-day roles.

He was also one of the first bloggers on Oracle BIEE at `http://www.obiee.info` and today runs the Addidici OBIEE consultancy, which has operations in the UK, Europe, and South Africa. Adrian runs one of the largest Oracle BI networking groups on LinkedIn -- *Oracle Business Intelligence*, is an active tweeter (`@Addidici`), is a speaker at Oracle conferences, and helps others learn.

In his spare time, he loves sailing at Hayling Island, skiing, enjoying life with his family, and learning new technologies.

I would like to dedicate this book to my wife Sarah, and wonderful children, Hugh and Harriet who are the coolest dudes in the world.

Many thanks to Christian and Haroun for their patience in writing the second book, I hope you enjoyed it as much as I did.

Christian Screen (@christianscreen) is an Oracle ACE, technologist, and Business Intelligence evangelist with over 20 years of experience in technology ranging from low-level programming, e-commerce, Data Warehousing, Hyperion Enterprise Performance Management, product management, IoT, and of course, analytics. Founder of Art of BI Software and Consulting Group, one of Oracle's top Oracle Analytics partners in North America, his company was acquired by Datavail (@datavail) Corporation in 2016.

In his spare time, he enjoys writing technical articles, learning new technologies, inventing new products, writing software, spending time with his family, trying to change the world, and running his blog and podcast which are read and heard all across the globe.

I would like to thank my co-authors on this book, in particular Adrian Ward, with extreme gratitude for completing many of the chores related to the care, watering, and feeding required to push the writing and publishing of this book along - ultimately over the finish line.

Indeed, I thank my wife and children for putting up with my late night writing sessions and booked-up weekends working on this book and the mental blockage that rides along with such a task. I thank my mother, brothers, and sister for their support in my endeavors, which in life attributes to the person I've been able to become, giving me the ability to contribute in such challenging enterprises.

Without the support of the user group communities such as ODTUG, IOUG, and UKOUG and great conferences such as Collaborate, KScope, and Oracle Open World, our message of great business intelligence wouldn't be as strong. Thank you all those who: purchased this book, support your local user group communities, follow us on social media, read our blogs, and attend our presentation sessions at conferences; you make efforts such as writing this book possible.

Haroun Khan is one of Europe's leading OBIEE consultants. A computer science graduate of Imperial College, London, he has been involved with OBIEE from its early days as an acquisition from nQuire by Siebel, and subsequently as part of the Oracle family. Haroun worked as a consultant on projects worldwide for Siebel and as a Principal Consultant for Oracle over a period of 10 years. He has specialized in BI and data warehousing over a longer period including time working at MicroStrategy.

Haroun is also an entrepreneur, successfully founding and currently running the online travel site `https://www.jrpass.com/`. His experience in e-commerce has given him new insight into how analytics is vital to the running of any business nowadays. He engages with cohort analysis, clickstream analytics, and conversion tracking.

He still freelances in leading and designing projects in the traditional BI and data warehousing space. In his downtime, Haroun likes to climb, is an avid squash player, and can sometimes be found prone, deep in despair, as he tries his hands at writing a novel.

About the Reviewer

Bill Anderson is a business analytics consultant with extensive experience in data visualization, Oracle BI, Oracle BI applications, BI cloud services, and Hyperion Essbase. He has a proven ability to integrate disparate heterogeneous data sources using Oracle Business Intelligence, Oracle Hyperion, and several relational database management systems. Bill has led multiple projects developing moderate-to-complex Oracle Business Intelligence solutions, working side-by-side with his clients in many industries. He is also a course instructor for a number of business analytics training courses. Outside of work, Bill dabbles in competition bar-b-que.

> *I would like to thank my family and friends for supporting me throughout my career and the authors for giving me the opportunity to work with them on this great book.*

www.PacktPub.com

For support files and downloads related to your book, please visit `www.PacktPub.com`.

Did you know that Packt offers eBook versions of every book published, with PDF and ePub files available? You can upgrade to the eBook version at `www.PacktPub.com` and as a print book customer, you are entitled to a discount on the eBook copy. Get in touch with us at `service@packtpub.com` for more details.

At `www.PacktPub.com`, you can also read a collection of free technical articles, sign up for a range of free newsletters and receive exclusive discounts and offers on Packt books and eBooks.

`https://www.packtpub.com/mapt`

Get the most in-demand software skills with Mapt. Mapt gives you full access to all Packt books and video courses, as well as industry-leading tools to help you plan your personal development and advance your career.

Why subscribe?

- Fully searchable across every book published by Packt
- Copy and paste, print, and bookmark content
- On demand and accessible via a web browser

Customer Feedback

Thanks for purchasing this Packt book. At Packt, quality is at the heart of our editorial process. To help us improve, please leave us an honest review on this book's Amazon page at `http://www.amazon.com/dp/1786464713`.

If you'd like to join our team of regular reviewers, you can e-mail us at `customerreviews@packtpub.com`. We award our regular reviewers with free eBooks and videos in exchange for their valuable feedback. Help us be relentless in improving our products!

Table of Contents

Preface	1
Chapter 1: Oracle BI 12c Architecture	9
Let's look at the big picture	9
Terminology differences from Oracle BI 11g	11
What is Oracle Fusion Middleware?	12
Why is there a database repository for OBIEE?	13
Overall components	14
Java components	15
Action Service	15
Visual Analyzer	15
Administrative Components	15
SOA Web Service	15
Oracle BI Office	15
Oracle Real-Time Decisions (RTD)	15
Oracle BI Presentation Service plugin	16
Oracle BI Publisher	16
Security Services	16
System Components	16
BI Server	16
BI Presentation Server	17
BI Scheduler	17
BI JavaHost	17
BI Server Cluster Controller	17
Essbase	18
WebLogic Server	19
A few WebLogic Server nuances	19
WebLogic Domain	20
WebLogic Administration Server	21
WebLogic Managed Server	21
WebLogic Node Manager	22
System tools controlled by WebLogic	23
Security	24
Managing by Application Roles	25
Security providers	25
Identity Store	26
Credential Store	26
Policy Store	27

System requirements	27
Client tools	28
Multi-User Development Environment	28
Certifications matrix	30
Scaling out Oracle BI 12c	31
Pre-configuration run-down	31
Shared storage	31
Clustering	32
Vertical versus horizontal	33
Oracle BI Server Cluster Controller	33
Failover and high-availability	34
Enterprise Deployment Guide	34
Directory folder structure	35
Log files / diagnostics	37
Configuration files	37
Download Oracle BI 12c	38
System requirements	39
References	40
A review - what I should now know!	40
Summary	40
Chapter 2: Installing the Prerequisite Software	**41**
Installation overview	42
Installation media	42
System requirements	45
Installing Java	46
Installing the WebLogic Server	47
Installing the metadata schemas	51
Creating the database and user	51
Installing the schemas	53
Gotchas	57
A review - what I should now know!	57
Summary	57
Chapter 3: Installing on Windows Server 2012	**59**
Installation overview	59
Installation media	60
Installing the BI Server software	60
Configuring the database for the BI Server schema	65
Configuring the BI application	69
What is installed?	77

Folder structure	77
Shortcut reference variables	78
Configuring start and stop links	78
A review - what I should now know!	80
Summary	80

Chapter 4: Reviewing the Features of the Reporting Repository — 81

Integrated tools	82
Answers	83
Dashboards	84
Published Reporting	84
Actionable Intelligence	84
Performance Management	85
Marketing	85
MapViewer	85
Administration	86
Briefing books	86
Visual Analyzer	87
Search	87
Help	87
Office integration	87
The home screen	88
Catalog	89
New	89
Recent	90
Help	91
Administration	92
Session Management	96
Maintenance and troubleshooting	97
Issue SQL	97
Catalog	98
Structure of the Presentation Catalog	99
Hidden items	100
File management	101
XML files	101
Object copying	102
Catalog deployments	103
Securing catalog objects	103
Multiple personal dashboards	104
Permission inheritance	105
A review - what I should now know!	106

Summary	106
Chapter 5: Installing and Configuring Client Tools	**107**
Installing the client software	108
Configuring a connection to the OBIEE Server	110
Configuring a connection to the database	114
Creating shortcuts	115
Testing the client software	115
A review - what I should now know!	118
Summary	119
Chapter 6: Understanding the Systems Management Tools	**121**
Let's talk management tools	122
WebLogic Server Administration Control	122
First access and checkpoint	123
Servers	124
Clusters	125
Machines / IP address or DNS	126
Data Sources / JDBC connections	127
Security Realms	130
WebLogic Server is its own application	132
Using WLST	133
Enterprise Manager Fusion Middleware Control	136
Getting around in EM	136
BI Foundation Domain Dashboard	137
Overview tab	138
Availability tab	138
Configuration	139
General	139
Performance	139
Presentation	139
Mail	139
Diagnostics	140
Log Messages	140
Log Configuration	140
Security	140
Oracle BI 12c Lifecycle Management	141
What is a BAR File?	142
Finding the default BAR files	143
Deploying, migrating, and backing up artifacts	143
Snapshot Service Instance artifacts - exporting to a BAR	143
Migrating a Service Instance Snapshot - importing the BAR	146
Moving just the RPD - no BAR necessary	148

Download the RPD only - no BAR	148
Uploading just the RPD - no BAR	149
Stopping and starting System Components	151
Stopping Oracle BI 12c	151
Starting Oracle BI 12c	152
Patching Oracle BI 12c	153
Upgrading Oracle BI 12c	153
Checking the logs	154
Creating users, roles, and associations	**155**
Creating users and groups in WebLogic Server	**156**
Assigning users to groups	**158**
Creating and assigning Application Roles	**159**
JMX, MBeans, Java, and interfacing Oracle BI	**162**
Migrating FMW Security to other environments	**163**
FMW Core Security files and OPSS	163
FMW Security Import/Export utility	**165**
Using the Security Realm migration utility	**165**
Oracle BI Publisher system management	**167**
Monitoring system performance	**167**
Have a backup plan!	**168**
Recommendations for further learning	**169**
A review - what I should know now!	**170**
Summary	**170**
Chapter 7: Developing the BI Server Repository	**171**
Prerequisites	**172**
Repository architecture	**172**
Physical layer	**173**
Creating an RPD and importing metadata	174
Elements of the physical layer	180
Database object	180
Connection Pools	183
Physical catalog and schemas	186
Physical tables	186
Physical join	191
Consistency check	195
Table aliases and naming conventions	196
Business layer	**198**
Business model	199
Logical tables	200
Logical table sources	203
Logical columns	203

Logical joins	207
Dimension hierarchies	211
Number of elements	214
Presentation layer	**217**
Subject areas	218
Best practices in the presentation layer	220
Aliases	223
Implicit Fact	224
Calculated measures	226
Logical column calculation	226
Expression Builder	229
Physical column calculation	231
Time series measures	233
Level-based measure	237
Federated and fragmented content	**239**
Vertical federation-aggregation or level-based	240
Horizontal federation	240
Fragmentation	240
Fragmentation example--content-based	241
Variables and initialization blocks	**246**
A review - what I should now know!	**254**
Additional research suggestions	254
Summary	**254**

Chapter 8: Creating Dashboards and Analyses — 257

Creating our first analysis	**258**
Creating our first Dashboard	**269**
Analysis building - more details	**272**
Views	284
Tables	285
Graphs	290
Pivot Tables	293
Narratives	295
Performance Tiles	296
Recap	300
Prompts	301
In analysis prompting	301
Result layout	308
Column hiding and showing	314
Conditional display	315

Recap	321
Master Detail linking	321
Saved Dashboards	324
Calculated data	324
Saved columns	331
Pretty useful stuff!	332
A review - what I should now know!	333
Summary	333
Chapter 9: Agents and Action Framework	**335**
Agents	336
Mail server setup	336
Creating the Agent	338
Actions	349
BI Navigation	349
Web navigation and passing a parameter	353
Adding some conditionality	356
Note on Invoke Actions	358
A review - what I should know now!	359
Additional research suggestions	359
Oracle documentation on Actions	360
Summary	360
Chapter 10: Developing Reports Using BI Publisher	**361**
Don't miss the installation integration checkpoint!	362
What's all this XML talk?	363
Where does BI Publisher excel?	363
Oracle BI Foundation versus Oracle BI Publisher	365
New features and enhancements	366
Improved Oracle BI 12c look and feel	366
Delivering documents to the cloud	366
Better encryption and security	366
Report design basics, terminology, and locations	367
Report design components	367
Data model	367
Layout	367
Properties	368
Translations	368
Where to administer BI Publisher	368
Default embedded BI Publisher configurations	369
Where to build a data model	369
Where to add a data source connection	370

What is a JNDI data source?	371
Let's get publishing	**372**
Administration management of BI Publisher	372
Accessing the BI Publisher Administration page	373
Verifying application roles	373
Creating the data source JDBC connection	374
Creating a file (XLS) data source	376
Verifying application role data source privileges	377
Setting up a data model	379
Creating a new Presentation Catalog folder	380
Creating a new data model	381
Creating an SQL query data set	384
Adjusting data set display names	387
Creating a parameter	388
Creating a list of values	391
Connecting the parameter to the list of values	392
Getting the sample data	393
Creating a BI Publisher report using the Layout Editor	396
Auditing and monitoring BI Publisher	401
Modifying a few configuration files	401
Enabling Audit Policy in the Fusion Middleware Control Enterprise Manager	**403**
Connecting to the Audit Framework	403
Viewing the auditing log file	404
Timeout issues	405
Connecting to Oracle BI server data sources	**405**
BI Publisher Application Programming Interface	406
BI Publisher Scheduler	406
High availability	406
A review - what I should now know!	**407**
Summary	**407**
Chapter 11: Usage Tracking	**409**
What is usage tracking?	**409**
Setting up usage tracking	410
Setting up database tables	410
Setting up the BI Server repository	411
Updating the BI Server configuration	416
Analyzing usage	**418**
Usage measures	418

Customizing your setup	420
Additional data	421
A review - what I should now know!	422
Summary	423

Chapter 12: Improving Performance — 425

What is poor performance?	425
Where can I improve the performance?	426
Hardware	427
Full speed ahead	428
More servers please	428
Database	429
BI Server	430
More performance tips	431
The use of cache	431
Setting up the cache	432
Web servers on top	433
Domain setup	433
A review - what I should now know!	433
Summary	434

Chapter 13: Using the BI Admin Change Management Utilities — 435

Problems with multiple developers	435
Merges	436
Three-way merge	437
Two-way merger	440
Multiuser development	441
Online development	441
Advantages and disadvantages	445
Multiuser Development Environment	446
Advantages and disadvantages	457
A review - what I should now know!	458
Additional research suggestions	458
Summary	458

Chapter 14: Ancillary Installation Options — 461

Oracle BI 12c on its own server	462
High availability and failover planning	462
Silent installation	463
Custom ports and port management	465
Installing Oracle BI 12c on *Nix	466
Listening on port 80	467
Configuring a HTTP proxy with the NGINX web server	468

Enabling compression on web servers	470
Setting up compression for the NGINX HTTP server	471
Automating starting and stopping	473
Scripting Windows Services	474
Ancillary application integration awareness	476
Recommendations for further learning	477
A review - what should I know now?	477
Summary	478

Chapter 15: Reporting Databases — 479

Theories and models	480
Reporting databases	483
Relational modeling	483
Dimensional modeling	484
Why is database theory important?	486
Designing your database - objectives, rules, and goals	486
Objectives	487
Rules	487
Rule 1 - complete dimensions	488
Rule 2 - build generic tables	489
Rule 3 - partition large tables	489
Rule 4 - prudent indexing	490
Rule 5 - aggregate everything	490
Rule 6 - constant analysis of usage and accuracy	491
Rule 7 - manage statistics	491
Rule 8 - understand the granularity	492
Goals	492
Goal 1 - keep it simple	493
Goal 2 - minimize Type 2 Slowly Changing Dimensions	493
Goal 3 - use data, not functions	493
Goal 4 - minimize joins	493
Goal 5 - reduce snowflaking	494
Goal 6 - make it flexible	494
Design summary	494
Creating a warehouse	495
Source system assessment	495
Warehouse design	498
Warehouse tables	498
The match star schema	499
The tournament star schema	500
Populating and tuning	501
Monitoring and maintaining	501
Some definitions	502
A review - what you should know now!	503

Summary	503
Chapter 16: Customizing the Style of Dashboards	**505**
Multiple skins and styles in one environment	506
Hands-on - go time!	507
Changing styles	507
Creating your own look and feel - overview	509
Creating your style	511
Modifying the code	512
Updating your style	522
Alternative deployment method	523
Custom messages	528
A review - what I should now know!	529
Summary	529
Chapter 17: Upgrading to 12c	**531**
Checking the 11g system and files	532
Generation	533
Export bundle	534
Bundle contents	534
Importing the bundle	535
Import via the Configuration Assistant	535
Import via the BI Migration Script	538
Connectivity	539
Consistency check	539
Security and manual migration	540
Regression testing	541
Unit testing	541
Full regression testing	541
User acceptance testing	541
A review - what I should now know!	542
Summary	543
Index	**545**

Preface

Oracle Business Intelligence Enterprise Edition (OBIEE) 12c is packed full of features and has a fresh approach to information presentation, system management, and security. You will be introduced to these features, through a step-by-step guide to building a complete system from scratch. With this guide, you will be equipped with a basic understanding of what the product contains, how to install and configure it, and how to create effective business intelligence. This book contains the necessary information for a beginner to create a high performance OBIEE 12c system with effective presentation of information.

What this book covers

Chapter 1, *Oracle BI 12C Architecture*, reviews the key areas of the Oracle BI system and its Fusion Middleware architecture, with WebLogic at the core of the system.

Chapter 2, *Installing the Prerequisite Software*, covers the steps to install the software needed before we can install the Oracle Business Intelligence Enterprise Edition (OBIEE) software.

Chapter 3, *Installing on Windows Server 2012*, provides step-by-step instructions for installing Oracle BI 12c on Windows Server 2012.

Chapter 4, *Reviewing the Features of the Reporting Repository*, introduces the new interface of the catalog and the tools that are integrated into the presentation services. It also explores the various aspects of the catalog administration.

Chapter 5, *Installing and Configuring Client Tools*, focuses on installing the client software, configuring a connection to the OBIEE server and the database, creating shortcuts, and testing the client software.

Chapter 6, *Understanding the Systems Management Tools*, goes into greater detail about the system management tools that tie everything together. We'll explain what these components are, what they do, and how they work together. We delve into the navigation of these tools so that you become more familiar with the interfaces and learn what components are specific to Oracle BI 12c. We will also explore which key controls are used to maintain the Oracle BI 12c environment.

Preface

`Chapter 7`, *Developing the BI Server Repository*, covers the development of a simple RPD, from importing tables in a database through to how these objects are presented to us when we move on to creating an actual request.

`Chapter 8`, *Creating Dashboards and Analyses*, shows us how to create analyses, and how to present them on Dashboards. We demonstrate the various ways of representing and formatting data that are available, along with advice on best practices gained from implementation experience.

`Chapter 9`, *Agents and Action Framework*, looks at a few functions that Oracle BI provides in an attempt to help organizations succeed at moving a user from a transactional reporting mindset to an analytical one.

`Chapter 10`, *Developing Reports Using BI Publisher*, covers the main features of BI Publisher in order to get you up to speed in using the tool. We also mention some of the new features of 12c.

`Chapter 11`, *Usage Tracking*, describes how to activate the usage tracking feature and create useful reports from it. We also learn how to fine-tune and improve the usage tracking feature.

`Chapter 12`, *Improving Performance*, looks at some common techniques to reduce common bottlenecks that can exist in the process of delivering dashboards and reports to the users. We look across the whole system, defining poor performance, and, where required, show the steps to improve performance.

`Chapter 13`: *Using the BI Admin Change Management Utilities*, describes some of the other utilities in the Administration tool that can aid and simplify the development process.

`Chapter 14`: *Ancillary Installation Options*, highlights some of the most common post-configuration installation options and discusses many of the real-world implementations that we've experienced.

`Chapter 15`: *Reporting Databases*, covers a brief introduction to the theory and guidelines for creating a warehouse, and an example of creating a warehouse.

`Chapter 16`: *Customizing the Style of Dashboards*, shows how to change a style and how to create and implement a new style.

`Chapter 17`: *Upgrading to 12c*, covers how to utilize the Upgrade Assistant in order to migrate some of the core components to 12c.

What you need for this book

To work through the steps in this book, you will need access to a Windows machine, preferably running Windows Server (but Windows 10 can cope), and a copy of SQL Server 2016. If you don't have one, Microsoft has now released the SQL Server 2016 Developer Edition as a free download, and it will work just fine for working through the recipes.

You can download the developer edition from `https://www.microsoft.com/en-us/sql-server/sql-server-editions-developers` or use the shortcut `http://bit.ly/sql2016dev`.

To mirror our setup, you also need the AdventureWorks 2014 multi-dimensional database. You can find the samples database at `https://msftdbprodsamples.codeplex.com/releases/view/125550`.

You will also need to register an account on Oracle.com – don't worry, its free!

If you would like to practice the install on Linux, then we recommend that you download the Oracle VirtualBox software and load an Oracle Linux virtual machine.

Who this book is for

A wide variety of users will find this book valuable. If you are an IT professional, business analyst, project manager, and/or newcomer to Business Intelligence who wish to learn from self-paced professional guidance and actual implementation experience, this book is for you. Ultimately, this book is for anyone who needs a solid grounding in the subject of Oracle Business Intelligence.

Approach: this book will take you from one feature to another in a step-by-step manner and will teach how to create effective business intelligence using Oracle Business Intelligence Enterprise Edition. You will be taught how to create BI solutions and dashboards from scratch. There will be multiple modules in the book, each module spread in chapters, each of which will cover each aspect of business intelligence in a systematic manner.

Preface

Conventions

In this book, you will find a number of styles of text that distinguish between different kinds of information. Here are some examples of these styles, and an explanation of their meaning.

Code words in text, database table names, folder names, filenames, file extensions, pathnames, dummy URLs, user input, and Twitter handles are shown as follows: "Select the BI Publisher Reports folder, which you created in the previous exercise."

A block of code is set as follows:

```
select dg.DepartmentGroupName,
           d.CalendarYear,
           sum(f.Amount)
      from
           DimDepartmentGroup dg,
```

When we wish to draw your attention to a particular part of a code block, the relevant lines or items are set in bold:

```
DECLARE @collate sysname
SELECT @collate = convert(sysname, serverproperty('COLLATION'))
IF ( charindex(N'_CI', @collate) > 0 )
BEGIN
select @collate = replace(@collate, N'_CI', N'_CS')
```

Any command-line input or output is written as follows:

```
C:Javajdk1.8.0_74binjava.exe -jar
fmw_12.2.1.0.0_infrastructure.jar
```

New terms and **important words** are shown in bold. Words that you see on the screen, in menus or dialog boxes for example, appear in the text like this: "Click on the **Save** button."

Warnings or important notes appear in a box like this.

Tips and tricks appear like this.

Reader feedback

Feedback from our readers is always welcome. Let us know what you think about this book-what you liked or disliked. Reader feedback is important for us as it helps us develop titles that you will really get the most out of. To send us general feedback, simply e-mail feedback@packtpub.com, and mention the book's title in the subject of your message. If there is a topic that you have expertise in and you are interested in either writing or contributing to a book, see our author guide at www.packtpub.com/authors.

Customer support

Now that you are the proud owner of a Packt book, we have a number of things to help you to get the most from your purchase.

Downloading the example code

You can download the example code files for this book from your account at http://www.packtpub.com. If you purchased this book elsewhere, you can visit http://www.packtpub.com/support and register to have the files e-mailed directly to you.

You can download the code files by following these steps:

1. Log in or register to our website using your e-mail address and password.
2. Hover the mouse pointer on the **SUPPORT** tab at the top.
3. Click on **Code Downloads & Errata**.
4. Enter the name of the book in the **Search** box.
5. Select the book for which you're looking to download the code files.
6. Choose from the drop-down menu where you purchased this book from.
7. Click on **Code Download**.

Once the file is downloaded, please make sure that you unzip or extract the folder using the latest version of:

- WinRAR / 7-Zip for Windows
- Zipeg / iZip / UnRarX for Mac
- 7-Zip / PeaZip for Linux

Preface

The code bundle for the book is also hosted on GitHub at `https://github.com/PacktPublishing/Oracle-Business-Intelligence-Enterprise-Edition-12c`. We also have other code bundles from our rich catalog of books and videos available at `https://github.com/PacktPublishing/`. Check them out!

Downloading the color images of this book

We also provide you a PDF file that has color images of the screenshots/diagrams used in this book. The color images will help you better understand the changes in the output. You can download this file from: `https://www.packtpub.com/sites/default/files/downloads/OracleBusinessIntelligenceEnterpriseEdition12c_ColorImages.pdf`.

Errata

Although we have taken every care to ensure the accuracy of our content, mistakes do happen. If you find a mistake in one of our books-maybe a mistake in the text or the code-we would be grateful if you could report this to us. By doing so, you can save other readers from frustration and help us improve subsequent versions of this book. If you find any errata, please report them by visiting `http://www.packtpub.com/submit-errata`, selecting your book, clicking on the **Errata Submission Form** link, and entering the details of your errata. Once your errata are verified, your submission will be accepted and the errata will be uploaded to our website or added to any list of existing errata under the Errata section of that title.

To view the previously submitted errata, go to `https://www.packtpub.com/books/content/support` and enter the name of the book in the search field. The required information will appear under the **Errata** section.

Piracy

Piracy of copyrighted material on the Internet is an ongoing problem across all media. At Packt, we take the protection of our copyright and licenses very seriously. If you come across any illegal copies of our works in any form on the Internet, please provide us with the location address or website name immediately so that we can pursue a remedy.

Please contact us at `copyright@packtpub.com` with a link to the suspected pirated material.

We appreciate your help in protecting our authors and our ability to bring you valuable content.

Questions

If you have a problem with any aspect of this book, you can contact us at `questions@packtpub.com`, and we will do our best to address the problem.

1
Oracle BI 12c Architecture

Fans of the Oracle BI suite of products will find **Oracle Business Intelligence (Oracle BI)** 12c a refreshing software version, both from its visual advancements and its technical foundation changes. This version of Oracle BI brings Oracle's flagship analytics system to the next level while maintaining its core enterprise-architecture concepts. The updated architecture allows for easier scalability of the solution across multiple servers, brings departmental BI and data visualization concepts into the mix, and strengthens its deployment processes with its new lifecycle-management tools. This chapter focuses on an overview of the Oracle BI 12c architecture, with occasional references to its predecessor to give some perspective as to how far the Oracle BI 12 release has come in terms of a more straightforward implementation process and increased functionality.

Let's look at the big picture

Going right for the guts of the platform, it is best to understand how the Oracle BI 12c system is laid out by looking at the logical interoperability of the architectural components. Oracle BI 12c is a combination of several core technologies, which reside as common software components within the **Oracle Fusion Middleware (FMW)** stack inside the Oracle software eco-system.

Oracle BI 12c Architecture

The following illustration shows some of Oracle BI 12c's logical architecture components. Users of Oracle BI 11g will find some of this topology familiar, yet clearly different in many ways:

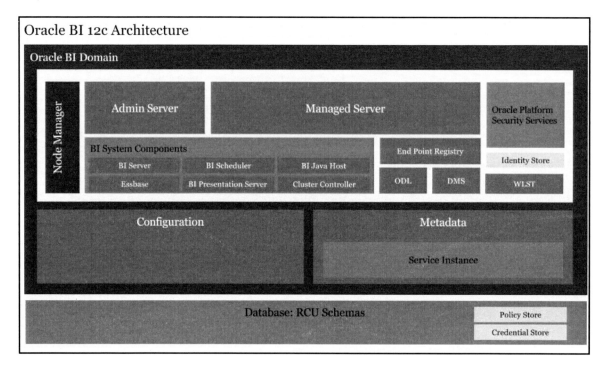

- **Oracle BI Domain**: This is the core architecture of Oracle BI 12c
- **WebLogic Server**: This is the chosen application server for Oracle BI 12c
- **Service Instance**: The structural housing for all critical Oracle BI artifacts (metadata) that would allow delineated movement from one environment to another (also multi-tenancy in future releases)
- **Java components**: These are the components which have been written in Java for Oracle BI 12c. They are deployed to the application server and WebLogic Server
- **BI System Components**: These are the components which have been written mainly in C++ for Oracle BI 12c
- **Oracle BI relational repository**: This is a set of database schemas (BIPLATFORM and MDS) that store metadata related to a specific Oracle BI 12c instance
- **Oracle BI filesystem**: This is the instructional set of physical files and directories containing configuration, logs, and metadata concerning the Oracle BI 12c instance

Similar to the Oracle BI 11g environment, once the software has been installed, all of the components in the architecture topology shown will exist. These components are transparent to the end users (that is, users in the organization who will view dashboards, reports, receive alerts, and so on). However, for the Oracle BI 12c administrators, and those that need to work with the technical aspect of the system, each of these areas of the Oracle BI 12c architecture is very important.

Terminology differences from Oracle BI 11g

There are a few noticeable changes in architecture terminology when comparing Oracle BI 11g to Oracle BI 12c. Let's call out a few of these key differences, as they are relevant to the language used throughout the book.

The first is that Fusion Middleware Home, as it relates to the installation of Oracle BI and the location of files in the file system, is now called **ORACLE HOME**. In Oracle BI 11g, Fusion Middleware Home was the base install folder for your Oracle BI 11g installation. The same concept is used in Oracle BI 12c; it is now rather more appropriately called the ORACLE HOME. This makes sense as traditionally, in an n-tier server architecture, the Oracle BI system is installed on its own application server. Therefore, it would be the only core Oracle technology application on a machine, not conflicting with any other Oracle home install locations from other applications.

The second is that the **Oracle Process Management and Notification Server (OPMN)** is no longer used to manage the Oracle BI System Components. This has been replaced by a more integrated process, which still allows start, stop, and status of Oracle BI to be controlled by the command line or through Enterprise Manager. These components, previously managed by the OPMN, are still referred to as the BI System Components (that is, BI Server, BI Presentation Server, and so on). This also means that the idea of instances is now replaced by Service Instances.

What is Oracle Fusion Middleware?

Oracle Fusion Middleware is taking on the enterprise challenge of bringing together the Oracle database and Oracle applications stacks. It is the middle-tier between them. Fusion Middleware is Oracle's go-forward foundation for the fusion of products between the database and application stack. Oracle has acquired many companies over the last decade for their technology or market share. This has taken it to a position of having excellent software. To achieve interoperability, a common layer had to be formed to fuse together the existing technologies, create efficiencies, and provide consistent delivery of software applications. The following figure illustrates the main categories of products making up the current Oracle product stack:

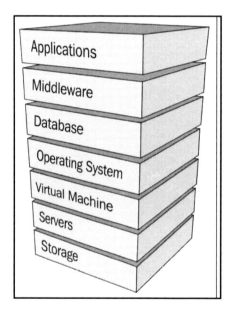

The Middleware product category contains **Oracle Fusion Middleware** (**FMW**), which forms the core of Oracle's **Application Integration Architecture** (**AIA**). It is the foundation for Oracle's fusion applications and software suites, such as Oracle BI, Oracle Hyperion Oracle Web Center, and so on.

Why is there a database repository for OBIEE?

Similar to the previous Oracle BI version, Oracle BI 12c requires a relational database repository schema to hold metadata concerning the installation, report scheduling, usage tracking, auditing, and other aspects of the environment. As an initial set of steps in the installation process, these very necessary repositories are created using the **Repository Creation Utility** (**RCU**) against the selected database server. Chapter 2, *Installing the Prerequisite Software*, goes into greater detail about this crucial repository structure. In Oracle BI 11g, two database schemas were installed with the RCU-**Metadata Services** (**MDS**) and BIPLATFORM. However, in Oracle BI 12c there can be up to nine database repository schemas for Oracle BI 12c that can be installed via the Oracle BI 12c RCU. There are now even more repository schemas that must be installed for Oracle BI 12c to be correctly installed and configured. The additional required schemas will have the suffixes WLS, WLS_RUNTIME, STB, and OPSS. Other schemas available are for auditing purposes, if optionally chosen for the implementation.

 Another interesting fact is that the **Oracle BI Metadata Repository** (**RPD**) is still a file, typically prefixed as RPD (that is, .rpd extension) and even in the latest version of Oracle BI the metadata is not stored in any database repository.

The Oracle BI Metadata Repository is the metadata storage mechanism in which Oracle BI developers model and map physical data sources to logical business representations in order for the resulting analytics to be easily consumed by end users.

The term Oracle BI Domain, as noted previously and shown in the illustration, is used as a way to group all Oracle BI 12c components within the Fusion Middleware (that is, WebLogic Server) architecture. This should not be confused with the WebLogic Application Server Domain, which is given the default name bi when following the default Oracle BI 12c installation options. The latter is a WebLogic Java Application Server term. The former is a Fusion Middleware term. Since Fusion Middleware is so closely related to the WebLogic Application Server, this is good to keep in mind from a technical perspective.

When learning about the overall component composition, a very important detail to keep in mind is the manner in which the components are managed. Since WebLogic Server is a Java application server, it manages all of the Oracle BI components developed in the Java programming language. The Oracle BI System Components are now managed by the **WebLogic Management Framework** (**WMF**) which is the same system that manages the **WebLogic Scripting Tool** (**WLST**) functionality.

Overall components

There are many components that comprise Oracle BI 12c. Oracle BI 12c can categorize these components by the class of programming languages in which they were developed. This is mainly either Java or C++. In comparison to previous versions of Oracle BI, where it seemed to be a somewhat compact environment, Oracle BI 12c is much more integrated into the larger platform of Fusion Middleware, which adds both value and complexity. Some of the same legacy component names persist; however, it should not be taken lightly that most legacy components have been renamed, removed, or placed under new management processes.

The following figure provides a high-level overview of the main components that comprise the Oracle BI 11g architecture. The components are clearly segmented by the processes in which they are managed, each of which ultimately comprise the Oracle BI Domain:

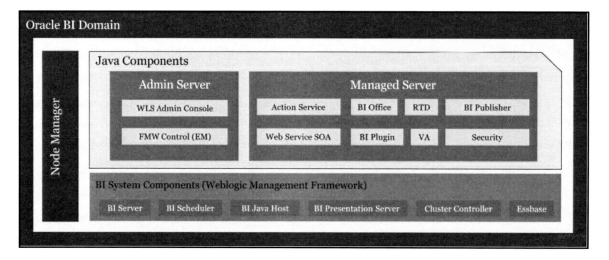

Java components

In relation to Oracle BI 12c, the Java components are those which have been developed in the Java programming language. These components are similar to Oracle BI 11g, with a few differences. The main Java for Oracle BI 12c components, in no particular order of importance, are described in the following sections.

Action Service

Primarily used by the **Action Framework**, it executes actions on behalf of Presentation Services and Oracle BI Scheduler. Actions may be invocations of third-party web services, or invocations of user-supplied Java code executed as EJBs.

Visual Analyzer

New to Oracle BI 12c, this JEE deployment provides the **Visual Analyzer** (**VA**) analytical graphics system, which allows for data visualizations.

Administrative Components

Java Management Extensions Managed Beans (**JMX MBeans**) allow dynamic API functionality for managing, configuring, and administering Oracle BI 12c.

SOA Web Service

SOA Web Service provides a web service interface to the contents of the Oracle BI Presentation Catalog. The tree of objects in the Oracle BI Presentation Catalog is exposed as a tree of web services, defined by a WSIL tree with WSDL leaves. An organization could use these services for **Business Process Execution Language** (**BPEL**) integration.

Oracle BI Office

Oracle BI Office provides integration between Microsoft Office and Oracle BI 12c.

Oracle Real-Time Decisions (RTD)

Oracle Real-Time Decisions (**RTD**) provides a decision-making rules engine that enables real-time business intelligence predictions and outcome analysis.

Oracle BI Presentation Service plugin

Presentation Services runs as a deployed JEE process, not as a web server, and does not communicate using any web server plug-in API. The Oracle BI Presentation Services Plug-in forwards HTTP requests to Oracle BI Presentation Services System Component to handle requests from HTTP traffic, such as browser-based user interfaces or SOAP requests.

Oracle BI Publisher

The enterprise reporting solution for authoring and delivering highly formatted documents.

Security Services

Security Services provides standards-based authentication and population services. It enables Oracle BI Server to integrate with the Fusion Middleware security platform, which includes the **Credential Store Framework** and the **Identity Store**.

System Components

There are many components that comprise Oracle BI 12c. These mainly need to be all in a running state in order for Oracle BI 12c to be considered in running condition - the only exception being the Essbase component. The Oracle BI System Components are those which are developed in a non-Java programming language. Most have been developed in the C++ programming language, as mentioned previously. The following sections cover a list of those components.

BI Server

This is a C++ process that does the data access and aggregates data from data sources. You can configure multiple BI Server processes, which share the load. No session replication takes place between the BI Server processes. This is the core of OBIEE, and provides the services for accessing and managing the RPD.

The BI Server does not maintain user session state. For high-availability deployments, query results are cached in the global cache.

BI Presentation Server

This is a C++ process that generates the user interface pages and renders result sets on behalf of the **Oracle BI Scheduler**. You can configure multiple Presentation Services processes, which share the load. No session replication takes place between the Presentation Services processes.

Presentation Services is almost stateless. The only significant state is the client authentication. If Oracle Business Intelligence is configured to use single sign on for authentication purposes, then users do not have to re-authenticate after a failover. For all other authentication schemes, when failover occurs, clients will have to re-authenticate. The client sees an interruption of service and is redirected to a login page.

BI Scheduler

This is a C++ process that runs jobs according to a configurable frequency. Jobs may be agents created in the Oracle BI Presentation Catalog, or jobs created by the job manager. This scheduler differs from the Quartz scheduler that BI Publisher leverages. When scaled, only a maximum of two instances (one active, one passive) can be configured.

BI JavaHost

This is a Java process that includes resource-intensive graph and PDF rendering. It also allows BI Presentation Services to support BI Publisher and Java tasks within BI Scheduler. You can configure multiple **JavaHost** processes, which share the load. No session replication takes place between the JavaHost processes. The JavaHost is a stateless process. In Oracle BI 12c, JavaHost enables query access between **Hyperion Financial Management** (**HFM**) and Hyperion planning data sources integrated in the OBIEE RPD.

BI Server Cluster Controller

This is a C++ process that manages the population of BI Servers and Oracle BI Schedulers. It also distributes requests to the BI Server and ensures that requests are evenly load-balanced across scaled-out BI Servers in the domain. When scaled, only a maximum of two instances (one active, one passive) can be configured.

Essbase

This is the Essbase server, which provides Oracle/Hyperion Essbase capabilities for the Oracle BI implementation.

It is important to understand how all of the components interact within the Oracle BI environment. Understanding such general concepts as which port numbers are defined to communicate within the default Oracle BI architecture, or how the Oracle BI Administration Tool communicates with the Oracle BI repository, will be quite helpful in your journey to becoming an Oracle BI professional. The following figure shows each of the components comprising the core Oracle BI architecture, the communication ports, and the communication direction:

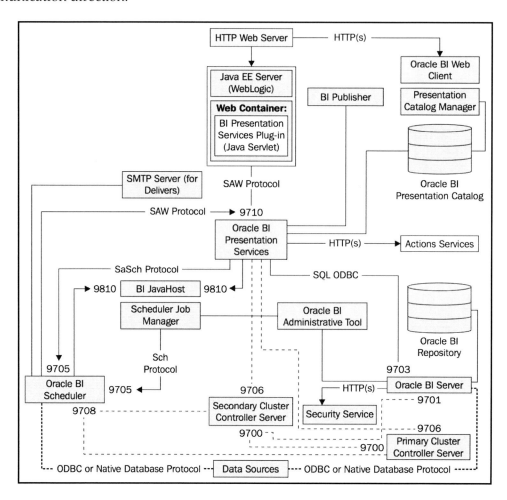

WebLogic Server

Let's talk a little more in detail about the enterprise application server that is at the core of Oracle Fusion Middleware, WebLogic. Oracle WebLogic Server is a scalable, enterprise-ready **Java Platform Enterprise Edition (Java EE)** application server. Its infrastructure supports the deployment of many types of distributed applications. It is also an ideal foundation for building **service-oriented architecture (SOA)**. You can already see why BEA was a perfect acquisition for Oracle years ago. Or, more to the point, a perfect core for Fusion Middleware.

The WebLogic Server is a robust application in itself. In Oracle BI 12c, the WebLogic Server is crucial to the overall implementation, not just from installation but throughout the Oracle BI 12c lifecycle, which now takes advantage of the WebLogic Management Framework. Learning the management components of WebLogic Server that ultimately control the Oracle BI components is critical to the success of an implementation. These management areas within the WebLogic Server are referred to as the **WebLogic Administration Server**, **WebLogic Manager Server(s)**, and the **WebLogic Node Manager**.

A few WebLogic Server nuances

Before we move on to a description for each of those areas within WebLogic, it is also important to understand that the WebLogic Server software that is used for the installation of the Oracle BI product suite carries a limited license. Although the software itself is the full enterprise version and carries full functionality, the license that ships with Oracle BI 12c is not a full enterprise license for WebLogic Server for your organization to spin off other siloed JEE deployments on other non-OBIEE servers. This book is hardly a guide to software licensing, but following are a few of those differences one should keep in mind when beginning or continuing an Oracle BI 12c implementation:

- **Clustered from the installation**: The WebLogic Server license provided with out-of-the-box Oracle BI 12c does not allow for horizontal scale-out. An enterprise WebLogic Server license needs be obtained for this advanced functionality.
- **Contains an Embedded Web/HTTP Server, not Oracle HTTP Server (OHS)**: WebLogic Server does not contain a separate HTTP server with the installation. The Oracle BI Enterprise Deployment Guide (available on `https://www.oracle.com/index.html`) discusses separating the Application tier from the Web/HTTP tier, suggesting Oracle HTTP Server.

Oracle BI 12c Architecture

These items are simply a few nuances of the product suite in relation to Oracle BI 12c. Most software products contain a short list such as this one. However, once you understand the nuances, the easier it will be to ensure that you have a more successful implementation. It also allows your team to be as prepared in advance as possible. Be sure to consult your Oracle sales representative to assist with licensing concerns.

Despite these nuances, we highly recommend that in order to learn more about the installation features, configuration options, administration, and maintenance of WebLogic, you not only research it in relation to Oracle BI, but also in relation to its standalone form. That is to say that there is much more information (books, blogs, and so on) at large on the topic of WebLogic Server itself than WebLogic Server as it relates to Oracle BI. Understanding this approach to self-educating or web searching should provide you with more efficient results.

WebLogic Domain

The highest unit of management for controlling the WebLogic Server installation is called a domain. A domain is a logically related group of WebLogic Server resources that you manage as a unit. A domain always includes, and is centrally managed by, one Administration Server. Additional WebLogic Server instances, which are controlled by the Administration Server for the domain, are called **Managed Servers**. The configuration for all the servers in the domain is stored in the configuration repository, the `config.xml` file, which resides on the machine hosting the Administration Server.

Upon installing and configuring Oracle BI 12c, the domain `bi` is established within the WebLogic Server. This domain is the recommended name for each Oracle BI 12c implementation and should not be modified.

The domain path for the bi domain may appear as `ORACLE_HOME/user_projects/domains/bi`.

This directory for the `bi` domain is also referred to as the `DOMAIN_HOME` or **BI_DOMAIN** folder.

WebLogic Administration Server

The WebLogic Server is an enterprise software suite that manages a myriad of application server components, mainly focusing on Java technology. It is also comprised of many ancillary components, which enable the software to scale well, and also make it a good choice for distributed environments and high-availability. Clearly, it is good enough to be at the core of Oracle Fusion Middleware. One of the most crucial components of WebLogic Server is WebLogic Administration Server. When installing the WebLogic Server software, the Administration Server is automatically installed with it. It is the Administration Server that not only controls all subsequent WebLogic Server instances, called Managed Servers, but also controls such aspects as authentication-provider security (for example, LDAP) and other application-server-related configurations.

WebLogic Server installs on the operating system and ultimately runs as a service on that machine. The WebLogic Server can be managed in several ways. The two main methods are via the **Graphical User Interface** (**GUI**) web application called WebLogic Administration Console, or via a command line using the **WebLogic Scripting Tool** (**WLST**). You access the Administration Console from any networked machine using a web-based client (that is, a web browser) that can communicate with the Administration Server through the network and/or firewall.

The WebLogic Administration Server and the WebLogic Server are basically synonymous. If the WebLogic Server is not running, the WebLogic Administration Console will be unavailable as well.

WebLogic Managed Server

Web applications, **Enterprise Java Beans** (**EJB**), and other resources are deployed onto one or more Managed Servers in a WebLogic Server Domain. A managed server is an instance of a WebLogic Server in a WebLogic Server Domain. Each WebLogic Server Domain has at least one instance, which acts as the Administration Server just discussed. One administration server per domain must exist, but one or more managed servers may exist in the WebLogic Server Domain.

Oracle BI 12c Architecture

In a production deployment, Oracle BI is deployed into its own managed server. The Oracle BI installer installs two WebLogic server instances, the Admin Server and a managed server, bi_server1. Oracle BI is deployed into the managed server `bi_server1`, and is configured by default to resolve to port 9502; the Admin Server resolves to port 9500. Historically, this has been port 9704 for the Oracle BI managed server, and port 7001 for the Admin Server.

When administering the WebLogic Server via the Administration Console, the WebLogic Administration Server instance appears in the same list of servers, which also includes any managed servers. As a best practice, the WebLogic Administration Server should be used for configuration and management of the WebLogic Server only, and not contain any additionally deployed applications, EJBs, and so on.

> One thing to note is that the Enterprise Manager Fusion Control is actually a JEE application deployed to the Administration Server instance, which is why its web client is accessible under the same port as the Admin Server. It is not necessarily a native application deployment to the core WebLogic Server, but gets deployed and configured during the Oracle BI installation and configuration process automatically. In the deployments page within the Administration Console, you will find a deployment named *em*.

WebLogic Node Manager

The general idea behind **Node Manager** is that it takes on somewhat of a middle-man role. That is to say, the Node Manager provides a communication tunnel between the WebLogic Administration Server and any Managed Servers configured within the WebLogic Domain. When the WebLogic Server environment is contained on a single physical server, it may be difficult to recognize the need for a Node Manager. It is very necessary and, as part of any of your ultimate start-up and shutdown scripts for Oracle BI, the Node Manager lifecycle management will have to be a part of that process. Node Manager's real power comes into play when Oracle BI is scaled out horizontally on one or more physical servers. Each scaled-out deployment of WebLogic Server will contain a Node Manager.

If the Node Manager is not running on the server on which the Managed Server is deployed, then the core Administration Server will not be able to issue start or stop commands to that server. As such, if the Node Manager is down, communication with the overall cluster will be affected. The following figure shows how machines A, B, and C are physically separated, each containing a Node Manager. You can see that the **Administration Server** communicates to the **Node Manager**, and not the **Managed Server**, directly:

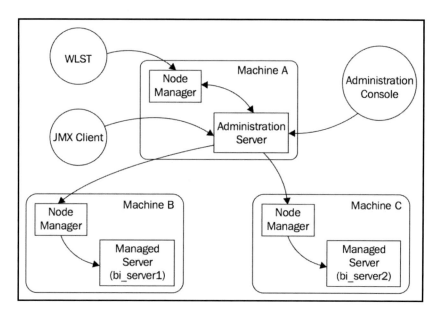

System tools controlled by WebLogic

We briefly discussed the WebLogic Administration Console, which controls the administrative configuration of the WebLogic Server Domain. This includes the components managed within it, such as security, deployed applications, and so on. The other management tool that provides control of the deployed Oracle BI application ancillary deployments, libraries, and several other configurations, is called the **Enterprise Manager Fusion Middleware Control**.

> This seems to be a long name for a single web-based tool. As such, the name is often shortened to **Fusion Control** or **Enterprise Manager**. Reference to either abbreviated title in the context of Oracle BI should ensure fellow Oracle BI teammates understand what you mean.

To discuss the vast amount of individual configuration points contained within the WebLogic Administration Console and Fusion Control warrants an entire book devoted to the subject. For further reading, we recommend the Packt Publishing Advanced WebLogic Cookbook.

Security

It would be difficult to discuss the overall architecture of Oracle BI without at least giving some mention to how the basics of security, authentication, and authorization are applied. By default, installing Oracle WebLogic Server provides a default **Lightweight Directory Access Protocol** (**LDAP**) server, referred to as the WebLogic Server Embedded LDAP server. This is a standards-compliant LDAP system, which acts as the default authentication method for out-of-the-box Oracle BI. Integration of secondary LDAP providers, such as **Oracle Internet Directory** (**OID**) or **Microsoft Active Directory** (**MSAD**), is crucial to leveraging most organizations' identity-management systems. The combination of multiple authentication providers is possible; in fact, it is commonplace. For example, a configuration may wish to have users that exist in both the Embedded LDAP server and MSAD to authenticate and have access to Oracle BI. Potentially, users may want another set of users to be stored in a relational database repository, or have a set of relational database tables control the authorization that users have in relation to the Oracle BI system. WebLogic Server provides configuration opportunities for each of these scenarios.

Oracle BI security incorporates the Fusion Middleware Security model, **Oracle Platform Security Services** (**OPSS**). This has a positive influence over managing all aspects of Oracle BI, as it provides a very granular level of authorization and a large number of authentication and authorization-integration mechanisms. OPSS also introduces to Oracle BI the concept of managing privileges by application role instead of directly by user or group. It abides by open standards to integrate with security mechanisms that are growing in popularity, such as the **Security Assertion Markup Language** (**SAML**) 2.0. Other well-known single-sign-on mechanisms such as SiteMinder and Oracle Access Manager already have pre-configured integration points within Oracle BI Fusion Control. A later chapter will go into an exercise for creating new users and groups, and assigning application roles, but for now, here are a few key concepts to know about security:

- Oracle BI 12c and Oracle BI 11g security is managed differently from the legacy Oracle BI 10g versions. Oracle BI 12c no longer has backward compatibility for the legacy version of Oracle BI 10g, and focus should be to follow the new security configuration best practices of Oracle BI 12c.
- An Oracle BI best practice is to manage security by Application Roles.

- Understanding the differences between the Identity Store, Credential Store, and Policy Store is critical for advanced security configuration and maintenance.
- As of Oracle BI 12c, the OPSS metadata is now stored in a relational repository, which is installed as part of the RCU-schemas installation process that takes place prior to executing the Oracle BI 12c installation on the application server.

The following sections discuss these few key concepts at a high level. Understanding these concepts is not critical at this moment for you to continue on with the remainder of the book; however, once you complete the book and are ready to engage in more advanced discovery, you will want to research and understand these items to be more versed in managing Oracle BI security.

Managing by Application Roles

In Oracle BI 11g, the default security model is the Oracle Fusion Middleware security model, which has a very broad scope. A universal information technology security-administration best practice is to set permissions or privileges to a specific point of access on a group, and not individual users. The same idea applies here, except there is another enterprise-level of user, and even group, aggregation, called an **Application Role**. Application Roles can contain other application roles, groups, or individual users. Access privileges to a certain object, such as a folder, web page, or column, should always be assigned to an application role. Application roles for Oracle BI can be managed in the Oracle Enterprise Manager Fusion Middleware Control interface. They can also be scripted using the WLST command-line interface.

Security providers

Fusion Middleware security can seem complex at first, but knowing the correct terminology and understanding how the most important components communicate with each other and the application at large is extremely important as it relates to security management. Oracle BI uses three main repositories for accessing authentication and authorization information, all of which are explained in the following sections.

Identity Store

Identity Store is the authentication provider, which may also provide authorization metadata. A simple mnemonic here is that this store tells Oracle BI how to *identify* any users attempting to access the system. An example of creating an Identity Store would be to configure an LDAP system such as Oracle Internet Directory or Microsoft Active Directory to reference users within an organization. These LDAP configurations are referred to as Authentication Providers.

Credential Store

The Credential Store is ultimately for advanced Oracle configurations. You may touch upon this when establishing an enterprise Oracle BI deployment, but not much thereafter, unless integrating the Oracle BI Action Framework or something equally as complex. Ultimately, the Credential Store does exactly what its name implies - it stores credentials. Specifically, it is used to store credentials of other applications, which the core application (that is, Oracle BI) may access at a later time without having to re-enter said credentials. An example of this would be integrating Oracle BI with the **Oracle Enterprise Management** (**EPM**) suite. In this example, let's pretend there is an internal requirement at Company XYZ for users to access an Oracle BI dashboard. Upon viewing said dashboard, if a report with discrepancies is viewed, the user requires the ability to click on a link which opens an Oracle EPM Financial Report containing more details about the concern. If not all users accessing the Oracle BI dashboard have credentials to access to the Oracle EPM environment directly, how could they open and view the report without being prompted for credentials? The answer is that the Credential Store is configured with the credentials of a central user having access to the Oracle EPM environment. This central user's credentials (encrypted, of course) are passed along with the dashboard viewer's request and presto, access!

Policy Store

The Policy Store is quite unique to Fusion Middleware security and leverages a security standard referred to as XACML, which ultimately provides granular access and privilege control for an enterprise application. This is one of the reasons why managing by Application Roles becomes so important. It is the individual Application Roles that are assigned policies defining access to information within Oracle BI. Stated another way, the application privileges, such as the ability to administer the Oracle BI RPD, are assigned to a particular application role, and these associations are defined in the Policy Store. The following figure shows how each area of security management is controlled:

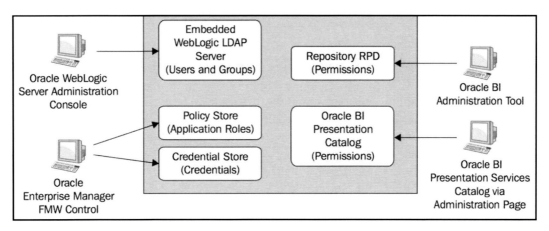

These three types of security providers within Oracle Fusion Middleware are integral to Oracle BI architecture. A chapter or more could be written on each provider, but that is beyond the scope of this book. Further recommended research on this topic would be to look at Oracle Fusion Middleware Security, OPSS, and the **Application Development Framework** (**ADF**).

System requirements

The first thing to recognize with infrastructure requirements prior to deploying Oracle BI 12c is that its memory and processor requirements have increased since previous versions. The Java Application server WebLogic Server installs with the full version of its software (though under a limited/restricted license, as already discussed). A multitude of additional Java libraries and applications are also deployed. Be prepared for a recommended minimum 8 to 16 GB **Read Access Memory** (**RAM**) requirement for an Enterprise deployment, and a 6 to 8 GB RAM minimum requirement for a workstation deployment.

Client tools

Oracle BI 12c has a separate client tools installation that requires Microsoft Windows XP or a more recent version of the Windows Operating System (OS). The Oracle BI 12c client tools provide the majority of client-to-server management capabilities required for normal day-to-day maintenance of the Oracle BI repository and related artefacts. The client-tools installation is usually reserved for Oracle BI developers who architect and maintain the Oracle BI metadata repository, better known as the RPD, which stems from its binary file extension (.rpd).

The Oracle BI 12c client-tools installation provides each workstation with the Administration tool Job Manager and all command-line **Application Programming Interface** (**API**) executables.

In Oracle BI 12c, a 64-bit Windows OS is a requirement for installing the Oracle BI Development Client tools.

It has been observed that with some initial releases of Oracle BI 12c client tools, the ODBC DSN connectivity does not work in Windows Server 2012. Therefore, utilizing Windows Server 2012 as a development environment will be ineffective if attempting to open the Administration Tool and connecting to the OBIEE Server in online mode.

Multi-User Development Environment

One of the key features when developing with Oracle BI is the ability for multiple metadata developers to develop simultaneously. Although the use of the term simultaneously can vary among the technical communities, the use of concurrent development within the Oracle BI suite requires Oracle BI's **Multi-User Development Environment** (**MUDE**) configuration, or some other process developed by third-party Oracle partners. The MUD configuration itself is fairly straightforward and ultimately relies on the Oracle BI administrator's ability to divide metadata modeling responsibilities into projects. Projects -- which are usually defined and delineated by logical fact table definitions -- can be assigned to one or more metadata developer. In previous versions of Oracle BI, a metadata developer could install the entire Oracle BI product suite on an up-to-date laptop or commodity desktop workstation and successfully develop, test, and deploy an Oracle BI metadata model. The system requirements of Oracle BI 12c require a significant amount of processor and RAM capacity in order to perform development efforts on a standard-issue workstation or laptop.

If an organization currently leverages the Oracle BI Multi-User Development Environment, or plans to with the current release, this raises a couple of questions:

- How do we get our developers the best environment suitable for developing our metadata?
- Do we need to procure new hardware?

Microsoft Windows is a requirement for Oracle BI client tools. However, the Oracle BI client tool does not include the server component of the Oracle BI environment. It only allows for connecting from the developer's workstation to the Oracle BI server instance. In a Multi-User Development Environment, this poses a serious problem as only one metadata repository (RPD) can exist on any one Oracle BI server instance at any given time. If two developers are working from their respective workstations at the same time and wish to see their latest modifications published in a **rapid application development** (**RAD**) cycle, this type of iterative effort fails, as one developer's published changes will overwrite the other's in real-time.

To resolve the issue there are two recommended solutions. The first is an obvious localized solution. This solution merely upgrades the Oracle BI developers' workstations or laptops to comply with the minimum requirements for installing the full Oracle BI environment on said machines. This upgrade should be both memory- (RAM) and processor- (MHz) centric. 16GB+ RAM and a dual-core processor are recommended. A 64-bit operating system kernel is required. Without an upgraded workstation from which to work, Oracle BI metadata developers will be at a disadvantage for general iterative metadata development, and will especially be disenfranchised if interfacing within a Multi-User Development Environment.

The second solution is one that takes advantage of **virtual machines** (**VM**) capacity within the organization. Virtual machines have become a staple within most information technology departments, as they are versatile and allow for the speedy proposition of server environments. For this scenario, it is recommended to create a virtual-machine template of an Oracle BI environment from which to duplicate and stand up individual virtual machine images for each metadata developer on the Oracle BI development team. This effectively provides each metadata developer with their own Oracle BI development environment server, which contains the fully deployed Oracle BI server environment. Each developer then has the ability to develop and test iteratively by connecting to their assigned virtual server, without fear that their efforts will conflict with another developer's.

The following figure illustrates how an Oracle BI MUD environment can leverage either upgraded developer-workstation hardware or VM images, to facilitate development:

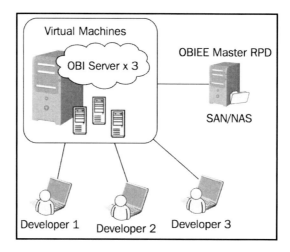

Certifications matrix

Oracle BI 12c largely complies with the overall Fusion Middleware infrastructure. This common foundation allows for a centralized model to communicate with operating systems, web servers, and other ancillary components that are compliant. Oracle does a good job of updating a certification matrix for each Fusion Middleware application suite per respective product release.

 The certification matrix for Oracle BI 12c can be found on the Oracle website at the following locations: http://www.oracle.com/technetwork/middleware/fusion-middleware/documentation/fmw-1221certmatrix-2739738.xlsx and http://www.oracle.com/technetwork/middleware/ias/downloads/fusion-certification-100350.html.

The certification matrix document is usually provided in Microsoft Excel format and should be referenced before any project or deployment of Oracle BI begins. This will ensure that infrastructure components such as the selected operating system, web server, web browsers, LDAP server, and so on, will actually work when integrated with the product suite.

Scaling out Oracle BI 12c

There are several reasons why an organization may wish to expand their Oracle BI footprint. This can range anywhere from requiring a highly available environment to achieving high levels of concurrent usage over time. The number of total end users, the number of total concurrent end users, the volume of queries, the size of the underlying data warehouse, and cross-network latency are even more factors to consider. Scaling out an environment has the potential to solve performance issues and stabilize the environment. When scoping out the infrastructure for an Oracle BI deployment, there are several crucial decisions to be made. These decisions can be greatly assisted by preparing properly, using Oracle's recommended guides for clustering and deploying Oracle BI on an enterprise scale.

Pre-configuration run-down

Configuring the Oracle BI product suite, specifically when involving scaling out or setting up high-availability (HA), takes preparation. Proactively taking steps to understand what it takes to correctly establish or pre-configure the infrastructure required to support any level of fault tolerance and high-availability is critical. Even if the decision to scale-out from the initial Oracle BI deployment hasn't been made, if the potential exists, proper planning is recommended.

Shared storage

We would be remiss not to highlight one of the most important concepts of scaling out Oracle BI, specifically for high-availability: shared storage. The idea of shared storage is that in a fault-tolerance environment, there are binary files and other configuration metadata that need to be shared across the nodes. If these common elements were not shared, if one node were to fail, there is a potential loss of data. Most importantly is that in a highly available Oracle BI environment, there can be only one WebLogic Administration Server running for that environment at any one time. A HA configuration makes one Administration Server active while the other is passive. If the appropriate pre-configuration steps for shared storage (as well as other items in the high-availability guide) are not properly completed, one should not expect accurate results from their environment.

Oracle BI 12c Architecture

OBIEE 12c requires you to modify the **Singleton Data Directory** (**SDD**) for your Oracle BI configuration found at `ORACLE_HOME/user_projects/domains/bi/data`, so that the files within that path are moved to a shared storage location that would be mounted to the scaled-out servers on which a HA configuration would be implemented. To change this, one would need to modify the `ORACLE_HOME/user_projects/domains/bi/config/fmwconfig/bienv/core/bi-environment.xml` file to set the path of the bi:singleton-data-directory element to the full path of the shared mounted file location that contains a copy of the `bi` data folder, which will be referenced by one ore more scaled-out HA Oracle 12c servers.

For example, change the XML file element:

```
<bi:singleton-data-directory>/oraclehome/user_projects/domains/bi/bidata/</bi:singleton-data-directory>
```

To reflect a shared NAS or SAN mount whose folder names and structure are inline with the IT team's standard naming conventions, where the `/bidata` folder is the folder from the main Oracle BI 12c instance that gets copied to the shared directory:

```
<bi:singleton-data-directory>/mount02/obiee_shared_settings/bidata/</bi:singleton-data-directory>
```

Clustering

A major benefit of Oracle BI's ability to leverage WebLogic Server as the Java application server tier is that, per the default installation, Oracle BI gets established in a clustered architecture. There is no additional configuration necessary to set this architecture in motion. Clearly, installing Oracle BI on a single server only provides a single server with which to interface; however, upon doing so, Oracle BI is installed into a single-node clustered-application-server environment. Additional clustered nodes of Oracle BI can then be configured to establish and expand the server, either horizontally or vertically.

Vertical versus horizontal

In respect to the enterprise architecture and infrastructure of the Oracle BI environment, a clustered environment can be expanded in one of two ways: horizontally (scale-out) and vertically (scale-up). A horizontal expansion is the typical expansion type when clustering. It is represented by installing and configuring the application on a separate physical server, with reference to the main server application. A vertical expansion is usually represented by expanding the application on the same physical server under which the main server application resides. A horizontally expanded system can then, additionally, be vertically expanded.

There are benefits to both scaling options. The decision to scale the system one way or the other is usually predicated on the cost of additional physical servers, server limitations, peripherals such as memory or processors, or an increase in usage activity by end users. Some considerations that may be used to assess which approach is the best for your specific implementation might be as follows:

- Load-balancing capabilities and need for an Active-Active versus Active-Passive architecture
- Need for failover or high availability
- Costs for processor and memory enhancements versus the cost of new servers
- Anticipated increase in concurrent user queries
- Realized decrease in performance due to increase in user activity

Oracle BI Server Cluster Controller

When discussing scaling out the Oracle BI Server cluster, it is a common mistake to confuse the WebLogic Server application clustering with the Oracle BI Server Cluster Controller. Currently, Oracle BI can only have a single metadata repository (RPD) reference associated with an Oracle BI Server deployment instance at any single point in time. Because of this, the Oracle BI Server engine leverages a failover concept, to ensure some level of high-availability exists when the environment is scaled. In an Oracle BI scaled-out clustered environment, a secondary node, which has an instance of Oracle BI installed, will contain a secondary Oracle BI Server engine. From the main Oracle BI Managed Server containing the primary Oracle BI Server instance, the secondary Oracle BI Server instance gets established as the failover server engine using the Oracle BI Server Cluster Controller. This configuration takes place in the Enterprise Manager Fusion Control console. Based on this configuration, the scaled-out Oracle BI Server engine acts in an active-passive mode. That is to say that when the main Oracle BI server engine instance fails, the secondary, or passive, Oracle BI Server engine then becomes active to route requests and field queries.

Failover and high-availability

High-availability of the Oracle BI system can be difficult to achieve, but may be necessary based on increased system demands on concurrent usage or other factors. Providing a 24x7 up-time of server operations for some organizations is a must. High Availability is the type of architecture associated with an environment when attempting to maintain a high-level of application availability and minimal downtime.

Failover is the process that takes place when a server node in a cluster fails, and application traffic otherwise intended for the downed server flows to the other active clustered server nodes. Failover also requires some level of load balancing, and the concept can vary depending on desired architecture within an organization, but the general concept should be roughly the same in most topologies. As part of an enterprise deployment strategy, taking failover and high-availability into consideration is usually part of the architecture-planning process. Step-by-step configuration instructions for a high-availability or failover environment are an advanced infrastructure topic and beyond the scope of this book. However, it is important to note that because Oracle BI is part of the Fusion Middleware stack, it has the ability to capitalize on all fault-tolerance features offered by that common architecture.

Enterprise Deployment Guide

In an effort to relay best practices and strategic deployment of large-scale enterprise Oracle BI deployment, Oracle lends a big helping hand and provides a topology referred to as the **Enterprise Deployment Guide** (**EDG**). This guide is not to be taken lightly. When deciding on the major factors of a full-scale, enterprise-wide Oracle BI deployment, this topology is what should be referenced first. Use the EDG to plan for required resource skills, procurement of hardware, and as a gauge to estimate the effort involved in achieving the architecture your requirements demand. The topology includes pertinent information regarding load balancing, virtual IP addresses, separation of HTTP servers from application servers, and other fully vetted infrastructure recommendations. It is especially recommended to view this guide before embarking on any deployment involving extranet access to your Oracle BI implementation or a large user base of an internal deployment.

Directory folder structure

As you get started with installing, configuring, and deploying Oracle BI 12c in the subsequent chapters, you will see several references to files inside of the Oracle Home (for those familiar with Oracle BI 12c, this is the same concept as the Fusion Middleware home location, which is now redefined as Oracle Home) folder structure. It is recommended that, as you progress in your learning of Oracle BI 12c, you take note of which folders contain files pertinent to modifying the environment or assisting with troubleshooting efforts. The following figure illustrates the standard logical deployment structure for Oracle BI 12c:

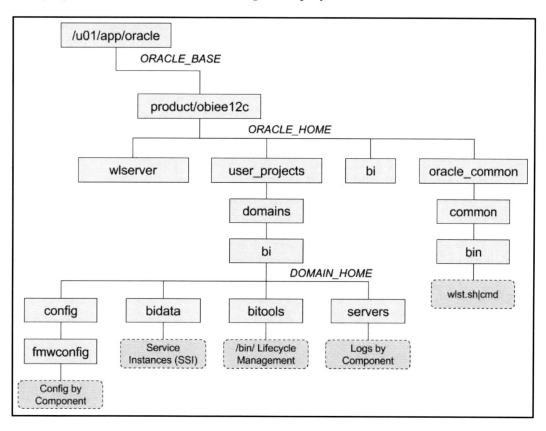

Here are a few key directories that are worth remembering as, during an Oracle BI 12c implementation, you will reference them frequently:

- `ORACLE_BASE`: This is the directory where you have chosen to install Oracle BI on the server as the base directory from which you have access. Typically, you will install into the main folder off one of the drive letters in Windows, or a sub-folder of a mounted directory in Linux, following some standard or best practice, for example: `C:oracle` or `/mount01/apps/oracle/`. Obviously, for maintenance purposes, create a base directory folder that is not too far from the main mount or drive letter.
- `ORACLE_HOME`: This is the location where Oracle BI 12c is installed from the installation process. There should only be one `ORACLE_HOME` for Oracle BI 12c on each physical server installation. For example: `C:/oracle/obiee12c/`, where child folders under this are `user_projects`, `wlserver`, `oracle_common`, and so on.
- `DOMAIN_HOME` (`BI_DOMAIN`): This is the location of the established Oracle BI 12c WebLogic Server domain created to house the managed server information and BI System Components.

  Singleton Data Directory (**SDD**) is the location of the metadata for the Oracle BI 12c domain. It also holds information regarding clustering across multiple host servers.

- `BI_CONFIG_HOME`: This is the location for all central configuration files related to the Oracle BI 12c. Such files found in all legacy versions of Oracle BI such as `instanceconfig.xml`, `NQSConfig.INI` and so on are located within sub-directories of this folder `DOMAIN_HOME/config/fmwconfig/biconfig/`.

  BI Tools is the directory location which has the main lifecycle-management tools and options for deploying, migrating, starting, and stopping the Oracle BI 12c system. The lifecycle-management-tool executables are located in the folder `DOMAIN_HOME/bitools/bin/`.

Log files / diagnostics

As you begin developing and deploying your Oracle BI 12c solutions, you will eventually run into some issues down the road. Face it: you are implementing technology! Issues, no matter how minor, are bound to arise. No one plans for them. But here is a list of log file locations where best to begin troubleshooting in Oracle BI 12c. If you have experience with a previous version of Oracle BI, you'll notice how some of the file names have changed to better reflect the new approach to functionality in Oracle BI 12c, although the general content of the log files is similar:

`<OBI_LOGS> = DOMAIN_HOME/servers/`

Log name (`.log`)	Location
NQQuery (`query.log`)	`<OBI_LOGS>/obis1/logs`
NQServer (`obis1.out`)	`<OBI_LOGS>/obis1/logs`
NQSUDMLGen	`<OBI_LOGS>/obis1/logs`
RPD Migration Utility	`<OBI_LOGS>/obis1/logs`
SAW Log	`<OBI_LOGS>/obips1/logs`
Java Host (`jh.log`)	`<OBI_LOGS>/obijh1/logs`
NQScheduler	`<OBI_LOGS>/obisch1/logs`
NQCluster	`<OBI_LOGS>/obiccs1/logs`

Configuration files

Those who are familiar with previous versions of Oracle BI might be surprised that several legacy-named physical-configuration files still reside in the Oracle BI 12c architecture. These files can still be manually manipulated to configure the Oracle BI environment; however, much of the basic configuration is handled via the Oracle BI Enterprise Manager, which will be discussed in more detail in `Chapter 5`, *Installing and Configuring Client Tools*. If there is a need to locate these configuration files, they can be found at `DOMAIN_HOME/config/fmwconfig/biconfig/bi_component_name`, where the `bi_component_name` could be OBIS, OBIPS, and so on.

Oracle BI 12c Architecture

Here is a list of the main Oracle BI configuration files based on the central Oracle BI 12c instance path of the `BI_CONFIG_HOME` path:

- `OBICCSccslogconfig.xml`
- `OBIJHlogging_config.xml`
- `OBIPSinstanceconfig.xml`
- `OBISCHschedulerconfig.xml`
- `OBISNQSConfig.xml`
- `OBISlogconfig.xml`
- `essbasecluster.properties`

Download Oracle BI 12c

The download files for Oracle BI 12c can be found at the **Oracle Technology Network** (**OTN**), `http://www.oracle.com/technetwork/index.html` or on `http://edelivery.oracle.com`, both of which require a login with an Oracle account, which is free to create for anyone with a valid e-mail address:

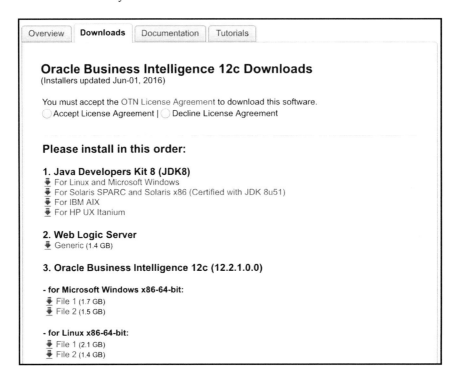

Once you have downloaded these files, unzip them using either the Windows native zip utility or a utility such as 7-zip (http://www.7-zip.org/).

Make sure you have enough space to store, unzip the files, and install the software, as follows:

- Recommended free disk space: Minimum 50 GB

System requirements

For a full list of system requirements, hardware, software, operating systems, and so on, see the following guide: http://www.oracle.com/technetwork/middleware/ias/downloads/fusion-certification-100350.html.

Here's a quick checklist of items before you get started installing and configuring OBIEE:

1. Has the RCU been run to create the OBIEE 12c required database repositories?
2. Is the database running?
3. Do you have sufficient privileges to install the software (such as administrator privileges on the machine)?
4. Have you downloaded the correct operating-system binary files for OBIEE 12c?
5. Is your machine using DHCP or does it have a static IP address?

> The instructions in this chapter are for a static IP. If you are using DHCP, you'll need to install a Loopback Adapter. For instructions on installing the Loopback Adapter, see http://technet.microsoft.com/en-us/library/cc708322(WS.10).aspx.

During installation on a Windows OS, it is best practice to use the command prompt to access the folder structure and executable files for each part of the installation and configuration. Be sure to use the right-click function to execute the executable files using the **Run as administrator** option.

References

There are a few terms used in this chapter we believe every reader should research at their leisure after you've gone through the content in this book. Here are the ones we think are worth learning more about:

Weblogic Management Framework: `http://www.oracle.com/pls/topic/lookup?ctx=fmw121400&id=ASCON11260`

A review - what I should now know!

The following points are very important for you to remember:

- What Oracle Fusion Middleware is
- Why there is a repository database
- What the main components of the OBIEE System are
- What the main components are for system security
- Where to get the OBIEE Software

Summary

In this chapter, we reviewed the key areas of the Oracle BI system and its Fusion Middleware architecture, with WebLogic at the core of the system. You'll find that it is equally important to understand the infrastructure and architecture of both WebLogic Server and Oracle BI 12c for where they intersect, and where the additional power of WebLogic may be leveraged for more advanced technology operations such as lifecycle management and programmability.

In the next few chapters, you will install the Oracle BI 12c software. It might seem like a lot to digest at first, but in the end you'll have your own private sandbox, free to play with, and occasionally break, at your own discretion.

2
Installing the Prerequisite Software

This chapter will cover the steps to install the software needed before we can install the **Oracle Business Intelligence Enterprise Edition** (**OBIEE**) software. OBIEE can be installed on a variety of operating systems, either directly or on a **virtual machine** (**VM**) (see the Oracle site for details on all supported operating systems).

We will install a **Java Development Kit** (**JDK**), which underpins the server software and is actually used to install the software. We will then install the Application Server - Oracle Fusion Middleware.

We have already installed a SQL Server database that will host the metadata tables. We used a trial version of SQL Server 2016, but you can use MySQL if you prefer (MySQL is free to use). Oracle XE is not supported for the metadata.

The final task is to install some schemas in the SQL Server database that will be used by the OBIEE system.

Before we begin, though, make sure you have suitable tools on your machine to undertake the tasks. The downloaded media will be in ZIP format, so you will need an unzip tool. My favorite is 7-Zip, and this is often the tool recommended by Oracle. You will also need a text editor, which could be the built-in Notepad (or vi on Linux). We normally install TextPad or Notepad++. Finally, you will need a browser that is compatible with the OBIEE answers and dashboards tool. This will probably be **Internet Explorer** (**IE**) 11+, Chrome 45+ or Firefox 31+. See the certification matrix for details.

Be sure to check the licensing costs when installing on a virtual machine versus installing directly on a physical server.

Installing the Prerequisite Software

Installation overview

In this chapter, the main tasks that we will perform are as follows:

- Download the required software
- Install Java
- Install the WebLogic Server
- Install database schemas for Fusion Middleware metadata

Installation media

All of the software you will need can be downloaded from the Oracle Business Intelligence 12c **Downloads** page at `http://www.oracle.com/technetwork`.

Before you can download the software, you will need to log in to the Oracle website and accept the license terms:

If you don't have an Oracle account then you can easily sign up for one - it's free!

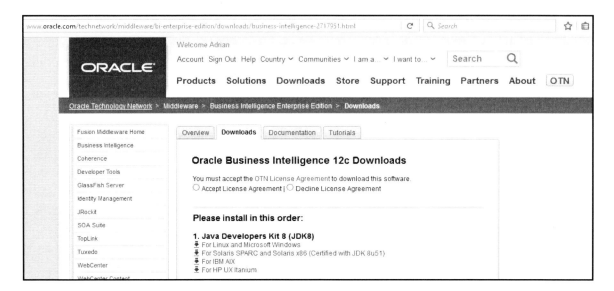

[42]

Chapter 2

Let's get all the software, including the software for the next chapter:

1. Create a folder for the downloads, for example, `C:obiee_downloads`.
2. Download all the OBIEE installation media to the previously created directory:
   - The Windows JDK (we used Version 8 Update 74)
   - WebLogic Server
   - Oracle Business Intelligence 12c, File 1 and File 2
   - Oracle Business Intelligence Developer Client Tool

   There is a link on the 12c **Downloads** page for the Java distributions.

3. Follow the links, accept the license, and download the Windows 64-bit version (`jdk-8u74-windows-x64.exe`):

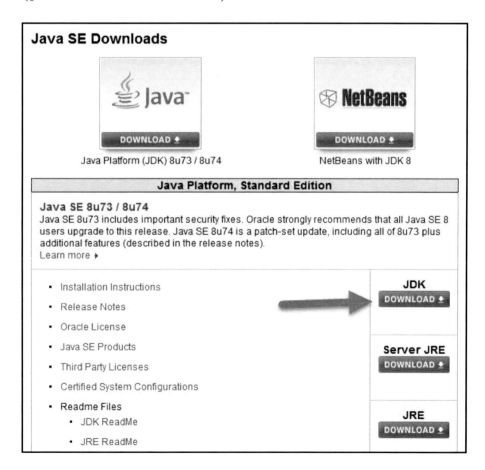

Installing the Prerequisite Software

4. You will end up with five files in the download folder, as shown in the following screenshot:

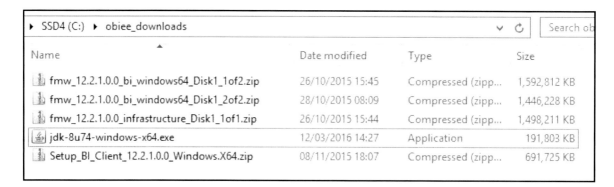

5. Once you have downloaded these files, unzip them using either the Windows native ZIP utility or 7-Zip (http://7-zip.org/). Unzip the files directly into the Downloads folder. The Disk1_2 of 2.zip file contains another file, which does *not* need to be unzipped:

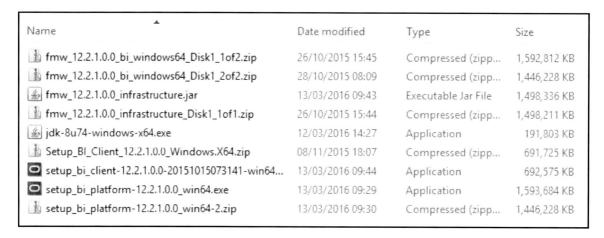

System requirements

Make sure you have enough space to store, unzip the files, and install the following software:

- **Zip files**: 5.42 GB
- **Unzipped files**: 5.47 GB
- **Recommended disk space**: 20 GB

> This has been mentioned because if you attempt to perform this installation on Amazon's EC2 service, you are allocated 30 GB of space initially. You may have to add a second disk if you want to install all the components (database/RCU and OBIEE) on a single machine.

For a full list of system requirements--hardware, software, operating systems, and so on-- see the following guide: `http://book.obiee.info/sysrequirements`.

That page links to the most up-to-date requirements and certification documents.

> For our installation, we used a server that uses a **Solid State Drive** (**SSD**) and 14 GB RAM with an Intel i7 eight-core CPU. The machine hosts the database, as well as the OBIEE components, and performance is good.

Here's a quick checklist of items before you get started installing and configuring OBIEE:

- Is the database installed and running?
- Do you have sufficient privileges to install the software?
- Is your machine using DHCP or does it have a static IP address?

The instructions in this chapter are for a static IP. If you are using fully dynamic DHCP, you'll need to install a Loopback Adapter. For instructions on installing the Loopback Adapter, see the following document:

`http://technet.microsoft.com/en-us/library/cc708322(WS.10).aspx`

Installing the Prerequisite Software

Installing Java

We are now ready to install, so let's get the Java Development Toolkit installed first:

1. Open the `downloads` folder.
2. Find the `jdk-8u74-windows-x64.exe` file.
3. Double-click on the file.
4. Follow the instructions.
5. When you are prompted for the install location for the JDK, change the path to one that does not contain a space. We always install in a `C:Java` folder:

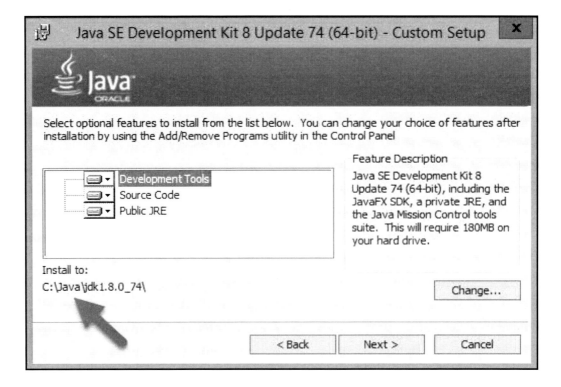

Installing the WebLogic Server

Now that Java Development Kit and JRE are installed, we can use this to install the Fusion Middleware software, that is, the WebLogic Server:

1. Open a `cmd` window.
2. Change directory (`cd`) to the `obiee_downloads` folder.
3. Enter the following command:

   C:Javajdk1.8.0_74binjava.exe -jar fmw_12.2.1.0.0_infrastructure.jar

4. Follow the on-screen instructions:
   1. Click on **Next**.
   2. I have chosen to **Skip Auto Updates**, but you can link to your support account.
   3. Change the directory where the Oracle Home will be installed. We are not planning to share this Fusion Middleware with any other software, so I have called ours `C:fmw_obieeOracle_home`. Write down this location, because we will need it later for the OBIEE installation. I have chosen to install in the `C:fmw_obieeOracle_home` folder. This is because my `C:` drive is a **Solid-State Drive** (**SSD**). You can choose any drive, but try to use an SSD so that you make your system as fast as possible:

> Do not include spaces in the name of your `Oracle_home` directory; the installer will give you an error message if your `Oracle_home` directory path contains spaces.

[47]

Installing the Prerequisite Software

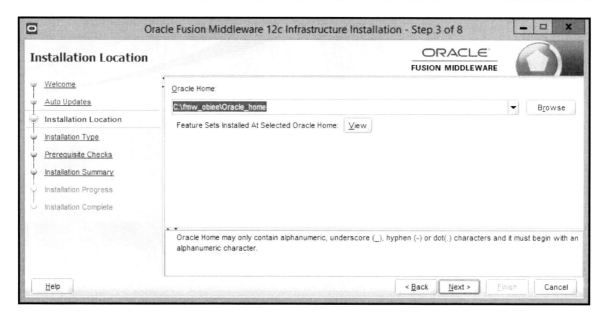

4. Choose the **Fusion Middleware Infrastructure** option.
5. Make sure that the checks are successful:

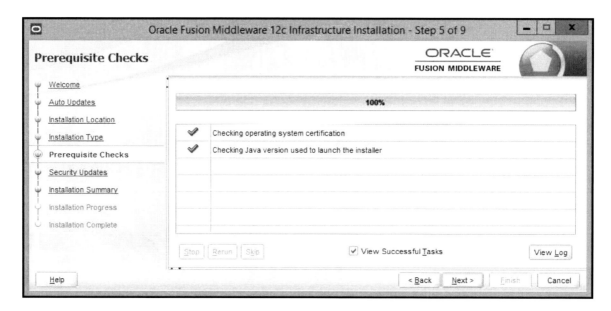

6. You can enter your e-mail address or leave it blank.

Chapter 2

7. You can save your responses, which we do as standard practice because we will always record install steps when creating a production environment. After saving, click on the **Install** button.

8. In this step, all of the installation work actually happens. This may take about 15 minutes. At the end, you'd be looking for green ticks across the board:

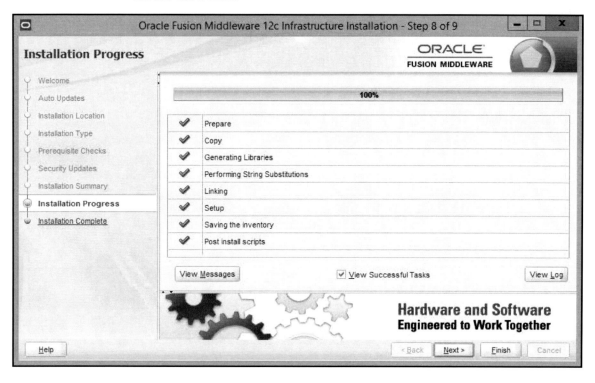

Installing the Prerequisite Software

9. In this step, we are looking for the phrase **Oracle Fusion Middleware 12c Infrastructure installation completed successfully**:

You have now successfully installed the Fusion Middleware platform software.

5. Check the folder for the following structures, and familiarize yourself with the contents:

[50]

The main folders you may use over time are as follows:

- `oracle_home`: This contains all the binary files to run the WebLogic Server. It will also contain useful tools, such as WebLogic Scripting Tool and Repository Creation Utility. This folder is referred to as `ORACLE_HOME`.
- `wlserver`: This is the WebLogic home directory, also known as `WL_HOME`. It contains all the WebLogic Server product files.
- `OPatch`: This is a tool that helps to keep your system up-to-date; that is, it helps to apply patches from Oracle.
- `em`: This is an application that runs on the WebLogic Server.

Installing the metadata schemas

The final installation task in this chapter is the creation of the schemas that will be used by the WebLogic part of the Fusion Middleware software. For this step, we will use the **Repository Creation Utility** (**RCU**) that has been installed as part of the Fusion Middleware system software.

Creating the database and user

Before we begin, let's create and configure a user and database in our SQL Server database:

1. Open SQL Server Management Studio.
2. Create a new login, called `obiee_sa`, which uses SQL Server Authentication. Make a note of the password you create for this user.
3. Create a new database.
4. Enter the database name of `obiee_book`.
5. Set the owner as `obiee_sa`.
6. Select **Options** in the left-hand panel.
7. Scroll to the **Miscellaneous Section** in the right-hand panel.
8. Change the value for **Allow Snapshot Isolation** to **True**.

9. Change the value for **Is Read Committed Snapshot On** to **True**:

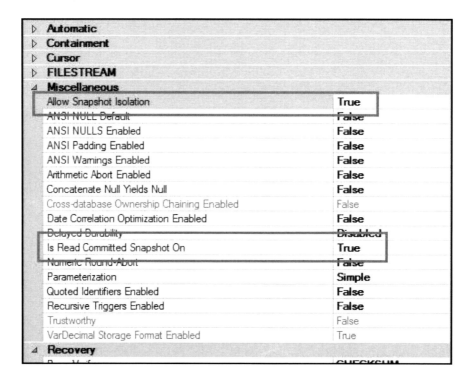

10. Click on **OK**.

    You will also need to code on your SQL Server Database to set the collation; open a **New Query** window.

11. Enter the following command (enter all commands):

```
        DECLARE @collate sysname
SELECT @collate = convert(sysname, serverproperty('COLLATION'))
IF ( charindex(N'_CI', @collate) > 0 )
BEGIN
select @collate = replace(@collate, N'_CI', N'_CS')
exec ('ALTER database obiee_book COLLATE ' + @collate)
END
GO
```

12. Execute the command by pressing *F5*.

Installing the schemas

Now we can proceed with running the **Repository Creation Utility (RCU)**.

The utility can be found in the C:fmw_obieeOracle_homeoracle_commonbin folder:

1. Open a cmd window.
2. Change directory to C:fmw_obieeOracle_homeoracle_commonbin.
3. Run the rcu.bat command:

1. Click on **Next**.

2. In this step, we can choose the method that will create the schemas. We will choose the **System Load and Product Load** option because we have DBA access to our database:

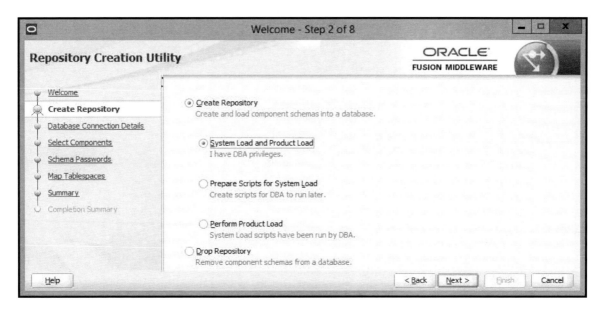

Installing the Prerequisite Software

3. Now we can enter the connection details for our database. Note that we have the option to install in Oracle, IBM DB2, MS SQL Server, or MySQL. We have a SQL Server database installed here, but you can use any supported database that suits you.

Oracle XE is not supported by the RCU.

4. Enter the details of an existing user in SQL Server--one that has DBA rights. Use the same user we created previously - `obiee_sa`.
5. Click on **Next**:

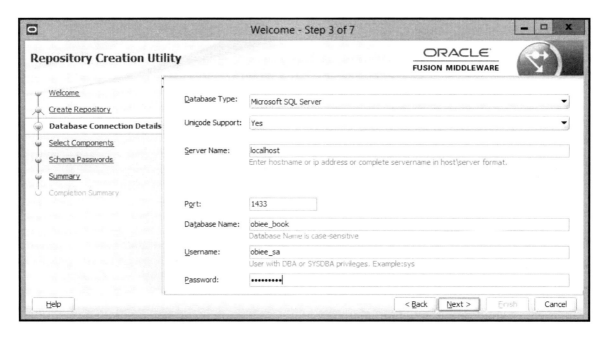

You will now see a screen full of green ticks!

6. Click on **OK**:

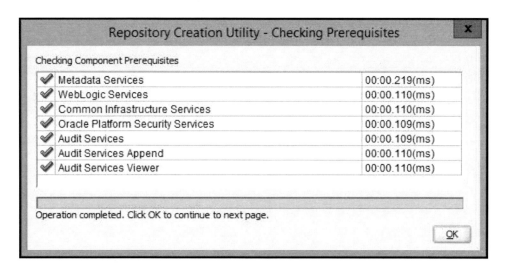

7. Now, set the **Schema Passwords**. You can choose any of the three options available in *step 5*, but just make sure you make a note of the passwords!

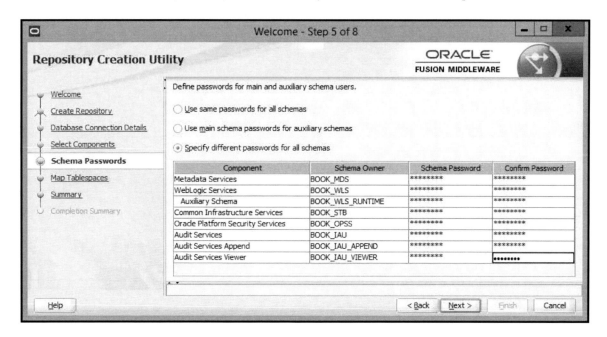

Installing the Prerequisite Software

8. We choose a different password here to demonstrate best practice when securing a production system. In development, you can choose one of the other options.
9. Finished!

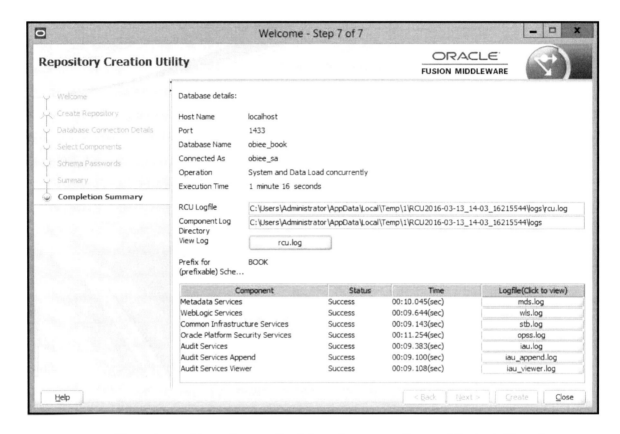

 There is an alternative method for schema creation; while installing the OBIEE software, you can ask it to create the schema for you. This is not as flexible as the method we just saw, which is why I recommend that you run the RCU as an independent step here. It's also important to know which schemas are just for WebLogic Server, and which have been added for OBIEE.

Gotchas

The most common issue with installing OBIEE on Windows seems (in this author's experience) to be setting up the database for the schema. You will encounter issues with the installation unless you have set the following in your SQL Server database:

- **Allow Snapshot Isolation = True**
- **Is Read Committed Snapshot On = True**

A review - what I should now know!

The following points are very important for you to remember:

- How to download all the required software
- How to install WebLogic Server
- How to install the database schemas

Summary

In this chapter, we went through the creation of the Fusion Middleware platform on Windows Server 2012, from downloading the files to installing Java and the binaries.

There are four steps that we covered: downloading the software, installing the Java Development Toolkit, installing the Fusion Middleware platform, and installing the schema for Fusion Middleware.

The installation of OBIEE 12c depends on a working Fusion Middleware (WebLogic) Server. This chapter showed you how to create a Middleware installation that will be dedicated to the OBIEE software.

You can now move on to `Chapter 3`, *Installing on Windows Server 2012*, to install your OBIEE software.

Later in the book, in `Chapter 14`, *Ancillary Installation Options*, we will cover other options for the installation of the RCU.

3
Installing on Windows Server 2012

This chapter will serve to provide step-by-step instructions for installing Oracle BI 12c (release 12.2.1 at the time of writing) on Windows Server 2012.

We have assumed that most readers will have skills around, and have access to, a Microsoft Windows environment, which is why the Windows operating system was chosen for this book. Chapter 14, *Ancillary Installation Options*, will highlight some advanced installation options, including Linux-based installations, and some post-upgrade options you may find of interest once you have worked through this chapter's first-time installation.

This chapter will walk you through the standard installation of Oracle BI 12c, which is the **Single Enterprise** installation that contains an Administration Server and a Managed Server. Don't worry about the terminology; basically, this is the only way 12c is installed, and this will allow you to work/play with all the features seen in a production Oracle BI 12c environment.

The Oracle Fusion Middleware GUI installation wizard is the default interface for Oracle BI 12c installation and provides a consistent installation experience regardless of the operating system, so the steps will be the same even if you are installing on Linux.

Let's get started!

Installation overview

The process that we will follow consists of the following tasks:

- Installing the BI Server software

- Configuring the database for the BI Server schema
- Configuring the BI application
- Configuring start and stop links
- Configuring a connection to the server
- Testing the system

Installation media

We downloaded the required files in the previous chapter. There are three files in our download folder:

- `setup_bi_platform-12.2.1.0.0_win64.exe`
- `setup_bi_platform-12.2.1.0.0_win64-2.zip`
- `setup_bi_client-12.2.1.0.0-20151015073141-win64.exe`

Installing the BI Server software

Here are the steps to install BI Server software:

1. Double-click on the BI platform `setup_bi_platform-12.2.1.0.0_win64.exe` execution file:

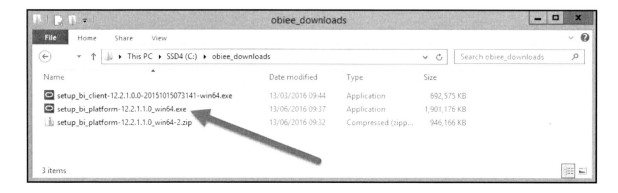

Chapter 3

You will be presented with the **Welcome** page, as shown in the following screenshot:

 You can also run the command using the DOS cmd Window. This may help you see any responses.

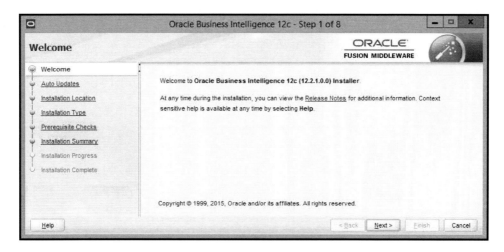

2. Select **Skip Auto Updates** and click on **Next**:

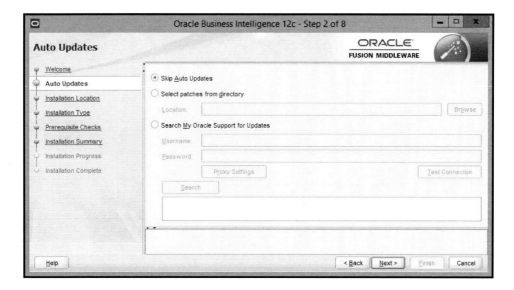

[61]

Installing on Windows Server 2012

3. Enter the location to install the software by selecting the **Oracle Home** path. This will be `C: fmw_obiee_Oracle_home`:

This is the path we created in `Chapter 2`, *Installing the Prerequisite Software*, in the *Installing the WebLogic Server* section.

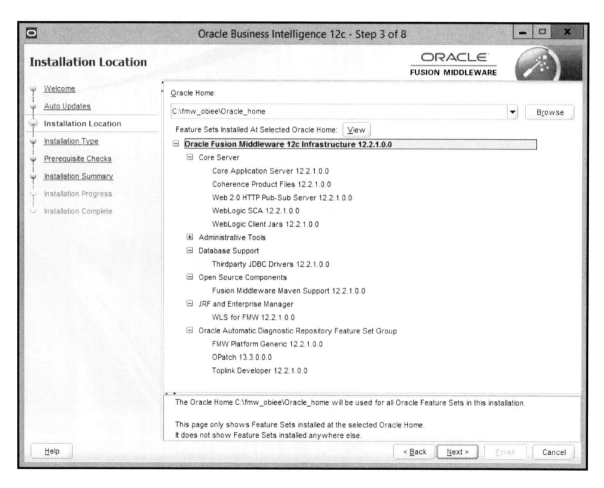

4. This step allows you to choose whether to install **BI Platform Distribution with Samples**. In this case, we will install them. If you were installing on a server that will be part of a cluster, you would not normally install the samples. Choose the second option and click on **Next**:

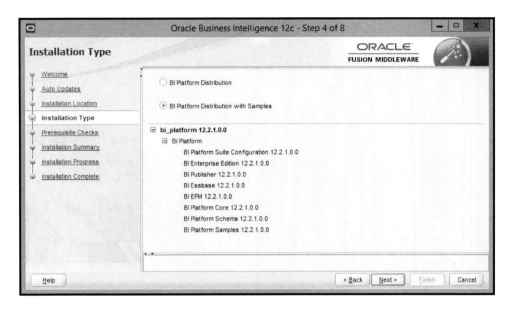

5. The installer will perform a quick check. You will need green ticks to proceed. If your checks are successful, click on **Next**:

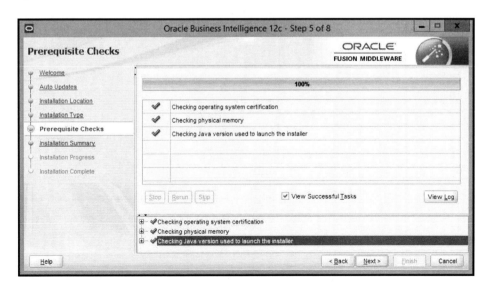

Installing on Windows Server 2012

6. The next screen is a little surprising but, essentially, it enables the installation to work. If you do get this popup, we recommend that you click on **Next**. If it does not appear, ignore this step:

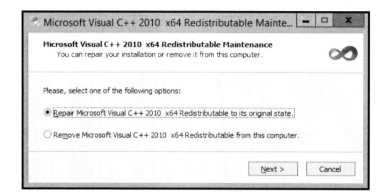

Over the last few years, there have been reported instances of slight difficulties in configuring the OBIEE software, and one common way to fix installation problems is to run the Visual C++ Redistributable Maintenance program. If you experience problems later, try downloading and running `vcredist_x64.exe` (available from Microsoft).

We have now reached the end of the installation of the BI Server software!

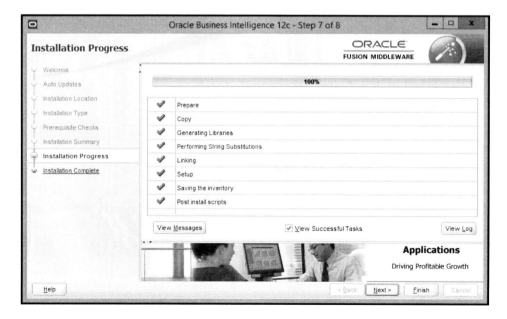

Chapter 3

At this point, nothing is actually running, or even capable of being run. We have simply installed the binaries. Our next task is to create an area in our metadata database for some OBIEE components. After that, we will be able to create the OBIEE domain.

Configuring the database for the BI Server schema

To create the metadata schema we will again use the **Repository Creation Utility** (**RCU**) that we used in `Chapter 4`, *Reviewing the Features of the Reporting Repository*. The command is the same one we ran in that chapter, but this time there will be one more schema to choose from-the `BI_PLATFORM` schema:

1. Open a cmd window.
2. Change directory to `C:fmw_obieeOracle_homeoracle_commonbin`.
3. Run the `rcu.bat` command.
4. When the **Welcome** dialog box appears, click on **Next**.
5. On the *Step 2* page, select **System Load and Product Load**. Click on **Next**:

Note that the second option available is for creating the scripts for a **Database Administrator** (**DBA**). If you do not have DBA access, you use this option to create scripts that you send to your friendly DBA.

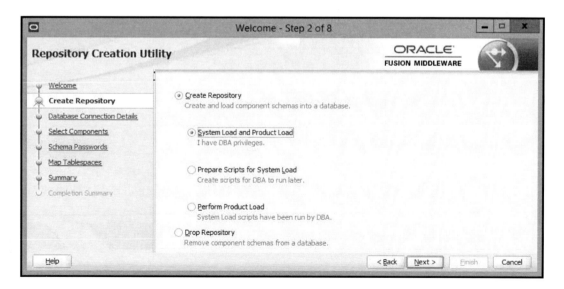

[65]

6. On the *Step 3* page, enter the connection details for your database. We used `localhost`, port `1433`, because that's where our database is installed. If you have installed your database on another server, then put that server's details in here.
7. Click on **Next**:

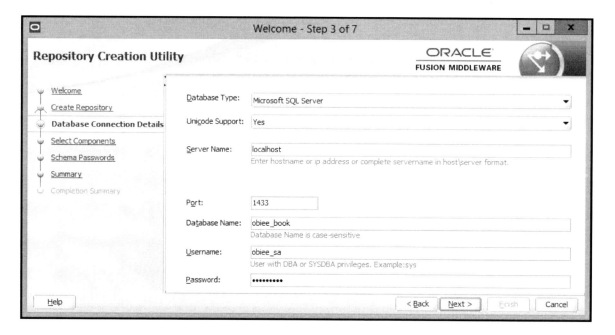

The installer will now run a quick check to make sure your database is compliant.

8. On the *Step 4* page, select the existing prefix that we created in the previous chapter-in our case, we called it **BOOK**.
9. Make sure the **Oracle Business Intelligence** option is selected.

Chapter 3

10. Click on **Next**:

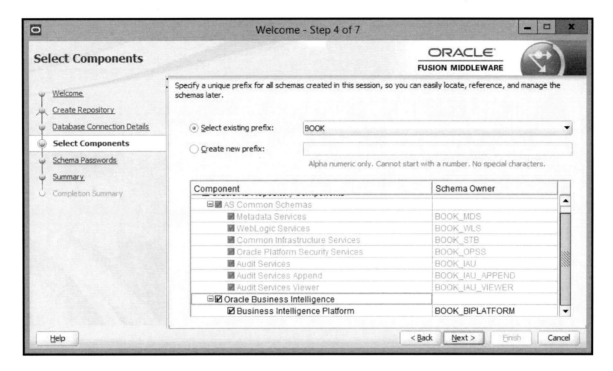

Another quick check for the prerequisites will pop up.

RCU Schema creation

At this point, it is worth pointing out that there is the option to install all of the schema at this time. You can select the **Create new prefix** option, then enter a value in the input box, for example, DEV. We ran the installation in the previous chapter to highlight that the BI_PLATFORM is related to the OBIEE installation, whereas the other schema is related to the Fusion Middleware platform.

[67]

Installing on Windows Server 2012

11. On the *Step 5* page, enter a password for the schema:

 Make a note of your password!

12. On the *Step 6* page, we can check our selected options and click on the **Create** button:

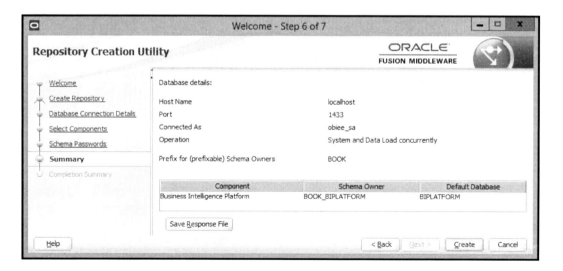

Once the create step has completed, you will have finished the installation of the schema that supports OBIEE.

Configuring the BI application

OK, let's recap what we have done so far:

- We installed the Fusion Middleware software (in the previous chapter)
- We installed the OBIEE Server software into the Fusion Middleware home
- We installed a new schema in a database that supports the OBIEE Server

We installed OBIEE as a *domain* in the Fusion Middleware system, and now we are in a position to create the BI domain. The installer you need for this step has been installed as part of the OBIEE Server software:

1. Open a cmd window.
2. Change the directory to the path for the installation by typing `cd C:fmw_obieeOracle_homebibin` and pressing *Enter*.

> Do not use the wrong `config` command, which you will see in the `oracle_commoncommonbin` folder.

3. Type `config.cmd` and press *Enter*.

4. The installer will fire up. Select all three options. Click on **Next**:

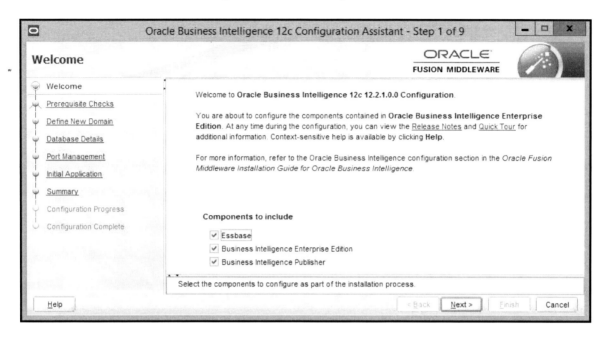

5. The next screen is just a confirmation that the prerequisite checks have completed. Oracle likes its prerequisite checks! Included with the components will be the **Enterprise Management** (**EM**) application that controls the OBIEE domain.
6. On the *Step 3* page, we set the location and user for our new BI domain. The default of C:fmw_obieeOracle_homeuser_projectsdomains in the Domains directory input field should not be changed. We also recommend leaving the domain name as bi for now. We have chosen weblogic as the username, but you can choose any name. We have seen biadmin, bidomainowner, and many more. Enter the username and password, and click on **Next**:

Remember the username and password!
Do not forget to make a note of the username and password entered here, because you will need it for all administration tasks later on.

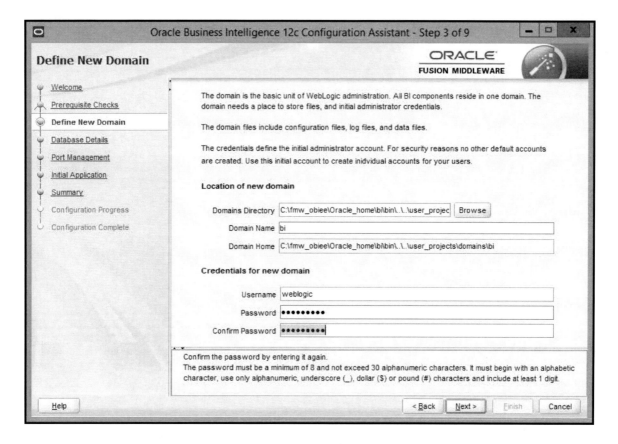

7. On the *Step 4* page, we select the database where we created the BI_PLATFORM schema:

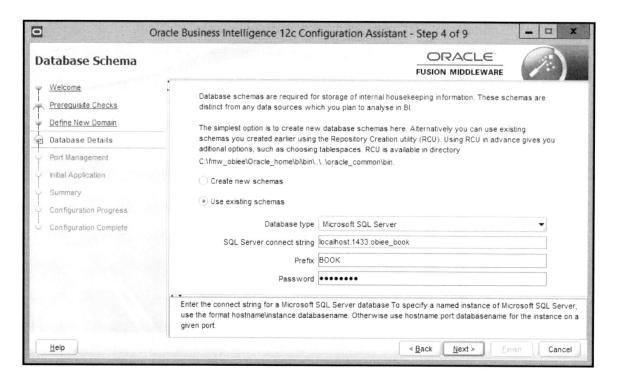

RCU schema creation

Note that there is an option to create schema at this point. We have already created ours using the RCU already, but Oracle have given you the choice if you prefer to run schema creation here as part of the domain creation.

8. On the *Step 5* page, we can change the default port numbers that are allocated to this domain. Port `9500` is the default access port for the WebLogic Administration server. If you accept the defaults, the OBIEE components will use the following ports:
    - `9500`: Administration Server
    - `9501`: Administration Server (using SSL)
    - `9502`: Managed Server
    - `9503`: Managed Server (using SSL)
    - `9507`: Presentation Services
    - `9508`: OBIEE Servers Cluster Controller
    - `9510`: JavaHost
    - `9511`: BI Scheduler
    - `9514`: BI Server

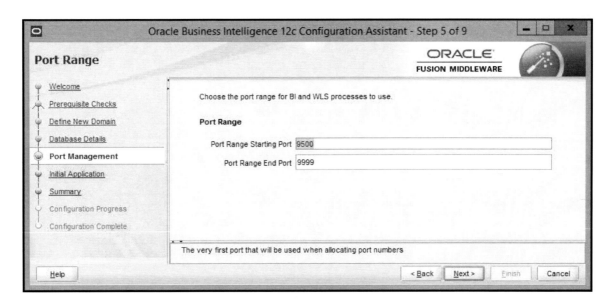

9. On the *Step 6* page, we choose the application that we would like to install along with the domain. We will choose the **Oracle sample application** option, because this is a development installation:

For a production installation, you would not include an application (choose the clean-state option). We have chosen to install a sample application, supplied by Oracle, to show you the features available, and it also means you can prove your system is working before moving to subsequent chapters. A production environment will use your own application, which you will upload.

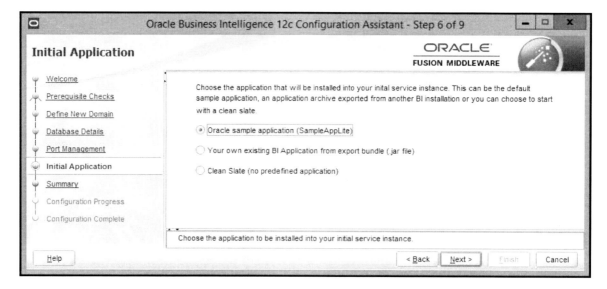

10. The *Step 7* page is useful to show what ports are being used, which could come in handy if you use non-default port-range settings. Note that you can save the responses made so far in a file, which could be used for a silent installation script.

11. At this point, you can click on the **Configure** button:

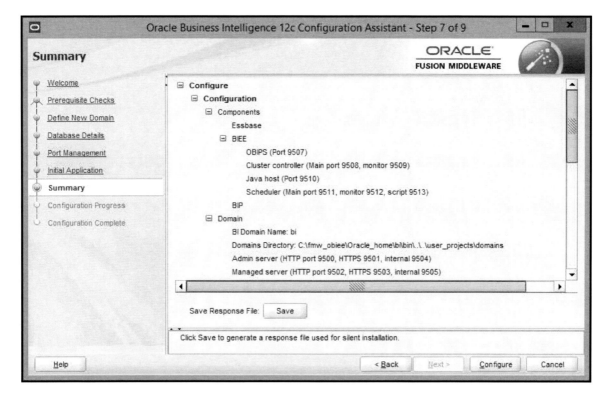

The configuration process may take a few minutes to complete. Be patient!

Installing on Windows Server 2012

12. When it has completed all the tasks, a browser window with a login page should appear:

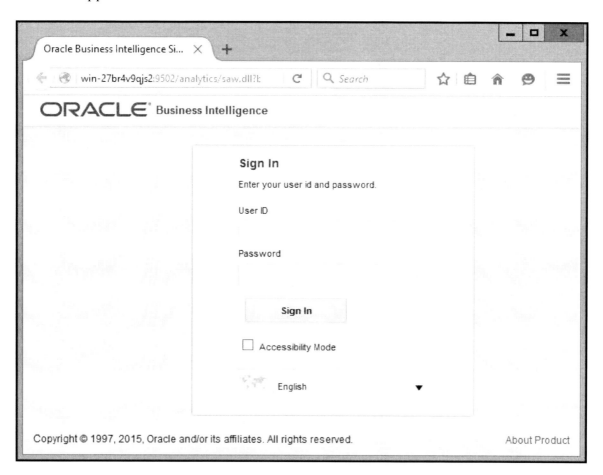

 This page does not always appear automatically. If it does not, open a browser, type http://localhost:9502/analytics in the address bar, and press *Enter*.

When you get this page, you can sign in with the credentials you set in *Step 3*.

Congratulations! Your environment has been built.

What is installed?

Let's recap what we have got so far. To begin with, we had a Windows 2012 server with a SQL Server database.

Then we installed Java version 8, so that we could then install the Fusion Middleware platform, that is, WebLogic.

After the Fusion platform, we installed the OBIEE software in the Fusion Middleware folders. Next, we ran the configuration tool, which put the BI applications into the server folders. The configuration tool also put the OBIEE client software in place.

This means that we now have a working OBIEE system ready to use and develop with, except that there are no connections in place for the client admin tool. If we had installed on a Linux system, then we would need to install the client tools separately on a Windows machine. We will cover how to install the client software and create the connections in `Chapter 6`, *Understanding the Systems Management Tools*.

Folder structure

Before we go into the details of the components, let us see what folders we have created for the OBIEE software.

After the Fusion platform installation, we had `C:fmw_obieeoracle_home`. Remind yourself by looking back at the folders screenshot in `Chapter 4`, *Reviewing the Features of the Reporting Repository*. There are many new folders installed as part of the OBIEE software, including the following:

- `bi`: The main folder for the OBIEE software.
- `bifoundation`: Found inside the `bi` folder, this folder contains the main executables for OBIEE; for example, inside the `serverbin` folder, you will find the `nqserver.exe` file.
- `user_projects`: In a standard Fusion Middleware build, this folder is created when needed, to host the domain and any application that is installed by a particular product. In the case of OBIEE, there is a version of the Enterprise Manager application (`em.ear`) that is specifically for managing the business-intelligence domain. The BI domain we created in the preceding steps is placed in this folder.

Shortcut reference variables

Most of the internal files will use pointers (or variables) to the folders in our build. This is because there is no set place to put the root folder, or set name for the BI domain. In our installation, these variables are pointing to the following locations:

Variable	Location
ORACLE_HOME	C:fmw_obiee
DOMAIN_HOME	C:fmw_obieeOracle_homeuser_projectsdomainsbi
JAVA_HOME	C:Javajdk1.8.0_74
BI_PRODUCT_HOME	C:fmw_obieeOracle_homebi
MW_HOME	C:fmw_obiee
WL_HOME	C:fmw_obieeOracle_homewlserver

There is no requirement to set these variables on your machine, because each script will set the value when it needs it. However, there is no known downside of having environment variables in place with these values, if you prefer to set them.

Take a look and familiarize yourself with the folders.

Configuring start and stop links

Finally, we end this chapter with some tips on how to set up a couple of useful links.

The installation process creates files that control the starting and stopping of the various services, including a command file that will start the WebLogic servers and all the OBIEE components. These control scripts exist in the software folders, and therefore, to access them, we would have to navigate to the full path they are in.

The `start` command is found within the `domain` folder, in `C:fmw_obieeOracle_homeuser_projectsdomainsbibitoolsbin`.

The command is as follows:

`start.cmd`

Therefore, the full command to run is as follows:

`C:fmw_obieeOracle_homeuser_projectsdomainsbibitoolsbinstart.cmd`

We will now create a shortcut to this file to place on the Windows Start screen:

1. On the Windows desktop, right-click and select **New | Shortcut**.
2. In the **Location** box, enter the following:

   `cmd.exe /K`
   `C:fmw_obieeOracle_homeuser_projectsdomainsbibitoolsbinstart.cmd`

3. Enter a name for the item, `OBIEE 12c Start`, and click on **Finish**.
4. Now find the shortcut on your desktop, and right-click on it.
5. Click on **Pin to Start**.

   Now you will be able to go to the Windows start menu and see your shortcut. The `/K` part of the command prevents the window from closing, and is optional.

6. Repeat this for the `stop.cmd` and `status.cmd` entries.

   You can edit the shortcut; for example, you can change the icon by right-clicking on the shortcut on the **Start** menu and selecting `Open File Location`. This will take you to the shortcut object in the folder, which for us is `C:UsersAdministratorAppDataRoamingMicrosoftWindowsStart MenuPrograms`. Here you can change the properties of the shortcut, again by right-clicking.

A review - what I should now know!

The following points are very important for you to remember:

- How to install the BI Server software
- How to install the repository database schema
- How to configure the BI Server

Summary

In this chapter, we learned how to install the OBIEE software in the Fusion Middleware home. We also learned how to use the **Repository Creation Utility** (**RCU**) to install the schema in a database that OBIEE uses; this is called the metadata schema.

There are other options. The first task we undertook, when the software was installed, was to configure a new OBIEE Domain.

Finally, we learned where the installation files are and how to create useful Windows shortcuts.

As you can see from the steps in this chapter, it is very simple to run the installation software supplied by Oracle to create the Oracle Business Intelligence system.

In the next chapter, we will review the Oracle BI reporting system and consider what the features are.

4
Reviewing the Features of the Reporting Repository

So far, we have given you an overview of the Oracle OBIEE 12c components and discussed how those objects relate to each other. We have also shown you various configuration options. As we discuss in more detail as the book progresses, you will have installed all the software, readied the requisite database, set up your users, and have a BI server repository ready to go. Then you will be ready to use the reporting part of the system--the **Presentation Catalog**. The Presentation Catalog is controlled by the Presentation service, which now has a bigger role in managing the Presentation Catalog and the applications that form OBIEE 12c.

This chapter will introduce the new interface of the catalog and the tools that are integrated into the Presentation services. We will also explore the various aspects of the catalog administration. The Oracle 12c BI system has such a large number of features that we need to examine what they are before deciding which ones to use. Some features may be too advanced for certain readers at this moment, so feel free to go forward to other chapters and come back as needed.

The security of data available for reporting is controlled by the BI server that allows access to the entire OBIEE 12c system. There is also security available at the object level, that is, the dashboards and reports themselves. So, later in this chapter, we will explore the security administration of the catalog.

The Presentation Catalog can be thought of as a comprehensive file-management system that includes folders and files with attributes such as security controls. The files contain XML and the folders relate to the real folders in your operating system.

Presentation Services is a web-based system that contains various tools integrated with the security of the WebLogic platform and the Presentation Catalog itself. For example, you can use one of the report-creation tools, called Answers, to create an analysis report, and then save it in the catalog, in a secure folder.

Integrated tools

Several BI tools are now integrated into the Oracle BI main Presentation Server application. The tools and features that are integrated into the Presentation Server (using the Oracle-defined names) are as follows (you can see some of them in the following screenshot):

- Dashboards
- Analysis and Interactive Reporting
- Published Reporting
- Mobile Application
- Actionable Intelligence
- Performance Management
- Marketing
- Administration
- Briefing books
- Search
- Help
- Mapping
- RSS feeds
- Office integration

- **Data Exploration and Discovery - Visual Analyzer** (new in 12c)

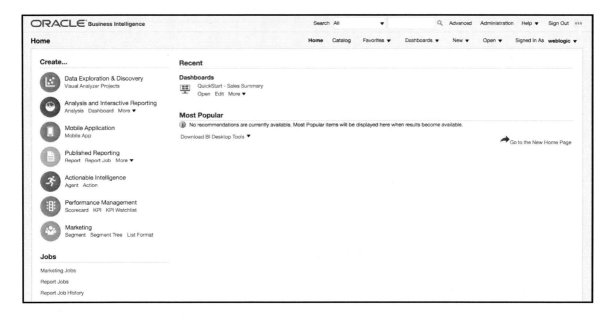

Answers

Answers is a part of the system that enables the creation of analysis objects. These are the queries and requests for information that return rows of data from a data source (such as an Oracle database). The resulting set of records can be presented by the analysis in a variety of layouts, for example, in a table of columns or as a chart. The important point to note is that the request for information is saved in the catalog, not in the data. Each time the request is run, it fetches the data in the source system at that time. You can save the results by downloading them as an Excel file, as a PDF, or even as a web page, but OBIEE does not store the result in an analysis. Analyses are saved for later reuse by opening them directly or by placing them on a dashboard. They can also be used by the Actionable Intelligence tool (refer to the *Actionable Intelligence* section in this chapter). Analyses are normally created by more advanced users of the system, but you do not need to have highly technical IT skills it's mainly click, drag, and drop.

We will cover in more detail how to create analysis objects in Chapter 8, *Creating Dashboards and Analyses*.

Dashboards

A dashboard is used to present information to users in a way that is simple to use and that can be conveyed to each user. Dashboards consist of one or more dashboard pages (also known as tabs), and can contain multiple pieces of analysis, embedded websites, URLs, text, actions, and folders.

Dashboards can be used by thousands of users, with each user seeing a view customized to them. They can be highly interactive, and provide end users the ability to drill into the data and investigate the results in a personalized way.

There is a chapter dedicated to the building of dashboards, as this is the core feature of most OBIEE implementations (refer to `Chapter 8`, *Creating Dashboards and Analyses*).

Published Reporting

Published Reporting consists of highly formatted reports that are normally available for printing. You could use reports for invoices, statements, pick lists, and so on, as well as formatted reports on company performance. These are created using BI Publisher, a formerly standalone product that is now well integrated into OBIEE.

For more information, refer to `Chapter 10`, *Developing Reports Using BI Publisher*, later in this book.

Actionable Intelligence

One of the great uses of OBIEE is to set up a report and have it delivered to your e-mail inbox every day. Better still, have the report e-mailed to you only if you need to take some action, for example, order new stock or chase debtors! The term for delivering triggered content to users is *agents*. Agents are scheduled jobs that decide who to send the content to, as well as when and where, based on criteria the creator sets. For example, you can create a schedule that checks the stock levels in the database for various stores. If a certain level is reached in one store, an e-mail is sent to the controllers, showing them where and how old the stock is.

You can take this idea one step further, which enables you to take action directly from a dashboard. An action may be to navigate to another part of the system or to invoke a web service, or even some JavaScript. In our example, the action available to the user could be the use of a web service that makes an order in the distribution system to move the stock from one warehouse to the store.

Chapter 9, *Agents and Action Framework*, is dedicated to the creation of Actionable Intelligence.

Performance Management

The BI system is mainly used for reporting on company performance. Performance is measured in terms of financial activity, sales, HR, and other specific business drivers, such as churn rates. Certain measures that we report upon are fundamental to the success of the organization, for example, the profit margin on products sold or the acquisition of new customers each month.

These measures are known as **Key Performance Indicators** (**KPIs**).

The concept of presenting all KPIs together on one page is called a **balanced scorecard**. These scorecards were designed in the early 1990s and have been widely adopted throughout the world, in businesses, governments, and non-profit organizations.

Oracle has integrated the reporting on KPIs and the creation of scorecards into the Presentation Server and Presentation Catalog. The creation of these is out of the scope of this book, but there are some examples available in the sample application you can install (available at `https://www.oracle.com/index.html`).

Marketing

One of the early uses of OBIEE (when it was owned by Siebel) was in the Siebel Marketing tool. The concept is simple finding lists of people to send marketing information to. In marketing terms, this is known as *Segmentation*.

The idea is that OBIEE can identify customers with certain attributes that are desirable for our marketing department. For example, they want a list of all males over 50 living in London. This initial list can then be further reduced to those who have already had a letter sent to them in the previous month. Once the target list has been created, it is imported into the marketing system for the fulfillment process (sending out literature by mail or e-mail).

Siebel Email Marketing is still available from Oracle today, as part of the **Siebel Enterprise Marketing Suite**. You can also purchase Marketing Analytics.

MapViewer

MapViewer is also integrated into OBIEE 12c. End users can incorporate Map mviews into their dashboards without using complex coding and without any extra licenses. Typically, the data involved is address-related, for example, postal address, but you can also include custom areas to show on a map. Address-type information is normally subjected to geocoding, to make it usable by OBIEE. Mapping data is managed from the administration screen and the definitions are held in the catalog.

To use MapViewer, we have a type of analysis view, called, unsurprisingly, the **Map mview**. The Map mview normally contains a map of a location, and this is overlaid with colored shapes or pins. These overlays denote items or measures. For example, sales by state could be three-colored to denote low, medium, and high levels. Map mviews allow further analysis by allowing users to drill into the data points, or even to use actions.

MapViewer is also available directly with your installation of Oracle BI 12c. Try `http://[server]:<port>/mapviewer` on your environment.

Administration

The common interface and use of a single catalog for reports, analysis, alerts, and lists requires an administration tool for the creation of these objects, as well as for the catalog itself. The web-based administration area is used to control who can access which feature and what settings to use in Mapping mdata and BI publisher. The administration area also provides access to the current logged-in users and the queries they are running.

Briefing books

If you are out of the office with no connectivity to your OBIEE system, you can use briefing books to take some of your reports with you. Briefing books is a way of gathering analyses together in a PDF or MHTML file and saving locally for later use.

Visual Analyzer

New to 12c, and the feature that differentiates this release from 11g and previous versions, is the Visual Analyzer. It allows rapid data discovery from your OBIEE system, and also from external data sources such as ad hoc spreadsheets. This self-service function allows local users to blend (mashup) enterprise data with their own local data for very quick discovery and representation in a variety of formats. Currently, this requires a further license from Oracle.

Search

You can search for any object thanks to a common search tool. It is accessible from the common toolbar or from links on the home page. The search system can use wildcards, and can be limited by the type of object.

Help

The home screen itself has a whole section dedicated to all the information you need. The common toolbar also has a link to internal help, and links to the Oracle documentation. The help is contextual, and it decides which help page you need based on the page you are on at the time.

Office integration

OBIEE 12c is great for presenting information and enabling further analysis. Most deployments can be managed by using online data. Sometimes, users need to have their analysis in Excel or PowerPoint, and this release makes that easier than ever. Exporting into Office, PDF, HTML, and XML is quick and easy. You can also use Excel to connect directly to the OBIEE Presentation service.

Reviewing the Features of the Reporting Repository

The home screen

All of these features are available from the home screen, which you are normally presented with when you first log into OBIEE 12c.

Try typing `http://[server]:[port]/analytics` in your browser, and after the login screen, you should see the home screen. Remember to change the port number if you changed it during installation.

> Note that your browser version is important. Our advice is that you use Firefox 10 and Chrome 17 onwards. Please refer to the full Oracle Certification Matrix for a complete analysis of what is supported.

Looking at the **Home** screen, we can see access to the features described on the left-hand side:

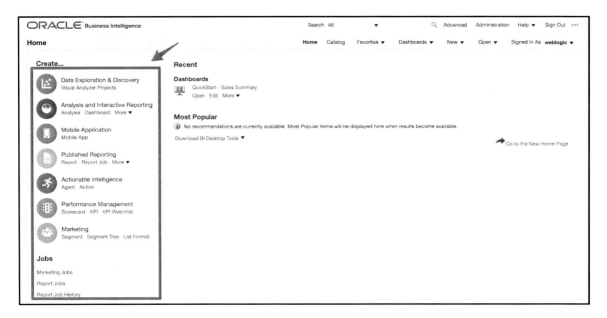

Catalog

This section contains object links to dashboards, analysis, briefing books, filters, published reports, and prompts. These can be personal to you (My `MFolders`), or objects that have been shared with you (Shared `SFolders`). It contains any catalog content that you have created and saved:

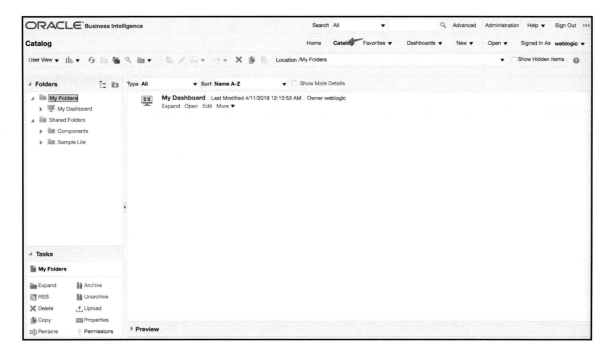

New

You can create new objects directly from the **Home** page using the **New** menu item. Along with the major types of object, such as dashboards, you can create related objects, such as prompts, filters, and style templates.

Reviewing the Features of the Reporting Repository

The only item links that are visible are the ones for which you have the rights to use:

Recent

The **Recent** section mainly contains links that are pre-defined searches. This includes a search for your analyses and reports. It contains any catalog content that you have recently created, edited, or opened:

Help

If you need help, you can find this in the local help files that were installed along with the application. Also in this section, there are links to the main Oracle website. You will also find links to download the Office Integration client tools.

The BI Desktop tools available to download are as follows:

- **Oracle BI for MS Office**: This enables direct access to OBIEE from Microsoft Office
- **Template Builder for Word**: This creates RTF templates for use in the published reporting:

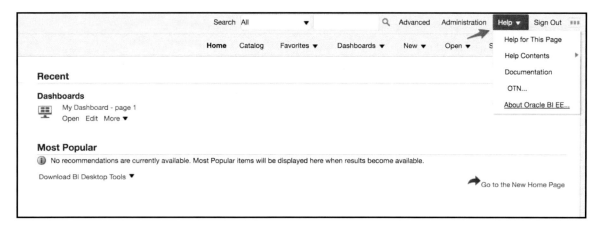

Administration

To the left of the Help link is the link to the **Administration** screen. You can also save a link to the address `http://[server]:<port>/analytics/saw.dll?Admin`:

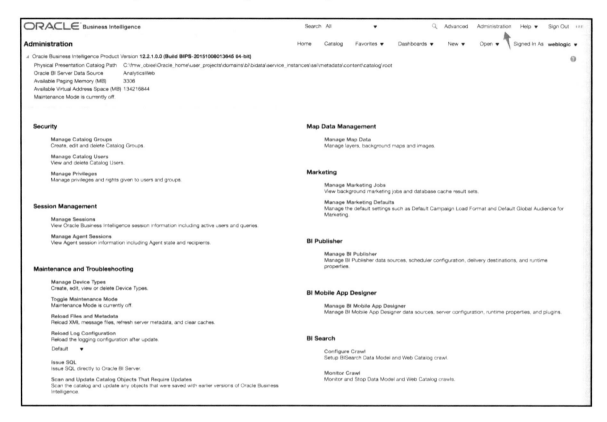

The content on the **Administration** screen is controlled and therefore, you will only see what the system administrator has privileged for you. A full-access user will see eight sections on the **Administration** screen.

The **Security** section provides links to the administration of catalog groups and system privileges.

Use the **Session Management** link to view currently logged in users and see what they are running. An active request could be canceled if they are taking too much time.

In Chapter 6, *Understanding the Systems Management Tools*, we will see that we can create **Users and Groups** in our security store (LDAP). The Presentation Catalog uses those groups and users that have been previously set up, but it also has the facility to create its own groups. This may be useful for certain types of special access that you want to set up, or to group various users together. This is not suitable in your LDAP system. An example of this could be giving some users extra administration rights on a temporary basis, for example, for a couple of hours during a deployment. Note that it is not the best practice to manage security in both the Presentation service and WebLogic Enterprise Manager. So, changes made directly in the Presentation Service Group Administration should be treated as temporary.

All of the features of the Presentation service can be secured by allowing access to certain individuals or groups that are using the **Manage Privileges** screen (accessed from within the **Administration** screen). These privileges are at a more detailed level than those set in the Enterprise Manager. Defining and maintaining the privileges is an important requirement for any OBIEE project. If you do not want to give access to untrained users to certain features or administration areas, you can choose the users carefully and the matrix can be created in advance to decide who can use what.

The **Manage Privileges** screen has various sections that relate to the parts of the system the named users can access or use. You can provide access to groups and/or users, and you can also deny specific groups or users access to a particular feature.

Reviewing the Features of the Reporting Repository

The main section to consider is the access rights. The first section of the **Manage Privileges** screen controls general access to the main tools, for example, dashboards:

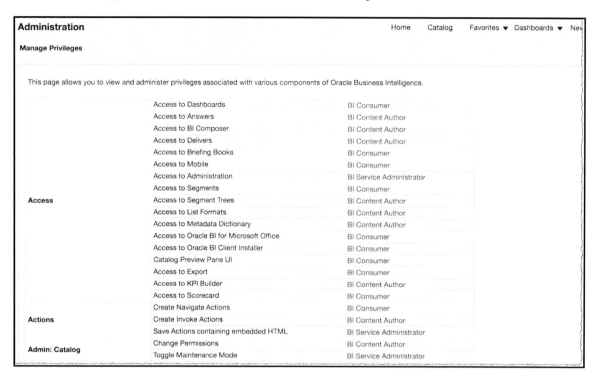

If you click on the link to the right of the item description, you can allocate or deny access. Try clicking on the **Access to Dashboards** link, which currently reads **BI Consumer**. Then, you will see a standard pop-up screen for allocating the rights to an object.

You can now click on the green plus sign to start adding more groups or users. This brings up the **Add Users and Group** form. Search for and select the role, group, or user to which you would like to give specific access. You can also select the role, group, or user for which you want to deny access.

Where possible, you should aim to assign permissions to roles. If this does not give sufficient granularity, choose groups. Again, if more granularity is required, choose individual users:

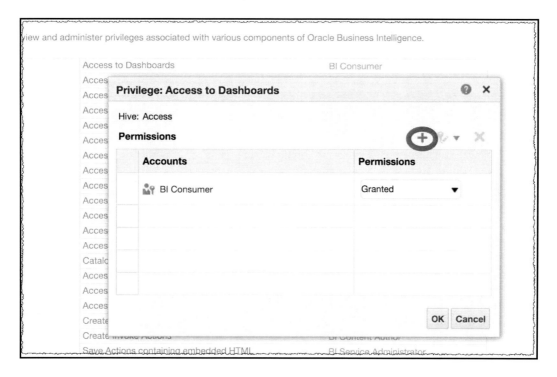

We will go into more depth on this in future chapters.

Session Management

On the **Administration** screen, there is a facility to view and manage the current sessions. Sessions are simple individuals that have logged in and are running analyses, dashboards, reports, and so on:

> **Session Management**
>
> Manage Sessions
> View Oracle Business Intelligence session information including active users and queries.
>
> Manage Agent Sessions
> View Agent session information including Agent state and recipients.

Clicking on the **Manage Sessions** link directs you to the session-listing screen. At the top of the list, there is a list of the sessions logged-in, and in a running system, you will see the recent requests that have been sent to the BI server. The list is also known as the **Cursor Cache** list.

In the column headed **Action**, you can see highlighted words on which you can click to invoke the action. For running requests, you can click on the **Cancel Running Requests** button to cancel the cursor. For finished requests, you can click on **View Log**, which will bring up a window showing the details of the requests. The level of detail depends on the logging level that is set for the user. We can set it to a level of granularity so that we can see the logical SQL being issued, and drill all the way down to see the native database SQL being issued.

We mainly use logging of queries to solve performance problems. The SQL sent to the database can be examined to check whether any bottlenecks exist in the database.

Maintenance and troubleshooting

This is a section on the **Administration** screen; it contains links to the following system settings:

- Managing mobile devices
- Loading metadata
- Toggling maintenance mode

Managing device types is not a common requirement, and in 12 years of OBIEE projects (new Siebel Analytics), I have never had a requirement to send data to a pager (!) or update the out-of-the-box settings.

Issue SQL

Under the **Maintenance and Troubleshooting**, there is a link to a significant feature-**Issue SQL**. The **Issue SQL** option is normally used to test the BI server, and is not normally made available to users. The SQL referred to here is the OBIEE Logical SQL, not ANSI SQL, but note that there is a subtle difference between the Logical SQL that can be run in an analysis and the logical SQL that can be run here. For example, the following statements make use of the * notation to select all fields in the presentation-layer tables:

```
SELECT * FROM Players
SELECT * FROM Tournaments
SELECT * FROM TIME
```

The following example uses the `SELECT_PHYSICAL` statement to query the physical layer object:

```
SELECT_PHYSICAL CALENDAR_DATE FROM "TENNIS".""""tennis"."W_DATE_D;
```

You can also use the * notation:

```
SELECT_PHYSICAL * FROM "TENNIS".""""tennis"."W_DATE_D;
```

Functions can also be used in the statement to count the number of records in the date table, for example:

```
SELECT_PHYSICAL count(*) FROM "TENNIS".""""tennis"."W_DATE_D;
```

We will cover more details on the Oracle BI SQL (also known as Logical SQL) syntax later in this book.

Catalog

All the tools mentioned at the beginning of the chapter store user-defined objects in a folder structure. This structure is bound together in a Presentation Catalog, also known as a **Web Catalog**. The catalog not only makes use of your operating system file and folder management, but also adds a layer of security and management. Each object is stored with a security reference and properties marker, which control when and how the objects are accessible:

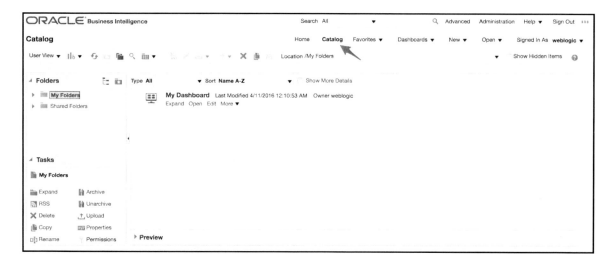

The catalog is managed by the web-based administration screens of the Presentation Server, or by using a Windows-based Catalog Administration tool (also known as the Catalog Manager).

All properties and controls are available directly in **Catalog View**. Tasks such as copying, renaming, and changing permissions are undertaken while browsing the catalog.

Structure of the Presentation Catalog

From a user's perspective, there are two main folders that contain the subfolders and stored objects. These folders are as follows:

- Users
- Shared

The users folder (`My Folders`) contains a subfolder for each user that logs in. This provides a space for the users to store their own analyses and other objects securely. The option to use personal storage folders can be disabled.

On a recent project, we had up to 50,000 potential users. This could make the user folder very difficult to navigate, so we implemented one of the advanced features, which arranges the user folders into subfolders. In this case, the subfolders were the first two characters of the user name. Users such as Daniel and Dave are available in the `DA` subfolder. For projects where you have more than 1,000 users, consider adding the `HashUserHomeHirectories` parameter to the instance `config.xml` file.

Click on the **Catalog** link on the common menu to explore the catalog. The default view includes your personal folders and shared folders to which you have access. If you have sufficient permissions, you can switch to **Admin View**. Click on the drop-down icon and select **Admin View**. Standard users do not have the option of **Admin View**:

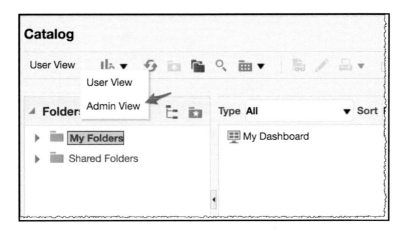

You are now presented with **Admin View**, which starts at a higher level of the Web Catalog **Catalog Root**. As an administrator, this allows you to see all the subfolders, but you will only be able to navigate to those folders if you have the permissions to do so. By default, you do not have permission to navigate to individual User Folders:

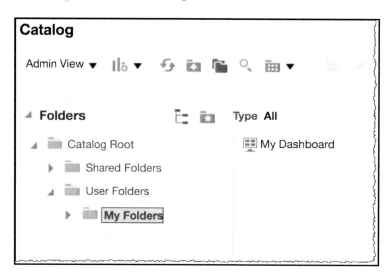

Hidden items

The objects you yourself create, such as your analyses or dashboard pages, are visible to you in your own User or Shared folders. There are also various hidden files that help to control your user experience. For example, users who have accessed the system using an iPad have their favorites stored in a hidden XML file.

To see the hidden items, tick on the **Show Hidden Items** checkbox in the top-right corner of the screen:

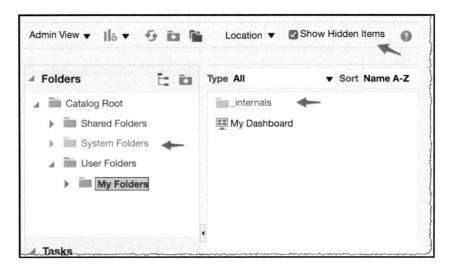

File management

Management of the catalog is undertaken using the Oracle-supplied tools, that is, the web-based Presentation Server. However, you can back up the whole catalog, or parts of it, such as a dashboard, using normal operating system tools. On Linux, I tend to use .tar to compress a folder and store this as a backup, or copy it into another environment.

XML files

The object definitions and hidden files contain XML. Using the Catalog Manager, you can view the XML being used, and can even edit it directly in the Catalog Manager. This is an advanced feature, which is not necessary on most projects, nor undertaken without fully understanding the XML structures.

The XML files are also visible in your normal file explorer, and they can be useful, for example, if you want to find which analyses use a particular column from your BI server.

Object copying

You can copy objects and complete dashboards. This feature speeds up the development cycles and encourages greater flexibility.

The method is widely available throughout the catalog, either in the **Tasks** pane (bottom-left corner) or by right-clicking on the object:

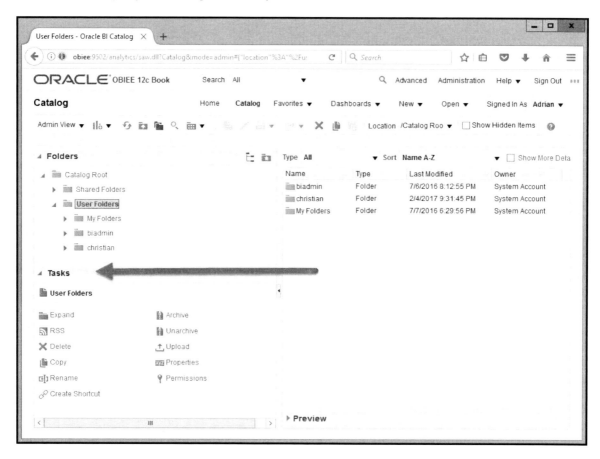

Users also have the ability to create more than one personal dashboard. For some power users, a single dashboard-**My Dashboard**-is just not enough. Having said that, it is also possible to create a dashboard in the **Shared Folders** and set the permissions so that you are the only person to see it; it has the same effect.

The downside of multiple personal dashboards is that only one dashboard **My Dashboard** is listed in the Dashboards menu. To navigate to other personal dashboards, you can locate them under **My Folders** in **Catalog View**.

Catalog deployments

One of the challenges we face on every project is how to develop, test, and deploy new dashboards and analyses without breaking the existing ones. Various approaches have been used at various companies, which either involve lots of downtime or, worse, no user-developed reporting. My preferred method is to use another part of the production system to create new dashboards, and only expose these when the testers have signed it off. This approach minimizes the risks of deploying from one network to another (which include permission issues and loss of user settings).

OBIEE 12c has a neat solution that allows users to archive their analysis, dashboards, folders, or other catalog objects, and save these archive files on the network. They can then be imported (unarchived) into another catalog. This process can be used to copy from a test catalog to a production one, for example.

Securing catalog objects

Each folder, dashboard, analysis, and report has permissions attached. In fact, every object in the catalog has a form of permissions. In a preceding section, we saw that access to the features in the Presentation Catalog and Presentation Server have specific permissions (set by the **Privileges** screen), but access to the feature does not automatically allow access to the objects in the feature (for example, a report).

Multiple personal dashboards

The permissions for the objects can be found under the right-click drop-down menu. The following screenshot shows the **Permissions** link for the `Sample Reports` folder:

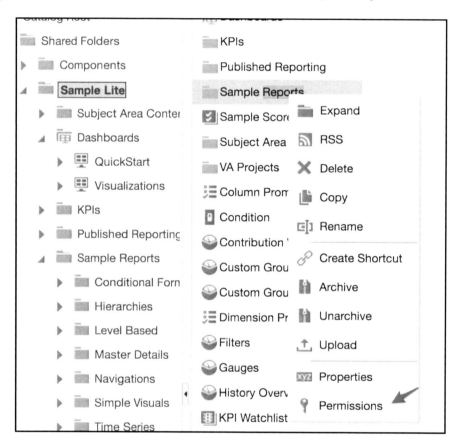

If you click on the **Permissions** link, you will be presented with the **Permissions** form. A standard layout is used for all the objects, as seen in the following screenshot:

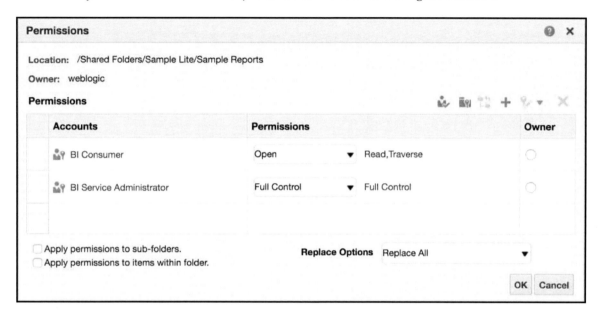

Here we can set permission levels (from full control to denied access). Note the options at the bottom of the form **Apply permission to sub-folders** and **Apply permissions to items within folder**. These are best left in the default mode of not applying.

Note that the dashboard sits inside a folder, so changing the folder can change the selection of users who can see your dashboard.

Permission inheritance

When a new object is saved in a folder, it inherits the permissions of that folder. You can overwrite the permission settings if required at the individual level, but in practice, this could end up in an administrative nightmare.

A review - what I should now know!

The following points are very important for you to remember:

- What reporting and analytical features are accessible from the OBIEE Home page
- What security options are available
- How the Presentation Catalog is organized
- How to set parameters and options for the BI tools
- What administration tools are available

Summary

In this chapter, we introduced the Oracle BI Presentation Catalog and all its features and tools.

Integrating published reporting allows a total reporting solution that fits the needs of each user, all from one place.

Managing security and deployments is simplified with integration, along with the ability for users to bring the Oracle BI reporting output to their desktops and into their daily routines.

If you are new to some of these concepts and it is confusing, be assured that we will go into far more detail on each reporting feature as the book progresses.

In the next chapter, we will look at installing the OBIEE system.

5
Installing and Configuring Client Tools

Up until this part of the book, we have focused on creating a server environment that will run the OBIEE system. As you have seen, you can already use the system by logging in to the frontend dashboards at `http://localhost:9502/analytics`. Now we want to control what is available for the frontend to display.

We need to install the tools that will be used to build the **metadata layer**. The metadata layer is the part of the system that converts database columns into user friendly fields we can use in the Answers web application.

The main tool that will be installed is the Oracle BI Administration tool, which is used to edit the repository (RPD) files. There are also several other RPD management tools that are installed, along with a Web Catalog manager and Jobs manager.

This chapter will cover:

- Installing the client software
- Configuring a connection to the OBIEE server
- Configuring a connection to the database
- Creating shortcuts
- Testing the client software

Installing and Configuring Client Tools

Installing the client software

The OBIEE Server software can be installed on Windows- or Linux-/Unix-/AIX- based systems, but the *client tools* can only be installed on Windows, and you will need to check the Certification Matrix for the versions that are supported. In this book, we have shown it being installed on the same server as the main OBIEE server, but you can install it on any Windows PC that can connect to the server where you installed the software. If you want to install on an Apple Mac, we recommend using VirtualBox from Oracle.

Installation is simple and quick:

1. First, locate the installation media you downloaded previously:

This will fire up the Oracle installer:

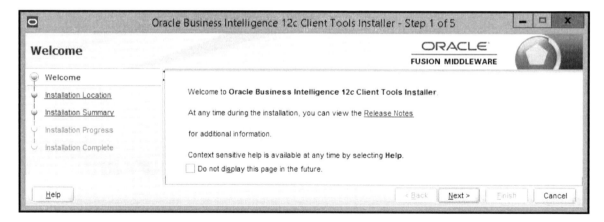

2. For step two, enter a folder for the client installation:

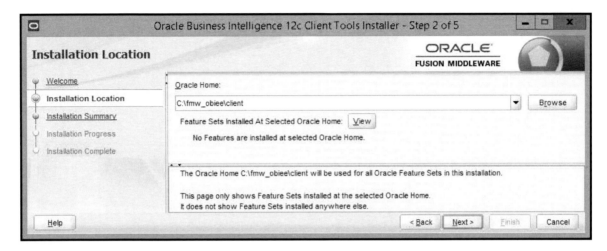

3. Step three is a simple confirmation. Click on the **Install** button:

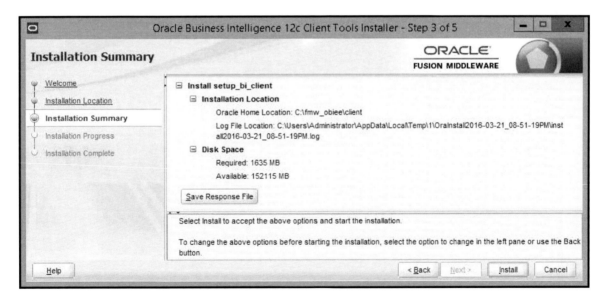

Installing and Configuring Client Tools

This will fire up the Oracle Installer:

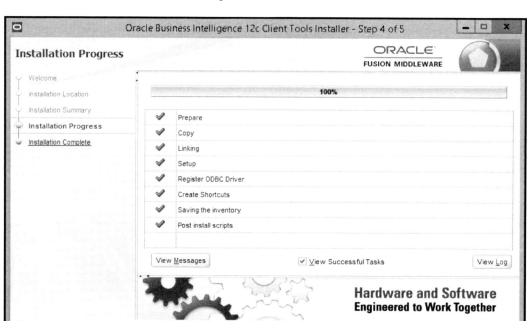

4. When you see all green ticks, you can click on the **Next** button; you are presented with a summary:

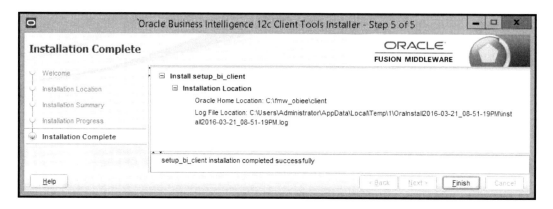

That's it: like I said, simple and easy! However, we now have several tasks ahead to make the system usable.

Configuring a connection to the OBIEE Server

In order to use our newly installed software, we have to tell it how to connect to our OBIEE Server. This is done through a simple **Data Source Name** (**DSN**), created on the PC where you installed the client.

We will create a new DSN, even if you have one installed:

1. Open the **ODBC Data Source Administrator (64 bit)**. This can be done from a link in the Control Panel or by typing `odbcad32.exe` in a Windows Run (windows key + R) command line.

   This opens the Administrator tool window on the **User** tab.

2. Select the **System DSN** tab:

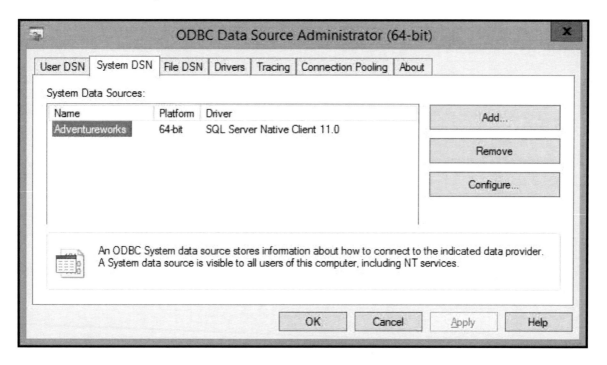

Installing and Configuring Client Tools

3. Click on **Add....**

    This will open the **Create New Data Source** dialog box:

    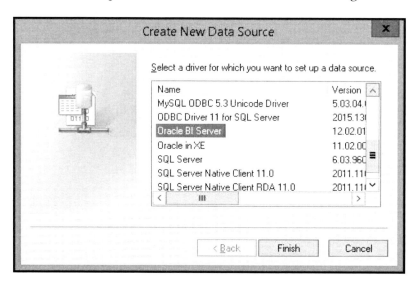

4. Select the **Oracle BI Server** from the list of available drivers. Make sure you select the 12c version if you have 11g already installed.
5. Click on **Finish**. Weird to click on finish already!

    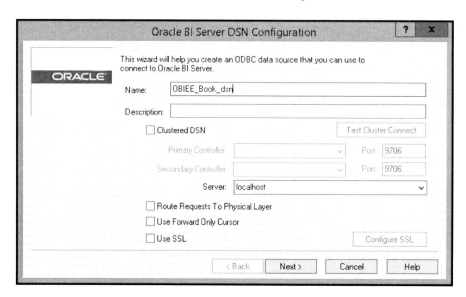

6. Enter the name (we have chosen to call it something meaningful).
7. Enter the details of the server (name or IP address).
8. Click on **Next**:

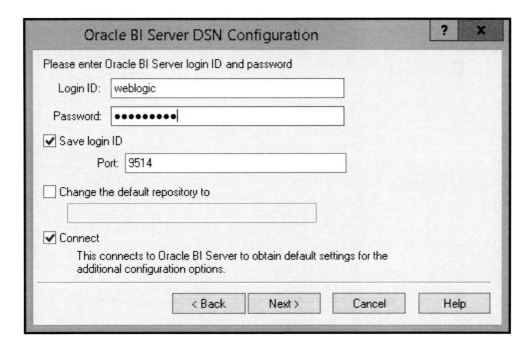

9. Now enter the username and password you created during the installation.
10. Change the port number to the one that was installed; in our case, it was 9514. If you are unsure, and 9514 did not work, go to the **BI Instance Availability** page in **Enterprise Manager**, where you will see what port numbers are in use.
11. Click on **Next**.

Installing and Configuring Client Tools

If your settings are correct, you will get the following dialog page. If you have an error on the screen, go back and make sure the port numbers, server name, username, and password are all correct:

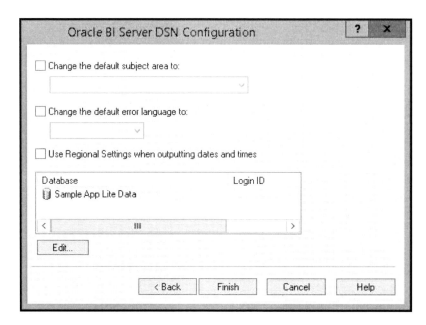

You now have a connection set up and nearly ready to use in the OBI Admin Tool.

Configuring a connection to the database

As you will see in the following chapter, one of the tasks that we set is to create a set of tables in the repository that mirror the tables in your database. This is best done when you can connect your client to the database you are modeling.

Creating a connection to your database is simple if you have the client software already installed on your workstation. For example, if you are connecting to Oracle, you will need the Oracle drivers on your machine.

We are connecting to the AdventureWorks database on SQL Server, which is on our local machine where the OBIEE client is installed; this means the software is already in place. In your installation, you may have to download the driver. Search `Microsoft.com` for an ODBC driver that matches your Windows version and database version, and install that first.

When the software is in place, create a new DSN using the SQL Server driver and you are ready to go.

At this point, you can move on to the next chapter, but if you want to connect to an Oracle database (and who wouldn't?), you will need to do some more work.

When you use the **Oracle Client (OCI)** connector, you can use a TNS name, and the system looks for the description of the TNS name in a file called `tnsnames.ora`. The default place it looks for the file is in the folder called `<<CLIENT INSTALL FOLDER>>\domains\bi\config\fmwconfig\bienv\core`, which in our example is `C:\fmw_obiee\client\domains\bi\config\fmwconfig\bienv\core`.

Copy your `tnsnames.ora` file into this core folder.

> An alternative method when connecting using the OCI connector is to use the full description instead of the TNS name. For example, use the following:
> `(DESCRIPTION =(ADDRESS = (PROTOCOL = TCP)(HOST = localhost)(PORT = 1521))(CONNECT_DATA =(SERVER = DEDICATED) (SERVICE_NAME = XE)))`.

Creating shortcuts

When you installed the client software, it probably created some of those icons on the main apps page in Windows 8 (or Windows 10). My advice, before you get stuck in the next chapters, is to put these shortcuts in the start area, and even on the taskbar. The two main shortcuts you will use are **Administration** and **Catalog Manager**. Right-click on those in the main **Apps** page and select **Pin to Start**.

Testing the client software

Now that we have configured all the connections, let's make sure they work properly before we head to the next chapter.

The first test is to check the connection to the live OBIEE Server:

1. Open the **Oracle BI Administration Tool**.
2. From the **File** menu, navigate to **Open | Online**.
3. Select the DSN we created earlier and enter the username and password.

4. Click on **Open**.

   You should now see the three panels of the repository:

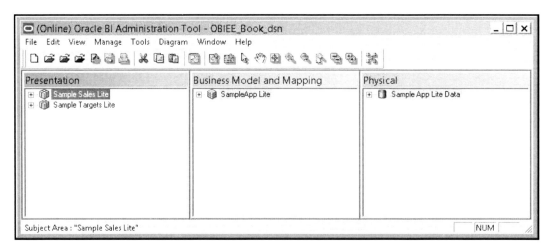

   The next test is to verify that you can see the **AdventureWorks** database.

5. Navigate to **File | Import Metadata**.
6. Select the **AdventureWork DSN** that we set up earlier.
7. Enter the username and password details.

   If you get to the following screen, then all is working okay and you can click on **Cancel** (we will show how to import fully in Chapter 7, *Developing the BI Server Repository*):

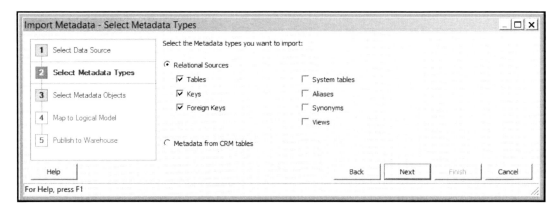

If, at any stage, you get an error, then again try making sure that the passwords are correct. If that still doesn't work, check the DSN. If it's still not working, then check the log files.

The log files that relate to the client Administration tool on our install are located in C:fmw_obieeclientdomainsbiserversobis1logs. The log is normally prefixed with the logged-in user's name. Make sure you check the file for any errors or warnings.

The next test is to try the catalog manager:

1. Click on the **Catalog Manager** link on the start menu.
2. When the Catalog Manager loads, navigate to **File** | **Open Catalog**.
3. Choose to open **Online**, and enter the URL of the Server. Our URL is http://localhost:9502/analytics/saw.dll:

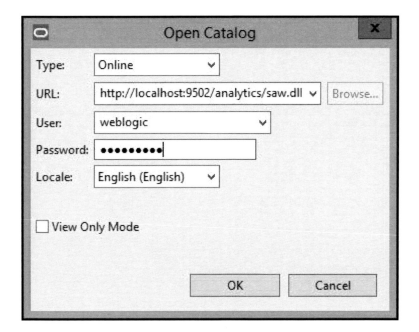

4. Click on **OK**.

You should now click on **OK,** and you will see the folder of the online catalog:

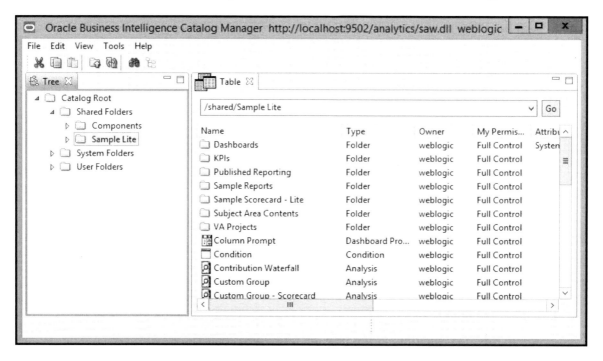

A review - what I should now know!

The following points are very important for you to remember:

- How to install the client software
- How to configure a Data Source Name
- How to open and test the client tools

Summary

In this chapter, we installed the client software in a Windows machine. There is no equivalent Linux install for the client tools. We installed an editor for the OBIEE repository and a specialist OBIEE catalog manager.

We then updated the configuration so that the software is usable, by creating a shared Data Source and a TNS entry to our Oracle database. Finally, we tested everything, to make sure that all the connections worked, by trying to connect to our database.

This chapter is crucial for the task set out in `Chapter 7`, *Developing the BI Server Repository*, but the client tools are not required if we just wanted to dive into the dashboard-creation tasks in `Chapter 8`, *Creating Dashboards and Analyses*.

6
Understanding the Systems Management Tools

Oracle BI 12c is an enterprise application suite and comprises several major application components that tie it all together. Together, the components operate as a system. These components typically run on a server and are configured by using a web-client interface, an API library, or a command-line interface. These tools, which configure the system, are referred to as System Management tools as they coordinate the operation of the entire Oracle BI 12c system. The WebLogic and Fusion Control administration interfaces were briefly covered in a previous chapter.

This chapter goes into greater detail about each. We'll explain what these components are, what they do, and how they work together. We will delve into the navigation of these tools so that you become more familiar with the interfaces and learn what components are specific to Oracle BI 12c. We will also explore which key controls are used to maintain the Oracle BI 12c environment. These components are slightly different from prior versions of Oracle BI and, in some ways, are more efficient.

Finally, this chapter contains security exercises for creating the users and groups that will be used to integrate the repository dashboards and reports you will develop in subsequent chapters, similar to what you would do in a real-world corporate environment.

Understanding the Systems Management Tools

Let's talk management tools

Oracle BI 12c is based on the Fusion Middleware architecture, which provides two core applications, **WebLogic Server** (**WLS**) Administration Console and **Enterprise Manager** (**EM**) Fusion Middleware Control. Oracle BI is deployed with a limited-use license for Oracle BI. This means that the WebLogic software itself is still the fully functioning product, but the implementation of WLS is bound to certain restrictions, such as a non-scaled-out environment, which would require the additional purchase (always consult your Oracle representative for these details) of an enterprise license for WLS. WLS and EM manage configurations that have a systemic impact. Basically, if those applications aren't online and available, neither is your Oracle BI 12c deployment. Yes, there are other management consoles that allow specific control of the individual applications, such as Oracle BI 12c server, BI Publisher, MapViewer, and so on. Those consoles are referred to as **Application Administration Tools**, all of which are part of a larger system that is managed by the System Management tools and are the topic of discussion for this chapter.

WLS and EM can be accessed through a standard web-based **Graphical User Interface** (**GUI**), as well as through command line and programmatic means. Access points for managing the system can be broken down into two classes: GUI and Programmatic.

The main programmatic interface tools for WebLogic are referred to as the Oracle BI Systems Management **Application Programming Interface** (**API**):

- **WebLogic Scripting Tool** (**WLST**): A command-line interface included with the WLS installation that provides a way to manage WLS domains, their objects, and artifacts. WLST leverages the Jython programming language and WLST-specific commands to script logic that executes against WLS.

Oracle BI 12c also introduces a **Representational State Transfer** (**REST**) protocol API. REST (or RESTful Web Services) relies on a stateless, client-server, cacheable communications protocol - and in virtually all cases the HTTP protocol is used. REST is an architecture style for designing networked applications and has become exceedingly popular in application-programming interfaces since 2010.

WebLogic Server Administration Control

If you have any WLS experience, you will understand that WLS is an application in its own right, and a server that runs other applications. If you don't have any WLS experience, don't be discouraged by the many options and configuration points that it offers. At the moment, only concern yourself with the WLS components that relate to the operation of the Oracle BI 12c environment.

The goal of this section is for you to familiarize yourself with the Oracle BI 12c System Management tools. You'll review the main areas of the system, which an Oracle BI administrator frequents, and gain a better sense of how Oracle BI 12c fits together with Fusion Middleware. Follow along from your Oracle BI 12c installation with the steps provided in the following subsections.

First access and checkpoint

Let's begin by getting into the WLS administration console. This is fairly straightforward; just complete the following steps:

1. Navigate to the WLS administration console via `http://<server_name>:<default port>/console/` (the default port is typically 9500 for Oracle BI 12c), where `<server_name>` is the name of the server where you've installed Oracle BI 12c.
    - For previous versions of Oracle BI, for example, 11g, the WLS port is 7001
2. Once logged in, you will see a navigation index on the left-hand pane of the GUI. You will use this navigation panel to move around WLS for these walkthrough exercises. Notice the `bi` domain under the **Domain Structure** section. BI is the default name of the WLS domain into which Oracle BI 12c is installed:

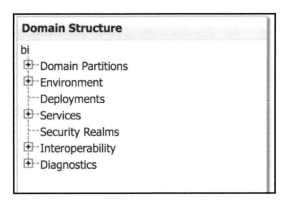

Please keep in mind the Change Center area above the **Domain Structure** menu shown in the preceding screenshot, since you will frequently use the **Change Center Lock & Edit** and **Release Configuration** options when administering WLS.

Understanding the Systems Management Tools

If your login was successful, continue with the steps. If not, make sure that your WebLogic Server has been started. We are operating under the premise that the Oracle BI 12c installation succeeded and all is operational from this point forward.

> **Let's get started!**
> As shown in an earlier chapter, the Oracle BI 12c system launches in the default browser after installation completes, in a Windows OS. At this time in the installation, the entire system, including WLS, is up-and-running. If you have restarted the machine and so on, you must start the Oracle BI 12c system via the command line. The easiest way to get Oracle BI 12c started is to open a terminal window or command prompt. Then, navigate to the ORACLE_HOME folder and the /bitools folder for your Oracle BI 12c installation,
> <ORACLE_HOME>\user_projects\domains\bi\bitools\bin, then execute the start.cmd|sh script.

You'll stay inside the WebLogic Server administration console during this walkthrough, until otherwise stated.

Servers

As an indication of how the Oracle BI 12c environment was installed and what scaled-out servers have been included in the post-installation configuration, the Servers page provides great insight into the current state of the infrastructure. No matter what installation type you choose, the **AdminServer** (admin) will always be found in this list. The Oracle BI 12c installation is always considered an Enterprise installation. Previous versions of Oracle BI, such as 11g, had installation concepts such as Software Only or Simple Installations, but these do not exist in the installation of Oracle BI 12c. As Oracle BI 12c is configured during the installation and configuration process, you should expect to see the bi_server1 managed server in this WLS Servers list as well:

1. Expand the Environment node under the bi domain in the navigation pane.
2. Click on the Servers link.

3. Click on the `bi_server1` managed server name, which is a link to its specific configuration page:

	Name	Type	Cluster	Machine	State	Health	Listen Port
☐	AdminServer(admin)	Configured			RUNNING	✔ OK	9500
☐	bi_server1	Configured	bi_cluster	AMAZONA-artofbi	RUNNING	✔ OK	9502

| New | Clone | Delete | Showing 1 to 2 of 2 Previous | Next |

- Notice the many tabs and options available to you on the Settings page for `bi_server1`. The **Configuration** | **General**, **Keystores**, and **SSL** sub-tabs, and **Monitoring** tab are where most of the advanced configuration for the Oracle BI 12c managed server will take place.
- On the **General** tab, you can see a position where the ability to change the default port numbers for Oracle BI 12c analytics exists. Often, Oracle BI customers change these ports, but technically they should be using an HTTP server tier with software such as OHS, Apache, or IIS, which are better options if you need a different port number to access the Oracle BI portal.

Next, let's talk about the WLS domain cluster for Oracle BI 12c.

Clusters

A WLS domain cluster establishes the context for the scalability and reliability that come from adding one or more managed servers to the domain. Oracle BI establishes a default cluster in WLS, `bi_cluster`. This cluster refers to a WLS domain cluster, which has the goal of allowing redundancy and high-availability to be configured. This domain-cluster configuration is for the application server nodes themselves. This should not be confused with clustering the Oracle BI Server system components. A domain cluster is required for scaling-out Oracle BI. The term scaling-out typically refers to either scaling-up vertically, for adding processing power on the same server, or scaling-out horizontally to one or more separate servers for high-availability and fault-tolerance.

Understanding the Systems Management Tools

Expand `bi > Environment > Clusters` to see the default cluster configuration established during the default installation configuration of Oracle BI. The name of the cluster is `bi_cluster`. The default configuration for the cluster should be left alone unless an advanced implementation specifically requires modifying it:

Name	Cluster Address	Cluster Messaging Mode	Migration Basis	Default Load Algorithm	Replication Type	Cluster Broadcast Channel	Servers
bi_cluster		Unicast	Database	Round Robin	(None)		bi_server1

New | Clone | Delete   Showing 1 to 1 of 1   Previous | Next

Next, we'll look at where the identifying address of the Oracle BI server(s) resides in WLS.

Machines / IP address or DNS

Knowing where and how an installation recognizes the server on which it resides is important. During an install or scale-out, the WLS administration console keeps track of its immediate location, as well as any other nodes in the cluster. Any changes to a server's IP address or DNS after installation can be painful to correct, so avoid doing so if at all possible. In a horizontal scale-out, Oracle recommends using a load balancer and virtual IP addresses to handle this complexity:

1. From the left-hand-pane navigation menu, expand `bi > Environment > Machines`.
2. In the **Machines** table list, you should see the name of the server on which you have installed Oracle BI.
3. In a horizontally scaled-out environment, multiple machine names would be listed here.
4. Click on the name of the machine in the **Machine** list.
5. Under the **Configuration** main tab, click the **Node Manager** sub-tab.
6. Notice that this area provides insight into the Node Manager, which should reside on each managed server associated with a WLS domain. By default, the Node Manager communicates over SSL on port `9506` (the previous version of Oracle BI 11g listened on port 9556 by default). The earlier chapter on the installation process discussed how this port could have been modified using the advanced custom-ports configuration during the installation of the software.

7. Click the Monitoring main tab and then the **Node Manager Log** sub-tab.
8. On the Node Manager Log page, you can see the status and log information for the Node Manager on that machine. This is often helpful for diagnosing more advanced integrations and modifications made to the SSL or port configurations.

Next, let's explore the easily overlooked data-source connection settings that are seldom, if at all, modified for a standard implementation.

Data Sources / JDBC connections

WLS is a Java application server. One of the biggest benefits from WLS hosting JEE applications (such as BI Publisher and other Oracle-BI-related applications) is the performance gain achieved by reducing the opening and closing of database connections via leveraging connection pools. WLS controls the connection pooling. The deployed JEE applications typically access the JDBC data-source connections created in the Data Sources area of WLS by calling the JNDI name associated with the JDBC connection:

1. From the left-hand-pane navigation menu, expand `bi` > `Services`.
2. Click on **Data Sources**.

   The resulting page is the **Summary of JDBC Data Sources** management area. Here are the application server-registered Data Sources, which can be leveraged by one or more applications deployed on the WebLogic Server.

3. On the **Data Sources** table, look at the column, **Targets**. As you can see, each of these **Data Sources** is deployed to (that is, accessible from) the server names listed in the **Targets** column. `bi_cluster` is listed as one of the targets, which means that any managed server included in that cluster is a candidate.

   The default web-based applications and/or libraries deployed to the same target(s) as the JDBC connections, such as Oracle BI and BI Publisher, are programmed to reference these default Data Sources. For example, the **mds-owsm** connection is set up as a default connection, which we know is a reference to the MDS metadata repository created by the RCU. BI Publisher and Oracle BI both communicate with that scheme in some way. Although you may not see a configuration setting for the connection within the Oracle BI application itself, the underlying program code has a reference.

4. The following screenshot shows mainly the default connections list configured during an installation or Oracle BI 12c. The **JNDI Name** column is usually the specific reference to this data source used within the application code, so do not modify any of these names or settings. Multiple repository schemas are deployed during the Oracle BI 12c installation, via the RCU, including `BIPLATFORM_DATASOURCE` and `MDS-OWSM`, with which users of the legacy Oracle BI 11g system will be familiar. However, there are several new schemas in Oracle BI 12c. One new change is that the OPSS data store now resides in a database schema repository and no longer in file-system storage:

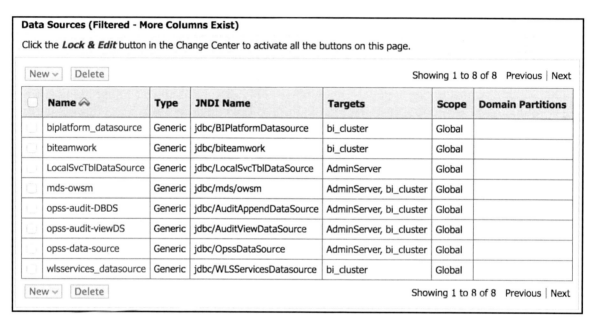

5. Click on the **biplatform_datasource** data source under the **Name** column.
6. Click the **Configuration** tab and then the **Connection Pool** sub-tab.
7. Scroll down to the **URL** input field and notice the connection string that was established during the installation configuration process.

8. Scroll down a bit further and notice the **Properties** box.

   Here you can see that an explicit reference to the BIPLATFORM schema created during the installation via RCU is made. The data source you clicked on is used for Oracle BI metadata, and the reference to this scheme is due to the fact that several tables hold metadata, such as scheduler information specific to the BI tools.

9. Click on the **Monitoring** main tab in this section. Then, click on the **Testing** sub-tab.
10. Click on the radio button in the **Server** table list corresponding to the managed server, for example, `bi_server1`, on which this data source is deployed:

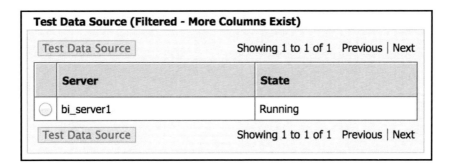

11. Click the **Test Data Sources** button:
    - A connection success message should appear above the tabs of this section

Next we'll take a look at exactly how and where the Fusion Middleware security model for Oracle BI 12c is managed.

Security Realms

Management of the over arching system security will take place in the Security Realms area. A Security Realm is basically a configuration area to manage how WLS resources are protected. This is where you configure users, groups, and other security profiles that determine how access to applications deployed on the WLS server and the WLS administration console itself is achieved. More than one Security Realm can exist, but only one can be used as the active realm from which the security configuration for the application server is sourced. Thus, during the Oracle BI installation configuration, only one Security Realm, **myrealm**, is created. It is within this realm that we will configure and manage authentication providers such as a company's LDAP directory and so on.

> Note that WLS itself contains an Embedded LDAP directory. This is also referred to as the **DefaultAuthenticator**. It follows the open standard LDAP v3 protocol, and could indeed support custom build directories for a small organization to host users (10,000 or fewer) and groups. Although most organizations use a more enterprise LDAP standard such as those offered by Microsoft or Oracle, it is always good to know the capabilities of a tool.

Later in this chapter, we will conduct a step-by-step exercise in assigning an enterprise LDAP directory - **Microsoft Active Directory** (**MSAD**) - as a WLS identity provider to show how an organization's core network-identity authentication repository can be used with the Oracle BI Fusion Middleware architecture. Let's take a look at navigating through the Security Realm area to understand where the key points of activity reside:

1. From the left-hand-pane navigation menu, expand **bi** > **Security Realms**.
2. Click on the solo Security Realm, **myrealm**, under the **Name** column in the **Realms** table list.
3. The default landing sub-tab is **Configuration** > **General**. This area highlights a few of the global Security Realm settings, which can be left alone for a basic Oracle BI configuration.
4. Click on the **Users and Groups** main tab, then click the **Users** sub-tab.

5. This will show the WLS-embedded LDAP server users. There should, by default, be three users established during the installation configuration: **weblogic** (biadmin, or whatever you decided to call this administrative user during the installation), **OracleSystemUser**, and **LCMUser**:
   - There is no longer a default BISystemUser, which is a change from the previous Oracle BI 11g version
6. Additional users can be added to this list at any time by clicking the **New** button and completing the resulting Add new user form:

Name	Description	Provider
LCMUser	This is the default service account for WebLogic Server Lifecycle Manager configuration updates.	DefaultAuthenticator
OracleSystemUser	Oracle application software system user.	DefaultAuthenticator
weblogic	This user is the default administrator.	DefaultAuthenticator

7. Click on the **Groups** sub-tab.

   Similar to the users established by default within the embedded WLS LDAP directory, several groups are also established. The default installation propagates three core Oracle BI groups: **BIAdministrators**, **BIAuthors**, and **BIConsumers**.

8. Click on the **Providers** main tab. Ensure the **Authentication** sub-tab is selected as the default. If not, click it.

   You should be able to see the three default identity providers, **Trust Service Identity Asserter**, **DefaultAuthenticator**, and **DefaultIdentityAsserter**. These default to the WLS installation. It is here under this **Providers** > **Authentication** sub-tab where you may configure an LDAP directory, described later in this chapter:

Name	Description	Version
Trust Service Identity Asserter	Trust Service Identity Assertion Provider	1.0
DefaultAuthenticator	WebLogic Authentication Provider	1.0
DefaultIdentityAsserter	WebLogic Identity Assertion provider	1.0

9. Click on the main **Migration** tab.

   Here you can see that the possibility to import and export security-provider information is available. This is good to know when copying some security credentials from one server environment to another. Security migrations in Oracle BI 12 are emphasized by the documentation as requiring to be conducted using the new lifecycle management tools in this version and not previous version techniques.

WebLogic Server is its own application

Working with WLS in the context of Oracle BI for the first time, it is easy to miss the fact that WLS is its own Oracle product. In the case of Oracle BI 12c integration, it is WebLogic Server 12c. To exemplify WLS's ability to act as a standalone product, a company may license WebLogic Server Enterprise Edition solely to service their internally developed application (typically, Java/JEE) deployment needs. Here are a few items that often get overlooked:

- As mentioned previously, after the default Oracle BI installation, a default set of users and groups is created in the WLS-embedded LDAP. The users and groups established by default here are a mix of users and groups for Oracle BI and the WebLogic Server application itself. Looking at the list of groups within the groups table, you see a group named **Administrators**, but also a group named **BIAdministrators**.
- The **Administrators** group is specific to the WLS application. That is to say that a WLS user belonging to this group will have administration rights to log in to the WLS administration console and manage it.
- The **BIAdministrators** group signifies a bucket for users established within the WLS-embedded `LDAP` directory that should have access to certain administration rights within the Oracle BI application.
- The WebLogic user exists in both the **BIAdministrators** and **Administrators** groups by default, which is why that user is the *God-like* user on the system. If you recall from the installation chapter, the name of this user is created during the installation and is arbitrary, although the default and recommended name is **weblogic**.
- WLS contains an Embedded `LDAP` directory and as such it can be accessed via standard LDAP-browsing tools. Leveraging an open-source tool such as **JXplorer** will allow you to view information about the repository, such as its users and groups.

- After conducting the preceding walkthrough in the WLS administration console, you can clearly see that there are many tabs and configuration sections available to manage the application server. Most of the other sections and tabs not mentioned are for advanced configurations. Any sections that were not mentioned in the preceding walkthrough are most likely not crucial to a basic Oracle BI configuration or administration routine.

Using WLST

Every Oracle BI Administrator should know the WLST. Eventually, the need will arise to use some advanced features against the application server - WLS - that hosts Oracle BI in order to automate or make short work of repetitive functions. In Oracle BI 12c, it's the lifecycle-management tools where administrators will make the most use of WLST. WLST is one of the ways in which you can interface with the application server. WLST is fairly straightforward to use. Its command-line interface is launched from a directory underneath the ORACLE_HOME installation root of Oracle BI 12c; typically, on the server for which the installation resides. However, WLST, when located on a networked server, may communicate with any another WebLogic Server located on the network.

Let's conduct a quick exercise that will show you how to launch the WLST interface. In addition, you'll run a few quick commands to return some simple data from the WLS server.

1. Launch WLST from a Terminal or command-prompt window on the server where Oracle BI 12c is installed, using the path and command, `<ORACLE_HOME>\oracle_common\common\bin\wlst.cmd`:

   Example: `C:\obiee\oracle_common\common\bin\wlst.cmd`

   On a Nix OS, launch WLST using the `./wlst.sh` command in the similar path, `<ORACLE_HOME>/oracle_common/common/bin/`.

The script first attempts to load a series of environment variables into the Terminal session so that WLST's required libraries can be assessed. This is all part of the program's procedure before the WLST engine can be ready for use on the command prompt or Terminal. As the launch message states, it can take up to a few minutes for the WLST prompt to ready itself for use.

Once the environment variables have been loaded, you will be presented with a command-prompt cursor and are ready to access the WLST program in offline mode.

Be sure to launch the WLST command from the file path specified above. Use the command-prompt or Terminal window so that you can view the output in real time. There are other ways to launch WLST, but those methods will not provide you with the access that you need for Oracle BI.

2. At the command prompt, connect to the WLS server by entering the following and pressing Enter:

```
connect('weblogic', '<password>','<server_name>:<port>');
```

Example:

```
connect('weblogic', 'Admin123','localhost:9500');
```

```
C:\Oracle\OBIEE12cHome\oracle_common\common\bin>wlst.cmd
Initializing WebLogic Scripting Tool (WLST) ...
Welcome to WebLogic Server Administration Scripting Shell
Type help() for help on available commands
wls:/offline> connect('weblogic', 'Admin123','localhost:9500
Connecting to t3://localhost:9500 with userid weblogic ...
Successfully connected to Admin Server "AdminServer" that be
Warning: An insecure protocol was used to connect to the ser
To ensure on-the-wire security, the SSL port or Admin port s
wls:/bi/serverConfig/>
```

If the WLS server is running and the credentials are valid, a successful connection message will be returned. With a successful online connection, there are many commands that could be entered to explore the WebLogic Server, and to a small degree the Oracle BI server. To keep your first foray into WLST simple but powerful, let's programmatically create an embedded WLS LDAP user.

3. Enter the following code lines into the command prompt; each line break should be a new line by pressing Enter:

```
dauth=cmo.getSecurityConfiguration().getDefaultRealm().lookupAuthenticationProvider("DefaultAuthenticator")
dauth.createUser('obi12cbook','Admin123','OBI 12c Book User')
```

4. The result should be the silent (that is, no response message) creation of a new user within the WLS embedded `LDAP` directory.

5. Quickly breaking down the preceding code, the first line instantiates the look-up function call for the identity provider defined as the argument. As we saw when walking through the WLS administration console, there are two default identity providers, one of which is named `DefaultAuthenticator`.

6. The second line makes reference to the now instantiated `dauth` object and calls the `createUser` function, passing three arguments to the parameters: `username`, `password`, and `username alias`.

> Syntax errors are bound to happen when working with WLST as the code is case-sensitive. One point to note is that the majority of WLST commands comply with the camel-case coding convention.

7. Open the WLS administration console and navigate to the **myrealm** Security Realm **User and Groups** tab. Refresh the page if needed to see the new user that you just created:

obi12cbook	OBI 12c Book User
OracleSystemUser	Oracle application software system user.

8. You could nearly manage all WLS operations via WLST. There is an entire document, `http://docs.oracle.com/cd/E15523_01/web.1111/e13813/toc.htm`, dedicated to WLST, which comes with the WLS offering from Oracle. The information we've offered gives you a practical insight into how to get started with WLST, as well as giving you an idea of what else it can do for you. For quick assistance, you can always type the, help(), command from the WLST prompt to get more information on using the tool.

Enterprise Manager Fusion Middleware Control

The WebLogic Administration Console's complementary web-based console, rounding out the System Management GUI tools, is the **Fusion Middleware Control** (**Fusion Control**). First introduced in Oracle BI 11g for OBIEE, it still exists in a similar capacity for Oracle BI 12c. It is the main interface to configure advanced Oracle BI options and to monitor and troubleshoot the Oracle BI system.

Presentation Catalog is a term introduced in Oracle BI 11g that continues to get used in version Oracle BI 12c. It is synonymous with the legacy term **Web Catalog**, referring to the Oracle BI Presentation Services' artifacts file repository for dashboards, reports, and so on.

This section will guide you through the Fusion Control console and explain each section as you navigate through it. Let's start by logging in to the EM console to have a look around.

Getting around in EM

The Fusion Control console is not WLS. It is a completely separate JEE application that is deployed into the **AdminServer** of the WLS system deployed. In the following steps, you'll learn how to log in to the EM console and navigate around the interface:

1. Navigate to the URL `http://<server_name>:9500/em`.
2. Enter the `weblogic` user credentials in the prompt and click the **Login** button:

Chapter 6

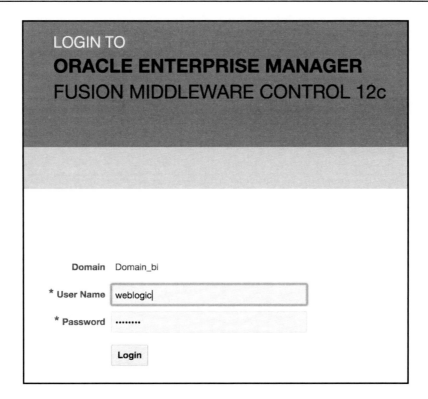

 Once logged in to EM, the main landing page is the server information dashboard page. This provides basic statistics on the running managed servers in the WLS server.

BI Foundation Domain Dashboard

The main page provides an overview of the management console and all paths from which you get more insight into the environment. The dashboard is broken up into left and right panes. The right pane always contains some core content information, while the left pane is used for high-level KPIs regarding the environment:

1. Click on the menu icon to the left of the **bi** domain name:

2. Click on the link for **Business Intelligence** > **biinstance** in the left-hand pane.
3. Review the **Overview** tab, which should be the default tab area presented:

Overview tab

The **Overview** tab provides a quick glance at the server status, capacity statistics, diagnostics of most recent errors and warnings, and general responsiveness of the Oracle BI instance(s). Initially there will not be much to do from this page, but it is good to know that, once the environment begins to operate, this is a good resource for getting a high-level status.

Click on the **Availability** main tab.

Availability tab

The Availability tab is a section that the Oracle BI Administrator may reference frequently during development and normal activity. Two sub-tabs are available: **Processes** and **Failover**. The **Processes** sub-tab provides information regarding the status of each individual System Component. Expanding the component using the triangle to the left of the component's name shows the respective port and host machine name. More importantly, this is the area of the management console where you can stop, start, or restart one or all of the Oracle BI System Components as an alternative to using the command-line utility. The **Failover** tab highlights the current redundancy status of the environment by listing potential points of failure, either from not having the environment scaled-out or not using the Oracle BI Server application clustering option.

Click on the **Configuration** tab.

Configuration

The following section covers the various Configuration sub-tabs.

General

The **General** tab shows only the general settings for Oracle BI 12c. In the release discussed in this book, only the option for **11g Compatibility Mode** exists in this tab area. The 11g **Compatibility Mode** checkbox, when checked, aligns with the 11g Compatibility Framework in Oracle BI 12c. More about this can be found in Oracle Support Doc ID 2189375.1.

Performance

Specific to the Oracle BI application, the **Performance** sub-tab allows for several of the main performance-related configurations to be modified. Applying changes in this section transparently updates the Oracle BI `instanceconfig.xml` configuration file for each Oracle BI instance configured. Although there are many other configurations that could manually be adjusted in the physical `instanceconfig.xml` files, this GUI interface captures the most-used performance-configuration settings deemed most useful to any organization's implementation of Oracle BI. Popular updates in this tab are configuring the **Global Cache path**, and increasing the **Maximum Number of Rows to Download**.

Presentation

This area of the configuration tab provides global configuration settings for how the presentation layer of the Oracle BI graphical layer is viewed, or its interactions used. Currently, several **Dashboards Defaults** and **Analysis** (Answers) **Defaults** can be configured.

Mail

This section allows for the **Simple Mail Transfer Protocol** (**SMTP**) Server configuration in order for an Oracle BI Agent to e-mail content from **Oracle BI Delivers**. Credentials and the **SMTP server** hostname used within your organization can be configured here, along with ancillary attributes such as leveraging SSL or limiting the number of sending retries before failing the sending of an e-mail.

Click on the **Diagnostics** main tab.

Diagnostics

The following section covers the various Diagnostics sub-tabs.

Log Messages

This sub-tab shows all errors and warnings relating to all underlying components of the Oracle BI system. Viewing this section is very useful when experiencing any issues within the Oracle BI environment. In addition, it is this section that you will visit when you want to access log files critical to the Oracle BI environment, such as the Oracle BI Server or Presentation Services log files. The section at the bottom, **View Log Messages**, provides the starting point to launch the **Log Viewer** for all logs, or one specific log, relating to the System Components.

Log Configuration

Log Configuration is quite essential to configuring how log files are generated and at which level of detail they will be created. This section enables you to manage a log file's file size and length of time (**Maximum Log Age**) to which each log file can be written. Most importantly, the **Component Specific Log Levels** section on this sub-tab allows management to control the amount of detail each log file will store as it is being written. By controlling the level of file-storage granularity, the log-file size will grow or shrink, but the more granular the logging, the more detailed the diagnostic information.

Click on the **Security** main tab.

Security

This section allows you to manage the **Single Sign-On** (**SSO**) system configuration for Oracle BI. It also provides navigation links to other parts of the Oracle BI System Management tools, such as the WebLogic Server Security Realm, in order to manage users and groups, and links to manage application policies and application roles.

Previous versions of Oracle BI, such as Oracle BI 11g, contained more tabs in the Business Intelligence Instance area of EM, such as an area to deploy the RPD or configure the location of the web catalog. This has been removed from Oracle BI 12c, and the tools to manage such dynamic features are now controlled via the Oracle BI 12c lifecycle management APIs or Command Line Interfaces.

Chapter 6

Oracle BI 12c Lifecycle Management

Lifecycle Management (**LCM**) is a fairly new concept for many administrators and developers of Oracle BI. All core transferable objects in a software application such as Oracle BI are defined as artifacts. Artifacts for Oracle BI 12c are items such as the RPD, Presentation (Web) Catalog, and so on. Since these are a few of the most critical artifacts to the operation of Oracle BI, this section discusses how they are managed in Oracle BI 12c.

LCM includes the many different areas of patching, backup, and recovery, and the general migration of Oracle BI artifacts from one environment to another. In Oracle BI 12c, there has been a concentrated effort to increase the ability to deliver a consistent, manageable Oracle BI application through the use of programmatic capability. In Oracle BI 12c, there are now several options to do so: Application Programming Interface Web Services via SOAP and REST, and **Command Line Interfaces** (**CLI**) through the Oracle BI 12c **BI Tools**.

The BI Tools are located in `<ORACLE_HOME>\user_projects\domains\bi\bitools\bin`. These tools are available on the fully installed Oracle BI 12c server installation.

When a developer installs the Oracle BI 12c client tools on their workstation, not where the Oracle BI server is not installed, they will have access to some basic programmatic client tools but only a portion of the tools provided with the full Oracle BI 12c server installation:

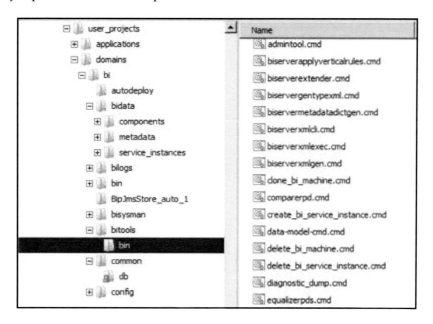

[141]

The Oracle BI Client Tools, when installed, are available from a similar folder path location, `<CLIENT TOOLS HOME>\bi\bitools\bin`; for example, `C:\OracleBIClient1221\bi\bitools\bin`.

One of the critical objects in the Oracle BI 12c LCM process is the `BI Archive` (BAR) file. This file type was introduced in the Oracle **BI Cloud Service** (**BICS**) solution prior to its release for the on-premise Oracle BI 12c solution. It operates on the similar principal of having one file to contain security information, the RPD file, and the Web Catalog files, for a compartmentalized way to move the critical artifacts of one Oracle BI environment to another.

All the exercises in this section will be done from the command prompt (Terminal window) on the server where the full version of Oracle BI 12c has been installed. After installing the Oracle BI 12c, the Sample Sales Lite subject area and respective RPD are deployed automatically to the Oracle BI server. As a developer, you would seek to make changes to the RPD and create several new reports and dashboards based on business requirements. Once the changes are made, you'll seek to migrate into the next highest level environment (for example, from Development to Testing) in order to have your changes tested, or begin in the approval process. Here you'll learn how the LCM tools will help you achieve such a goal.

What is a BAR File?

The **Business Intelligence Application Archive** (**BAR**) file is a single file that contains a set of BI metadata artifacts (data model, content model, and authorization model). The general idea is that Oracle BI 12c (and BICS) maintains a service instance, and that the BAR file can be imported and exported from a single instance and transferred into another instance with relative ease. There is no data, only metadata, contained in the BAR file by default, so it is really a means to move the essential metadata required to have an operational Oracle BI portal's content deployed. Granted, a data source will still need to be referenced from the RPD of the BAR file.

Finding the default BAR files

During an implementation, there is often the need to either start from scratch or have a standard OBIEE interface from which to begin development efforts. Oracle BI 12c comes with a few BAR file examples once Oracle BI 12c is installed. You can find these BAR files in the following directories, below the `<ORACLE_HOME>` installation path; use them as a baseline when conducting your own development efforts:

- `..\bi\bifoundation\admin\provisioning\empty.bar`
- `..\bi\bifoundation\samples\sampleapplite\SampleAppLite.bar`
- `..\bi\bifoundation\samples\usagetracking\UsagTracking.bar`

Deploying, migrating, and backing up artifacts

Developing in a sandbox or development environment means that you will eventually need to migrate the work you've done with the Oracle BI metadata, security, or reports and dashboard development to another environment for testing and, ultimately, to a production live environment. This section discusses the use of the BAR file for transporting artifacts during a deployment and making use of the other LCM commands for backing up and otherwise working with real-world Oracle BI.

This section will focus on capturing a BAR file, downloading and uploading the RPD, exporting a service instance, and importing a service instance. You'll also learn, through discussion, how and when each respective operation is used.

Snapshot Service Instance artifacts - exporting to a BAR

Just remember, a BAR technically has one or more of the following: a RPD, the Web Catalog, an Application Role security structure, and, potentially, other information about the Oracle BI environment that allows your instance of Oracle BI to be restored as fully as possible, providing the infrastructure of the Oracle BI system is otherwise in place.

Let's look at how this is accomplished.

Understanding the Systems Management Tools

Almost all the Oracle BI 12c LCM functionality is based on the interoperability of the WebLogic Server. The LCM functionality for exporting the Oracle BI instance artifacts to a BAR file requires use of the WLST:

1. Open a command-prompt Terminal window, change the directory to the `BI Tools` directory, and execute the WLST command to start the WLST interface, `<ORACLE_HOME>\oracle_common\common\bin\wlst.cmd`.
2. Enter the following command, and be very careful with the use of double-quotes and single-quotes, as shown in the execution command:

   ```
   exportServiceInstance( 'C:/OBI12cHome/user_projects/domains/bi'
   ,'ssi', 'C:/tmp/BAR/OBI12cBook/', 'C:/tmp/BAR/OBI12cBook/',
   'ssi.OBI12cBook', 'OBI 12c Book BAR File', '3.0', true,
   'Admin123')
   ```

3. Press the *Enter* key to execute the preceding command.
4. If the syntax was entered correctly, the script will run a series of tasks and this can take up to 10 minutes to complete, depending on how much metadata is configured in your instance.

The result of the preceding command execution will use WLST to call the function `exportServiceInstance` to reference the Oracle BI 12c domain home (`'C:/OBI12cHome/user_projects/domains/bi`), the `serviceInstanceKey` (ssi), `work` directory (`C:/tmp/BAR/OBI12cBook/`), and the `export` directory (`C:/tmp/BAR/OBI12cBook/`), It will create an application name (`ssi.OBI12Book`), add a description (OBI 12c Book BAR file), give the BAR file a version (3.0), determine to export user folder information in this BAR file (true), and create a password to secure the RPD, which in turn allows the RPD to maintain its connection pool credentials (Admin123).

The results of your export should be that you have a BAR file now residing in the `exportDir` (export directory) path, in this example, `C:/tmp/BAR/OBI12cBook/`.

In some circumstances, you may want to use a different path value for `exportDir` and `workDir`, but for most purposes using the same directory serves the same purpose.

The following are the parameters for the `exportServiceInstance` function that was just called:

```
exportServiceInstance
(
domainHome,
serviceInstanceKey,
workDir,
exportDir,
```

```
applicationName=None,
applicationDesc=None,
applicationVersion=None,
includeCatalogRuntimeInfo=false,
includeCredentials=None
)
```

The `exportServiceInstance` is the command that creates a BAR file. It always captures the core elements and artifacts described previously. It is on importing the service instance BAR snapshot that it can be determined which of the artifacts should be deployed into a target environment.

The following are the parameters for the `exportServiceInstance`:

Parameters	Description
`domainHome`	Path to BI domain home.
`serviceInstanceKey`	Key for the service instance.
`workDir`	Work directory for the run.
`exportDir`	Directory where the BAR file is to be exported.
`applicationModuleName`	Reserved for future use, but use as used in preceding code.
`applicationModuleDesc`	Reserved for future use, but use as used in preceding code.
`applicationModuleVersion`	Reserved for future use, but use as used in preceding code.
`includeCatalogRuntimeInfo`	Optional - If this flag is true, catalog runtime info (for example, user folders) is included in exports. Otherwise, catalog runtime info is skipped. The default value of this flag is false.
`includeCredentials`	Optional - This is the password to encrypt the exported metadata repository content. The default value for this field is None. If you do not specify this value, connection credentials are not exported; otherwise, connection credentials are exported.

Migrating a Service Instance Snapshot - importing the BAR

Now that you have exported your Oracle BI service instance, ssi, to a BAR file and you can see the physical file in the directory, it is time to import the BAR file back to Oracle BI. This can, of course, be done on the same server you conducted the `exportServiceInstance` exercise on, because ultimately you are just restoring a snapshot. Surely, the real-world example would be to conduct the steps for the `importServiceInstance` on a different server having an Oracle BI 12c installation, but for now the principle of the process is the equal. Let's import the BAR file and include all the artifacts:

1. Use the existing command prompt Terminal window and change the directory to the `BI Tools` directory, or open a new one.
2. Execute the WLST command to start the WLST interface, `<ORACLE_HOME>\oracle_common\common\bin\wlst.cmd`, if using a new window.
3. Enter the following command, and be very careful with the use of double-quotes and single-quotes, as shown in the following execution command:

    ```
    importServiceInstance( 'C:/OBI12cHome/user_projects/
    domains/bi','ssi', 'C:/tmp/BAR/OBI12cBook/ssi.OBI12cBook.bar',
    true, true, true, 'Admin123' )
    ```

4. Press the Enter key to execute the preceding command.

If the syntax was entered correctly, the script will run a series of tasks and can take up to 10 minutes to complete depending on several factors such as size of the RPD, size of the Web Catalog, and so on.

The result of the preceding command execution will use WLST to call the function `importServiceInstance` to reference the Oracle BI 12c domain home (`C:/OBI12cHome/user_projects/domains/bi`), the `serviceInstanceKey` (`ssi`), the absolute file location on the server where the BAR file to import resides (`C:/tmp/BAR/OBI12cBook/ssi.OBI12cBook.bar`), decision to import the RPD (true), the decision to import the Web Catalog (true), the decision to import the application roles and policies (true), and the password used to decrypt the RPD metadata content, such as the connection pool credentials (`Admin123`).

Restarting the Oracle BI components and, technically, the entire Oracle BI system, is highly recommended to ensure that all artifacts are completely recognized by the Oracle BI system. Also, please understand that, with the import process, importServiceInstance will overwrite the existing artifacts on the target server based on the import option parameters (rpd, web catalog, security) marked as true. A best practice is to conduct an exportServiceInstance on the target server prior to conducting an importServiceInstance.

The importServiceInstance is the command that takes an existing BAR file and moves its contents, as directed, into the Oracle BI 12c ecosystem. By setting the optional parameters of the function, you effectively determine which of the artifacts to deploy into a target environment.

The following are the parameters for the importServiceInstance:

Parameters	Description
domainHome	Path to BI domain home.
serviceInstanceKey	Key for the service instance.
barLocation	Exported service instance BAR (absolute path).
importRpd	Optional - The value of this parameter can be true or false. The default value is true. This parameter supports selective import of metadata. If this flag is set to false, the command run does not import the repository metadata.
importWebcat	Optional - The value of this parameter can be true or false. The default value is true. This parameter supports selective import of the catalog. If this flag is false, the command does not import the catalog.
importJazn	Optional - The value of this parameter can be true or false. The default value is true. This parameter supports selective import of the Jazn. If this flag is false, the command does not import the Jazn.
includeCredentials	Optional - This password is used to decrypt the imported RPD content. The default value for this field is Admin123.

Understanding the Systems Management Tools

The last four parameters are optional. Entering those parameters with explicit values allows the execution of your code to be consistent in nature, and very visibly helps any readers of your code understand specifically what you are trying to accomplish. Only the first three arguments of the function are required, so in theory you only need to call importServiceInstance with the domain home, server instance name, and the BAR file location.

Because exportServiceInstance and importServiceInstance can be called via WLST, it also means that these items can be programmatically integrated into a scheduled process or into a custom-developed solution. For now, the basics are that capturing a BAR file is great for snapshot backups of the Oracle BI system and for migrating from one server to another.

Moving just the RPD - no BAR necessary

The method of using importServiceInstance to move Oracle BI artifacts from one Oracle BI server instance to another is a great concept. There is the option with importServiceInstance to set only the option for importing the RPD and no other artifacts. This could be the preferred approach. However, one would still need to run the exportServiceInstance command, which technically will always take a snapshot of all artifacts even if you do not intend to reimport all of the artifacts. This command will look similar to the following code if attempting to import just the RPD from an exported service-instance BAR snapshot file:

```
importServiceInstance( 'C:/OBI12cHome/user_projects/domains/bi','ssi',
'C:/tmp/BAR/OBI12cBook/ssi.OBI12cBook.bar', importRpd=true,
importWebCat=false, importJazn=false, includeCredentials='Admin123' )
```

Download the RPD only - no BAR

Because the importing and exporting of the services is known to be time-consuming for immediate metadata repository development, there is an option to upload and download the RPD without using WLST.

An LCM CLI tool that resides in the BI Tools for moving the RPD is called data-model-cmd (data-model-cmd.cmd|sh). This command is multipurpose, but its primary use in this section is to move the RPD back and forth as simply as possible.

Important: Command File Name Change

In the initial release of Oracle BI 12c, the BI Tool file, `data-model-cmd`, was introduced. It was changed in subsequent releases to a shorter file name, `datamodel` (that is, `datamodel.sh` or `datamodel.cmd`). This book will use the original file name. Please note they are interchangeable in the steps that follow.

To download the RPD from the Oracle BI server, follow these steps:

1. Open a Terminal window command prompt and change the directory to `<ORACLE_HOME>\user_projects\domains\bi\bitools\bin`; for example, `C:\OracleOBIEE12c\Home\user_projects\domains\bi\bitools\bin`.

2. Execute the following command:

   ```
   data-model-cmd.cmd downloadrpd -O obi12cbook_dwnld.rpd -W
   Admin123 -U weblogic -P Admin123 -SI ssi
   ```

3. Verify the file has been downloaded into the BI Tools directory; as the `-O` argument did not specify a different path, it will be downloaded into the same directory in which you currently reside.

4. The `downloadrpd` option has the following structure for arguments passed into it:

   ```
   downloadrpd -O RPDname [-W RPDpwd] -SI service_instance -U
   cred_username [-P cred_password] [-S hostname] [-N port_number]
   [-SSL] [-H]
   ```

Uploading just the RPD - no BAR

When not editing the RPD in online mode and a developer needs to move the RPD from one Oracle BI server to another or even swap out their RPD in development, the straightforward approach is to upload the single RPD using the BI Tools, `data-model-cmd`, command using the `uploadrpd` option.

You can open the recently downloaded RPD in offline mode and make a change to one of the Subject Area names so that you will be able to determine if the rpd is actually uploaded to the server after running the command in the following steps. Save the RPD and upload it with the following instructions:

1. If not already open and set to the `BI Tools` directory, open a Terminal window command prompt and change the directory to `<ORACLE_HOME>\user_projects\domains\bi\bitools\bin`; for example, `C:\OracleOBIEE12c\Home\user_projects\domains\bi\bitools\bin`.

2. Execute the following command:

   ```
   data-model-cmd.cmd uploadrpd -I obi12cbook_dwnld.rpd -W
   Admin123 -U weblogic -P Admin123 -SI ssi
   ```

   It will take a few minutes for the file to be uploaded by the command.

3. Open the Oracle BI portal, /analytics/, web page, and click to begin creating a new analysis. Determine if the subject area is changed to the updated name, which will only exist in the RPD that you briefly modified.

The `uploadrpd` option has the following structure for arguments passed into it:

```
uploadrpd -I <RPDname> [-W <RPDpwd>] -SI <service_instance> -U
<cred_username> [-P <cred_password>] [-S <hostname>] [-N <port_number>] [-
SSL] [-H]
```

As a straightforward test, you can see how this process for uploading the RPD is relatively intuitive. You may have also noticed that the RPD changed without having to restart any of the Oracle BI system components. Oracle BI has a refresh that takes place by default every 10 minutes in the system, and it looks for changes to the RPD or changes based on BAR file updates in order to determine what it may need to refresh based on an administrator making changes to the system.

> The BI Tools directory can be added to the `PATH` environment variable on your server so that you can easily call the commands, such as data-model-cmd.cmd|sh, from anywhere on your operating system, thus alleviating the need to specify an absolute path for the output argument, such as when you download the RPD.

Stopping and starting System Components

Oracle BI 12c gives you several approaches to stop, start, or restart the Oracle BI System Components: via **command-line interface** (**CLI**), via JMX, and via the **Enterprise Manager** (**EM**) GUI. One approach is to use the EM as discussed in the preceding section. Another is to use the CLI executable that installs with Oracle BI. The last is a programmatic approach that is easily executable from Jython or Java coding.

In the Fusion Middleware Control (EM) console, restarting all components simultaneously using the **Restart All** button ensures that the Fusion Middleware Control will handle all serial communication with the **WebLogic Management Framework** (**WMF**) in order to correctly stop and start the system components in the necessary order.

However, there is a more advanced approach, which can be achieved by calling an executable on the server where the Oracle BI server is installed. This executable is located in the BI Tools path, `<ORACLE_HOME>\user_projects\domains\bi\bitools\bin`; for example, `C:\OracleOBIEE12c\Homeu\ser_projects\domains\bi\bitools\bin`.

You can get a list of all components and their names by running the following status command from the command prompt within the preceding directory:

```
status.cmd
```

Please take note of all the component names, since they will be relevant in the stopping and starting of the system components.

Stopping Oracle BI 12c

To stop the Oracle BI system and all its system components, open a command prompt Terminal window. Then, execute the following command: `stop.cmd`, if on a Windows **Operating System** (**OS**), or `stop.sh`, if on a Linux or Unix OS.

The `stop.cmd|sh` command will stop all Oracle BI components in a specific order to prevent locking conflicts. It will also stop the node manager, the BI-managed Server, and the WebLogic Admin Server, to fully bring the Oracle BI system to a halt.

Understanding the Systems Management Tools

If you want to stop just a single component of the Oracle BI system, for example, if you need to restart the Presentation Services component after you've made a change to a configuration file, then use the -i switch in the stop command: stop.cmd -i obips1. In this case, only the component name that follows the -i will be acted upon for the action. If you need to stop multiple components, use the -i argument/switch and enter the names of the components, separated by a comma, but without spaces in between the comma or the names. For example, to stop the presentation services and BI Server services, use the following command:

```
stop.cmd -i obips1,obis1
```

Starting Oracle BI 12c

Starting the Oracle BI system and all of its system components follows the exact same process as the stop command. Open a command prompt terminal window then execute the following command, start.cmd, if on a Windows Operating System, or, start.sh, if on a Linux or Unix OS.

The start.cmd|sh command will start all Oracle BI components in a specific order to prevent locking conflicts. It will also start the **Node Manager**, WebLogic Admin Server, the BI Managed Server and all of the system components to fully bring the Oracle BI system into operation.

If you need to start just a single component of the Oracle BI system, for example, if you the WebLogic Server is running and you need to need to restart the Presentation Services component after you've made a change to a configuration file, then use the -i switch in the start command: start.cmd -i obips1, after you execute the stop command. In this case, only the component name that follows the -i will be acted upon for the action. If you need to start multiple components, use the -i argument/switch and enter the names of the components, separated by a comma, but without spaces in between the comma or the names. For example, to start the presentation services and BI Server services use the following command:

```
start.cmd -i obis1,obips1
```

In the case of the start command, notice how, because the order of the components is specific, the syntax starts the Oracle BI Server Component first and the Presentation Services component second. This is a best-practice sequence for Oracle BI. It is illustrated here to show that, when specifying the start and stop processes, the sequence of components can make a difference.

Patching Oracle BI 12c

As with most software, there can be bug fixes or new features that allow requested functionality in the current version of the software. These items would be considered patches and typically released in a patch download for your current software. A patch is normally associated with a particular version and involves updating from one minor version of the product to a newer minor version of the same product (for example, from version 12.2.1 to version 12.2.2). A patch set is a single patch that contains a collection of patches designed to be applied at the same time.

This would not necessarily be considered an upgrade to the current version of your software. Oracle releases immediate hotfix patches for Oracle BI software sporadically as customers with production-halting issues need them. Oracle releases quarterly patches that fix issues or apply general functionality improvements. And, once a year or so, they provide an upgrade of the solution to the next major or minor version of the software.

Typically, patches, when applied to Oracle BI, do not impact configuration files or non-design-time schema-based metadata such as scheduler, web catalog, and RPD files. Patches can be rolled back. One would roll back a patch, for example, if the new patch version actually causes issues when applied, even if it fixes the problem you anticipated the patch would resolve.

The patching process is beyond the scope of this book, but you can find more information about patching in the Oracle BI 12c documentation, at `https://docs.oracle.com/middleware/1221/biee/BIESG/patching.htm`.

Upgrading Oracle BI 12c

This book will cover the basics of upgrading to Oracle BI 12c from a previous version of Oracle BI toward the end. However, there is the possibility that an upgrade from one version of the Oracle BI 12c system to another core release of Oracle BI 12c may be imminent. If so, the best instruction that can be provided is to follow the instructions included with any upgrade version of the software that may come along. As always, be sure to back up your artifacts and move all configuration files, artifacts, and customization files out of the ORACLE_HOME directory in which you installed Oracle BI 12c. Placing them outside that main folder should ensure that they will not be replaced or overwritten during the upgrade.

Checking the logs

Oracle BI allows almost every crucial log file regarding the runtime of its artifacts to be visible from the Fusion Middleware Control EM console. This is very important when diagnosing issues, since you don't need to navigate to the file system in order to locate the respective service's log files. Oracle BI does something very clever with its log files, by using an **Execution Context ID** (**ECID**), which ties all log files together around one transaction or event. This way, a single error or failure will allow you to look across all components based on a particular event, using the ECID, to determine what caused an issue. Use the following steps to see how to get at some basic Oracle BI log information:

1. Navigate to the **Diagnostics** > **Log Messages** sub-tab.
2. Here you will see the most recent warnings and error messages across all system components and more.
3. Scroll toward the bottom of this sub-tab section and notice the header **View Log Messages**.
4. Click the **Server Log** link.
5. This takes you to the Log Messages viewer specifically predicated on the Oracle BI Server logs. If no records are immediately shown, click the search icon above the table and change the **Date Range** fields to **Most Recent 20 Days**, or modify the day filter to a range that will have captured data since your Oracle BI installation, and click the **Search** button.
6. Notice the results section is now populated. Scroll through the results looking for both errors, if any, and warnings, under the column heading **Message Type**. There should always be a few warnings, most of which can be ignored.
7. Above the log messages table is a button drop-down labeled **Export Messages to File**. Click the drop-down button and select the option **As Oracle Diagnostic Text (.txt)**.
8. The log file contents from the search will process and a save file prompt will appear asking you to download or open the file.

9. Download this file for later use when making a snapshot of issues or reporting issues to Oracle Support:

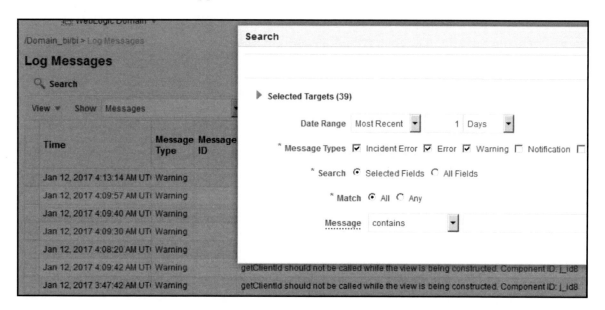

The Log Viewer is predicated on the target log file selection made, in this case, Server Log, as selected in Step 3. In order to view other log files within this area, click the **Search** button above the left side of the table to open the search window. Then expand the **Selected Targets** triangle area. Next, for example, scroll down and locate **bi_server1**, click the row, and click the respective **Target Log Files** icon to view the list of log files for **bi_server1**. Click on `bi_server1.log` toward the top of the table-list of log records, and then click on the **View Log File** button at the top of the table to view the log file in question.

Creating users, roles, and associations

In the previous section, you've briefly reviewed the embedded WebLogic LDAP Server, and also completed an exercise using WLST to create a new user via scripting. There is one other operation that is integral to managing users and groups within Oracle BI - Application Roles.

Application Roles provide a means to associate universal privileges to users and groups, regardless of which identity provider (for example, MS Active Directory, Oracle OID, and so on) they may stem from. That is to say, we can assign an embedded WLS LDAP user and a user from our Active Directory LDAP to a single application role. We could then assign certain privileges within the Oracle BI application to that specific application role. In addition, you can assign application roles to another application role in order to provide a hierarchy of authorization.

Oracle BI 12c comes with three broad-range core application roles out-of-the-box that should not be deleted or modified: BIServiceAdministrator, BIContentAuthor, and BIConsumer.

> Users of the previous Oracle BI 11g version will notice that the BI System application role is no longer a default application role out-of-the-box. This was removed in Oracle BI 12c.

The application role names are quite indicative of what each role's capabilities are, except, maybe, BIServiceAdministrator. BIServiceAdministrator has administrative ability over the Oracle BI environment; BIContentAuthor may read/write reports and create most types of content, and BIConsumer can read/consume content such as reports but is restricted as to what it is able to create.

As a WebLogic Server administrator, in Enterprise Manager, you can create new application roles from scratch, or you can mimic the properties from any of the default application roles to assume those capabilities into your own custom application roles.

Creating users and groups in WebLogic Server

In this exercise, we are going to create several users and groups in the WLS embedded LDAP directory. Then we will navigate to the Enterprise Manager Fusion Control console and associate those users and groups with application roles we create from scratch:

1. Launch the WLS Administration Console by navigating to `http://<server_name>:9500/console`.
2. Log in using the WebLogic administrator credentials.
3. Navigate to the **Security Realms** > **myrealm** > **Users and Groups** > **Groups** sub-tab.

4. In the **Groups** sub-tab, click the **New** button to create a new group.
5. On the **Create New Group** page:
    - Enter in the **Name** field: **Sales Team**
    - Select or make sure **Default Authenticator** is chosen from the **Provider** drop-down
    - Click the **OK** button to save the new group
6. Using the same technique as in Steps 4 and 5, create the following groups:
    - **Store Manager**
    - **Bicycle Technician**
7. Navigate to the **Users and Groups** > **Users** sub-tab.
8. On the **Users** sub-tab, click the **New** button to begin adding a user.
9. On the **Create New User** page:
    - Enter in the **Name** field: **Eddy Merck**
    - Select **Default Authenticator** from the **Provider** drop-down
    - Enter in the **Password** and **Confirm Password** fields: `Admin123`
    - Click the **OK** button to save the new user
10. Using the same technique as you just completed in the preceding steps, use the same password, Admin123, to create the following users:
    - **Binard Hinalt**
    - **Greg Limon**
    - **Sean Kelly**
11. Verify in the **Users** sub-tab that three new users exist.
12. Verify in the **Groups** sub-tab that two new groups exist.

Understanding the Systems Management Tools

After more identities are added to this list of available users or groups, the **Users** sub-tab or **Groups** sub-tab page table will paginate at 10 records per page. This can become annoying when looking for certain records:

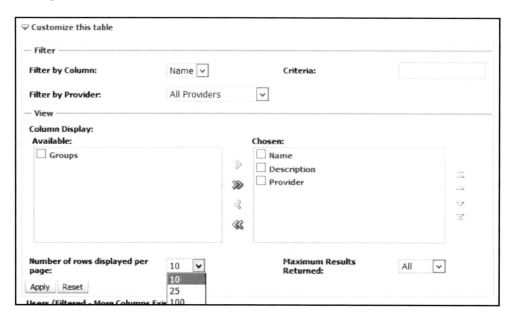

To increase the limit of records shown per user or group, click the **Customize this table** link above the **Users** or **Groups** table to expand the option. Next, change the value of the **Number of rows displayed per page** drop-down to a higher value (for example, 100) and click the **Apply** button for the change to take effect.

Assigning users to groups

When users and groups are created, it is straightforward to add a user to one or more of the groups to create an association in WLS LDAP:

1. On the **Users** sub-tab, locate, under the **Name** column, **Greg Limon**.
2. Click the **Groups** tab within the Settings for the **Greg Limon** page.
3. Assign the **Sales Team** group by placing a check in the checkbox of the **Sales Team** option in the Available box.
4. Using the middle arrows, click on the right-hand arrow so that the value of **Sales Team** appears in the Chosen box.

5. Click the **Save** button.
6. Return to the **Users and Groups** > **Users** sub-tab by using the breadcrumb navigation at the top of the page under the **Home, Log Out, Preferences** menu.
7. Repeat Steps 1 to Step 5 to assign the remainder of users to groups, using the following matrix to guide you:

Users	Groups
Greg Limon	Sales Team
Binard Hinalt	Bicycle Technician
Sean Kelly	Sales Team
Eddy Merck	Bicycle Technician, Sales Team

Creating and assigning Application Roles

Once the users and groups have been created and properly associated with one another based on the matrix provided in the previous section, you have completed LDAP assignment only. This in effect emulates the LDAP directory relationship that would already be established in an organization's LDAP directory, such as Microsoft Active Directory. You've simply leveraged what is already built into WLS in order to showcase that using the embedded LDAP is a solution for managing a small number (really, up to 1,000 it is still quite functional) of users and assigning them to groups. Next, you'll associate groups you've created to the Oracle BI Application Roles used to delegate privileges for the Oracle BI system. This is done using Fusion Middleware Control Enterprise Manager as follows:

1. Navigate to Fusion Middleware Control and log in with the WebLogic administrator user's credentials.
2. Click on the WebLogic Domain drop-down icon under the **bi** label to the right of the navigation menu icon to expand the menu options.
3. Select **Security** > **Application Roles** from the menu.
4. On the **Application Roles** page, if no roles are shown in the table grid:
    - Select **obi** from the **Application Stripe** drop-down
    - Click the **Play image** button to the right of the **Role Name** field to search for application roles within EM

5. The default OBI application roles should appear.
6. Click the row for **BIConsumer** to select it, and it should highlight the row.
7. Click the **Create Like...** button above the **Application Role** table.

   This will technically duplicate the application role so the same properties and system privileges associated with the **BIConsumer** role will be given to the new application role you'll create in the next step.

8. On the Create Application Role Like : BIConsumer page:
   - Enter **AdvWorksConsumer** in the Role Name field.
   - Edit the **Display Name** and **Description** fields, making them unique to the **AdvWorkConsumer** purpose:
     - Enter **AdvWorks Consumer** for the Display Name
     - Leave the **Description** field as-is
   - Below the **General** section, locate the **Members** section.
   - Click the **Add** button to begin adding a new member to this application role.
   - Change the Type drop-down value to Group.
   - Leave the Principal Name and Display Name fields blank.
   - Click the play/submit button showing to the right of the Display Name field.
   - This will reveal all groups from the WLS identity provider(s).
   - Click on the row for Sales Manager and then click the OK button.
   - Click on the row for Sales Team and then click the OK button.
   - Repeat the preceding steps, clicking the **Add** button, adjusting the Type drop-down to Group, and searching for the groups. This time, click **Sales Team** as the group to add, and click the **OK** button.
9. Review the two new groups added to the application role you are creating.
10. Click on the row for BIContentAuthor and then click the **Delete...** button above the table to remove that entry from the **Members** table.

11. Repeat the preceding step for the authenticated-role member to remove it from the members list.

    The **authenticated-role** member is an important role that is installed by default with Oracle BI. It basically means that any user that can log in successfully into the Oracle BI portal will be placed into this role once authenticated. Any application roles that have this role as a member will automatically give such an authenticated user any assigned privileges provided by that application role. So, one must be cautious about keeping this role in any of the custom-created application roles. Often, as a best practice, the authenticated-role is also removed from the **BIConsumer** application role before migrating the solution into production.

12. Click the OK button in the upper-right corner of the **Create Application Role Like : BIConsumer** page to return to the main application role page again:

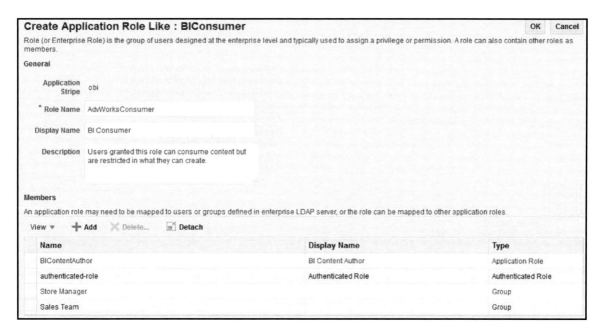

13. Repeat Steps 4-12, but this time create two more application roles and only assign the users or groups (that is, principals) as described in the following matrix below:

Application Role	Group Name
AdvWorksSalesTeam	Sales Team
AdvWorksTechnician	Bicycle Technician

14. The final Application Role list should look similar to the following screenshot:

Role Name	Display Name	Description
BIServiceAdministrator	BI Service Administrator	This role confers privileges required to administer the sample a...
BIContentAuthor	BI Content Author	Users with this role can create most types of content.
BIConsumer	BI Consumer	Users granted this role can consume content but are restricted ...
AdvWorksConsumer	BI Consumer	Users granted this role can consume content but are restricted ...
AdvWorksSalesTeam	AdvWorks SalesTeam	Sales team application role based on BIConsumer role. Remov...
AdvWorksTechnician	AdvWorks Technician	Users granted this role can consume content but are restricted ...

That wraps up the security assignments we needed to create in order for users to access the reports and dashboard you'll create in a later chapter.

Now that we've completed the embedded LDAP identity-provider configuration of users and groups, created new application roles, and assigned WLS Embedded LDAP groups to them, let's read some more about the advanced security features available to you in Oracle BI.

JMX, MBeans, Java, and interfacing Oracle BI

Similar to WLST, when there comes a time for automating processes that interface with WLS or Fusion Control EM, there is an opportunity to look at the System Management API Java programming. Again, using a handy-dandy IDE such as NetBeans or JDeveloper, putting together a custom Groovy or Java program that can be executed via command-line is a cinch for a Java programmer.

Previous versions of Oracle BI, 11g, used JMX and MBeans that are no longer used for interfacing with the Oracle BI 12c system. The legacy means interfacing with administrative functions of Oracle BI has been replaced with RESTful services, SOAP web services, and the WebLogic Management Framework.

Migrating FMW Security to other environments

In previous versions of Oracle BI, migrating all components of security and other Oracle BI artifacts took place simply by moving the RPD and/or Web Catalog from the source to target server until Fusion Middleware was introduced. Oracle BI is much broader in scope and does not come with such a luxury. This section takes a glance at the files that comprise FMW Security within the System Management tools, leveraging the WebLogic security import/export utility to aid in simplifying security migration.

Please note that this section mainly discussed the users and groups in the WLS Embedded LDAP security provider. Application Roles are migrated mainly by the BAR file concept you learned earlier.

FMW Core Security files and OPSS

In order for Oracle BI 12c to store system-specific metadata and security information that requires some level of encryption to communicate between the many interoperable areas of Fusion Middleware, it uses (**OPSS**Oracle Platform Security Services (OPSS). Security policy information and audit information are stored so that they can be easily retrieved by the Oracle BI system and its components.

Basically, all of the Application Roles, Application Policies, and assignments of users and groups you conducted in Enterprise Manager are stored in the OPSS.

In Oracle BI 11g, the OPSS file was primarily file-system based. And, if you needed to migrate the security from one environment to another, you could use the process of copying files and executing some logic on the target environment that incorporated the source security.

In Oracle BI 12c, Oracle recommends using the BAR file process to handle any migration of Application Role or Application Policy migrations from a development/source to the target system. It is good to know where and why these files exist, purely from a technical administration perspective.

Understanding the Systems Management Tools

To view where the OPSS is configured or to view the database schema and the security stores associated with the OPSS for your installation, follow these steps:

1. Log in to EM.
2. Click the menu for WebLogic Domain and expand **Security** > **Security Provider Configuration.**
3. Expand **Security Stores.**

Note how the Store Type value states a database, that the Location is based on a jdbc/OpssDataSource connection, and there is a Database URL configured, which is the same database connection information you provided during the configuration of Oracle BI 12c. Also note that the jdbc/OpssDataSource is a reference to the WLS Data Sources configuration you can view by opening WebLogic Server Admin Console:

To see for certain that the OPSS schema is storing the application roles information:

1. Log into your favorite SQL IDE, such as SQL Server Management Studio (or SQL Developer if using an Oracle DBMS).
2. Submit the following query to the OPSS schema on your database as indicated by the Database URL from the previous steps:

   ```
   SELECT * FROM JPS_DN WHERE RDN LIKE '%ADVWORKS%'
   ```

3. View the record for the application role you created previously:

ENTRYID	RDN	PARENTDN
13081	cn=advworkstechnician	cn=opssroot,cn=jpscontext,cn=opsssecuritystore,cn=obi,cn=roles,

FMW Security Import/Export utility

WebLogic Server provides a mechanism for exporting and/or importing a full Security Realm, that is, users, groups, identity provider configurations, and so on, for the purposes of backup or migration to another Security Realm. Remember, the Security Realm, **myrealm**, handles the Identity Store portion of FMW Security, but the Enterprise Manager Fusion Control handles the configuration of the Policy Store. To migrate the security-realm security-provider information from one environment to another, you'll use the export and import functionality found within the WebLogic Admin Console.

Using the Security Realm migration utility

When migrating security, there are really two scenarios proposed to artifacts on your target environment: clean or dirty. If you have already done a clean migration (that is, the first time) to your target once, then the environment is now dirty. So, subsequent migrations must take into consideration the possibility of overwriting or replacing existing items. Regarding Security Realm migration, the WLS Security Realm migration utility handles all of this for you. For example, if you export a Security Realm from Development and it contains a group named BIAdministrators that also exists in the Production environment, the import into Production will not overwrite the BIAdministrators group already existing there.

Understanding the Systems Management Tools

To understand how to migrate the default Security Realm from one environment to another, follow these steps:

1. Open the WLS Administration Console and navigate to **Security Realms > myrealm**.
2. Click the **Migration** tab.
3. Click the **Export** sub-tab.
4. Enter a temporary path on the physical server where the Oracle BI implementation resides, for example, `C:TempMyExport`, in the **Export Directory on Server** field. The file path you enter must already exist:

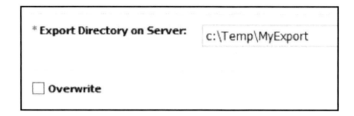

5. Click the **Save** button.
6. A success message should appear at the top of the page, below the breadcrumbs section of the WLS Admin console. The resulting directory should have several DAT files now created inside it, and should appear similar to the following screenshot:

Name	Type	Size
DefaultAuthenticator.dat	DAT File	9 KB
DefaultCredentialMapper.dat	DAT File	1 KB
exportIndex.dat	DAT File	1 KB
XACMLAuthorizer.dat	DAT File	116 KB
XACMLRoleMapper.dat	DAT File	170 KB

7. To import this Security Realm's exported metadata to a target system, copy all DAT files to the target environment and place them in a similar location, for example, `C:TempMyImport`.
8. Open the WebLogic Administration Console in the target environment and navigate to **Security Realms > myrealm**.

[166]

9. Click the **Migration** tab and the **Import** sub-tab.
10. Enter the folder path on the target server, where you placed the exported files from the source environment in the **Import Directory on Server** field.
11. Click the **Save** button; the import will begin and fairly quickly return a message towards the top of the page denoting success.

Following the preceding steps, you have successfully migrated a single Security Realm from one environment to another. Unless you checked the **Overwrite** checkbox when you exported the Security Realm, WLS will automatically use a difference algorithm to ensure that no users, groups, and so on are overwritten in the target environment.

Oracle BI Publisher system management

Oracle BI Publisher can be embedded within Oracle BI or stand on its own as a solo installation. Based on the initial installation and configuration you conducted earlier in the book, BI Publisher's System Management tools are primarily the same as those used for Oracle BI. The WLS Administration Console and Fusion Control Console are used to monitor, deploy, and set some data source configurations for BI Publisher.

Monitoring system performance

Ideally an application server environment will monitor itself, regulate itself to optimize performance, and resolve any issues automatically if they occur. However, this is, of course, just wishful thinking! But luckily, WLS does at least provide mechanisms to monitor the environment and perhaps programmatically integrate monitoring with some of your existing IT standards for monitoring software. The ability to monitor WLS is available from the WLS Dashboard. This can be a very helpful means of gauging request loads, most active applications, and peak load times, all of which can contribute to a better understanding of when and in which direction to optimize the server(s).

Another approach to monitoring Oracle BI is under the analytics server itself. By entering the URL, `http://<bi_server>:9502/analytics/saw.dll?Perfmon`, a diagnostic view is displayed. This information provides insight into current activity and peak uses within the Oracle BI System Components. Taking this information into account, combined with information from the WLS Dashboard, and possibly other sources such as Windows Server's Perfmon logs, the load-balancing servers and database-monitoring services, you should have enough data to make an informed decision on tuning the Oracle BI environment for optimal performance:

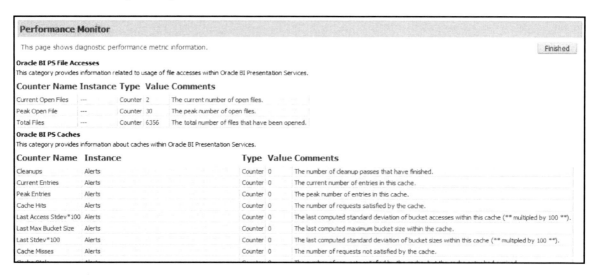

Have a backup plan!

It's hard to get out of a chapter about managing a system without discussing backing up and disaster recovery. Again, an entire chapter could be filled with content on this subject, but that would be beyond the scope and intent of this book. Let's first be aware that backing up the FMW (that is, Oracle Home) folder structure and the Oracle BI artifacts is a good thing. The frequency is up to each organization, but once a week at a minimum is a good recommendation. Back up these items daily for high-availability or critical environments. Each application delivered with the Oracle BI Suite has its own backup consideration. Although OBIEE and BI Publisher comprise the main Oracle Business Intelligence Enterprise Edition software (don't forget Essbase, RTD, and the other analytics tools such as Interactive Reporting, and so on), they have some common metadata elements and some which are sole references.

If an outage were to occur after your Oracle BI environment has been placed in production, typically, the gross loss of effort will usually stem from any development in the RPD or Presentation Catalog artifacts. The `.rpd` file and the Presentation Catalog folder should be continually backed up in line with the development and deployment lifecycle. From a database perspective, the relational schemas created during the Oracle BI installation by the RCU will also need to be backed up. Typically, this falls into line with other backups conducted on the database server where these schemas reside. Using Oracle BI 12c's BAR-file export procedure with the `ExportServiceInstance` WLST command to back up the instance components, which include the RPD, Web Catalog, and Security application role assignments, is also a good measure to take. We also recommend using a Source Control Management system such as Git or SVN.

Ultimately, a full monthly BAR backup and a backup of the entire FMW folder structure is simply the minimum that should be done in any enterprise production deployment of Oracle BI. Disk storage is relatively inexpensive these days; rebuilding an environment due to an outage is not.

Recommendations for further learning

This chapter looked at basic-to-advanced aspects of the Oracle BI System Management components. There were a few sections limited in coverage because of the advanced nature of the topics, but a high-level review was provided. As a step in the right direction, please explore the following recommendations for a chance to further your learning:

- WebLogic Scripting Tool:
    - http://docs.oracle.com/middleware/1221/biee/BIESG/bi_wlst_cmd.htm
- Understanding Oracle BI Security:
    - http://docs.oracle.com/middleware/1221/biee/BIESC/toc.htm
- LDAP Tools: JXplorer or Apache Directory Studio:
    - http://jxplorer.org/
    - https://directory.apache.org/studio/
- LDAP Configuration:
    - http://download.oracle.com/docs/cd/E14571_01/bi.1111/e10541/toc.htm
- Oracle BI SampleApp (OBIEE 12c):
    - http://www.oracle.com/technetwork/middleware/bi-foundation/obiee-samples-167534.html

- System Management API:
  - https://docs.oracle.com/middleware/1221/biee/BIESG/index.html
- Service Instances in Oracle BI 12c
  - http://docs.oracle.com/middleware/1221/biee/BIESG/configrepos.htm#BIESG2889

A review - what I should know now!

For self-review and a recap of the chapter, here are a few questions. No answers are provided. These questions are for your own reflection on the chapter:

- What is the method used to deploy the Oracle BI RPD and Presentation Catalog in Oracle BI 12c?
- From what tool do you launch and execute the ExportServiceInstance command?
- How many Security Realms are configured with the default Oracle BI installation?
- What are the key files that need to be backed up for Oracle BI?
- In WLS, what is the WLS Embedded LDAP directory?
- What is the Oracle BI 12c REST API, and what is WLST?

Summary

In this chapter, we explored the System Management tools required to administer the core components of the Oracle BI environment.

We discussed each main section of the Weblogic Server Administration and the Enterprise Management consoles. We provided insight and an example on how the application interfaces (APIs) can interface with Oracle BI to manage the environment programmatically. Finally, we took a look at deploying the core Oracle BI metadata components, migrating security, and monitoring performance. These management concepts should have provided you with an above average understanding of how to administer your Oracle BI environment and speculate on future activities you may need to facilitate within your organization. Weblogic Server and Weblogic Scripting is a large subject in its own right, and therefore we encourage you to undertake further reading. There are several books from Packt Publishing covering WebLogic, for example, *Getting Started with Oracle Weblogic Server 12c Developer Guide*, which you can get from https://www.packtpub.com.

7
Developing the BI Server Repository

Finally, we get to the heart of the OBIEE system, the metadata repository that resides within the RPD file. The RPD contains all information regarding the physical tables that are held in our database or data warehouse, whether this is from a single source or a heterogeneous set of sources. It stores their relationships, additional business logic, and the structure of how columns are presented via the frontend to the dashboard creators. As well as physical database tables, the RPD can also utilize other data sources, such as Essbase, Oracle OLAP, and Excel sheets.

The RPD also holds variable definitions, various security and cache settings, and drill/dimensional hierarchies that affect the end functionality of reports. All of these settings and metadata are used by the Oracle BI server choosing the content and structure of database queries when presented with a request via OBIEE Answers.

Once a system is installed and has gone live, a good amount of development time will be spent on the metadata repository. An RPD developer is given a large amount of freedom in modeling and enhancing physical objects in a way that can satisfy the most complex business requirements.

In this chapter, we will cover the development of a simple RPD, from importing tables in a database through to how those objects are presented to us when we move on to create an actual request. This will be carried out via the Oracle BI Administration Tool, which is the primary method of accessing and modifying an RPD file. This tool provides an inviting graphical interface for developing and administering the RPD. By the end of this chapter, you will be able to complete the major tasks associated with RPD development. We will also briefly describe some of the more advanced options that are available. This will give you a foundation on which you can investigate these tasks under your own supervision.

Prerequisites

The example we will be using stems from a Star schema design for a data warehouse. It is expected that you are already familiar with terms such as Star, Snowflake, Fact, and Dimension, and that you have an understanding of data warehouse schemas. The vast majority of development projects out there will use such a design as the basis for their BI projects. If you are not familiar with this, we would recommend studying one of the seminal texts on this subject beforehand - *The Data Warehouse Toolkit* by *Ralph Kimball*.

Repository architecture

Before we embark on developing a new repository, let's have a look at how the RPD is structured. The fundamental structure of an RPD is made up of three layers for modeling data:

- **Physical layer**: This contains the information, for example table/column names and keys, for your data sources, as they exist in their database along with their connectivity details. No data is actually stored in the RPD, just references to your data sources, that is, it is metadata that is stored in it.

    If needed, we can also connect to other data sources, for example, Flat files and Excel spreadsheets.

- **Business layer**: The main purpose of this layer is to create an abstract and simplified model of the physical layer objects. This is especially valuable if we need to combine data from varying data sources. The business layer allows us to integrate these different sources and then present them to an end user as a coherent and unified whole.

    OBIEE supports federated querying, so we can query and stitch together data from multiple data sources. For example, we may need to combine multiple data sources into one logical object, such as Geography or Business Department.

We can add business logic to the set of objects that we have described in the physical layer. We can also restructure them as necessary and enhance them via OBIEE server-based calculations and functions.

The final business model that we produce in this layer should be organized as per your business requirements. It should reflect how your business sees and organizes itself.

- **Presentation layer**: In this layer, we can choose how we present the business layer objects to end users when they actually create reports. We can customize the view of the business layer for those end users, for example, renaming data objects as they pertain to the end user's business requirements.

That was a brief overview of the RPD structure. As we will proceed to actually develop a new project, you will gain more clarity on the role of each metadata layer in the RPD. The example project that we will be developing is that of a fictitious bicycle manufacturer called Adventure Works. This scenario is provided by Microsoft (yes, we know!) and covers an organization that has sales, purchasing, manufacturing, and HR data amongst others. It is typical of the type of project that you yourself will be developing in the BI industry, and provides us with a workable data warehouse structure. We will use this DW schema to create aggregated measures that are reported across multiple dimensions. The tools and techniques that we will teach you in the next chapters can be used in any environment that has a requirement of being able to mine data and generate intelligent insight. So let's start!

Physical layer

Firstly, we will be creating the physical layer of our RPD.

Creating an RPD and importing metadata

The procedure is as follows:

1. Start the Oracle BI Administration Tool by navigating to **Programs** | **Oracle BI** | **BI Administration**. As shown in the following screenshot, in Oracle BI Administration Tool by clicking on **File** | **New Repository...**:

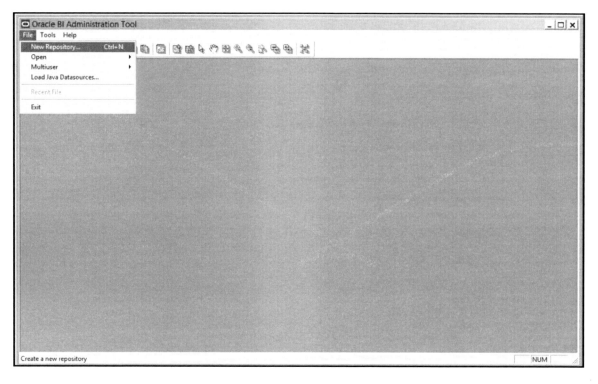

2. This leads us to the start of the **Create New Repository** wizard. The first screen is an input screen for **Repository Information** where you need to input the following information:
    - **Name**: Choose something sensible in this field according to the project or subject matter. For our purposes we will name the RPD as `AdventureWorks`.
    - **Location**: Leave this field as it is, but this can be changed to anything that you require, such as a shared area or mapped drive.
    - **Repository Password**: You must have at least eight characters and one numeral.

- **Retype Password**: Enter the same password that you entered in the **Repository Password** field.
- **Import Metadata**: If you choose **Yes**, you will automatically be prompted to import metadata (physical layer table definitions). If you choose **No**, a completely empty RPD will be created:

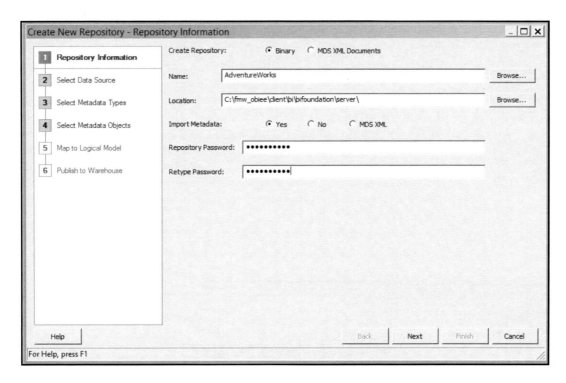

Go ahead and choose **Yes**. You will be presented with screens enabling you to automatically import physical table definitions, from a data source to the physical layer. We can create all of these definitions manually, using the Administration Tool, but a vast amount of time will be saved if the initial set of tables is imported with this method.

Within projects it is common to initially import a first draft of the schema directly from the database and then to make manual changes when needed as that schema is enhanced.

The **Import Metadata** wizard can also be instigated at anytime from the Oracle BI Administration Tool by navigating to **File** | **Import Metadata**.

3. In the first screen of the wizard, as shown in the following screenshot, you will need to choose the following:
    - **Connection Type**: This can be a native driver for the major databases or via ODBC.
    - **Datasource Name**: If we have chosen a native driver, for example Oracle, we will generally need to present this information.
    - **User Name**: It is the user information for the data source.
    - **Password**: It is needed for the Administration Tool so that it can access the data source. There are other bits of information that are required if you natively connect to other sources, for example, Essbase or Oracle OLAP. Have a play and choose other options from the **Connection Type** dropdown, and you will see those other requirements. For our purposes, we are using an SQL Server database and connecting to it via ODBC. This requires us to have SQL Server drivers installed on the local machine and a system DSN set up in the ODBC Data Source Administrator in Windows. These are quite common Windows/ODBC tasks, so we will not go into detail on setting this up. As you can see in the screenshot, we have an `Adventureworks` DSN available that connects to our Data Warehouse schema. You have to input your **User Name** and **Password**. Then, click on **Next**:

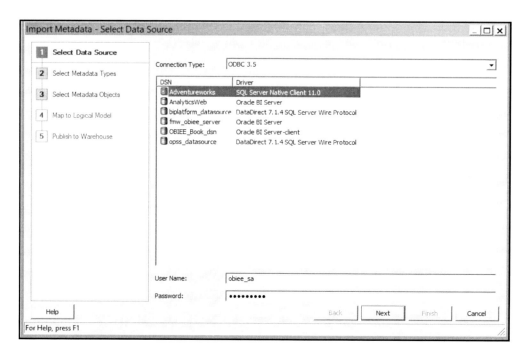

Chapter 7

4. In the following screen, choose which types of objects you want to import into the RPD. These are all common database terms that you should (hopefully!) be familiar with. For example, if you choose **Views**, in the next screen you will be able to import view definitions from the database. If you wish to import joins between tables, choose **Keys** and **Foreign Keys**:

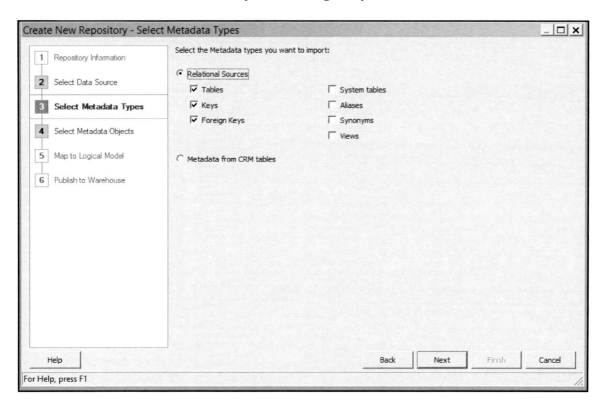

The only non-generic option here is **Metadata from CRM tables**. If this is chosen, upon clicking the **Next** button, the Administration Tool will read the table definitions in a legacy Siebel CRM system, from that CRM system's metadata dictionary. This is as opposed to reading these definitions directly from the database itself. Although this option is not widely used, it is important to note the distinction here. A CRM table may be different in definition at its application metadata layer compared to its implementation in the database, and project requirements may mean that the CRM application relationships are more pertinent.

Developing the BI Server Repository

We will ignore that CRM metadata. For our example, we have a very simple database schema, so we will only need to choose **Tables**, **Keys**, and **Foreign Keys**. Note that all foreign keys have not been set up in our database, so we will show you how to manually implement these in the Administration Tool as the chapter progresses.

5. Once you are happy with our chosen options, click on **Next**. At this point, in the left-hand pane, you will see all the objects within the data source that we have provided details for, filtered by the options chosen in the previous screen:

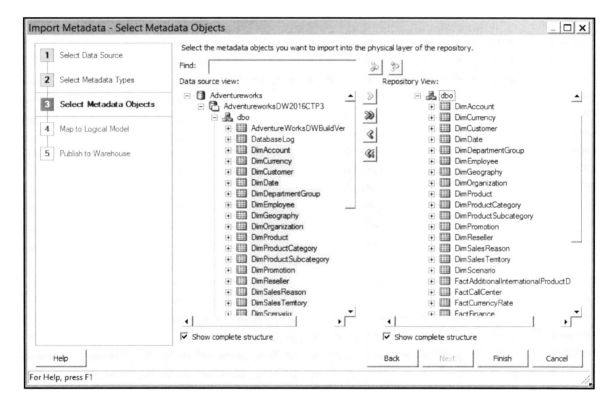

If we were rerunning this wizard in the future, we may selectively choose objects and use the single arrow icon to move them to the right for importing. As we are starting from scratch, we will need all of these tables, so we can use the double arrow button to move everything into the right-hand pane. Once you do this, you can click on **Finish** and these table definitions will be imported.

You will be actually using only the import objects. You should not get confused or make your workspace unwieldy to manage by adding extraneous objects.

6. As shown in the following screenshot, at this point you will be in the main view of the RPD that you will see every time you return to open it. Note the structure, there you will see the base (physical) layer on the right-hand pane and the layers that build upon this flow to the left-hand side. Although initially this may be anti-intuitive to Western readers, this order does make sense when you consider how the metadata in the RPD actually works in a live environment. When building reports, we choose objects in the **Presentation** layer. The tool then constructs an OBIEE-specific logical SQL that filters through the **Business Model and Mapping** layer. This, in turn, informs OBIEE how to turn that logical SQL into actual physical queries against our sources in the **Physical** layer.

These panes are, of course, empty at the moment, but we should see our imported tables in the **Physical** layer, waiting for us to check and finalize details such as the keys and joins.

Elements of the physical layer

Before we create joins, let's go through the **Physical** layer objects that have been automatically created by the Import Metadata wizard:

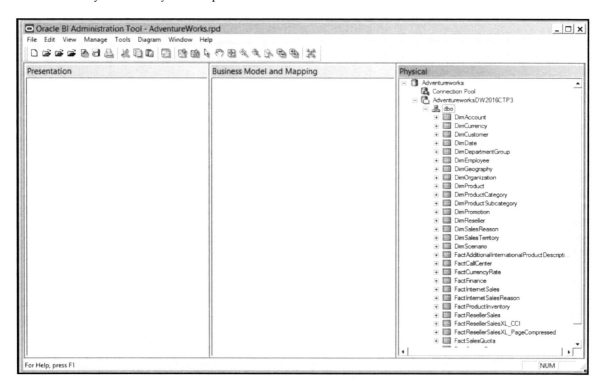

Database object

If you double-click on the topmost object, the Database object will open. This is more generically known as the **Datasource**, as we can have different types of source, for example, Flat files. Have a look at the following screenshot: in the **General** tab, we can set and amend features for that individual database connection. You can change the name of the object and if you decide to use another database type, we can inform OBIEE by changing that definition.

Chapter 7

On this tab, there are also some useful advanced features, which we will briefly describe:

- **Allow populate queries by default**: This allows the use of this database to run and populate SQL.
- **Allow direct database requests by default**: This allows the execution of actual physical SQL queries directly against this database by passing the RPD metadata. Be extremely careful with this option, because if the connection rights within the connection pools (which we will discuss shortly) are too powerful, users will be able to do anything including dropping tables and updating data:

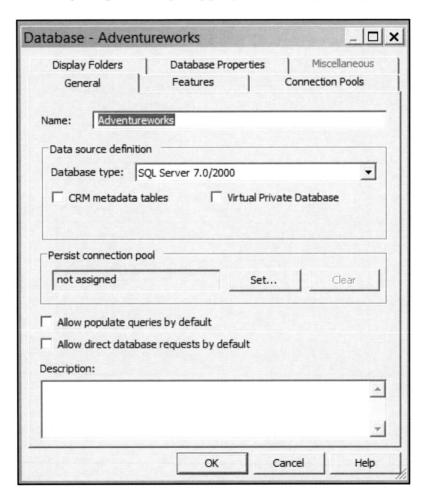

[181]

Moving onto the next tab--**Features**. Although this is an advanced part of the RPD, it is well worth quickly exploring this capability in the Database object. When we imported our table definitions, we stipulated the database type. The types of query that are supported by this specific database are populated, as shown in the following screenshot. You can then turn on or off supported types of query capability as you please. This results in the OBIEE server producing SQL that is restricted to the set of chosen features. This is sometimes really useful when fine-tuning queries against a certain database. However, be warned that this is an advanced feature and unless you are an experienced database developer or have DBA support, you should leave the default settings alone.

The next two tabs list the child objects of the database object, and we will cover these in the following sections.

> Note that you can also manually create a new database object in the physical layer by right-clicking in the white space in that pane, and choosing the **New Database...** option.

Connection Pools

Referring back to our physical layer, under the `Database` object we can see an item called **Connection Pools**. This contains authentication details for the database object and allows multiple users to use the same data source. We can also create multiple connection pools for the same data source. This may be helpful if you want to access the same data source, but with different users and their associated rights.

As shown in the following screenshot, in the **General** tab under **Connection Pool**, you can see the following fields:

- **Name**: It contains the name of the `Connection Pool` object.
- **Permissions**: This button can be useful if you have multiple connection pools and want to restrict their use to certain groups of users. Be careful with this, as users will be able to access cached reports regardless of the permissions set here.
- **Call interface**: This field describes the method of connecting to the database object.

> Try and use native drivers in **Call interface**, wherever possible. This will be helpful to increase the performance, when compared to ODBC.

- **Maximum connections**: This determines the maximum number of connections that the server can open in the database through this connection pool. Before going live, take some time to get this setting right for your environment. You do not need to allow so many connections that query performance is degraded, or so few that users are frustrated as they cannot run queries. You will need to look at the capacity of your database to handle multiple concurrent sessions, and the size/memory of your servers. To get you started, we would say that it is useful to multiply the number of users on the system by the average number of queries on a dashboard.

> For example, a system has 100 users. Typically, 20 percent of them will be online, running an average of four reports at a time. So, our **Maximum connections** parameter will be as follows: *(100 x 20 percent) x 4 = 80*. Then, amend this number depending on our database capacity and as we assess how the system is used in a production environment.

- **Timeout**: Along with **Maximum connections**, this is an important setting as the time set here affects how often OBIEE opens and closes new connections. It is the field where we can stipulate how long a connection to a data source remains open. If a request is received within the set time, the associated query will use an open connection rather than creating a new one:

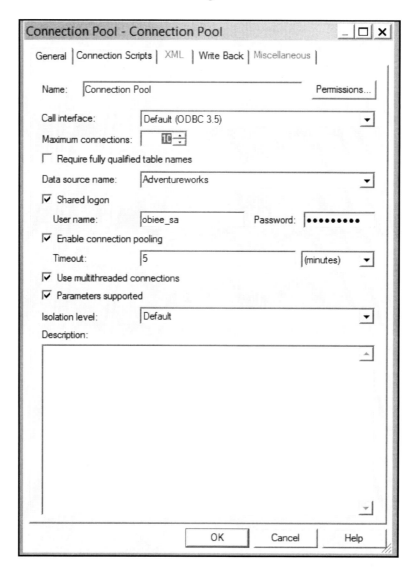

Chapter 7

For our purposes, we are happy with the defaults that have been automatically created. Other advanced options are not relevant for our example project or most development activities, but it is worth having a look at the **Connection Scripts** tab (refer to the following screenshot). Here, it is possible to run commands on the database before and after the initiation of a query or database connection. This gives an opportunity to enhance the performance of requests against this connection pool. One example, from a recent project run by the authors of this book, is that we needed to improve the performance of a set of queries running against a specific connection pool. It was found to be really helpful to run the Alter Session command on the Oracle database to allow parallelism for SQL queries. Again, such a change would only be made after a very mature period of development and in consultation with your database experts:

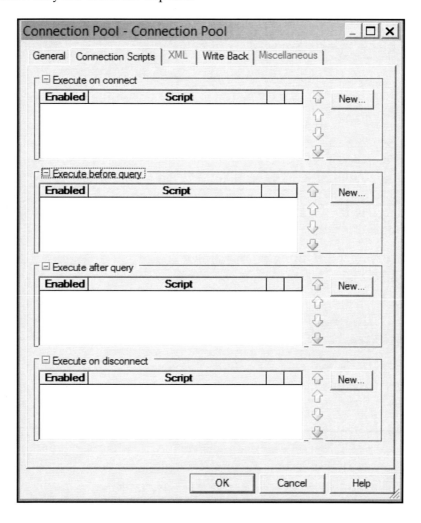

Connection pools can also be created within the **Connection Pool** tab of the `Database` object, or by right-clicking on the `Database` object and selecting **New Object** | **Connection Pool**.

Physical catalog and schemas

Referring again to the objects that have been created automatically by the Import Metadata wizard, you can see an object called **Adventureworks**. This is called a **Physical catalog**. A catalog contains all of the definition information (metadata) for a particular data source (in our case, the database objects).

However, if we have vast amounts of metadata and want to organize objects that exist within the same schema in the database, we can optionally create a `Physical Schema` folder.

We have a small set of objects, so it is fine if we continue with the sole catalog, as the **Import Metadata** wizard has created.

`Physical Catalogs` and `Physical Schema` (display) folders can be created by right-clicking on the data source. Additionally, `Physical Schema` folders can be created via the **Display Folders** tab within the `Datasource` object. A catalog contains information for a whole database object, while a schema contains metadata information for a schema owner. Model this in the same way that your database is designed.

Get your groups organized in advance. It is difficult to amend this afterwards, and if you decide to use folders instead of a catalog, you will not be able to rearrange and create a catalog.

Physical tables

Either of the previous objects will contain **Physical tables**. As we have mentioned in the preceding section, these are the definitions of the actual tables within our database. If you double-click on a `Physical table` object, you can see the basic properties of the table.

As with other objects, we can create physical table definitions manually by right-clicking on the `catalog` or `schema` folder. We can manipulate the definitions of columns and keys via their associated tabs or by expanding the physical table definitions and double-clicking on the individual columns.

We can also add foreign key relationships via the **Foreign Keys** tab. Let us take a look at the **General**, **Columns**, **Keys**, and **Foreign Keys** tabs in the following screenshots:

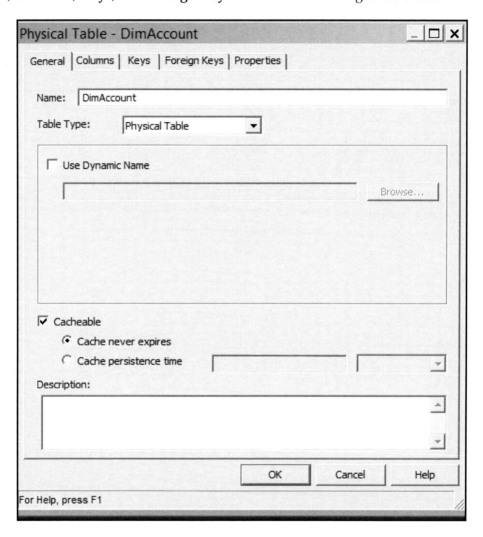

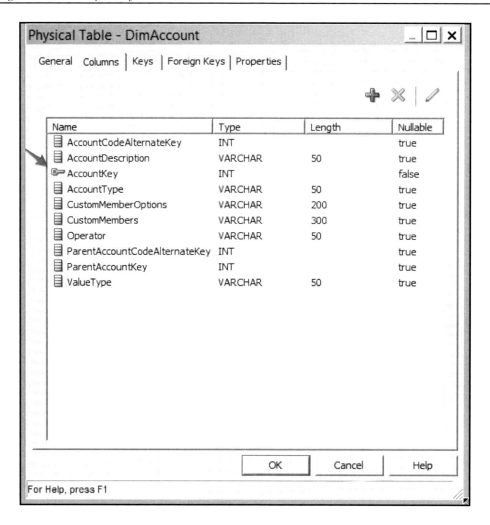

Chapter 7

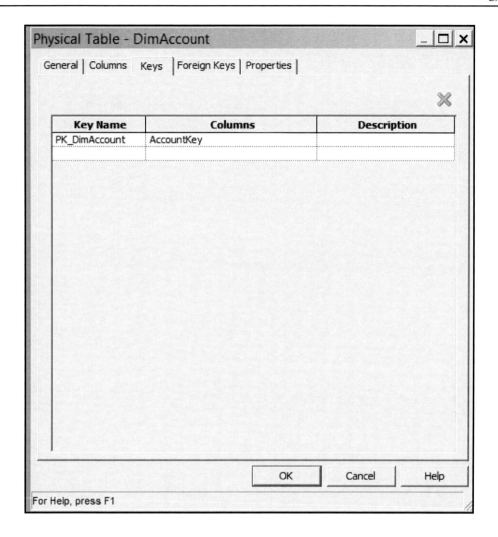

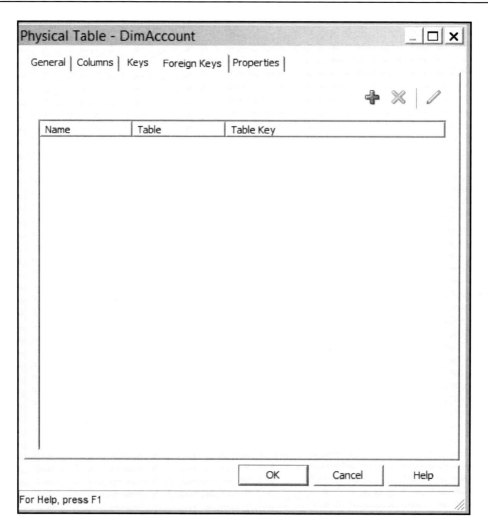

We can see that our column definitions have been imported correctly with a primary key (as denoted by the golden key sign). However, we do not seem to have any foreign keys. So, we will have to create these relationships (also known as physical joins) ourselves via the Administration Tool.

Physical join

We could create the relationships between the tables by using the **Foreign Keys** tab, but the Administration Tool provides a far easier way of changing these relationships. This method uses what is called the **Physical Diagram**. During any development cycle, you will spend a lot of time in here. The Physical Diagram graphically represents relationships between tables. It will show basic cardinalities as with an Entity Relationship Diagram, that is, 1:M or 1:1 signifiers.

So, let's open the diagram. We can choose all of the tables that we want to model, then right-click on **Physical Diagram** | **Selected Objects Only** (actually, in this instance, any of those final options will suffice). Note that instead of a contextual right-click, we could have also used a button on the toolbar that looks like a mini-ERD diagram:

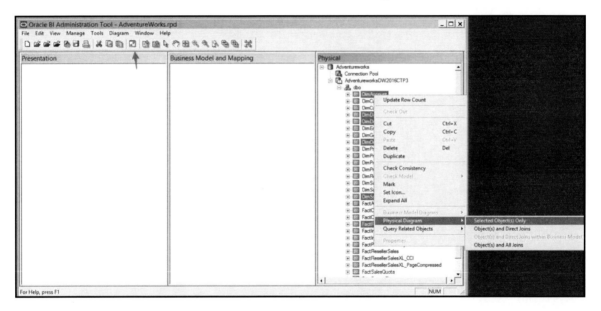

As you can see in the following screenshot, we are now presented with a graphical representation of the table definitions. We can double-click on the tables to open the previous screens that we discussed, but the most useful aspect of the diagram is that we can define the relationships between these tables in a visual manner:

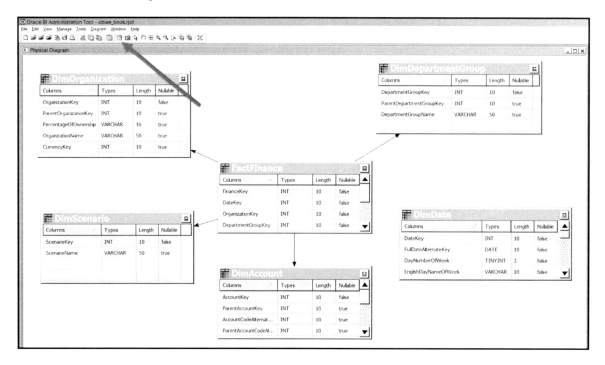

To do this click on the **New Join** button (as denoted by the tooltip in the preceding screenshot) and then click on our fact table (FactFinance) and drag the pointer out to the table for which we want to define a join (in our case, the DimDate dimension).

As you can see in the screenshot, a line is drawn representing the relationship that exists between the two tables. The **Physical Foreign Key** screen prompts us. This is where we can stipulate the exact details of the join. OBIEE makes a pretty good guess of the join for single key tables, especially if we have already set up our primary keys properly.

In the following screenshot, we can see that it has guessed that we are joining on `DateKey` in both tables. This is correct, but if it had not been, we could easily change this in the **Expression** box. This would definitely need to be done if we were joining on compound keys. We would also have to check that the tables, columns, and join information are correct and have a look at the cardinality as well. Ensure that this is in line with your warehouse design: otherwise, redo the join:

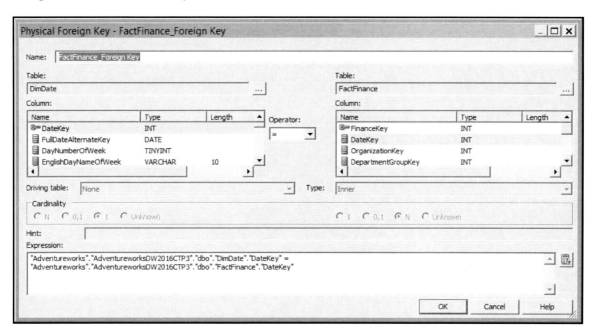

Once you are happy with the settings, you can click on **OK** and proceed to define the joins for all other tables as needed. For each star within a warehouse, we will end up with something like what is shown in the following screenshot. The **Physical Diagram** is a great tool with which you can model your data. Visualizing your data in this way adds clarity and eases the development process:

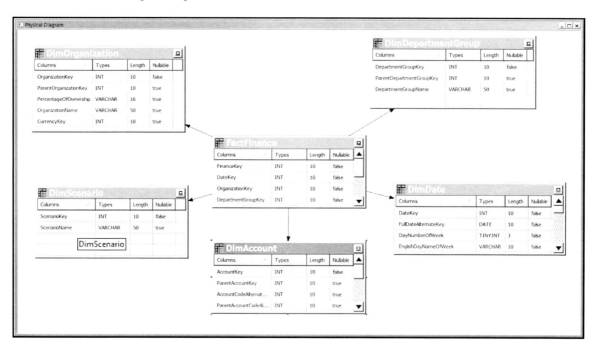

Now we are ready to proceed to the next layer of the RPD. We have set up the objects needed for data connectivity and defined the objects that exist in that data source. Having completed a large amount of work, it is easy to make errors when completing large swathes of development. So we should save and check our work periodically.

To this end, the Administration Tool provides what is commonly known as the consistency check, or in Oracle's own documentation as the **Consistency Check Manager**. This process will parse all of the metadata that we have developed, rather like one of the tasks a compiler may do for a programming language, and inform us of any errors. It will give us errors, which we must definitely fix before proceeding. Or it will create advisory warnings, where we can use our own judgment on whether it will impact our development negatively or not. Errors can range from missing object definitions, such as column types. Warnings can flag, as an example, a join that we have purposely disabled. We can also choose to have the process to give us best practice recommendations.

If you use the Import Metadata wizard for keys and foreign keys, and import joins rather than creating them manually, double-check the results. Ensure that these joins have been imported correctly.

Consistency check

Normally, you will be prompted to run the check when saving your work, but it must be stressed that it is good practice to run this check of your own volition regularly. Let's run the check now. Select **File** | **Check Global Consistency**:

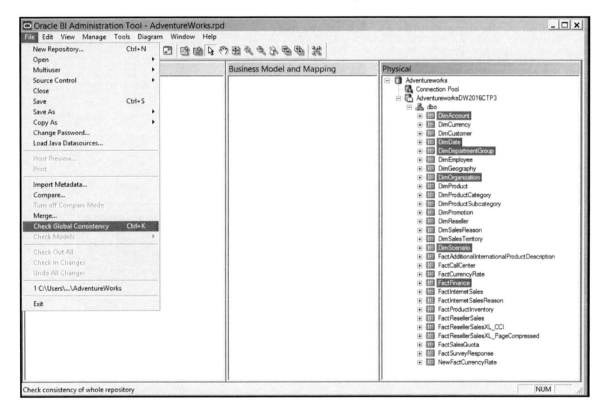

Ideally, next you should see the following message:

 Consistency check didn't find any errors, warnings, or best practice violations.

If not, and you see a list of errors and warnings, you will need to note this and look through your development to rectify these issues. There are too many possibilities to go through here, but as you increase in experience as an OBIEE developer, you will learn to recognize and solve these quickly.

 Clicking on an error or warning automatically takes you to the object concerned.

Table aliases and naming conventions

Before we move onto the business layer, let's quickly look at a couple of best practices in developing this layer:

- **Naming conventions**: For ease of use, your objects should have identifiable names. For example, our physical tables have Dim and Fact prefixes denoting whether they are a dimension or fact. Another common standard is to have table name _D and _F suffixes.
- **Aliases**: If your physical objects are not appropriately named, you can create aliases by right-clicking on the object and choosing the alias creation option, as you can see in the following screenshot:

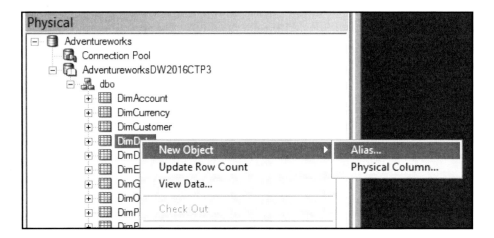

Chapter 7

This creates another object, or level of abstraction, that retains its reference to the original source object. Then we can name this alias in a more appropriate way. Note that the icon for an alias differs:

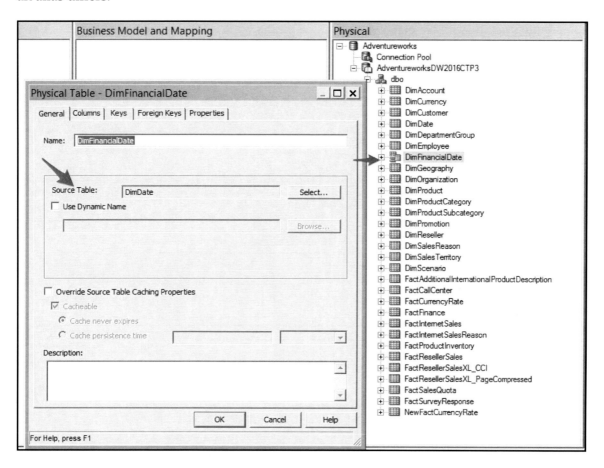

Developing the BI Server Repository

 By right-clicking on the icon and choosing **Set Icon** from the menu, we can change the icon to a custom setting if that helps to identify key tables quickly. You can see that we have chosen a traffic light icon for one of our tables in the following screenshot:

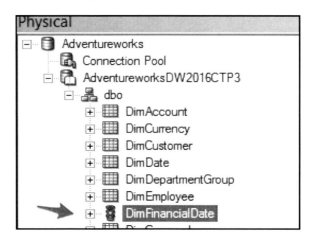

Aliases are also commonly used to create multiple physical models based on the same base objects. This is sometimes useful if we want to avoid circular joins or just want to organize our Star schemas in a clear manner.

Business layer

In this layer, we are not limited by the constraints of the actual physical tables in the database. We can restructure and consolidate sources that will inform the BI server on how to best handle the end user requests. Most of the metadata that affects SQL production by the BI server is handled in this layer.

Business model

The **business model** is the highest level in this layer and it contains a business view of the physical schema. You should be able to simplify the physical schema so that in the end you get to look at the business view of the data. Anything we do in this layer will not affect the work that has been done in the physical layer, but we can create multiple models based on the same physical sources.

To create a business model, right-click on the **Business Model and Mapping** pane in the middle and choose **New Business Model**. Then, we are prompted to give the model a name, as shown in the following screenshot:

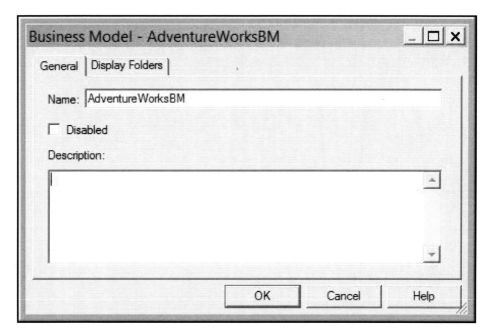

We will name our model as `AdventureWorkBM`, and will keep the **Disabled** flag checked, as this model is not ready to handle any queries. Once we click on **OK**, we will see a new business model has been created. In the following screenshot, note that the business model icon is supplemented with a no entry sign. This signifies that it is disabled. We are now ready to start adding the logical representations of the tables that we have already added in the physical layer:

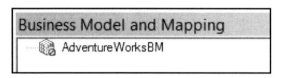

 In general, create different business models for different areas of reporting even if they are from the same source, for example, a separate model for HR and another for CRM data.

Logical tables

Within a business model, the most common object that you will create is called a **logical table**. This is a representation of one or more tables amalgamated into one logical group. A common best practice example would be if we have a Snowflake physical schema, we will be able to define that as a Star schema in the business model by combining multiple dimension tables as one logical dimension.

A logical table:

- Can be a fact table or a dimension
- Contains at least one logical table source, but can have many
- Is a business view of data

Initially, we are going to create a logical table for our Finance fact. Right-click on our new business model and select **New Object** | **Logical Table**:

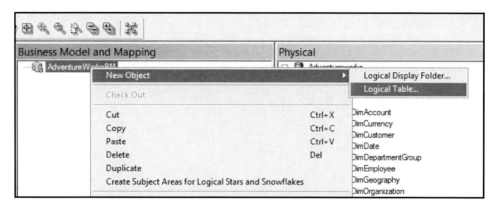

Name the new table as `Fact - Finance`. We want this fact to contain measures from the `FactFinance` physical table. So, as shown in the following screenshot, we pick the required columns (in our case there is only one measure here, called *Amount*) in the physical layer and drag them to our new logical table:

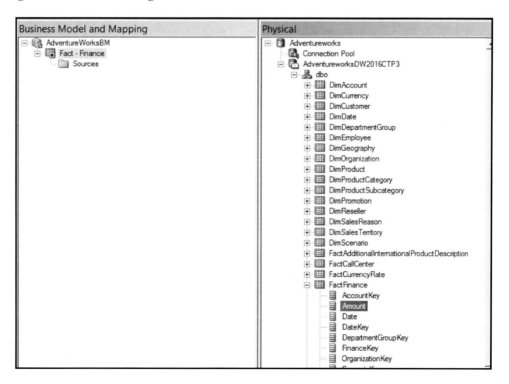

Developing the BI Server Repository

 Logical fact versus Logical Dimension Tables.

Ideally, fact tables should only contain aggregated measures and dimension tables should only contain descriptive attributes.

 You can name these logical tables whatever you want, but it is good practice to give sensible names that denote their purpose, for example, a Dim prefix for dimensions and a Fact prefix for facts.

As demonstrated in the following screenshot, after adding columns to that logical table, the `Sources` folder is now populated with a reference to the physical table that holds these columns. This is known as a **logical table source**:

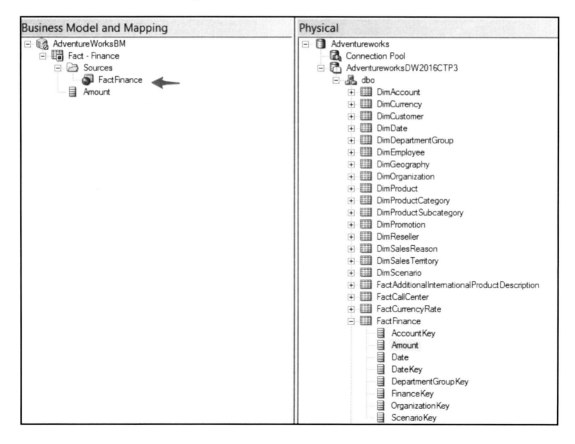

Logical table sources

A **logical table source** (**LTS**) is where you can map a logical table to one or more physical tables. As we will see later, we can use an LTS in the following ways:

- Map and transform data, for example, adding calculations on top of the physical columns
- Define aggregation rules for measures in fact tables
- Add other physical tables for purpose of aggregation or fragmentation

Logical columns

We will cover these LTS scenarios as the chapter progresses, so let's concentrate on our current example. We have bought the measure over, but we need to tell the OBIEE server that these are metrics that should be shown in queries in an aggregated format defined by dimensions.

We will cover these LTS scenarios as the chapter progresses, so let's concentrate on our current example. We have bought the measure over, but we need to tell the OBIEE server that these are metrics that should be shown in queries in an aggregated format defined by dimensions. We do this by double-clicking on a column to get to the tabs shown in the following screenshot:

We will rename the column to something that makes more sense from a reporting point of view--Revenue. Note that this does not change the name of the physical column and that the mapping to that column will remain unaffected:

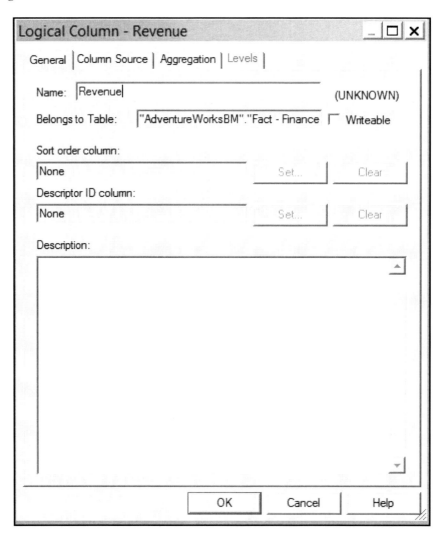

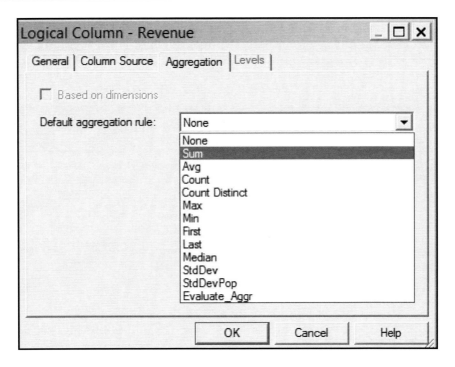

Then in the **Aggregation** tab, we will set the **Default aggregation rule** field to **Sum**, as this measure is an additive and we want to report on aggregated sales. Note that if we also want to treat this measure in a different manner, for example an average, we could copy this column and have the aggregation rule set to **Avg**. This would result in two logical columns, which are mapped to the same physical column, and will yield different results in a report due to our varying definitions in the business model:

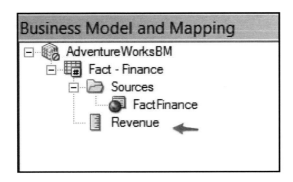

Developing the BI Server Repository

Note that in the preceding screenshot, the name of the logical column has changed (without changing the underlying physical mapping). More importantly, the column is identified by a yellow slide rule icon, which indicates that this column has been defined as a measure.

We will also go ahead and add a new logical table for a dimension. Rather than right-clicking, as we have done before, we can use the alternative method of dragging the whole physical table from the physical layer into the business model. Doing this for DimDate will result in what you can see in the following screenshot:

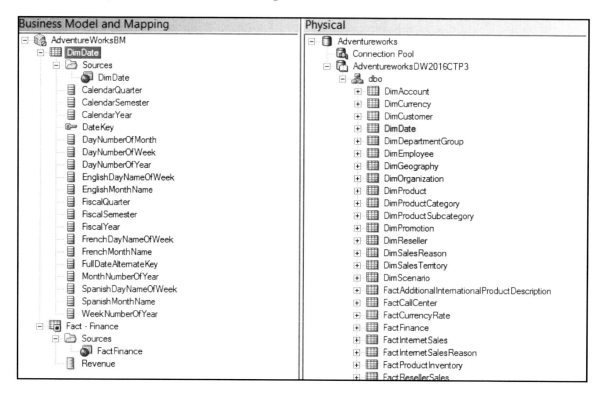

Note that when bringing the dimension table across, it also automatically sets one column (primary key) as a key for that logical table. Now, we do indeed need a logical key, but this should be something that has more of a business meaning. We can change this key in the same way that we did for a physical table: by opening the logical table, navigating to the **Keys** tab, and changing the key definition.

Fact tables generally do not need logical keys.

Dimension tables do need a key, but generally the physical key should be deleted from the business model and a key with more of a business meaning should be set.

Logical joins

As with the joins in the physical layer, we must also set the relationships between logical tables. Again, the Administration Tool provides a good visual interface for this.

We can choose our dimension and fact. Right-click and select **Business Model Diagram** | **Selected Tables and Direct Joins** (as currently we only have two tables in the business layer, any option would have sufficed):

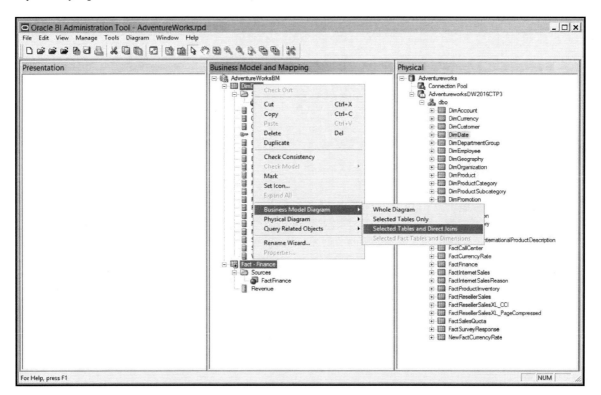

Refer to the way in which we set the joins between the tables in the physical layer. We can create joins in the business layer in exactly the same way. However, take a look at the join detail shown in the following screenshot. Notice that this time there are no columns stipulated in the **Expression** block for the join. This is because we previously already set up the physical relationships. The OBIEE server will use this information as well as the metadata that we have set up in the logical tables and logical table sources in order to ascertain what type of SQL query it should run:

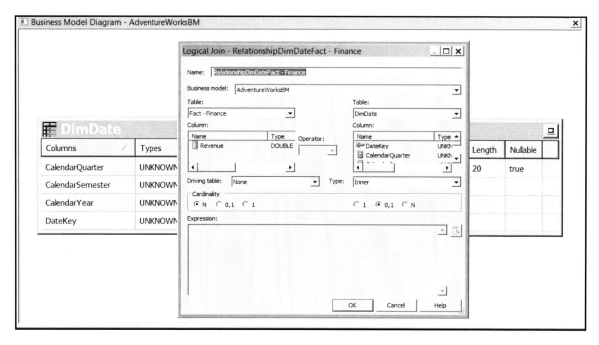

- **Physical join**: This is a join between two physical tables based on a stipulated relationship.
- **Logical join**: This is a join between two logical objects. These objects may be made up of many different physical data sources. This join is a symbolic way of letting OBIEE know that a relationship exists between these objects. The OBIEE server will utilize our settings within these logical objects, and subsequently the physical joins, in deciding how to best generate a query when joining these logical objects in a report.

Again, looking at the preceding information concerning a logical join, we do have a choice of what cardinality to set between these logical tables. This helps in providing the information to OBIEE on how to create queries. In general, you should leave this setting alone unless you are an advanced developer and understand the ramifications.

Now that we are comfortable with setting up logical facts and dimensions, let's go ahead and bring all of our **Physical** dimensions and facts into the business model:

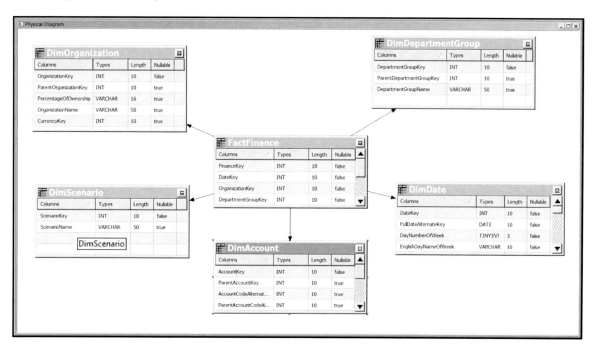

Once we have done this, our RPD should look something like what you can see in the preceding screenshot. Note that we are using easily identifiable names for the logical tables. Also, we can see in the **Business Model Diagram** for this star, that all the tables are joined.

Now, there is a bit more work to do regarding dimensions. We need to create a dimension hierarchy for each logical dimension table.

At this point you may have been thinking about how to represent levels in a dimension. For example, how do we show that a geography dimension has levels of country, state, and city, or that time has year, month, and day? Well, OBIEE allows us to set hierarchies in the business model. The most common hierarchy is level-based. This enables us the following:

- Creating measures aggregated at a certain level.
- Creating predetermined drill paths for the end users in reports. These levels will vary from dimension to dimension and will depend on your business requirements. For example, a business may need separate geography dimensions--one with different levels or groupings for their customers and another for their offices or stores. To create a logical dimension, right-click on the logical table for the dimension. Then, select **Create Logical Dimensional** | **Dimension with Level-Based Hierarchy**. You can see this in the following screenshot:

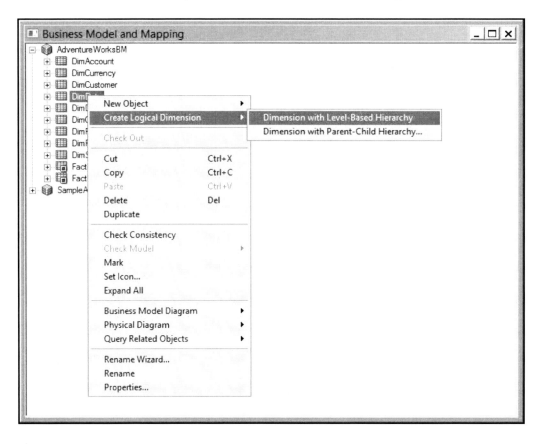

Chapter 7

Dimension hierarchies

This results in the dimension object that you can see in the following screenshot. Notice that currently there are only two levels--one for the grand total and another for the lowest level of granularity. We need to have levels that correspond to a year, month, week, and so on. So there is a bit more work for us to do:

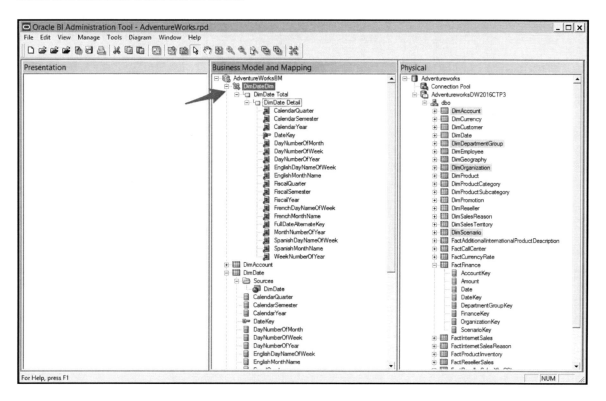

[211]

Build up the levels by starting at the lowest level and adding parents between that level and the grand total. We can do this by right-clicking and selecting **New Object** | **Parent Level...**:

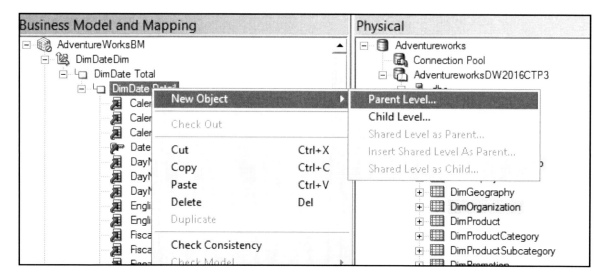

As you can see in the following screenshot, we will be presented with the detail tabs. Our lowest level is **Date**, so we will name this next level up **Week**. Note that there is an entry called **Number of Elements at this level**. This entry does not affect the results that will be brought back in a query, but when we go on to include multiple table sources (especially aggregates), these figures will help the OBIEE server to optimize that query. Don't be worried about an exact number, all that matters are the ratios between levels. The grand total is defaulted to, and system set at **1**. The lower levels should have numbers that are progressively higher.

In the example shown in the following screenshot, we are looking at the **Week** level. For our requirements, the next level will be **Month**. So, the final number that we input here will be just above four times of the number that we input at the **Month** level, as that is the ratio between a month and a week:

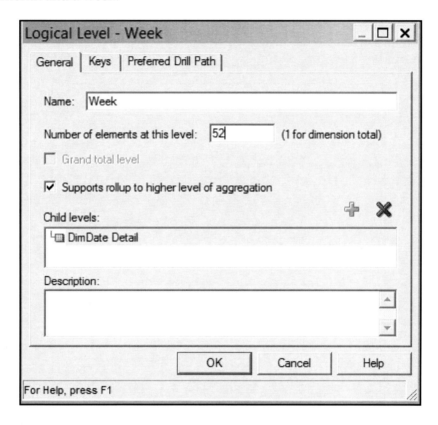

Number of elements

Remember that the ratio between levels matters more than the actual numbers.

If we do this for all of our new levels, we will end up with something resembling that is shown in the following screenshot. However, we also need to inform the OBIEE server about how to identify those levels using the columns that we have brought into the business layer. This requires us to set keys at each level:

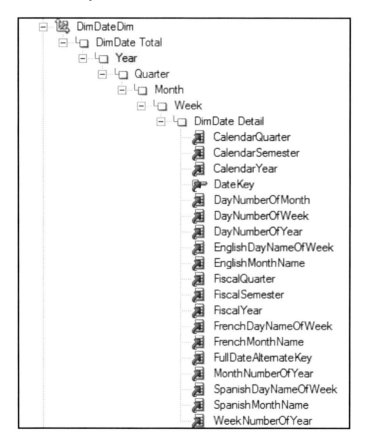

Remember that we can also set drill paths within dimensions that can be utilized by the end users in their final reports. In addition to the level keys, it is at this point that we can set these keys:

So we need keys that uniquely identify a level, and we should not have columns at a level that differs from their grain. So, as an example, for our Time dimension, we have a very straightforward hierarchy of **Year** | **Quarter** | **Month** | **Week** | **Date**. We can see that we have unique identifiers such as **MonthNumberOfYear** for the month, **WeekNumberOfYear** for the week, and so on. These will be great for our level keys. Notice that we also have some descriptive columns, for example, **EnglishMonthName**. We need to ensure that these exist at the right level, so these will have to be moved as well. If we do that for all of the levels, we will get a hierarchy, as shown in the following screenshot:

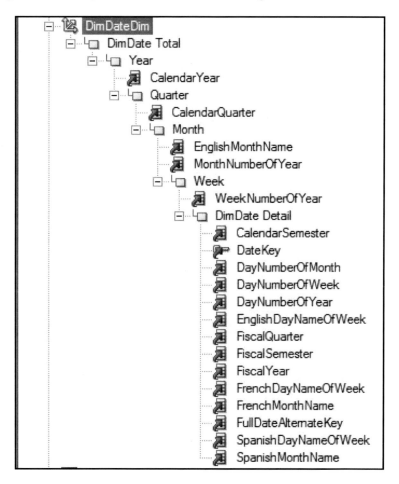

At this point, we have still not stipulated which columns are keys and which are to be used in a drill path. We can do this by right-clicking on a column and choosing **New Logical Level Key**. We will then get a screen, as shown in the following screenshot. A **Year**, such as 2016, is both a unique identifier and a description that we would be happy to click on and drill down in a report. Therefore, we will set it as key, and check the **Use for Display** box to indicate that this is what we will be using for drilling in a report:

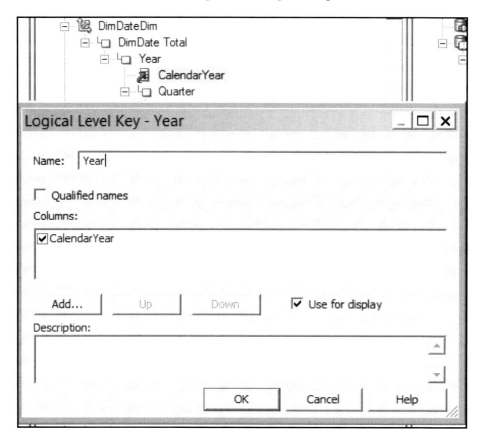

If we do this for all our levels, we will get a hierarchy, as shown in the following screenshot. Note that the icons have changed to a golden key, indicating that these are now keys. The keys that will uniquely identify these levels for optimization purposes are **CalendarYear | CalendarQuarter | MonthNumberOfYear | WeekNumberofYear | DateKey**. The drill path that we have set is **CalendarYear | CalendarQuarter| EnglishMonthName | WeekNumberOfYear | EnglishDayNameOfWeek**. Note that we have also removed superfluous columns, for example, French and Spanish **Name** columns:

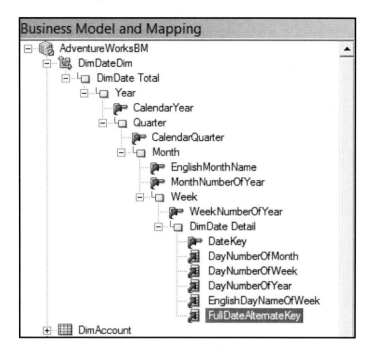

Once we repeat this for all of our dimensions, we are ready for the final part of developing an RPD--the presentation layer.

Presentation layer

If we try to do a consistency check at this point, we will find that it throws up an error, as we do not have anything in the presentation layer. So far, we have mapped our data sources and de ned the physical objects. Then, we proceeded to add some business logic and tell the OBIEE server how to handle the physical objects in a way that relates to our business requirements. Now, we need to expose this to our end users.
In this layer, we can customize the view of the business model for the end users. This includes renaming objects sensibly without affecting the logical and physical names that will be used to generate queries. To reinforce the point, the names and definitions of presentation tables are separate from logical tables, that is, we can rename the columns to whatever we want without changing the mapping to their associated logical column and onward to their physical column.

We can also choose to widen or limit the scope of the parts of the business model that can be seen by the end reporting users at any time by only showing a partial amount in the presentation layer. The presentation layer names will be stored and used as references in the Presentation Catalog metadata when creating reports.

Subject areas

A subject area is a grouping of objects from the business model. Note that, this can be a subset if required. We can do this by right-clicking in the presentation layer area and choosing the option to create a new subject area. We can then drag folders and columns across. We can also automatically create a subject area for the whole business model straight from the business layers. We do this by right-clicking in the **Business Model and Mapping** area and choosing **Create Subject Areas for Logical Stars and Snowflakes**:

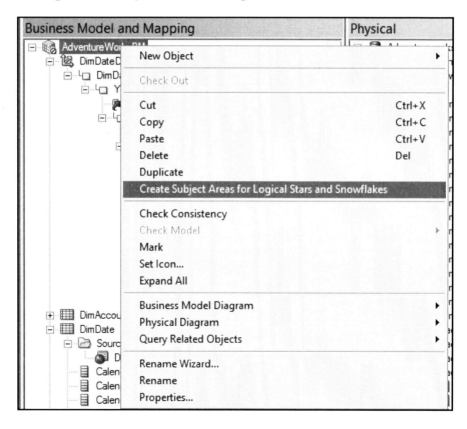

Chapter 7

This option automatically creates a separate subject area for each logical star that is detected. This can be a great way to start creating your subject areas.

As you can see in the following screenshot, we have one subject area for our Finance star. Note that we have renamed that, and our `AdventureWorks` business model has a green 3D cube icon, which indicates that it has passed the consistency check and is now ready to generate queries. And also note that we have renamed our Time dimension hierarchy as **Time Dim**:

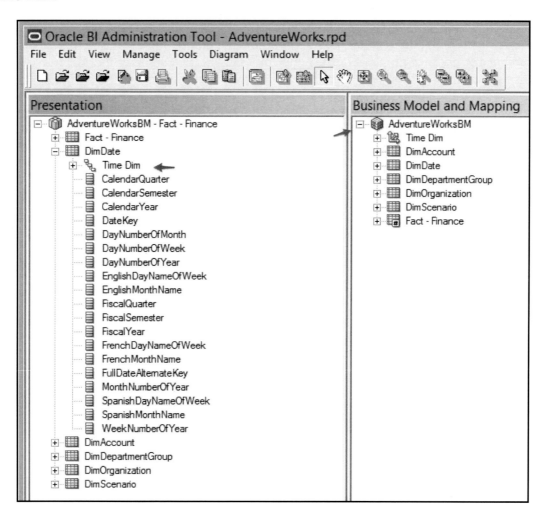

Also note the object in the presentation layer that is arrowed in the preceding screenshot. This is called a hierarchical column, and we will discuss this further in Chapter 8, *Creating Dashboards and Analyses*.

Best practices in the presentation layer

Development in this layer is not as involved as it is in others. It mostly involves considering how you wish to present your logical columns to the end user. End users will see tables and columns exactly as you arrange/name them in the presentation layer. Due to this flexibility, it's beneficial to go through some of the better practices that we have found through our own experience:

- Keep column names relevant to the business. Try and do this renaming at the business model layer rather than at the presentation layer.
- Order your dimensions and facts in the same way in all subject areas. For example, we would recommend always having Time first. If dimensions appear in multiple subject areas then keep their order the same in all of those areas.
- Keep fact tables at the bottom, with dimensions preceding.
- Rename tables to remove dimension and fact pre x indicators, that is, remove Dim as this looks ungainly to the end users.

To enable the editing of presentation table names, go to **Tools | Options** and enable the **Edit presentation names** checkbox:

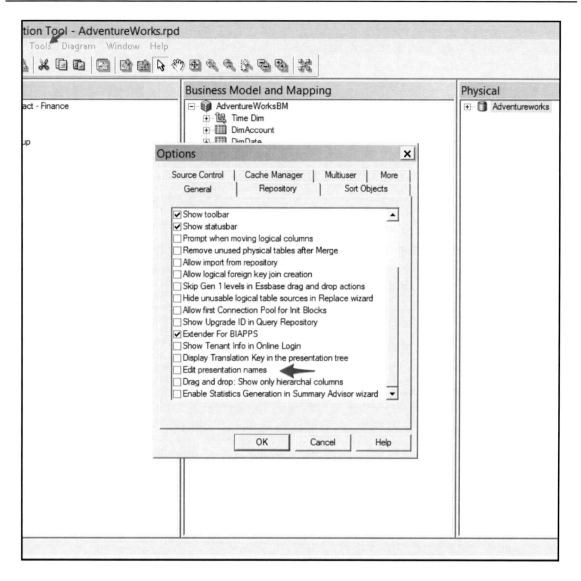

- Ensure that every possible combination of columns chosen in a subject area will produce a coherent result. It is not possible to run a query when errors occur due to errant metadata configuration. If this happens, your credibility in front of users will diminish.
- Keep subject areas as small and as targeted as possible.

Developing the BI Server Repository

If you follow these guidelines with our example RPD, you will end up with something similar to what is shown in the following screenshot, in the **Presentation** layer:

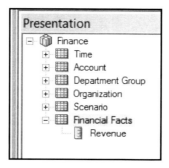

Note that we have removed the Dim prefixes and the columns have names with business meanings. We can reorder and rename tables by double-clicking on the subject area and navigating to the **Presentation Tables** tab, as shown in the following screenshot:

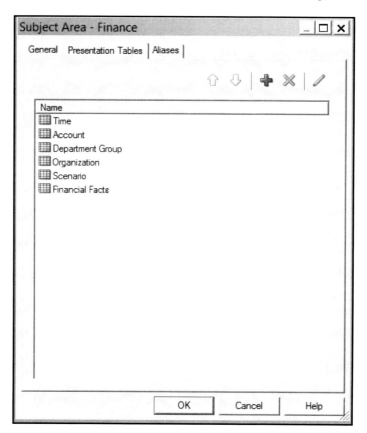

As you can see in the preceding screenshot, we can click on the pencil icon to rename a table. We can use the arrow buttons to reorder them.

We can make a subfolder by using a hyphen at the start of the presentation table name. This is especially useful as it is common to have an empty fact folder at the bottom with nested tables separating different types of measures.

Aliases

Have a look at the following screenshot:

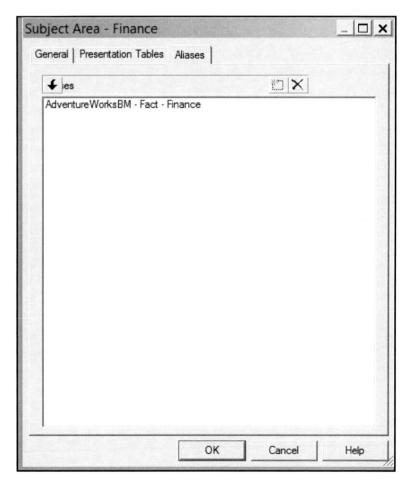

Developing the BI Server Repository

We can see that there is also an **Aliases** tab. Here, we can rename a column without ever losing its mapping to a logical column. Every time we rename a column or table in the presentation layer, we retain a reference to the old presentation layer name here. This ensures that if we have already created reports and dashboards using these names, they will not create an error using the new names.

However, this also means that you cannot create a column/table with the old name unless that alias is deleted. This is a common source of errors, so be aware of this. Presentation aliases are easy to forget about, so you should use these very sparingly and keep in mind the drawbacks of using it. They should not be used as a quick way to fix badly named presentation objects. These have to be agreed with the business beforehand.

In the preceding screenshot, you can see the old name for the **Finance** subject area as an alias.

Implicit Fact

Many times users will try to choose columns from two or more dimensions in a report without choosing a fact. OBIEE will then choose a fact accordingly. However, this may not always be the fact that we desire the query path to run through. An example would be when you have multiple facts in one subject area that share conformed dimensions. Our current RPD doesn't have multiple facts. Let's say it did with shared *Account* and *Scenario* dimensions and we wanted to ensure that a query using those same two dimension always utilized the Finance fact. OBIEE allows for this by enabling the selection of an Implicit Fact for each subject area. We do this by double-clicking on a subject area and choosing **Set** for the **Implicit Fact Column**:

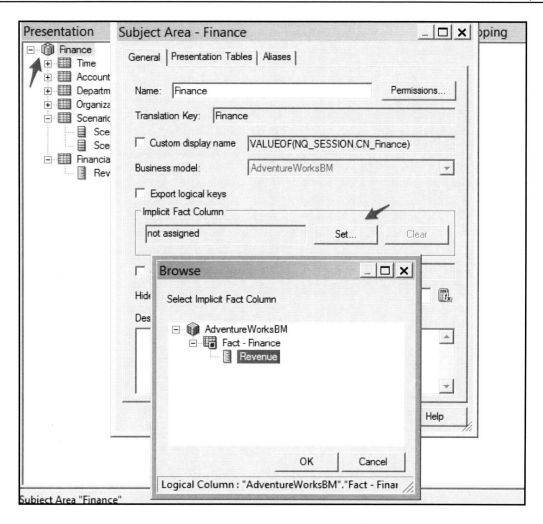

Then we choose any column from the fact that we want our default query to join to. So in the preceding example, you can see that we have opened the Finance subject area and are choosing a column from the Finance fact. Now, whenever we try to run a query in this subject area that consists solely of dimensions (that is, we don't specifically choose a measure from a fact table), this column and fact will be used for generating the query even if the OBIEE engine has a choice of multiple facts.

Note that this is not a mandatory step in development. An important part of a BI project involves educating end users. In general, properly educated users will not choose queries without a fact and they will have an awareness of their star structures. However, if you notice that this errant choice does commonly occur, think about implementing this feature.

Calculated measures

Congratulations! We have finally completed the RPD. In albeit a simple example, we have gone through the process from start to finish. You can use this as a starting point in any environment. It's now time to delve into slightly more complicated examples of OBIEE functionality. As well as giving you greater insight into the full capability of OBIEE, it will also serve to reinforce concepts that we have already visited in this chapter.

Logical column calculation

So far, the columns and measures in our example RPD have had a one-to-one relationship with physical columns. We have added aggregation information, but we can also make new columns using already created logical columns and without the need to create new physical sources in the database.

For this example, we will use the **InternetSales** fact. We won't step through the modeling from the physical layer to the presentation layer as the methods are exactly as for the Finance fact that we have already completed. Please refer to the sample `AdventureWorks` RPD if you need to reference.

Chapter 7

In this fact, we have measures for **Sales Amount** and **Total Product Cost**, but let's say that we have a requirement to understand what the profit margin is on a product. To do this, right-click on our logical table and choose **New Object | Logical Column...**:

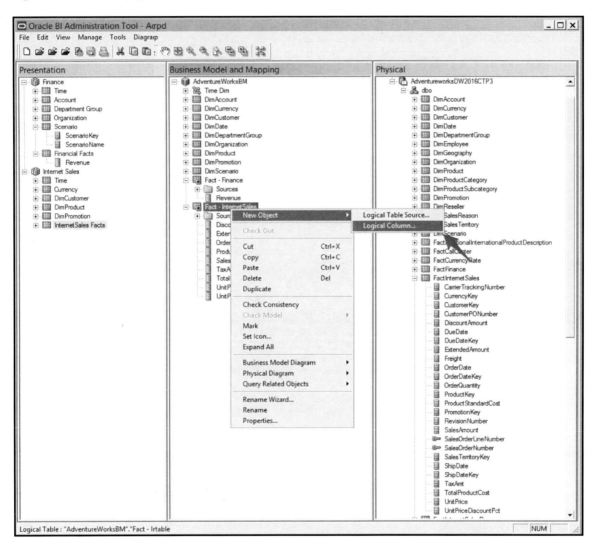

Then you will get the screen shown in the following screenshot. In the **General** tab, name our new measure as **Gross Product Profit**. Then proceed to the **Column Source** tab. Note that there is no physical column currently mapped. Remember from the preceding section that we dragged objects from the physical layer to the business layer, automatically creating logical columns with their appropriate physical mapping:

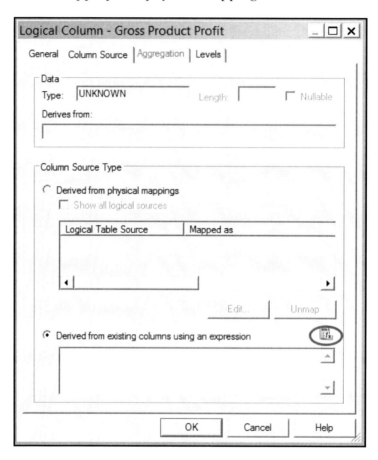

This time, we are creating a column directly in the business layer. We are not worried about physical mappings or columns as we can deduce the information for the new measure from two current logical columns. So, as you can see in the preceding screenshot, we have checked the **Derived from existing columns using an expression** option. If you are familiar with the syntax needed, you can type that into the input box straightaway. Alternatively, you can invoke the Expression Builder by clicking on the icon with the **fx** indicator on the bottom right of the screen, shown in the preceding screenshot.

Expression Builder

You will come across the Expression Builder in many places during project development. It exposes functions and methods of manipulating data that the OBIEE server provides. We can use these to create new definitions in a repository. One function enables us to manipulate strings in an attribute column, for example, concatenating the first name and last name for a customer. Another function allows us to convert a column data type. In fact, there are many possibilities here, and you are well advised to take the time to explore the functionality available here. You can have a look at the various functions and objects by changing the choice in the **Category** box in the top left of the screen shown in the following screenshot. Then you will be given further options in the other two boxes:

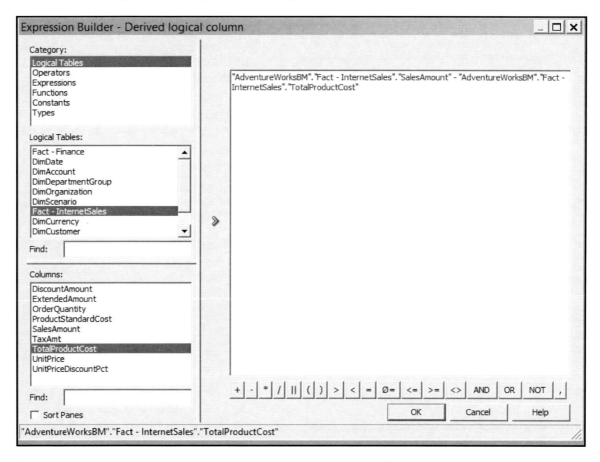

Developing the BI Server Repository

In our case, we want to refer to two logical columns. So choose **Logical Tables** as our **Category** and then choose the table (**Fact - InternetSales**) and columns that we require. We can then make a calculation that represents the profit margin. You can see that calculation in the preceding screenshot.

Once you click on **OK**, the Expression Builder will check that our syntax is coherent and if it parses successfully then you can proceed to drag this new measure to our physical layer. Note that in the **Column Source** tab, the column automatically gets a data type of INT and the **Aggregation** tab is grayed out. Both of these are derived from our base columns.

So now we have a new measure that our business can use without having to alter our original physical data source. All the required development has taken place within OBIEE:

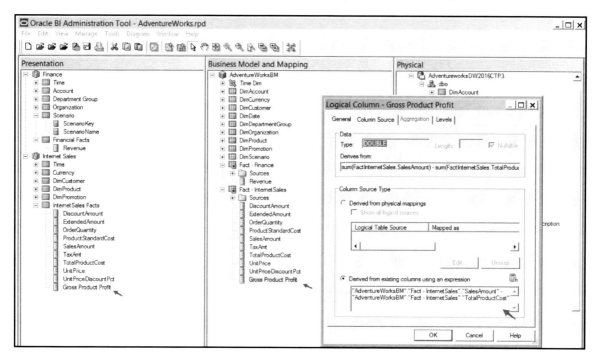

Physical column calculation

We can create the same calculation, but this time using physical columns rather than logical columns as our base. So we will create a new logical column exactly as before; however, let's name it as **Gross Product Profit (Physical)**. Note that this time we have to set an aggregation rule as we are deriving the information straight from physical columns instead of logical ones. After this, we need to open the logical table source. We can do this via the **Column Source** tab and edit the logical source from the **Derived from physical mappings** section (previously we used the Expression Builder), or we can double-click on the **LTS** (**Logical Table Source**) itself. Then we proceed to the **Column Mapping** tab, as you can see in the following screenshot:

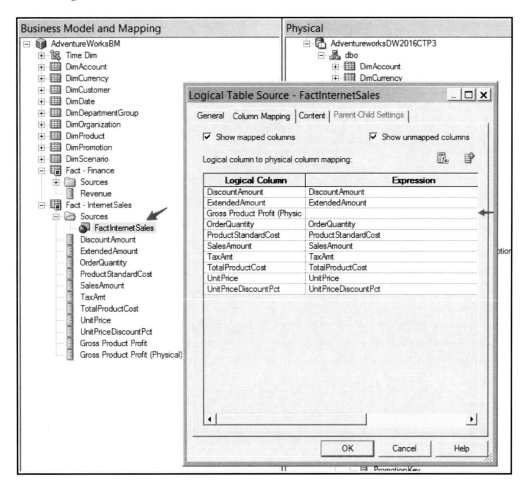

In the preceding screenshot, you can see the mappings from physical to logical columns. If you check the **Show unmapped columns** box, you will see our new logical column. To create the mapping and calculation, choose our new column and again click on the Expression Builder icon:

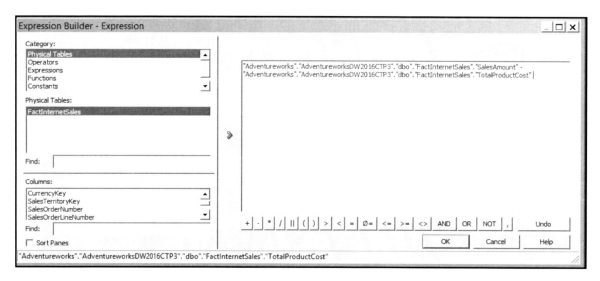

This time we do not have access to logical columns and tables. They have been replaced by physical tables, but we have access to the same functions and operators. If our syntax is correct, we can drag this column to the presentation layer.

Although we have discussed two separate methods to produce the exact same calculation, you have to be careful when choosing the solution for a live environment. The rather more correct method in this case would be to use a physical calculation. Why? Well, because we want to know the aggregated profit margin and then aggregate upwards. So, it is better that we set an aggregation rule after our calculation, rather than setting it before, as it is in the first case. If we had another example, for example, finding a percentage between two already aggregated amounts, then the logical calculation would be better as we are aggregating before the final calculation:

- **Logical calculations**: Use when you need an aggregation before your calculation
- **Physical calculations**: Use when you need an aggregation after your calculation

However, the best advice, as always, is to test your results and experiment freely as you learn so that your knowledge of the system, its capabilities, and its limitations increases. Both of these methods will be utilized as needed according to your project requirements. Ensure that you test the results properly before you expose such development to the users.

Time series measures

OBIEE also provides several functions that allow you to make comparisons between different time periods. For example, we may have a report based on the current month's sales, but we also want to include a column for last month's sales as well so that we can compare. OBIEE offers the following time series functions:

- `AGO`: This is used when we have a requirement such as the one we have just described, that is to compare current time periods with previous time periods.
- `TODATE`: This function is used when you need to aggregate a measure from the beginning of a specified time period to the lowest grain in a report that we have created, for example, a year-to-date calculation.
- `PERIODROLLING`: Here you can stipulate the length of the period to cover. For example, we could set a period of 3, which would cover three months or three years depending on the grain of the report. This function is useful when you need something like a rolling average in a report. We are going to create a new measure using the `AGO` function. Firstly, this requires a slight change to the Time dimension hierarchy that we previously set up. In the preceding section, we discussed how to set up a generic dimension hierarchy; however, when we start using time series functions, we need to inform the OBIEE server that this dimension is specifically associated with time.

Developing the BI Server Repository

We do this by double-clicking on the Time dimension hierarchy in the business layer and ensuring that the **Time** box is checked under the **Structure** options. This will then give us the option to set a chronological key at each level of the dimension, as shown in the following screenshot:

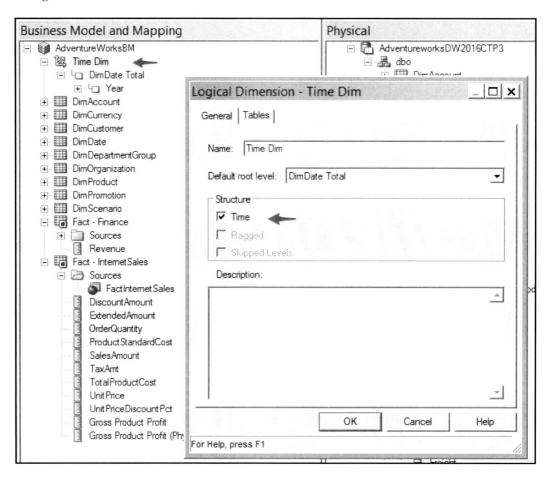

The OBIEE server requires a chronological key to be set for each level of our Time hierarchy. Oracle describes this key as monotonically increasing, which for our purposes means a key that increases in chronological order. This key will enable the server to produce efficient SQL when creating the time series queries:

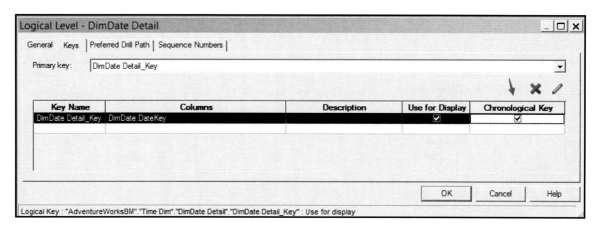

As you can see in the preceding screenshot, we have opened the detail level of our hierarchy and set the key. Then proceed to do the same for all of our levels. At this point, we are ready to create our new measure.

First, create a new logical measure in the business layer. We will be doing this in our `Fact - Finance` logical fact table. As we showed you in the preceding section, we will open the Expression Builder to create our calculation from an already existing logical column. If we choose **AGO** from the time series function, the builder will ask us to create a calculation based on this syntax:

```
Ago(<<Measure>>,<<Level>>,<<Number of Periods>>)
```

The measure we want to make a comparison with is `Revenue`, and let's say our requirement is to see the previous year's sales. Choose the `Year` level from our Time dimension (as you can see in the following screenshot). The number of periods will be `1` as we wish to have a time-shift of one year:

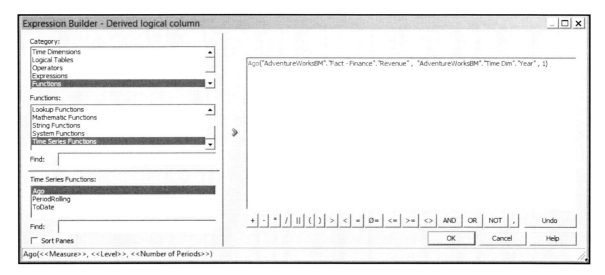

Drag this measure to the presentation layer, and there you go, we have a new measure based on the `AGO` function. We now can show current revenue and last year's revenue for the same chosen dimensions in the same report. Note that we could have built this measure upon a column that was calculated from two other logical columns, for example, from our **InternetSales** fact as previously shown. This shows how you can increase complexity in the business layer without changing physical columns, and how quickly you can increase the sophistication of your offering to the end users.

Now you may remember that we set the **Number of elements at this level** for each logical level. That helps the server with general queries. You can also help the server specifically optimize time series functions by adding Sequence Numbers for each logical level. This is new to 12c and can be done via the **Sequence Numbers** tab. You have two choices of sequencing that you can input:

- **Absolute**: Where you know the exact (or rough) numbers at each level
- **Relative**: Where you know the numbers at each level relative to each other

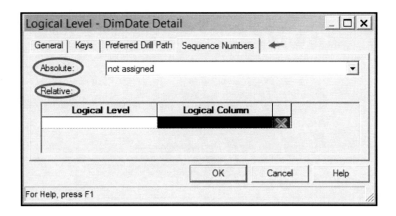

Level-based measure

The AGO measure will show us last year's results for the lowest grain in our report. So if we were looking for a report by month, that measure would show us the data for the same month last year. How about if we wanted to show data for the whole previous year, in spite of the grain that we choose for our report? Well, we can leverage our dimensional hierarchy and create a measure that always covers an entire year. This is done by creating a measure and setting its content level to the desired level in one of our dimensions.

Again, we will build upon our previous work. As you can see in the following screenshot, you can copy the whole definition of our AGO measure by right-clicking and choosing **Duplicate**:

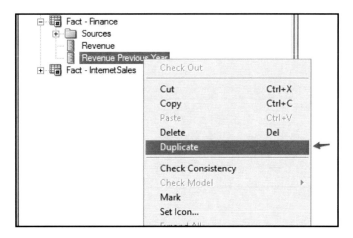

Then open this new logical column, rename it, and navigate to the **Levels** tab. The **Levels** tab shows us all of the levels for the dimensions that we have connected to this logical table:

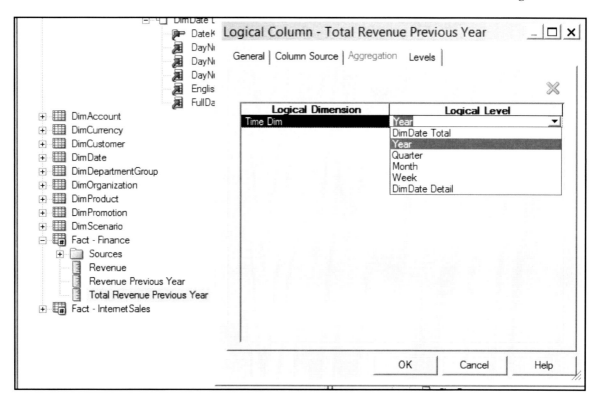

In our case, as you can see in the preceding screenshot, choose the **Year** level from the Time dimension. This means that this measure will always show results for an aggregated level of **Year**. This functionality is extremely useful when dealing with many requirements. For example, a business may need to compare the sales performance of a store against that of its parent region, but they are in different levels in the same dimension. We could create a level-based measure for the parent region and still show results for the store.

Once you have clicked on **OK**, our new measure is created:

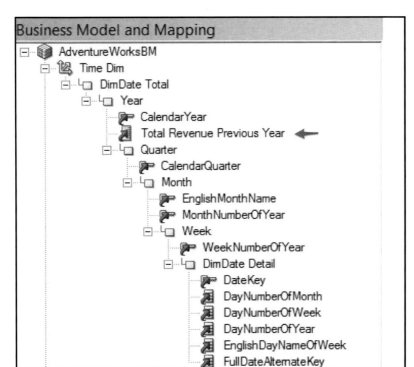

As shown in the preceding screenshot, this new measure now appears in our dimension hierarchy for Time and at the **Year** level. This shows that this column/measure is always aggregated at this level of the Time dimension. Note that rather than changing the settings in the **Levels** tab, we could also have dragged this new measure to the **Year** level in the hierarchy. Both methods yield the same end result.

Federated and fragmented content

We have talked a little bit about how we can have multiple logical table sources behind each logical table. This supports the federation and fragmentation of data, and is an extremely important part of OBIEE's capability. This is an advanced topic, but we will provide an introduction to advanced LTS functionality with an example of fragmentation. There are three main scenarios where we require multiple logical table sources.

Vertical federation-aggregation or level-based

This is used when we have aggregate tables in our schema. An aggregate table is a summary of our base data at a higher level of one or multiple dimensions. This is usually created to improve query performance. We can introduce an aggregate table as a new LTS. As we have done with our previous level-based measure, we can set the content for the whole LTS to the appropriate level in one of our dimensions. Logical columns will be mapped to both sources and OBIEE will then choose to utilize the appropriate source depending on the grain of the query run. This is an extremely common scenario, and as such we will go into more detail and a step-by-step example of this in `Chapter 12`, *Improving Performance*.

Horizontal federation

This is where a fact or dimension has multiple table sources at the same grain, but they contain different column information. Columns will be mapped to one of the sources and OBIEE will choose a single source table or combine them depending on which columns are chosen in the query.

An example of horizontal federation is where we want to combine two sources at the same granularity as one logical table. An example would be that we have financial actuals information and budget figures in different sources, but want to be able to report on them as a whole. These physical sources would not even need to be in the same location, that is, we could combine data from two different databases.

Fragmentation

This is where we have multiple physical tables for a dimension or fact, but this time these tables have the same set of columns and they differ in the information or rowset contained in each column. For example, this is quite commonly used when we have a set of data that is rarely accessed and we want to save it on the database I/O.

Fragmentation example--content-based

So let's look at a scenario for content-based fragmentation. Our data warehouse development team have come back to us and said that for performance reasons they would prefer if they present the information for Accounts in two different tables--one for accounts in the East and another one for those in the West. We have created two new physical tables--`DimAccountEast` and `DimAccountWest`. These supersede the old dimension table of DimAccount. Firstly, we import them and add the appropriate joins in the physical layer, as shown in the following screenshot:

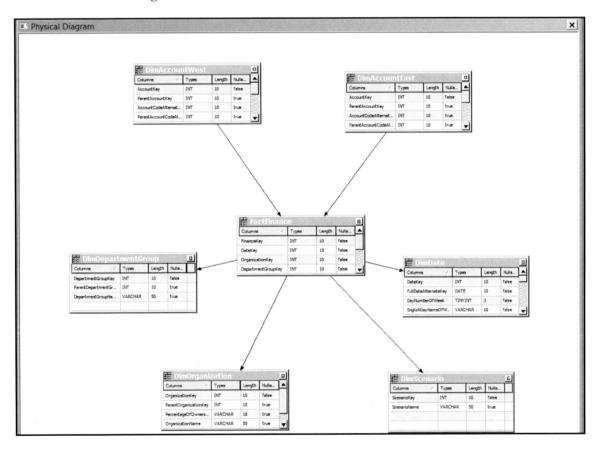

Developing the BI Server Repository

At this point, we could delete the current logical table source for Account in the business model and add the two new tables as two new sources. However, to save a bit of time we can rename and repoint the current source to one of the new tables. As you can see in the following screenshot, we have opened the **Account** logical table source. Note that in the **Map to these tables** section, we have deleted the reference to the `DimAccount` physical table and added a mapping to the new table for accounts in the East:

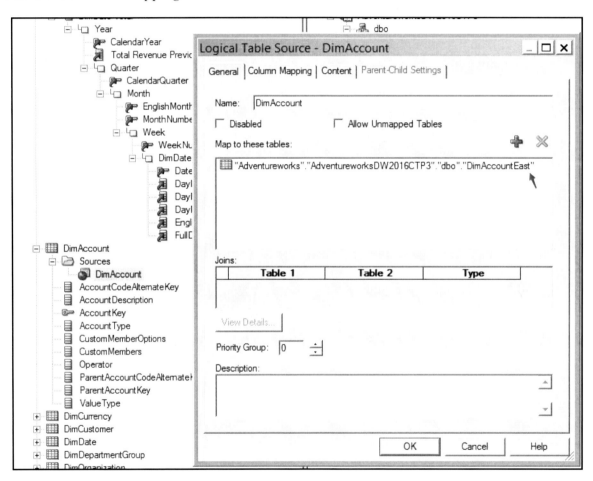

Now we move onto the **Column Mapping** tab and ensure that it is showing both mapped and unmapped columns (check boxes). The change in the LTS mapping to the underlying physical table means that some logical columns may not be mapped correctly to a physical column (or previous expressions). OBIEE will make a best guess by comparing column names, but if we have renamed the logical tables to use names with business meaning, it will struggle to map all of the columns. So we must ensure that all of these columns are mapped successfully:

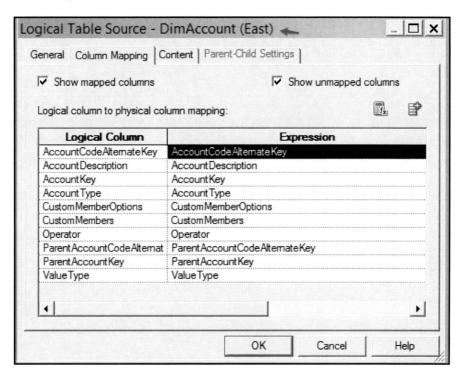

In the preceding screenshot, we can see that we have now mapped all of the existing columns correctly. Note that we have also renamed the source **DimAccount (East)** so that it is clear what this LTS represents.

Developing the BI Server Repository

Now create a new LTS called **DimAccount (West)** and map it to the `DimAccountWest` physical table. We can do this by right-clicking on the `Sources` folder of the logical table and choosing **New Logical Table Source...**:

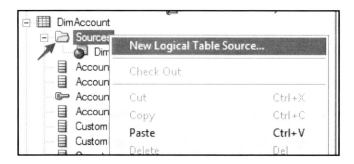

Name and map the table and then the individual columns accordingly. As you can see in the following screenshot, we now have two logical table sources for one logical table. Also, if we open a logical column as we have done in the following screenshot, we will see that each one is now mapped to two physical columns. So how does the OBIEE server know which physical table and column to use?

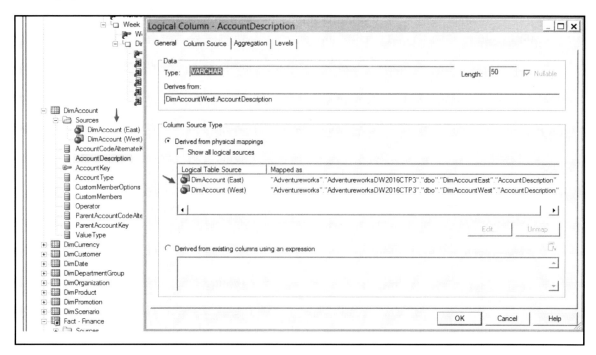

Well, as you may have seen in the **General** tab, there is a priority option for the LTS called **Priority Group**. We could set one as a higher priority over another, and the OBIEE server would choose that one first. However, that does not make sense in this case as these tables are of equal priority, they just differ in their datasets. So we need to give an indication to the server of how they differ. We do this in the **Content** tab of each LTS. We can set a condition based on a column in the **Fragmentation Content** pane. Once this condition is satisfied, the associated LTS will be used in the query. We have added a physical varchar column to the tables called `Region` that has a value of `E` or `W` to differentiate between the two datasets. Let's bring that in to the logical layer and ensure it is mapped to both East and West tables. We can then use it in our condition, and also add it to the presentation layer.

You can see the condition set up in the following screenshot. Note that you can use the Expression Builder to create your condition. Also, we have to do the same for our other LTS, but this time the condition will be as follows:

```
AdventureWorksBM"."DimAccount"."Region" = 'E'
```

This is because we are denoting that this LTS has records for our East records:

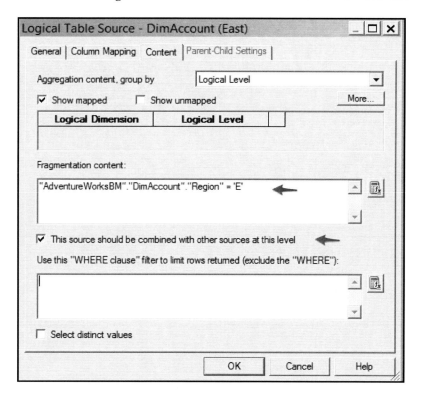

Note that we have ticked the **This source should be combined with other sources at this level** option. This is important because if a query is made that does not filter on **Region**, we will need OBIEE to combine record sets from both of these sources in order to produce a result.

Repeat the same step for the **DimAccount (West)** LTS, but with the condition being `"AdventureWorksBM"."DimAccount"."Region" = 'W'`.

With that we are done with fragmentation for these tables. Note that at no point should you delete a logical column. This means that no presentation columns were affected and all of this work was hidden from the end users. It would not have impacted them in any way, and any previously created reports would have worked seamlessly.

Variables and initialization blocks

Outside of the three layers of RPD development, there are also other sections of functionality that help to support the report and dashboard creation. The most important of these are the ability to create variables that end users can use in their reports. There are two types of variable:

- `Repository`: Set for the system as a whole and is refreshed at set periods.
- `Session`: Individual to the user or session when they login. To create either of these, we need to create what is called an **initialization block** in order to instantiate these variables. Create a repository variable. The first step is to click on **Manage** | **Variables**:

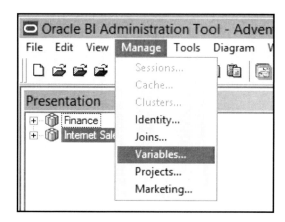

This brings us to the **Variable Manager** screen. Here, create a new **Init Block** by navigating through **Action** | **New** | **Repository** | **Initialization Block...**:

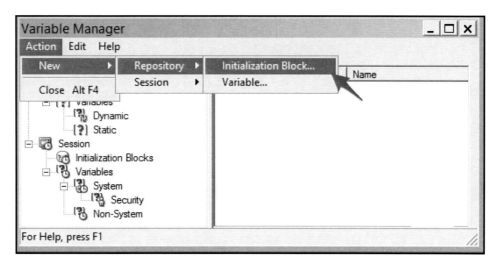

This brings us to the main initialization block screen, where you can set up the data source and actual variables. Provide a name for the block. In our example, the name is `initTimeComparison`. You can also set up how often you want the variable values to be refreshed:

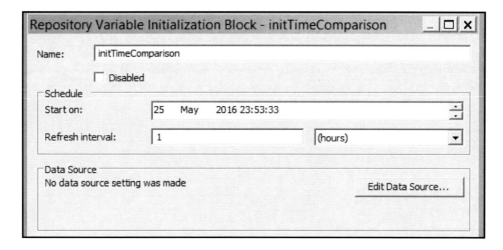

In this screen, first click on **Edit Data Source...**. This opens up the data source screen:

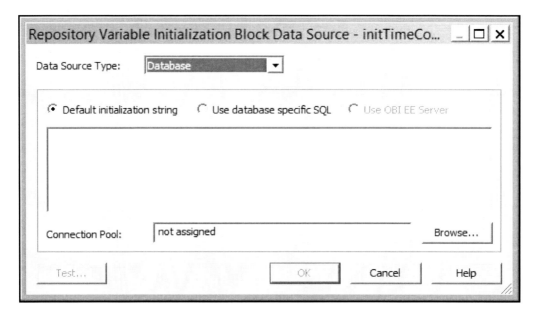

In this area, we need to inform OBIEE about the following:

- **Data Source Type**: It gives the location from where we are getting the data for our variables. In our case, this is a normal database.
- **Default Initialization String**: It is the query that we will run on our data source in order to populate variable values.
- **Connection Pool**: It is the connection pool in the physical layer against which we will run our query. As you can see in the preceding screenshot, we have already set our **Data Source Type**.

Let's go ahead and choose one of our connection pools by clicking on the **Browse...** button:

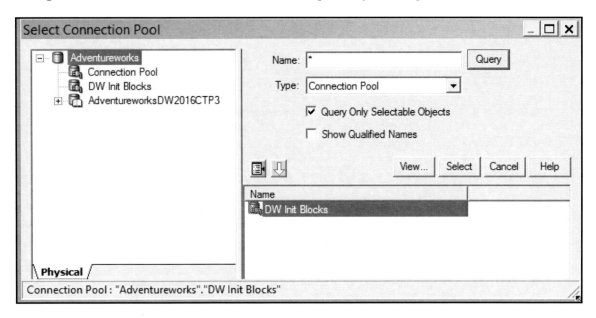

This provides us with a list of our physical layer connection pools. It is best to create a separate connection pool solely for variables. This reduces contention with your main connection pools. So, for our purpose, we will select a new pool called **DW Init Blocks** that we created especially for variables:

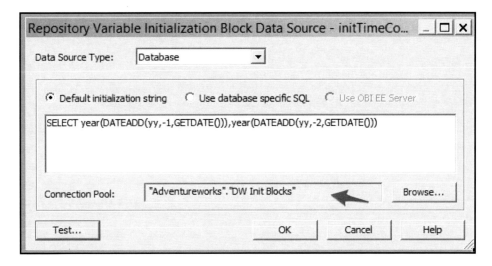

Developing the BI Server Repository

Note that our connection pool has been recorded. We can now write a statement to populate our variables. As you can see in the preceding screenshot, we have written a simple example for an SQL Server database. This returns two values retrieving the last two years. We can test that our query and Init Block are working by clicking on **Test...**:

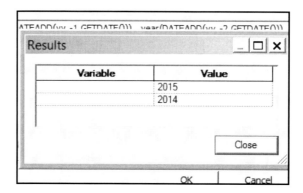

Our values have returned successfully, but we now need to assign them variable names. We do this by returning to the block's main screen and clicking on **Edit Data Target...**:

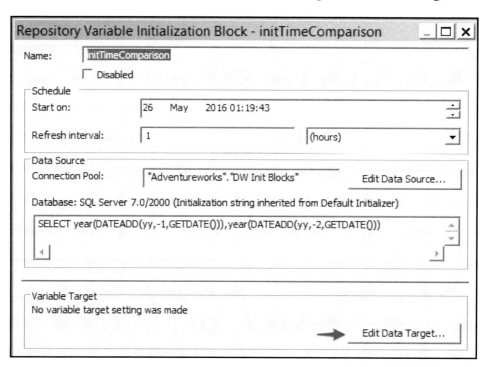

This brings up the **Repository Variable Initialization Block Variable Target** screen. Here, click on **New** and you can proceed to define our variable names. These names will be used as references to the variable in reports and analyses when we come to making the:

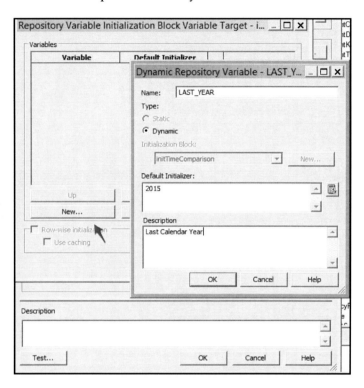

We can also set a temporary default value if we require. Once we have created both variables, make sure that they appear in the same order as the values are returned within our SQL query:

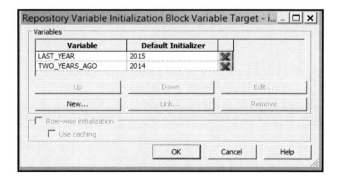

Developing the BI Server Repository

Clicking on **OK**, we can return to a fully completed **Repository Variable Initialization Block Variable Target** screen. We can click on **Test...** here to check whether the whole block works:

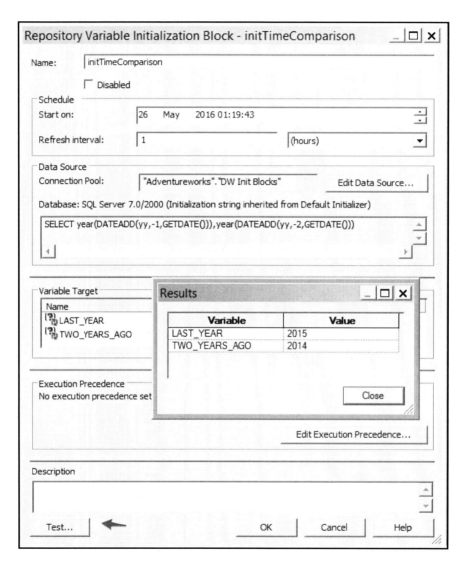

Chapter 7

As you can see in the preceding screenshot, our whole block works and the returned values have associated variables.

Returning to the **Variable Manager** screen, you can see our new objects:

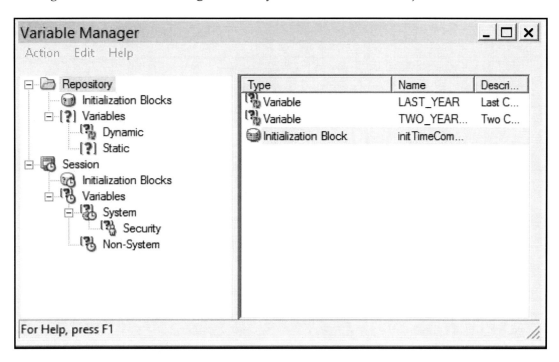

We will see an example of a variable in use when we come to create reports in Chapter 8, *Creating Dashboards and Analysis*.

A review - what I should now know!

For self-review and recap of the chapter, here are a few questions based on important topics covered in this chapter:

1. What are the three layers of an RPD?
2. How do you define physical joins?
3. How do you set up the levels of a dimension?
4. How do you create a level-based measure?
5. What is a way of using functions to compare time periods in a report?
6. How do you ensure that a fact-less query is routed properly?
7. How and why do you add multiple sources to a logical table?
8. How do you check that an RPD is consistent?

Additional research suggestions

The following are some additional research suggestions that may help you in understanding this chapter in more detail:

- Help files in the Administration Tool
- Oracle documentation at `https://docs.oracle.com/middleware/1221/biee/BIEMG/`

Summary

As you can see in the final screenshot, we have covered a lot of ground in this chapter. This will be enough to get a developer going on any project, yet we hope that this material has opened your eyes to the vast amount of development options within the RPD, and also the massive scope for you to gather further experience and knowledge. Be patient. Learning new functionality and skills takes time to sink in. Also, some of the topics covered in this chapter, for example, variables, will make a lot more comprehensive and cohesive sense once we show you how to make dashboards and reports and use those objects.

Chapter 7

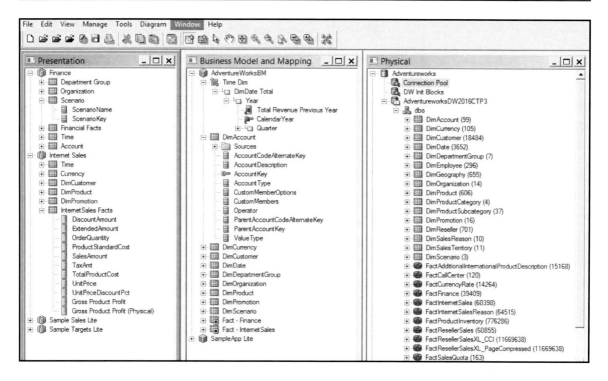

In summary, we went through setting up a new project from importing physical tables to adding extensive business logic, and then through to configuring the presentation for our end users. We created advanced objects, adding layer upon layer of complexity, each time iterating and building upon a previous piece of development. Again, don't be overawed by the amount of options, but take time to experiment and read up on all of the topics that we have discussed in this chapter.

Developing the BI Server Repository

Once you are up to speed in running queries (as we will show you later in this book), you can use OBIEE's query log (`NQQuery.log`) to check how the logical and physical SQL changes as we make RPD changes. This will strongly enhance your understanding of RPD development.

We also talked a lot about best practices. If you wish to become a valuable developer, take the time to develop your projects with this in mind. It is very easy to just drag a bunch of objects in quickly without thinking about the future iterative cycles and requirements. OBIEE has very powerful options, but do not be tempted to just put everything into the RPD.

Take time to understand whether something should be developed in the RPD or pushed down to the ETL or database.

Many times, an advanced metric or solution may perform better in a lower level of the system. Also keep in mind that advanced functionality can add a lot to the server load of your OBIEE installation. Although it can be difficult in a pressurized project, liaise with your ETL and database experts to try and reach the best and most performant solution for your overall system rather than grasping for the easiest option straightaway.

8
Creating Dashboards and Analyses

In the previous chapters, we have installed a new system, learned how to administer the system, and developed the metadata (the `.rpd` file) for a brand-new project. This chapter is the culmination of all that work in that we are finally ready to develop reports that can be delivered to our end users.

We will cover creating analyses, and how to group them in Dashboards. We will also look at the various ways of representing and formatting data that are available, along with advice on best practices gained from implementation experience.

The drive behind OBIEE and other BI tools is to create analytical reports where we are focused on gaining insights that are difficult to pick up on in our daily dealings. This often means that we are looking for patterns or information over a historical period in an aggregated format. Using the operational examples, we might want to look at call volumes over a whole Year, so that we can make better choices about the staff numbers needed. In retail, we might want to see what types of products sell better in certain countries over a certain time period. So in essence, we are looking at giving ourselves information that drives more strategic or longer-term decisions rather than those that concern day-to-day matters. This also means that we traditionally would be looking at a dataset that changes less often than that used for operational reporting.

Creating Dashboards and Analyses

Creating our first analysis

Time to get stuck into creating some content. We will now create a simple analysis.

1. Log into OBIEE.
2. Use the URL `http://[servername]:[port]/analytics`. In our case, this is `http://obiee:9502/analytics/`:

After log in, you are taken to the **Home** page. In the left-hand panel, you will see the **Create...** section:

3. Click on the word **Analysis**:

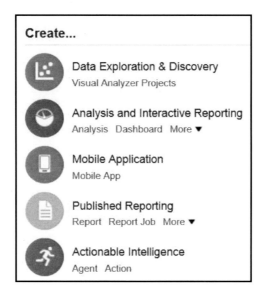

4. Select a Subject Area by clicking on **Sample Sales Lite**:

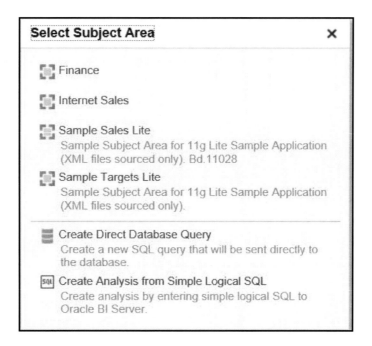

Creating Dashboards and Analyses

You are now presented with the designer window. On the left side, you will see all of the columns you can choose from in your analysis.

5. Click on the arrowhead to the left of the `Time` folder:

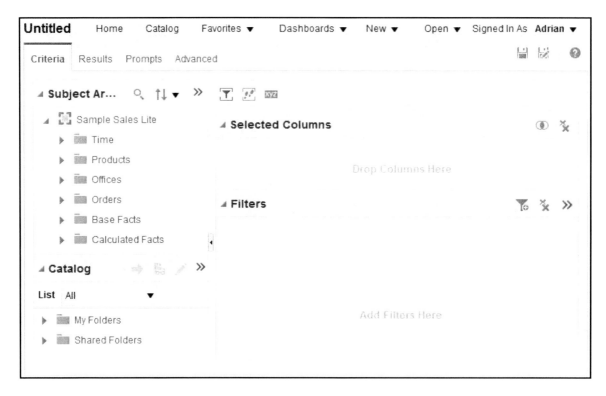

6. Double-click on the **Per Name Year** column (Note: You can also drag and drop the column into the right pane.)
7. Expand the `Base Facts` folder.
8. Double-click on the `Revenue` column:

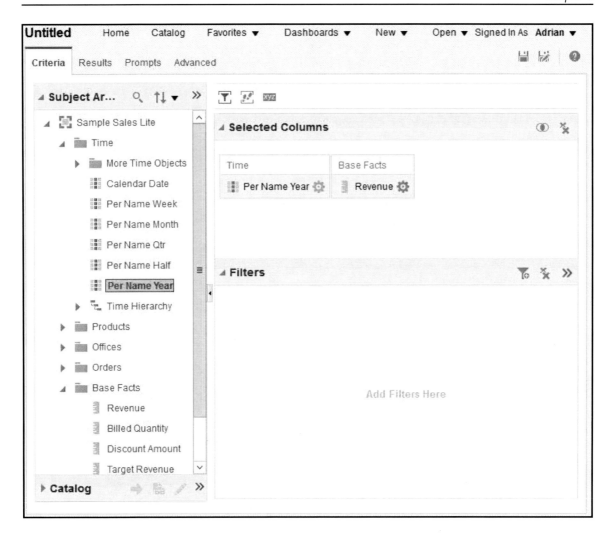

9. Now click on the **Results** tab.

Creating Dashboards and Analyses

10. You can now see the Revenue by year:

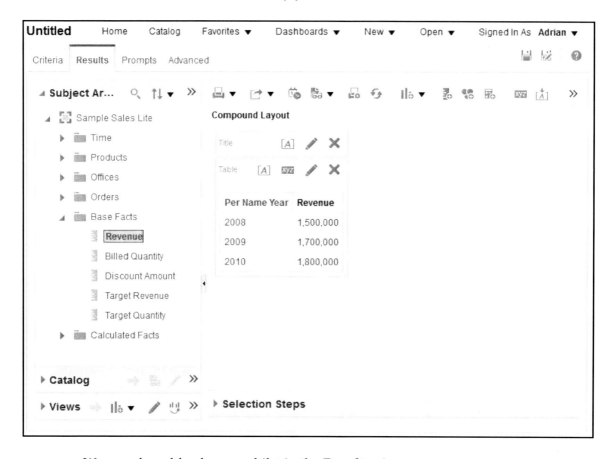

We can also add columns whilst in the **Results** view.

11. Expand the Time folder.

12. Drag the column **Per Name Month** over to the table, and place it to the left of the `Revenue` column:

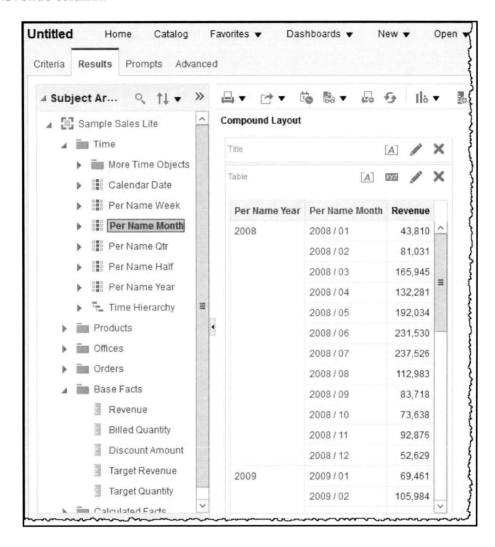

Let's add a Graph to the results view.

13. Click on the plus sign in the **Views** pane.
14. Click on **Graph**.

Creating Dashboards and Analyses

15. Click on **Line** Graph:

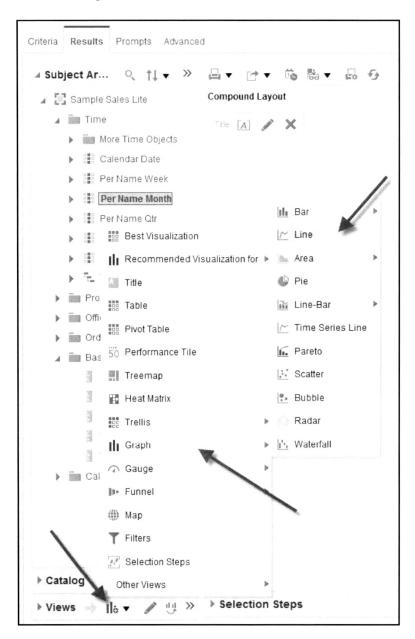

Chapter 8

You are now presented with the View Designer page.
Note the three separate panels:

- The folders are in the left-hand panel. You can add columns even in the view designer page.
- The layout panel is bottom-right. You can move columns around. Columns can be excluded from the view, or presented as Prompts.
- The preview panel is top-right. You can turn off the Graph preview by clicking on the mini Graph icon:

Notice that the `Year` column was placed into the **Sections** box and that the **Display as Slider** is ticked.

[265]

Creating Dashboards and Analyses

You can move the columns around, for example you could put the `Year` column into the **Graph Prompts** box. This would present you with a drop-down column on the Graph so that you choose which `Year` to view. You could also move the Year column to the horizontal axis (by dragging and dropping onto the **Line** box). This would give you all Years on one Graph:

1. Make sure the `Year` column is in the **Sections** box.
2. Click **Done**.

   At this stage, you go back to the results view, but your Graph is nowhere to be seen! We have to put the Graph onto the page ourselves.

3. Click on the **Graph** in the **Views** panel (bottom-left).
4. Click on the right arrow or drag the view onto the right panel:

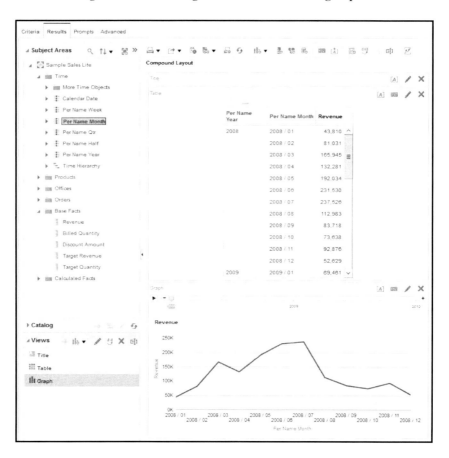

5. We are now going to save the analysis that we just built.
6. Click on the **Save** button (top right).
7. Click on the `Shared Folders` (in the left-hand panel)
8. Click on the **New Folder** icon, and enter a folder name (use `Book`). Click **OK**:

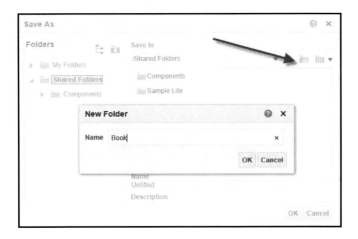

 When you save your analysis, you are saving the structure of the query. You are not saving the data.

9. Click **OK** to save your analysis in the `Book` folder:

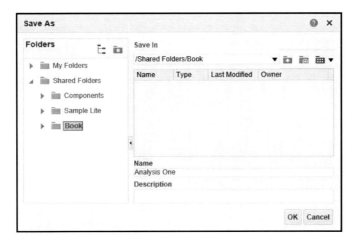

Creating Dashboards and Analyses

We have now created our first analysis called `Analysis One`. We put a Graph on the results page and saved it in a folder called `Book`.

This is a simple example which introduces the basic concepts involved.

Let's just have a quick look in the `Catalog` folder to see what we have just created:

1. Click on the **Catalog** link on the top bar.
2. Select the `Book` folder in the left-hand panel.
3. You will now see your analyses listed:

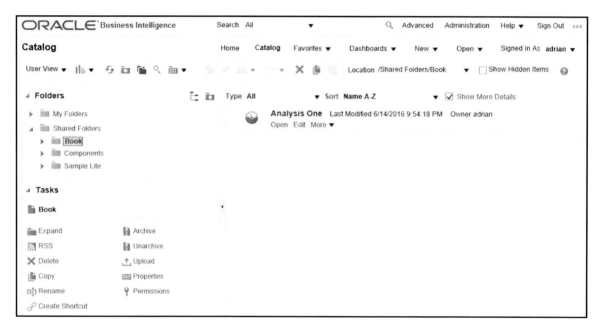

So, you now know how to create an analysis, save it in a folder of your choice, and find it in the catalog.

Take a minute to look at the options available when you click on the **More** link under your analysis.

Later in the chapter we will explore more options when creating analyses, but for now, in the next section, we will put your first analysis onto a new Dashboard.

[268]

Creating our first Dashboard

The Dashboard is the place that most of your users will be viewing the data. You create a Dashboard and usually place one or more analyses on a Dashboard page. You can have pages with just text on too. You can have several pages on a Dashboard, each with their own analysis.

Let's get stuck into creating:

1. Click on **New** on the top bar.
2. Select **Dashboard** from the list
3. Enter the Dashboard **Name** and **Description**, then choose the location of your Dashboard. Choose the `Book` folder which is in the `Shared Folder`.
4. Leave the **Content** option set to **Add Content Now**. Click **OK**:

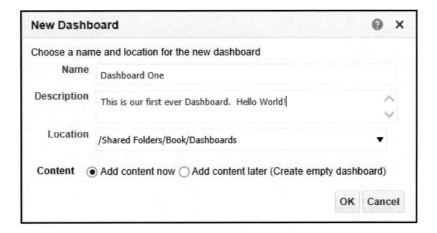

Creating Dashboards and Analyses

You are now presented with a blank Dashboard page:

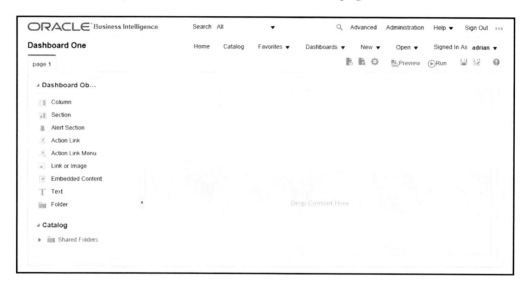

5. Expand the `Shared Folders` folder in the **Catalog** pane (bottom left panel).
6. Expand the `Book` folder.
7. Click on the `Analysis One` object, and drag it on the main blue panel. Drop it there:

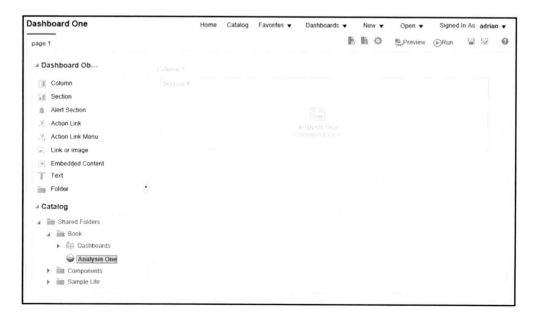

You will now see that **Column 1** has been created, with **Section 1** inside the column, and `Analysis One` is inside the section:

8. Click on the **Save** button.
9. Click on the **Run** button.

You are now presented with your first Dashboard, showing content from `Analysis One`:

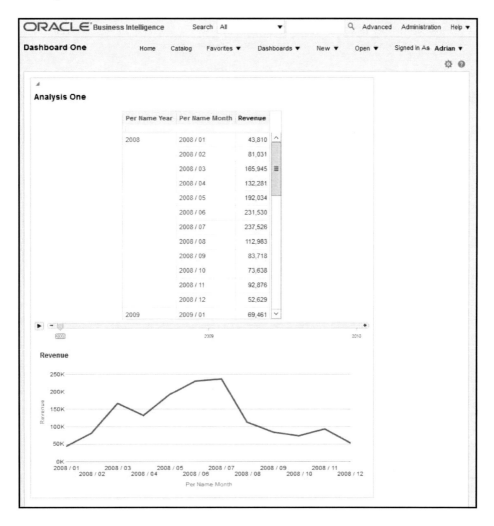

Congratulations - you have completed your first Dashboard.

Analysis building - more details

Now we have introduced the rudimentary basics of creating an analysis, let's look at the options when building effective analyses in more detail.

First, we need to create a new analysis to work on, in the same way we did in the preceding section:

1. Click on **New**.
2. Click on **Analysis**.
3. Pick the **Subject Areas** (choose **Sample Sales Lite** again).

    The page you are presented with has the following sections (marked here with green squares):

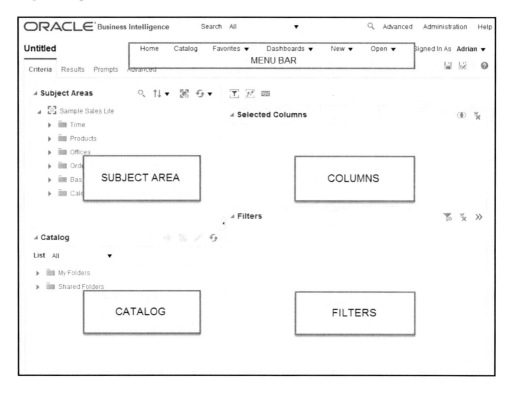

- **Menu Bar**: This is where we can navigate to other content, or create new content.

- **Subject Areas**: This is where we can explore and choose from the attributes and Measures that we previously set up in the .rpd file. Normally, you would use a single Subject Area, but you can add other Subject Areas by clicking on the little box icon. Subject Areas will consist of Measures that are on one or more Fact tables, and attributes, that come from one or more dimensions. The Subject Area was defined in the .rpd file.
- **Columns**: Once we have chosen objects from the **Subject Areas**, then these will appear in this pane and form the basis of our analysis. Columns can be dragged into this panel, or if you double-click they will appear. Dragging gives you greater control on where they end up.
- **Filters**: This is where we can add and amend any Filters which are applied to the result set produced by our **Selected Columns**. **Filters** are created either by clicking the Filter icon on a selected column, or by clicking on the Filter icon on the Filters header bar. **Filters** can be defined using the **Filter** dialog box, or they can be handcrafted SQL.

Filters can be saved for use in other analyses. This means that several analyses can use the same shared Filter which saves time if you need to make a change to the filtering.

- **Catalog**: Here we can access any previously created and already saved items; for example, Filters or calculations that we may want to use in our current analysis.

Let's explore the options available on each column:

1. Select the column Brand from the Products folder in the **Subject Areas** panel by double-clicking it. It will appear in the **Columns** panel.
2. Now click on the little cog wheel and you will see the menu shown below:

Creating Dashboards and Analyses

- **Sort**: Does what it says on the tin! Note that you can add sorts to an analysis that already contains a sort column. You can remove individual sorts or remove them all in one go.

3. Click on **Sort Descending**.

- **Edit formula**: Selecting this will open a dialog box with a large number of options, too many to cover in this book, but let's look at the most commonly used features.

4. Click on **Edit formula**:

You are presented with the following dialog box that has the available columns on the left panel, the main formula box on the right, and some quick link buttons at the bottom:

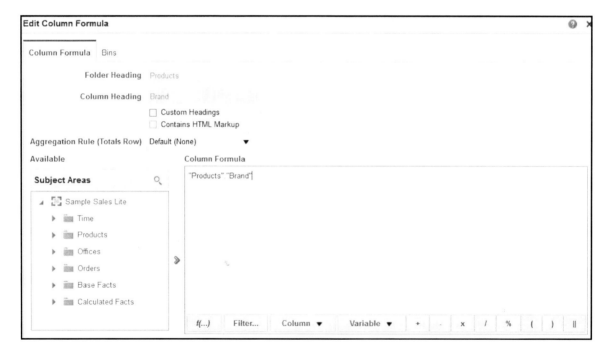

 Note the **Bins** tab at the top. Bins help us to group items together, and are a quick way of creating a case statement.

For now, we will enter a formula directly into the box:

5. Enter `"Products"."Brand"` into the preceding formula box.
6. Click **OK**.
7. Click on the **Results** tab to see the brands in capitals.

 When you have some free time, take a look at all the available functions by clicking on the **f(...)** button.

- **Column Properties**: It opens another dialog which provides many options on how the column is formatted. You may notice that the title for the `Brand` column is now, `Brand`, so let's change the title to something more friendly:

8. Click on **Column Properties**.
9. Click on the tab heading **Column Format**.
10. Check the box **Custom Headings** - This unlocks the preceding box.
11. Replace the words with `Brand`:

Note that **Suppress** is selected, which means that if two rows have the same value, they are merged into one box.

12. Click **OK**.

To explore the other **Column Properties** options, we will add some more columns into our analysis:

13. Double-click on the `Calendar Date` column twice to add it to our analysis.
14. Double-click on the `Revenue` column.
15. Check the results by clicking on the **Results** tab.
16. Click on the **Criteria** tab.

Column Style

17. Click on the **Column Properties** link on the first **Calendar Date** field.
18. Change the **Horizontal Alignment** to **Right**.
19. Font **Color** to blue.
20. Font **Style** to **Italic**.
21. Cell **Background Color** to grey:

Data Format

Now we will change the way the information in the Date column is presented:

22. Click on the **Data Format** tab.
23. Tick the **Override Default Data Format** box (which makes the option available to edit).

24. Select a format:

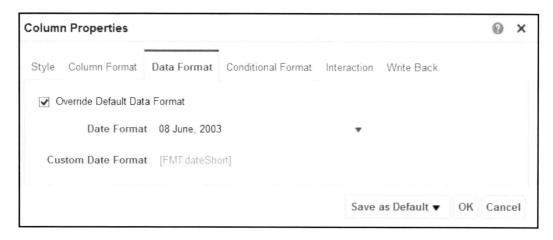

25. Click **OK**.
26. On the second `Calendar Date` column, set the **Date Format** option as **Custom** and enter `dddd` into the **Custom Date Format** box:

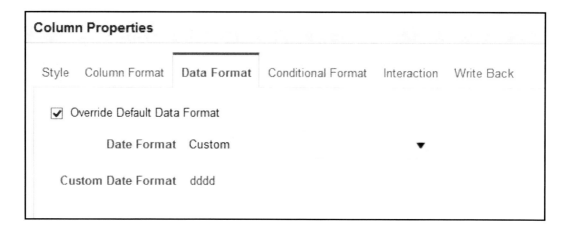

27. Click **OK**.

 After each setting change, you can check the results in the **Results** tab.

Conditional Format

Next, we will explore how to change the format of the data presented, based upon a condition. For example, make Revenue numbers red if they are below 1,000 and green if they are above 5,000:

28. Select **Column Properties** for the Revenue column.
29. Select the **Conditional Format** tab.
30. Click on **Add Condition**, and select Revenue.
31. Set the parameter, less than 1000:

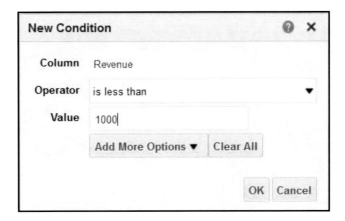

32. Click **OK**.
33. Now set the format we would like. Choose yellow bold font on a red background.
34. Click **OK**.
35. Add another condition.
36. Select Revenue.
37. Greater than 5000.
38. Set the format to a green background.
39. Click **OK**.

Creating Dashboards and Analyses

Let's see all those formatting changes now:

40. Click on the **Results** tab:

 Conditional Formats can also present images instead of, or as well as, the data in the column. See the **Select Image** button.

Interaction

The next column property to explore is the **Interaction** tab. This enables users to interact with the data they see, perhaps to see more details or view a web page. We will use an example link to a page on a Dashboard:

41. Click on **Column Properties** of the `Revenue` column.
42. Select the **Interaction** tab.

43. Change the value **Primary Interaction** to **Action Links**.
44. Click on the plus sign.
45. Enter a name in the **Action Name** box.
46. Click on the little plus sign (the left-hand running man):

Creating Dashboards and Analyses

47. Select the first option, **Navigate to BI Content**.
48. Select the **Sales Summary** page on the **Quick Start Dashboard** (located in folder `Shared FoldersSample LiteDashboardsQuick StartSales Summary`).
49. Click **OK**, Click **OK**, Click **OK**.

    At this stage, we need to save our work, so let's save it as `Analysis Two` in the `Book` folder:

50. Click **Save As**.
51. Navigate to the `Book` folder.
52. Enter the Name `Analysis Two`.
53. Click **OK**.

    Now you can test the link by running the report (click on the **Results** tab) and click on one of the `Revenue` numbers. It will now load the **Sales Summary** page.

    Reopen our `Analysis Two` by clicking on the breadcrumb link in the bottom left-hand corner.

Other ways to find your `Analysis Two` include using the **Open** link on the menu bar; it will show your recent edits. You can also click on the **Catalog** and navigate to the `Book` folder. Another method is to click on the **Home** link and you will see `Analysis Two` in the recent edit section.

Continuing with the **Column** options available...

Filters are used to pre-select data. You can use them to limit your results sets, and you can use them to allow users to limit results on a Dashboard. Let's see them in action:

54. Click the **Filter** option on the `Brand` column.

    This opens the **Filter** dialog box.

[282]

You can now click on the **Value** box and it will display available values:

55. Select **BIZTECH**.
56. Click **OK**:

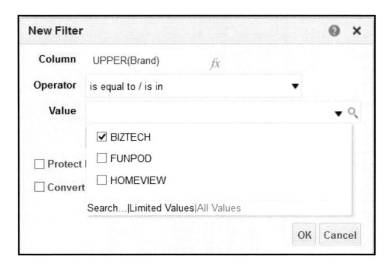

When you run the results now, only Biztech brands will be listed.

Filters can also be applied to columns that are not displayed in your analysis. In the bottom panel, you can see a **Filter** button (looks like a funnel).

57. Click on the **Filter** button.
58. Click on **More Columns...**.

It will open the **Select Column** dialog:

59. Select the column you would to Filter. We will choose `Per Name Year` from the `Time` folder.
60. Change the **Operator** to **is greater than**.

Creating Dashboards and Analyses

61. Enter 2008 in the **Value** box.
62. Click **OK**.

To create a SQL Filter, you tick the box **Convert to SQL** and press **OK**. This will display a SQL statement that represents the Filter you have created.

We will add some more columns to our analysis now. Find the column in the left-hand panel and then double-click it or drag to the right-hand panel:

63. Add the column Per Name Year between the Brand and Calendar Date columns.
64. Add the column # Of Orders from the Calculated Facts folder.

We now have an analysis ready to go:

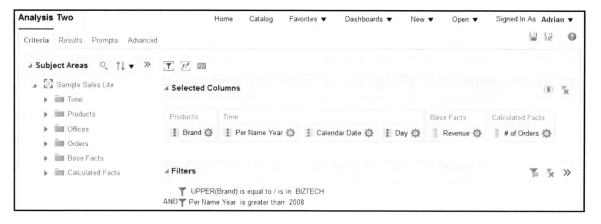

65. Save your analysis again.

After you have saved your work, let's see what it looks like:

66. Click on **Results**.

Views

You can now see a title and a table with our columns in. In the bottom-left panel (called **Views**) we can see the title and table object. Each analysis can have multiple views, including multiples of the same type.

As you build different views of your data, they are listed in the **Views** panel. You can add the same type more than once, for example, two Pivot Tables could be created, one with Years in columns, the other with Quarters.

After you create a view, you can drag it onto the right panel, wherever you like. You can move views around and you can format the view borders, alignment, background, and so on.

Views each have their own container which have layout and style properties. Looking at `Analysis One`, we can see that the default horizontal alignment for a table container is to the center.

Let's examine some of the most commonly-used views.

Tables

By default, you get one table.

The default properties for a table are that the column headings are fixed, and there is a scroll bar on the right side for viewing results further down the dataset. If we had lots of columns in our analysis, then only the first few would be visible, but there will be another scroll bar at the bottom to view more columns. There are alternative settings that we can set.

We will now edit the properties of the table:

1. Click on the **Edit Table Properties** icon (small pencil at the top-right of the view):

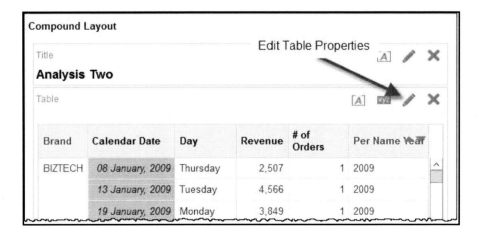

Creating Dashboards and Analyses

This will open the **Edit Table View** page:

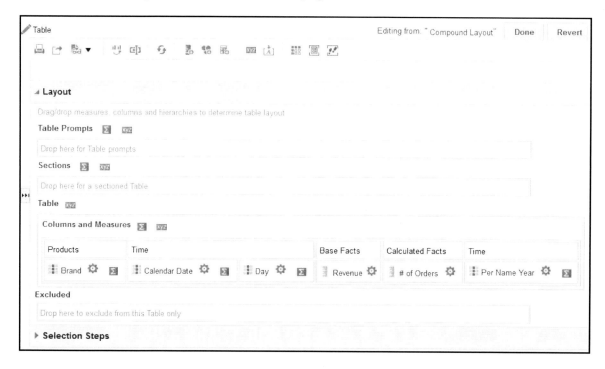

On this page, we can change what columns are presented, in what order, and where in the view. Note the **Table Prompts**, **Sections**, and **Excluded** boxes. In the preceding image, we are only showing the **Layout** and **Selection** steps. You can show or hide parts of the editor using the icons on the menu bar:

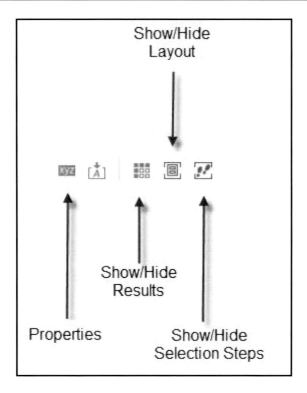

2. Click on the **Properties** icon.
3. Change the **Data Viewing** option to **Content Paging**.
4. Enter 5 into the **Rows per Page** box.
5. Check the box for **Row Styling** (the default is green and white rows).

6. Change the **Column headings** to **As separate rows**:

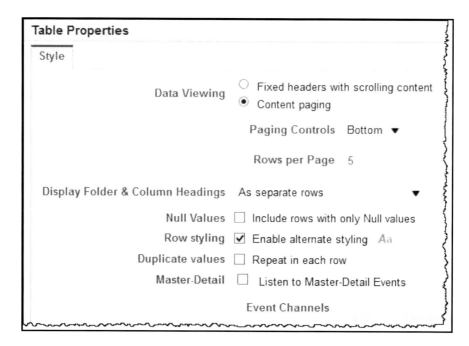

7. Click **OK**.

We will now move some columns around to see the effect:

8. Move (by dragging) the `Per Name Year` column to the **Table Prompts** box.
9. Move the `Day` column to the **Excluded** box.

Now add a total row at the bottom of the table:

10. Click on the sum sign next to **Columns and Measures**:

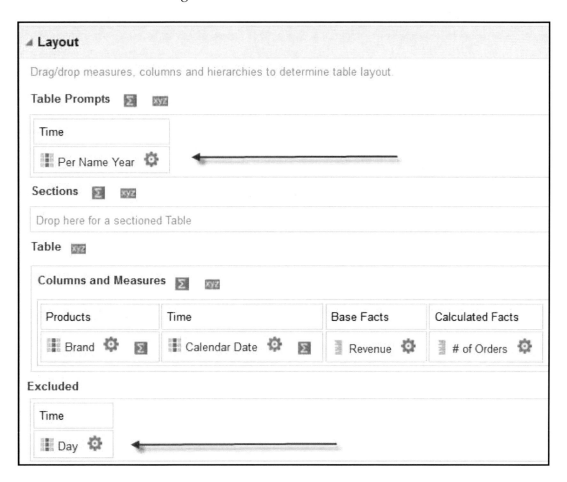

11. Click **OK**.
12. Click **Save**.

Let's see the results:

13. Click on the **Results** tab:

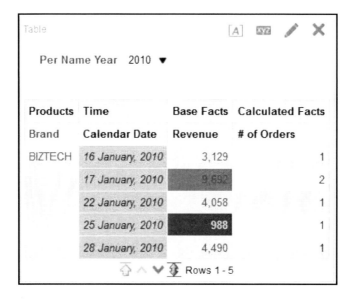

Try changing the Year Prompt and you will see the results changing.

Graphs

Click on the small **Graph** button on the top bar.

This displays all the possible ways of viewing the data we can retrieve in our analysis. In the following image we show the different types of **Bar** Graphs that are available:

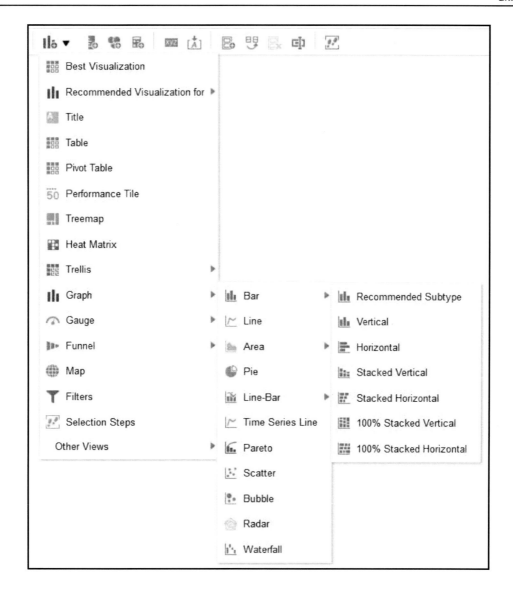

Creating Dashboards and Analyses

Like tables, Graphs have **Prompts**, **Sections**, and **Exclude** boxes:

1. Select the **Vertical B**ar Graph.
2. Take some time to explore Bar Graphs. Experiment with dragging the columns to the various boxes.
3. Change the Graph type to **Line**.
4. Move the `Year` column to the **Sections** box.
5. Move the `Date` column to the **Horizontal Axis**.
6. Click on the **Properties** box (the small xyz icon) and change the scale to **900** width:

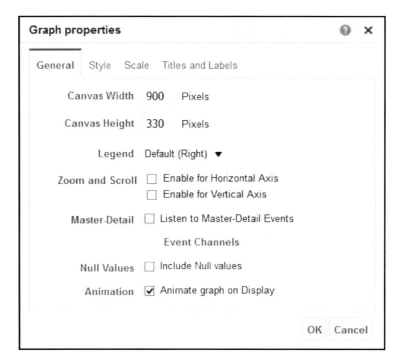

7. Click on the **Titles and Labels** tab.
8. Change the **Horizontal Axis Labels** (click on the icon next to the option).
9. Set the **Axis Labels** option to **Hide**.
10. Click **OK**, Click **OK**.
11. Click **Done**.

Your analysis now has three views on the page, a title, a table, and a Line Graph.

12. Save your analysis.

Pivot Tables

Pivot Tables are used to move values into columns, just like in Excel.

Here we show a pivot table with `Brand` in rows, and `Year` in columns. Pivot Tables also have **Prompts**, **Sections**, and **Excluded** boxes:

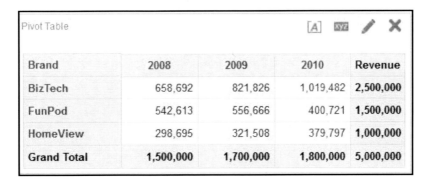

The preceding is created in a new analysis:

1. Click **New**.
2. Choose **Analysis**.
3. Select the **Sample Sales Lite** Subject Area.
4. Add the columns, `Brand`, `Per Name Year`, and `Revenue`.
5. Click on the **Results** tab.
6. Click on the Graph icon and select **Pivot Table**.

Creating Dashboards and Analyses

7. Move the `Year` column to the `Columns` section:

8. Click **Done**.
9. Now remove the table from the page by clicking on the little x in the top right corner.
10. Save your analysis as `Analysis Three`.

Removing a view from your page does not delete it; it can be used later but is not shown on this page.

[294]

Narratives

Narrative views are very useful for when you want to present your data in a precise manner, usually (but not always) using HTML and CSS. We can mix words, images, and column data to produce impressive output.

A simple narrative example:

1. Open `Analysis Three` and go to the **Results** tab.
2. Click on the Add View icon and select **Narrative** - you will find it in the **Other Views** list.
3. In the **Prefix** box enter `<font size=3>[u]Summary[/u]</font>[br/][br/]`.
4. In the **Narrative** box enter `[b]@1[/b] Sales in [b]@2[/b] were $@3[br/][br/]`.
5. Enter some text into the **Postfix** box.
6. Click on **Done**.

> The @ sign indicates a column in your analysis. @1 is the first column @2 second and so on.

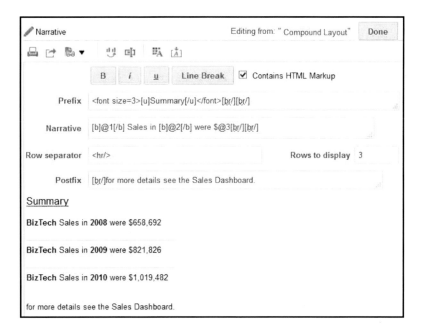

[295]

As you can see, **Narrative** views can provide flexibility in how one presents data.

 Narratives can be used to create statement-like output. We often use them to create forms that have boxes for signature blocks.

Performance Tiles

Performance Tiles present a single number in a box. This can be a very effective way to get an import measure presented to users. Any measure that is within an analysis can be used in a tile. We will create a new example analysis to explore performance tiles and also introduce the `Filter By` function:

1. Create a new analysis using the **Sample Sales Lite** Subject Area.
2. Add the `Revenue` column four times.
3. Add a Filter for `Per Year Name = 2010` (note we do not need the `Year` column in the analysis.
4. Edit the formula for the second `Revenue` column.
5. Click on the **Filter...** button at the bottom of the box.
6. Find **Brand** in the left pane and double-click it.
7. Select **BizTech** in the criteria.
8. Deselect the **Filter by Brand Key** option.

You should now have a screen like shown in the following screenshot:

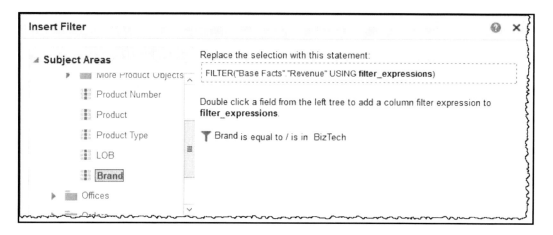

9. Click **OK**.

   The formula is set so that it will sum the Revenue column where the "Brand" = Biztech. Your formula will now look as follows:

   ```
   FILTER("Base Facts"."Revenue" USING ("Products"."Brand"
   ='BizTech'))
   ```

10. Change the column name to Biztech Revenue.
11. Edit the third Revenue column - this time we will sum the Target Revenue. Set the formula to:

    ```
    FILTER("Base Facts"."Target Revenue" USING ("Products"."Brand"
    = 'BizTech'))
    ```

12. Change the column name to BizTech Target.
13. Edit the fourth Revenue column. Create a variance percentage column which will show the percentage actual Revenue is under, or over, Target Revenue. Set the formula to:

    ```
    (FILTER("Base Facts"."Revenue" USING ("Products"."Brand" =
    'BizTech')) - FILTER("Base Facts"."Target Revenue" USING
    ("Products"."Brand" = 'BizTech'))/ FILTER("Base Facts"."Target
    Revenue" USING ("Products"."Brand" = 'BizTech')))*100.0
    ```

14. Change the column name to Variance.

    Now change the **Data Format** of the Variance.

15. Edit **Column Properties** for the Variance column.
16. Select the **Data Format** tab.
17. Tick the **Override Default Data Format**.
18. Change the option **Treat Number As** to **Percentage**, and set decimal places to one.

    Before we move on, we will add a conditional format on the variance column. We will create a simple red format when the Revenue is less than the Target Revenue. First, values less than zero, that is, poor performance against the target.

19. Click on the **Column Properties** for the **Variance** column.
20. Select the **Conditional Format** tab.
21. Add a condition.

22. Select the `Variance` column from the list.
23. Set the **Operator** to **is less than** and put 0 (zero) into the **Value** box.
24. Click **OK**.
25. Set the format of the font to red and bold.
26. Set the background color to `#ff8080` (you enter this directly into the box).
27. Click **OK**.

Now values more than 10 percent, that is, good performance against target.

28. Add condition.
29. Select the `Variance` column from the list.
30. Set the **Operator** to `is greater than` and put 10 into the **Value** box.
31. Click **OK**.
32. Set the background color to `#669966` (you enter this directly into the box).
33. Save the analysis as `Analysis Four`.

That's the data created, we will now add a **Performance Tile**:

34. View the results.
35. Add a view, selecting **Performance Tile**.
36. Set the **Measure** to the `Variance` column.
37. Untick the **Use Measure Description** option and edit the **Description** box. Set it to `Revenue vs Target`:

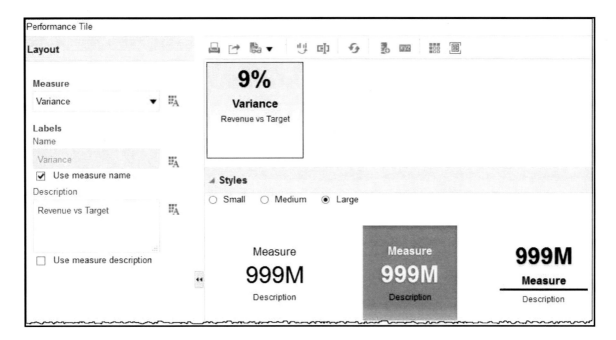

38. Click **Done**.
39. Save the analysis.

    We now have a **Performance Tile** which can be added to the page.

    Experiment now with different Years to see the results:

40. Change the Filter for `Year` to `2008`.

41. View the results.

You should now see a green box instead of a white one:

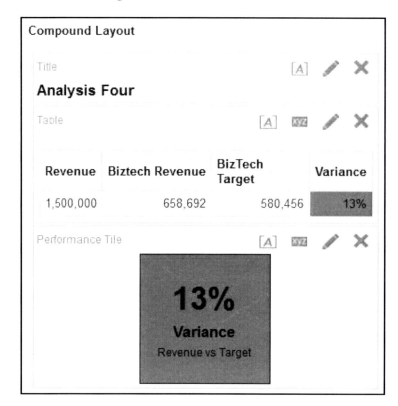

Recap

So far in this chapter, we have covered creating a simple analysis, adding a Graph, and saving as Analysis One. We then created a Dashboard and put our Analysis One onto a page. Next, we looked at column sorting, formulae, and column properties, which included the Data Formats, Conditional Formatting, and Interaction features. We also reviewed the most common views that an analysis can present; tables, Graphs, Pivot Tables, narratives, and Performance Tiles.

Chapter 8

There are 46 different view types in OBIEE 12c, so you should take some time to experiment with some of those we haven't covered in detail. Check out the Heatmap view and Gauge views for yourself.

In the next part of this chapter, we will look at how you present your analysis on Dashboard pages, and how users can interact with your Dashboards.

Prompts

In most of our example analyses, we have been setting Filters for specific values, for example, we added the Filter `Per Name Year is greater than 2008` into `Analysis Two`.

Instead of predetermining what `Year` the user would like to see, we can give the user the option of choosing the `Year` when the analysis is run. This turns a static analysis into an *interactive analysis*.

There are two ways to make an interactive analysis, either ask users within the analysis, by using the **Prompts** tab, or by placing the analysis onto a Dashboard which has a `Dashboard Prompt` object on it.

In analysis prompting

We will now examine the **Prompts** held within an analysis:

1. Create a new analysis, using **Samples Sales Lite**.
2. Add the columns, `Per Name Year`, `Per Name Quarter`, and `Revenue`.
3. Click on the **Prompts** tab.
4. Click on the green plus sign to add a new Prompt.
5. Select **Column Prompt** `Per Name Year`.
6. Change the **Label** to `Choose Year`.
7. Change the **User Input** to **List Box**.
8. Change the **Default Selection** to **Specific Values** and add `2009`.

Creating Dashboards and Analyses

9. Click **OK**:

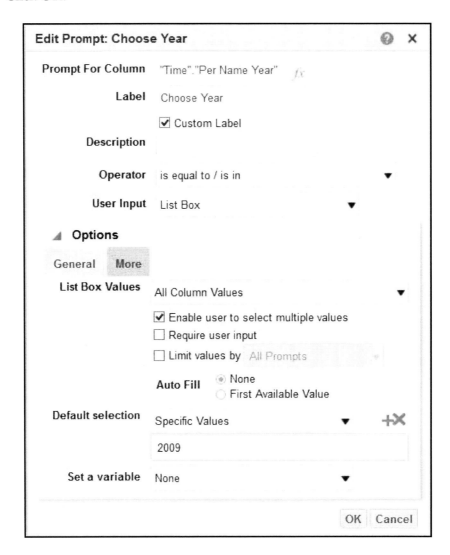

10. Save your work as `Analysis Five` in the `Book` folder.
11. Click on the **Home** tab.

    `Analysis Five` is listed in the recent section.

12. Click on the **Open** link under the title of `Analysis Five`:

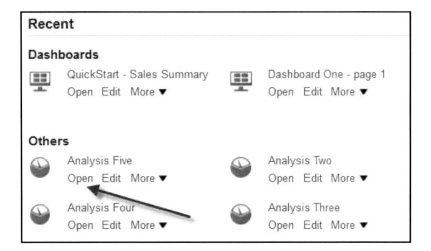

The analysis will now open with the Prompts page. You select the Years you are interested in seeing and when you press **OK**, the results will appear.

Use *Ctrl + click* to select multiple values.

We can also see similar behavior when we place the analysis onto a Dashboard page:

13. Edit Dashboard One (click on the **Edit** link on the home page).
14. Click on the Add Dashboard Page icon and select **Add Dashboard Page**.
15. Enter `Page Two` in the **Page Name** box.
16. Click **OK**.
17. Drag `Analysis Five` from the `Catalog` onto the page.
18. Click on the Save icon.
19. Click on the Run icon.
20. Select the `Year` from the **Prompt** box and click **OK**.

[303]

Creating Dashboards and Analyses

Now we will look at the other method, using a Dashboard Prompt object on the Dashboard.

There are two tasks when creating an interactive Dashboard. First, you make your analysis responsive by adding Filters, and then you create a corresponding Prompt on the Dashboard Prompt object. The good news is that you can set a column to any of the available Prompt types, including a simple **Is Prompted** option.

A column in an analysis will only respond to a Dashboard Prompt if the column has a Filter.

We will create the analysis first, which will be similar to `Analysis Five`:

1. Create a new analysis, using **Samples Sales Lite**.
2. Add the columns, `Per Name Year`, `Per Name Quarter` and `Revenue`.
3. Add a Filter to the `Per Name Year` column.
4. Set the **Operator** to **is prompted**:

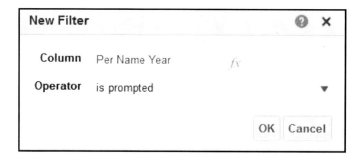

5. Save your analysis as `Analysis Six`.

   Now we create a Dashboard Prompt:

6. Click on **New**.
7. Choose **Dashboard Prompt**.
8. Pick the `Sample Sale Lite` Subject Area.
9. Click on the green plus icon to add a **Column Prompt**.
10. Select the `Per name Year` column.

11. Experiment with the available options. Choose a default specific value, and **Require User input**:

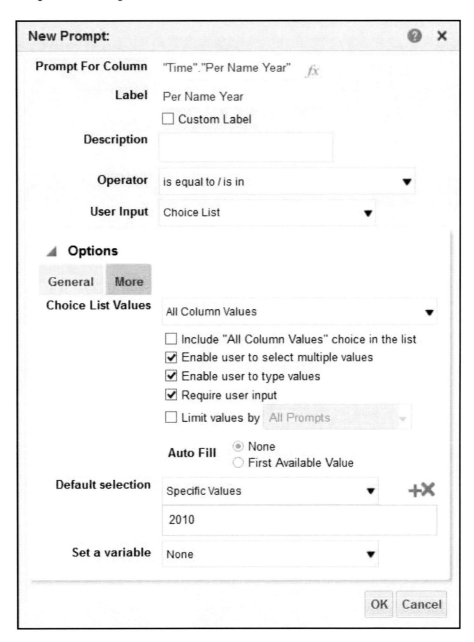

Creating Dashboards and Analyses

12. Click **OK**.
13. Save the Dashboard Prompt in the `Book` folder as `Prompt One`.

    Now we have created the two ingredients, let's put them together on a Dashboard page.

14. On the Home page, click on the **Edit** link for Dashboard One.
15. Add a new page, `Page Three`.
16. Drag the `Prompt One` onto the page, and then the `Analysis Six` below it:

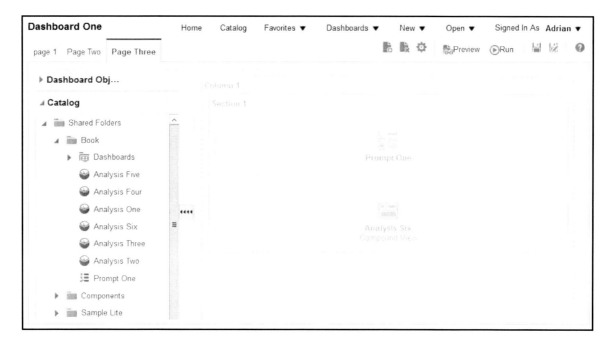

17. Save the page, then run it:

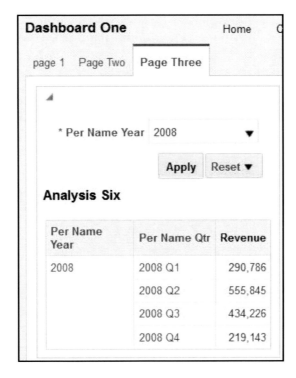

Experiment by selecting different Prompt values and pressing **Apply**. See how the results change depending upon what values you choose.

 Spend some time looking at all the different options available in a Dashboard Prompt both in the column, and in the **Prompt** properties.

Remember, only columns that have a Filter on will respond to a Dashboard Prompt.

Result layout

All of the analyses we have built so far have used the default way of presenting the results. The default place to see results is on the **Compound Layout** screen. This is a results page that has our views on. We can choose which views to place on the compound layout, and we can also create more than one compound layout screen.

To demonstrate this feature, we will create a new analysis, and on this analysis, we will create three separate layouts. We will then place these on a Dashboard page:

1. Create a new analysis based upon **Sample Sales Lite**.
2. Add the columns `Per Name Year`, `Brand`, `Product`, `Revenue`, `Target Revenue`.
3. Save it as `Analysis Seven` in the `Book` folder.
4. View the results.

   By default, you will see a title and a table view. We will now create a few more views so that we can place them on different layouts.

5. Create a new Table view using the Add View icon on the views menu bar:

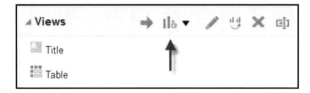

6. Remove the `Brand` and `Products` columns to the excluded section.
7. Click **Done**.
8. Rename the view using the rename icon on the **Views** menu bar:

9. Rename the Table to `Year Totals Table`.
10. Add a Graph view. Choose **Line G**raph and place `Brand` in the **Prompts** section, `Year` in the **Group By** section and **Measure Labels** in the **Vary Color by** section.
11. Click **Done**.
12. Rename the view as `Revenue Lines graph`.

We now have four views; one title, two tables and one Graph view.

Now we will create a new layout:

1. Click on the create **Compound Layout** icon:

When you create a new layout, the system will automatically create a new title view:

2. Rename the layout as `Year Layout`.
3. Drag the `Year Total` table over below the title.
4. Add another **Compound Layout**.
5. Rename it `Graph Revenue Layout`.
6. Add the Graph view, `Revenue Lines graph`.
7. Save it as `Analysis Seven`.

The analysis is now ready to place on a Dashboard:

8. Open Dashboard One in Edit mode.
9. Add a new page, calling it `Compound Example One`.
10. Drag `Analysis Seven` onto the new page.
11. Now click on the analysis properties (xyz icon).
12. Hover over **Show View** and the list of available views will appear.

Creating Dashboards and Analyses

13. Select **Year Layout**:

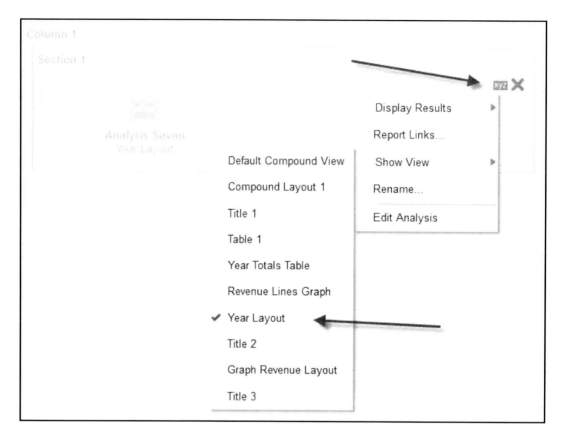

14. Save your page and run it.

What you are now looking at is the **Year Totals Table** and a title which are both on the Compound Layout - Year Totals Layout.

So far, we have viewed analysis results on the Dashboard page. Another option when viewing Analysis results from a Dashboard is to launch the analysis from the page and view in another window.

Let's see this in action using `Analysis Seven`, and also introduce the new 12c feature of sub pages:

1. Open the Compound Example page of the Dashboard in edit mode.
2. Add a sub page (available from the add page icon) and call it `Example Sub Page`.
3. Drag `Analysis Seven` onto the sub page.
4. Change the view shown to **Graph Revenue Layout**.
5. From the analysis properties icon, hover over **Display Results**.
6. Click on **Link - In A Separate Window**:

7. Save the page and run it.

All we see now is a link. To view the results, click on the link and a window will pop open showing the Graphs.

> If you rename the object on the Dashboard, there is an option to make the object name your link.

Creating Dashboards and Analyses

One feature to explore while we are here, is the **Report Links** option on the properties menu.

Report links are presented at the bottom of the view and can be customized for each view. The users' favorite link is the Export one!:

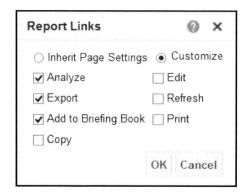

Add the links as shown above, then re-run the page and you will see the links at the bottom.

When we run a Dashboard page, we sometimes want to switch views quickly but stay on the page. The good news is that there is a feature for that in the analysis views:

1. Open `Analysis Seven` in edit mode.
2. View the results.
3. Add a view called `View Selector` (from the other views link).
4. Enter a **Caption** (`Select View`).
5. Select some views from the list in the left-hand box and move them to the right side (the first one will be the default view):

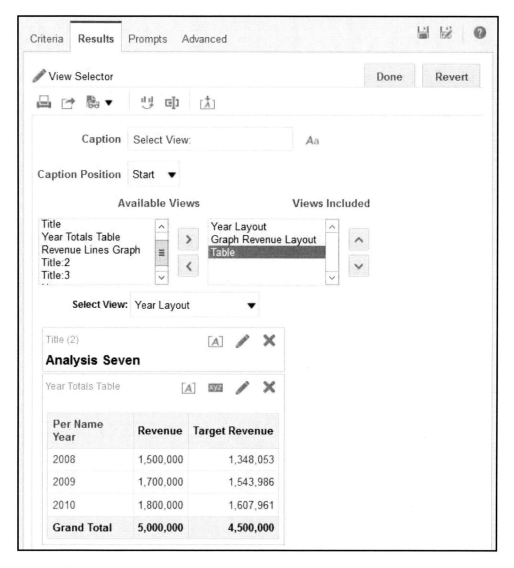

6. Save the analysis.
7. Open Dashboard One in Edit mode and add another page.
8. Call it `Selector Example`.

Creating Dashboards and Analyses

 View Selectors can include individual views (for example, tables) or complete compound layouts.

9. Drag `Analysis Seven` onto the page.
10. Change the view to `View Selector 1`.
11. Save and run the page:

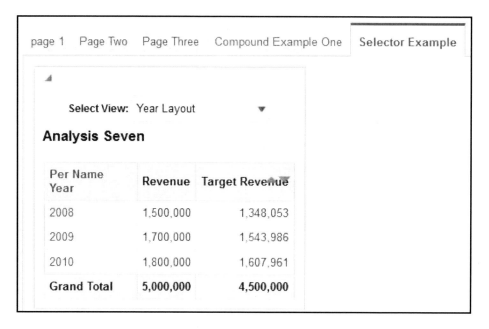

Now you can switch views quickly.

Column hiding and showing

When we place a view on a Dashboard, we set the default columns that are displayed. We can allow users to show columns that are excluded from the view, or exclude columns from the view.

To enable column hiding, set the **Interaction Properties** (available on the **Analysis Properties**):

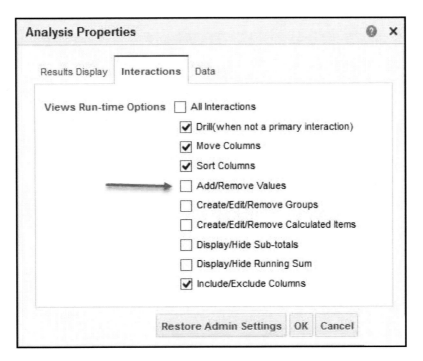

Conditional display

One of the best aspects of OBIEE is the ability to direct the user to the most useful information. Sections on a Dashboard page can be hidden or displayed conditionally. The condition can be a specific analysis or can be a saved condition object.

We will put together an example using the condition object. The steps will be the following:

- Create an analysis
- Create a condition object
- Create a Dashboard Prompt - we include this to help demonstrate the concept
- Create a Dashboard page
- Add a section and set it to conditionally display

Creating Dashboards and Analyses

Let's get on with it:

1. Create an analysis, based upon **Sample Sales Lite**.
2. Add the columns `Per Name Month` and `Revenue`.
3. Add a Filter to the `Year` column, set it to `2011 / 12`.
4. Add a Filter to the `Revenue` column, set it to `less than 100000`.
5. Save the analysis as `Analysis Eight`:

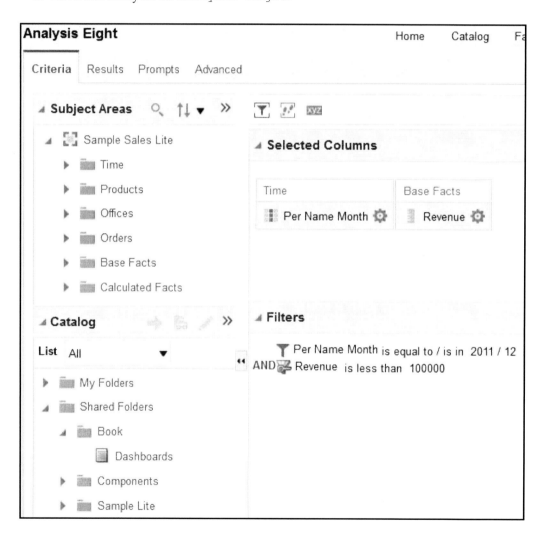

If you run the analysis, you will see there are no results.

Now create the condition:

6. From the **New** menu, select **Condition**.
7. Browse to and select the `Analysis Eight`.
8. Save it as `Condition One`.

Next, we create the Dashboard Prompt:

9. From the **New** menu, select **Dashboard Prompt**.
10. Choose the **Sample Sale Lite** Subject Area.
11. Add a **Column Prompt**.
12. Select `Per Name Month`.
13. Set the options that all are not ticked.
14. Set the **Default Value** to a specific month.
15. Edit the **Page Properties** (use the pencil icon).
16. Untick the **Show Apply Button** option.
17. Untick the **Show Reset Button** option.
18. Save the **Prompt** as `Prompt two`.

Putting it all together:

19. Create a new page on Dashboard One.
20. Call it **Condition Example**.
21. Add a Section (drag the Section object from the top-left panel).

22. Click on the properties icon and select **Condition...** from the drop-down menu:

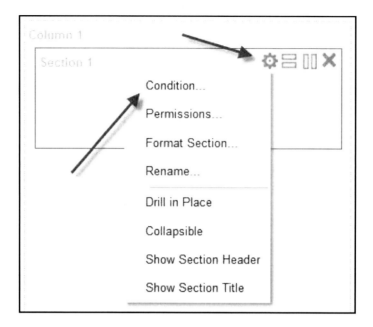

23. Click on the select **Condition** icon and find the Condition One object in the `Book` folder:

We will add some content into the section. A simple message will be sufficient in this example. You can add anything into a conditionally displaying section.

24. Drag text from the top left panel.
25. Enter some text:

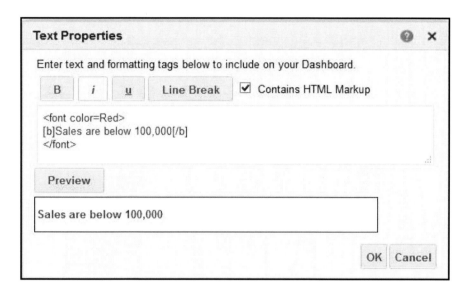

 You can enter normal text, HTML, and CSS in a text box.

26. Click **OK**.
27. Save the Dashboard.
28. Run it.

Creating Dashboards and Analyses

You will now see a blank page!

The condition returned false, because there are no records for 2011 / 12.

To prove it will show when `Revenue` is low, let's add another section:

1. Go back to Edit mode.
2. Drag another section onto the page.
3. Drag the Dashboard Prompt, `Prompt Two` into the second section.
4. Drag `Analysis Eight` into the second section.
5. Save the page.
6. Run the page:

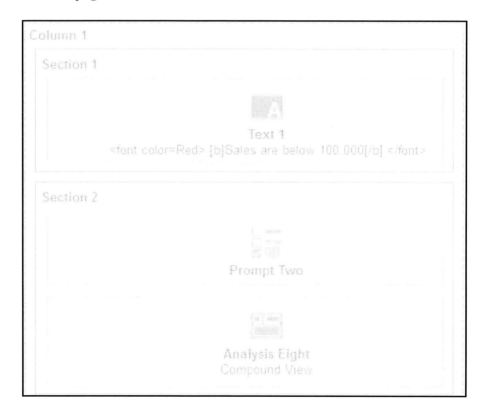

Default: you will see no results.

7. Change the **Prompt Value** to 2008 /10.

Our sales message appears!

Recap

We just built a Dashboard page that can conditionally display a section, depending upon the result of a condition, which is the checking of results of an analysis. We choose a simple example but this could be useful to highlight something to users that needs to be addressed, for example, sales orders not yet processed.

Conditionally displaying results means your users are informed when they need to be, and not when they don't. This changes the way people interact with their data. Do not give them all the data to determine what is good or bad, but present the messages that you need them to act on.

OBIEE is not just for presenting historical Graphs. OBIEE is great for day to day operational use, reporting to users any type of information that they need to do their job. We like to use the phrase, *"It is better to see the bunny in the headlights, than the roadkill in the mirror"*!

Master Detail linking

When presenting more than one analysis on a Dashboard page, you can link them together using the Master Detail feature. One analysis will be the master, and the other, the detailed analysis.

We will put together an example. The steps will be:

- Create the Master Analysis
- Set the communication channel identifier
- Create child views
- Set the Filter for the channel
- Place both on a Dashboard page

Creating Dashboards and Analyses

Let's get on with it:

1. Create an Analysis, based upon **Sample Sales Lite**.
2. Add the columns `Per Name Year`, `Per Name Month` and `Revenue`.
3. Edit the `Per Name Year` **Column Properties**.
4. Change the **Primary Interaction** on the `Year` column value to **Send Master-Detail Events**.
5. In the box that appears, put `salesyear`.
6. Save the analysis as `Analysis Nine`:

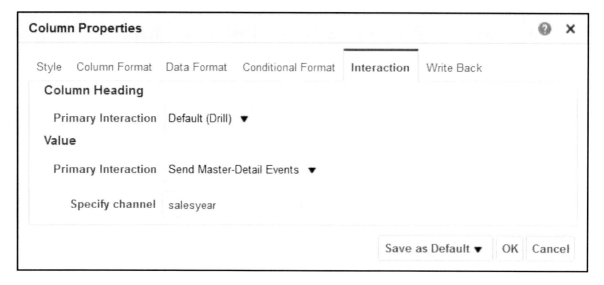

Now we create the child views:

7. View the results page.
8. Add a Graph View.
9. Place the `Year` column into the **Prompts** section.
10. Edit the View Properties.
11. Check the box for **Listen to Master-Detail Events**.
12. Enter `salesyear` into the **Channel** box.

[322]

13. Save the analysis:

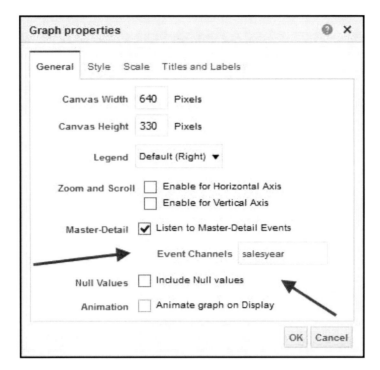

The analysis is now ready to use. We will demonstrate it on a Dashboard page:

14. Add a page to Dashboard One, call it `Master Detail Example`.
15. Add `Analysis Nine`.
16. Set the View to `Table 1`.
17. Add another column to the page (drag from the left panel).
18. Change the properties of the second column, removing the page break.

The above setting will place the second column to the right of the first one:

19. Drag `Analysis Nine` onto the page again, into the second column.
20. Change the view displayed to the Graph.
21. Save the page and run it.

Now, when you click on a `Year` in the table, the Graph will automatically update. Note that we could have also created a different analysis to listen to the Master Detail channel.

[323]

Saved Dashboards

When a Dashboard is loaded, the query runs with the default values if there are defaults set. This may not suit the user, so they set the Prompt to the value of their choice, for example, their office or region. The next time the page is run, the user does not want to have to repeat the process again, so they can save the settings applied. This is simply done by using the Dashboard properties wheel, and selecting the **Save Current Customization** option:

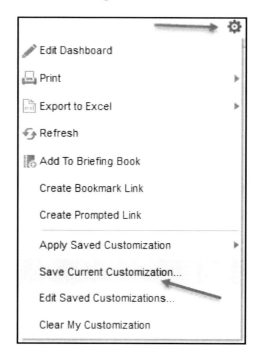

Select the **Use as default** option and your Filters will be applied automatically when you run the page. You can save many customizations, and switch between them using the **Apply Saved Customization** option in the menu.

Calculated data

So far, we have mainly used simple presentation of columns that are available in the Subject Area. We introduced the formula editing feature when we used the UPPER() function, and there are large number of functions available which can create a calculated result in a column. There is also a method available to calculate row totals.

Let's look at some typical calculations:

- `SUM`: You can sum any numerical column, from any of the folders, although you would normally operate on measure columns.

A typical `SUM` calculation would look as follows:

```
SUM("Base Facts"."Revenue" )
```

You can also set a level to aggregate by, for example a Year or a brand:

```
SUM("Base Facts"."Revenue" by "Time"."Per Name Year")
```

A typical use for the above calculation would be to create a `Percentage` column:

```
("Base Facts"."Revenue" / SUM("Base Facts"."Revenue" by "Time"."Per Name Year"))*100.0
```

Now we will create an analysis to demonstrate the function:

1. Create a new analysis using the Samples Sales Subject Area.
2. Add `Per Name Year` and `Brand`.
3. Add the `Revenue` five times.
4. Edit the formula on the second `Revenue` column, and change it to `SUM("Base Facts"."Revenue" by "Time"."Per Name Year")`.
5. Change the heading to `Revenue By Year`.
6. Edit the formula on the third `Revenue`, and change it to `SUM("Base Facts"."Revenue")`.
7. Edit the formula on the fourth `Revenue`, and change it to `( "Base Facts"."Revenue" / SUM("Base Facts"."Revenue" by "Time"."Per Name Year")) *100.0`.
8. Change the heading to `% of Year`.
9. Change the **Data Format** to Percentage.
10. Edit the formula on the fifth `Revenue`, and change it to `( "Base Facts"."Revenue" / SUM("Base Facts"."Revenue" by "Time"."Per Name Year")) *100.0`.
11. Change the heading to `% of Year`.
12. Change the **Data Format** to Percentage.
13. View the results.
14. Edit the Table View.
15. Set the Totals for the `Year` column and for the Columns (both After).

16. Save it as `Analysis Ten`:

Per Name Year	Brand	Revenue	SUM of Revenue BY Year	SUM of Revenue	% of Year	% of Total
2008	BizTech	658,692	1,500,000	5,000,000	44%	13%
	FunPod	542,613	1,500,000	5,000,000	36%	11%
	HomeView	298,695	1,500,000	5,000,000	20%	6%
2008 Total		**1,500,000**	**1,500,000**	**5,000,000**	**100%**	**30%**
2009	BizTech	821,826	1,700,000	5,000,000	48%	16%
	FunPod	556,666	1,700,000	5,000,000	33%	11%
	HomeView	321,508	1,700,000	5,000,000	19%	6%
2009 Total		**1,700,000**	**1,700,000**	**5,000,000**	**100%**	**34%**
2010	BizTech	1,019,482	1,800,000	5,000,000	57%	20%
	FunPod	400,721	1,800,000	5,000,000	22%	8%
	HomeView	379,797	1,800,000	5,000,000	21%	8%
2010 Total		**1,800,000**	**1,800,000**	**5,000,000**	**100%**	**36%**
Grand Total		**5,000,000**	**5,000,000**	**5,000,000**	**100%**	**100%**

You can see that the `Revenue by Year` total is repeated for each row of the `Year`, but the `Sum of Revenue` is repeated for every row.

You can also use the Aggregate Function to get a measure column total, for example `"Base Facts"."Revenue"/Aggregate("Base Facts"."Revenue" BY)*100.0` would also provide the overall percentage.

- `TimestampDiff`: A function that work with dates and times, it calculates the difference between two dates, and presents the result in Years, Months, Weeks, Days, Hours, Minutes or Seconds.

The format is as follows:

`TimestampDiff(interval, date 1, date 2)`, where interval is one of the following:

- `SQL_TSI_SECOND`,
- `SQL_TSI_MINUTE`,
- `SQL_TSI_HOUR`,
- `SQL_TSI_DAY`,
- `SQL_TSI_WEEK`,
- `SQL_TSI_MONTH`,
- `SQL_TSI_QUARTER`,
- `SQL_TSI_YEAR`.

We often use the function to Filter data for relative dates, for example, display the Total of Sales for the last two months.

- **TIMESTAMPADD**: `TIMESTAMPADD` is similar to the `TimeStampDiff` function, but it returns a date. You add or subtract an interval (For example, Week) to a date. The same list of intervals is used. The format is as follows:

    `TIMESTAMPADD(interval, number of intervals, date 1)`

If the number of intervals is negative, then you are subtracting from `date 1`. The example is as follows:

`TIMESTAMPADD(SQL_TSI_DAY, -1, date '2010-12-30')`

This will return the day before 30th December 2010.

Let's create an analysis using the `timeStampDiff` function:

1. Create a new analysis using the Samples Sales Subject Area.
2. Add `Calendar Date` twice and `Revenue`.
3. Edit the formula on the second date column, and change it to `TIMESTAMPDIFF(SQL_TSI_WEEK, "Time"."Calendar Date", date '2010-12-30')`
4. Change the Heading to `Week`.
5. Add a filer on the `Week` column, set it to `less than 6`.
6. View the results.
7. Add a Line chart.

8. Set it to be a curved line (use the icon on the toolbar).
9. Set the horizontal as the Week column.
10. Save it as Analysis Eleven:

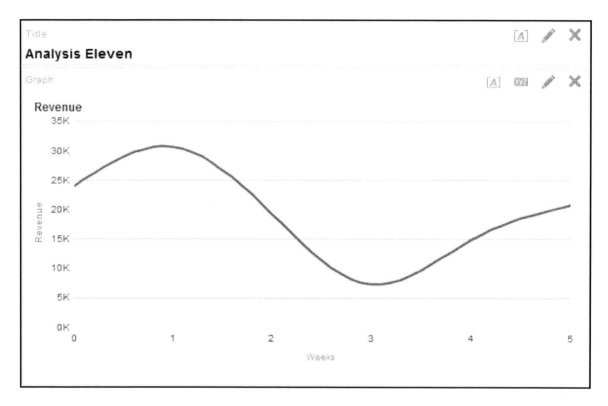

This example shows the trend of sales over 6 rolling weeks from December 30, 2010.

At this point, it is also worth mentioning the special functions of CURRENT_DATE(), CURRENT_TIME(), CURRENT_TIME(), and NOW(). Current date will return a date that relates to the server, without any time components. Current time will only return the time on the server, without any date element. Current_Timepstamp will return both the date and time. Now is exactly the same as current time-stamp.

These functions can be useful in creating a reference point for your other functions. For example, you may want to see the sales for the last three days, in which case you would use the function `TIMESTAMPDIFF(SQL_TSI_DAY, "Time"."Calendar Date", CURRENT_DATE)` and set a Filter on this column for less than four.

- RCOUNT: This useful function provides the user with a row count column in the results. Use `RCOUNT(1)` to have a simple row count for each row of the results. You can also use a group by clause in the functions, for example, `RCOUNT(1 BY Per name Year)` will reset the counter to one each time the `Year` changes.

This function can be useful to just display a small sample of the results, by having a Filter on the `RCOUNT(1)`:

- TopN: This is a combination of a Filter and a function at the same time. It determines the order of a measure, by its value from highest to lowest, and then Filters your recordset for the top N. For example, you can see a list of the top 10 months by `Revenue` using: `TOPN("Base Facts"."Revenue",10)`. If you just want to see how a number ranks overall, then set the Filter number to be larger than the expected number of total result rows. `BottomN` is similar to `TopN` but ranks from smallest to largest.

- NTile: `NTile(number,scale)` arranges numbers on a scale are presents where the row lies on the scale. For example, if you had a list of month numbers and used a scale of 6, that is, `NTILE(Month Number, 6)`, then January and February will be ntile 1, March and April will be 2, May and June will be 3, and so on.

- **Calculated rows**: So far, we have looked at some example functions that operate on a column value, in a single row. With OBIEE, we can also sum rows together, and not just using table properties. We can create Groups which bring data together.

Let's demonstrate this using `Analysis Ten` as a starting point:

1. Edit `Analysis Ten`.
2. Save As `Analysis Twelve`.
3. In the **Criteria** view, click on the Selection step icon (looks like a couple of feet!).
4. Click on **New Step** in the **Brand** section.

5. Select **New Group** from the sub menu:

6. Give the gsroup a name, `Biz and Home`.
7. Select the Brands, BizTech and HomeView.
8. Click **OK**.
9. Click **Save**.
10. View the **Results** tab.

You will now see a new row added to the table view, called Biz and Home, which shows the totals for those two brands only.

 The above example's use of functions demonstrates the principles. There are dozens of functions available to use, so please spend some time experimenting with them.

Saved columns

One of the cool new features in OBIEE is the ability to create a column and save it for use elsewhere. This feature enables a column to be created once and used in multiple analyses. Better still, any updates to the column can be made in one place and all analyses will reflect the changes.

Let take a quick look at Saved columns:

1. Create a new analysis.
2. Add the Office column.
3. Edit the formula, set it to be LEFT("Offices"."Office", 1).
4. Click on the **Bins** tab.
5. Click on **Add Bin**.
6. Set the **Operator** to **Less than**.
7. Enter H in the **Value** box.
8. Click **OK**.
9. Enter and Name, use A-G.
10. Add another bin for less than R.
11. Add another Bin for Equal to or less than Z.
12. Click **OK**.
13. Now save the column by clicking on the **Column Properties Wheel** and select the bottom option, **Save Column As...**
14. Choose a name for the saved object, use Office_Group.
15. Change the location to the Book folder. You will get a warning message about the location, you can safely ignore the message.

Creating Dashboards and Analyses

So, we now have a column created, and you can edit it as a stand-alone object. Navigate in the catalog to the `Book` folder and you will see the column you just created. You can right-click on it and you get two edit options, the formula or the Properties.

Now we will use the column:

1. Create a new analysis.
2. In the **Catalog** panel, locate the `Book` folder and click on the `Office_Group` object.
3. Click on the right-facing arrow to add the column to our analysis.
4. Add the `Revenue` column.
5. Save as `Analysis Thirteen`.

Pretty useful stuff!

Here we show an update to the shared column and how it automatically changes in `Analysis Thirteen`:

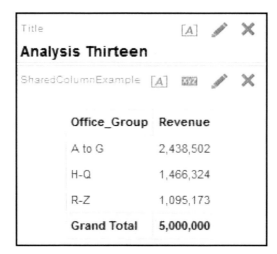

A review - what I should now know!

Here is a checklist of the things you should now be able to do:

- Create an analysis
- Create different results views
- Set column formats, including conditional formatting
- Create a new Dashboard and pages
- Place analysis onto Dashboards
- How to set Prompts
- How to add formulae to analyses
- How to create Shared calculated columns

Summary

In this chapter, we covered a lot of ground. We learned how to create an analysis and a Dashboard. We looked in depth at some of the options available to the OBIEE developer when building analyses and building Dashboards. There are dozens of features, with dozens of settings in each feature, so take some time to familiarize yourself with the option.

It might seem like a lot to digest at first, so you may want to re-read the chapter, and explore more features, for example, other available views. You can also create your own examples and experiment.

We covered analyses, including column display properties, Filters, different views, functions, and shared columns. We built Dashboards, including Dashboard Prompts, pages, conditional sections, and links.

In the next chapter, we will look at automating the production of analytical data.

9
Agents and Action Framework

Much of what is visible to end-users exists on the reporting layer and the development of those underlying components has already been discussed in previous chapters. This is all targeted at delivering business analytics to end-users by enabling them to cut through complex datasets in order to discover new insights about their business. These insights are often best realized when they can be acted upon. This chapter reviews a few concepts and functions on how to take the next step after the reports or dashboards are developed in order to create call-to-action analyses in OBIEE and how to further deliver data to individuals in the organization.

Oracle BI 12c has functionality that allows Oracle BI to be integrated into business processes to make the information more actionable directly from the Oracle BI system. In legacy versions of Oracle BI, there was the **Delivers** portion of OBIEE where you could invoke basic Actions, such as the delivery of reports via e-mail (also known as bursting) or to signal a dashboard alert. Oracle BI 12c uses Delivers concepts and enhances this capability through the **Action Framework**, where we are able to initiate a multitude of Actions; for example, calling web services, launching business processes workflows, or chaining delivery of other analyses and reports based on conditions or other logic.

The vision going forward for OBIEE is that it will provide a system that can deliver process interaction as well as analyses and reporting. This can often be described as a **closed-loop** system in that the Oracle BI platform moves a user from a transactional reporting mindset to an analytical one and the Action Framework moves Oracle BI further into an actual decision making processes initiator. This chapter looks at a few functions that Oracle BI provides in an attempt to help organizations succeed at this goal.

Agents

As said in the introduction, legacy versions of OBIEE, prior to Oracle BI 11g, contained functionality to deliver analyses to a targeted set of end-users. So delivery of reports through e-mail and alerts is not new. The object that was created to provide the Delivers method of delivery in those legacy versions was described as an **iBot**. This functionality has been retained and iBots have been renamed as **Agents**. To support this functionality, we need to have the **Scheduler** metadata tables (created by the RCU) and Oracle BI services running as we have covered previously as part of the start up process in order for the full process and following examples to work. So let's go through the process of creating an agent.

The example that we will go through involves e-mailing one of our previously created analysis reports to a user. To do this, we initially have to set up OBIEE with details of a mail server. If you do not have your organization's mail server information or do not wish to set up a sandbox mail server on your server you can skip to the Creating the Agent section, directly after the following Mail server setup section.

Mail server setup

To configure e-mail settings for delivering functionality, conduct the following process:

Open **Enterprise Manager** and expand the **Target Navigation** left panel to expose the list of folders.

Then expand the **Business Intelligence** folder and click on the **biinstance** option. When the **biinstance** area opens, click on the **Configuration** tab and then the **Mail** sub-tab for our application:

You can send a scheduled report as an alert without setting up the mail server. However, in order for a user to receive an e-mail, the mail server configuration must be completed in order for OBIEE to know how to send an e-mail. To get a basic mail server configured, you can use either a combination of freeware and open source tools such as **hMailServer** and **Apache Directory Service** or just hMailServer to handle the **Simple Mail Transfer Protocol (SMTP)** functions required for sending e-mails on a local server. To receive mail, install the Thunderbird mail client. All setup of the additional software mentioned for setting up capability on the server is beyond the scope of this book. If using the WebLogic Server LDAP users in combination with the SMTP server, you will need to modify each user's account profile Delivery options with corresponding e-mail addresses created for your testing to actually receive e-mails. Lastly, updating the hosts file on the server will allow you to create a mock DNS such as `obi12cbook.info` that references the localhost server.

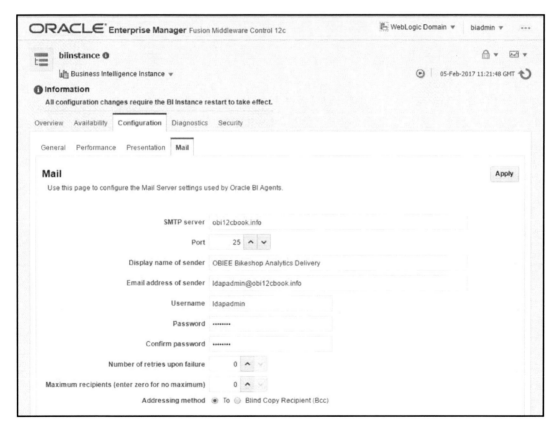

Agents and Action Framework

1. Lock and Edit the page.
2. Input the details of an SMTP server, including user and password details, and SSL information if required.
3. Click **Apply**.

OBIEE will use this mail routing server when sending out analyses via e-mail. We can also change the display name of the sending party.

For our example, we will use **OBIEE Bikeshop Analytics Delivery**:

1. Click the **Apply** button.
2. Expand the lock icon menu again and click on **Activate Changes**.

Once we have applied these changes, as learned in previous chapters, we can move to actually creating an Agent. You should stop and start all Oracle BI service components after applying this change to the mail tab.

Creating the Agent

Access the /analytics Oracle BI portal home page and view the **Actionable Intelligence** options on the left side of the page to notice the **Agent** and **Action** options. Just view this area for now, as you'll use a more direct method to create the Agent in the following steps:

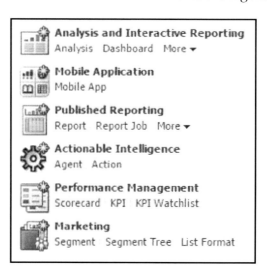

Next, navigate to the **Catalog** page.

Chapter 9

Expand the **Shared Folders** and **Book folders** where the exercises you have created from the previous chapters now reside. Locate the analysis report, **Analysis Ten**. This is the analysis that we will send out to one or more users through a dashboard alert and via e-mail if e-mail bursting is configured. On the **Analysis Ten** analysis row, right-click on the analysis and select the **Schedule** item from the options menu:

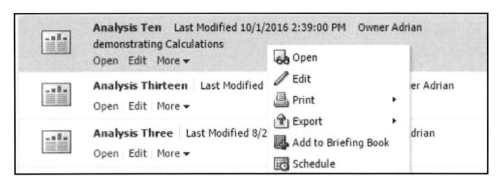

Selecting the **Schedule** option will take you to the new **Delivers Agent** form. On this new form with the name **Untitled Agent**, you will first encounter the **General** tab:

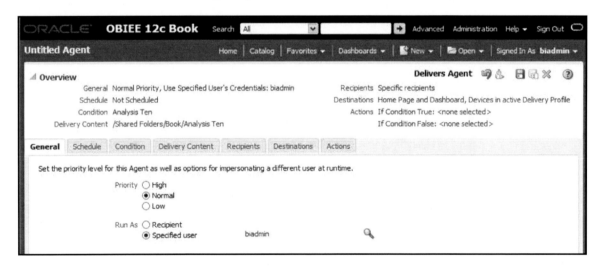

You can set the **Priority** for an Agent, which is analogous to the priority levels you might typically see in e-mails. This priority also relates to how each user has configured their **Delivery Profile** settings for how they wish to receive **Delivers Agents** based on level of priority. For example, they may stipulate that *High* priority Agents are sent to their mobile phone, while *Normal* ones are sent to their e-mail.

More importantly, in this tab, we can decide which user OBIEE will run this Agent as. In our example, we have stipulated our admin user. This means that every recipient of this Agent will receive the same report. However, if we had a report with some type of data-security, we could set the Agent to **Run As** the **Recipient**. This means that the content that is delivered will be filtered or personalized by that recipient user's or their respective security group's data visibility as defined in the RPD.

Be aware that much of what a user is able to configure in the Delivers Agent areas are controlled by security privileges defined by the Oracle BI Administrator in the Administration page. Several restrictions prevent users by default from gaining full control of Agent functions and/or attributes that can be selected.

For example, in this Agent we will be sending out the information from analysis report Analysis Ten showing Brand Revenue by Year. If we had a set of users with access to only BizTech data, and another set of users with access to only FunPod data, then using the **Run As Recipient** option would enact the relevant data-security, which would ensure that users only receive the appropriate Brand data when the Agent is executed.

Next, click on the **Schedule** tab:

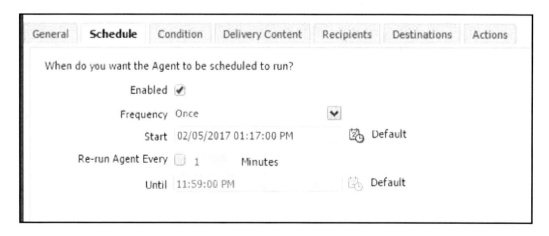

This tab is pretty self-explanatory in that, as well as ensuring that the Agent is turned on (**Enabled** checkbox), we can set a schedule for an Agent. We can decide whether the Agent runs once or is recurring, and on which days/times it occurs. This is useful, for example, if we have a sales report that needs to be sent out monthly with updated data. Changing the **Frequency** dropdown from **Never** to another option will enable the other attributes to become enabled. For now, change the **Frequency** dropdown value to **Once** by selecting it from the list.

Next, click on the **Condition** tab:

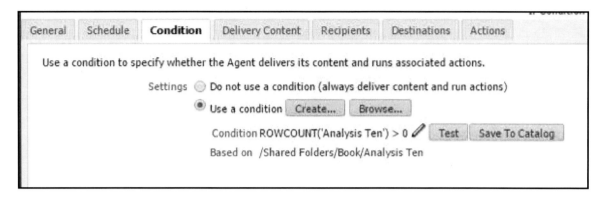

This is another tab that adds greatly to the flexibility of an Agent. A condition in this context is a check or validation run by OBIEE to determine if the Agent should be sent on its schedule frequency. This validation often is in the form of referencing another analysis, not just the one being sent. In this example, we'll use the default, which is using the actual analysis that we will be sending out, as a condition. It checks whether or not it produces a row count greater than 0, that is, whether it is producing any data at all. If the analysis has not produced any data then it is not worth sending out, so this is a handy condition. If it is true, in that the row count is greater than 0 (true), then it will be sent. If it is less than zero (false), it will not be sent. Note that we can save conditions and reuse them in other Agents. Also we can check the current status of a condition by clicking on the **Test** button:

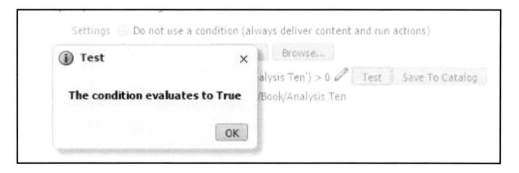

We can see that for our condition, our analysis currently does have a row count greater than 0, so when we run this Agent, the process will complete and send out our information in the format that we'll configure in the next tab, **Delivery Content**.

Agents and Action Framework

In the **Delivery Content** tab you decide what content and format will be used by this Agent to send out the information:

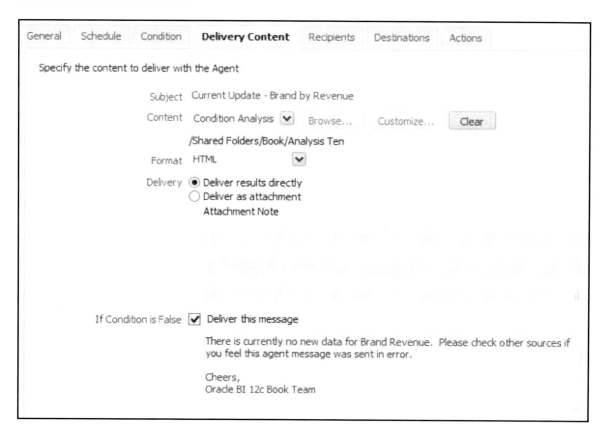

There are several attributes in the **Delivery Content** tab:

- **Subject**: Firstly we can set the **Subject**, this will show in the subject header of our e-mail.
- **Content**: If we created an Agent from the **Schedule** option of an analysis, then the Content will already show that analysis and the path from which the analysis resides. Otherwise you can change the dropdown to **Analysis** and browse the catalog to choose one. Note that our content dropdown shows the value **Condition Analysis**. This is due to the fact that we are using the default condition check in the previous **Condition** tab.

- **Format**: You can keep the Device Default format of the delivery **Format** option or override it and choose another value as we have done here by selecting **HTML**. We also have the choice of sending the content out as CSV data, an Excel document, a PowerPoint slide, PDF, or plain text.
- **Delivery**: Selecting the **Deliver results** directly option will place the output of the analysis or message that you are sending directly into the resulting medium (that is, e-mail, dashboard alert, and so on) rather than as an attachment, which is how most users will want to receive the content.
- **If Condition is False**: If our previous condition, via the **Condition** tab, proves false, then our Agent will not run. However, our users may think that something has gone wrong if they do not receive the delivered Agent one day, if having received it on a previous frequency such as on a daily basis when a condition was true. Using this option, we can send them a message, in this case, to allay these fears and tell them that there simply is no data currently for this analysis.

The next tab is for detailing the **Recipients** who will receive the Agents output:

Agents and Action Framework

In this tab, one can choose individual users, or Application Roles. In the preceding screenshot, we have an example of both. Your username as the author of the Agent should appear already by default in the list of recipients.

 Catalog groups used to be an option in Oracle BI 11g and legacy versions, but catalog groups are no longer a grouping concept supported by Oracle BI 12c.

Click the green + plus button to add a new recipient to add additional users or application roles to receive the information to be distributed from this Agent.

In this Recipients tab we also have the option to **Publish for Subscription.** This means that we can open Agent objects up to users and allow them to pick and choose which Agents they want to receive, or subscribe to, based on publishing this Agent to a group of users to select what information they'd wish to receive via whatever automated Agent bursting frequency. This centralizes report bursting, but also enables owners of data to have more control over how information is distributed and to whom.

Additionally, by clicking on the envelope icon, we can type in actual e-mail addresses for individuals who should also receive the Agent's output. E-mails here could include users that are outside the network such as third-party recipients.

The last major tab is the **Destinations** tab:

The main options here are to do with devices delivery selection. Again, we can allow users to choose their own methods of receiving data through their delivery profile (that is, **My Account** > **Delivery Options** tab), or we can override and choose a specific device option ourselves. Keep the **User Destinations** options set as the defaults to have **Home Page and Dashboard** and **Devices > Active Delivery Profile** selected for now.

There is, obviously, another tab labeled **Actions**. Clicking on this tab reveals a different set of attributes for evaluating a condition and based on the validity of that condition executing or rather invoking another Agent or executing some script, web service, or Java program. There is a decent amount of programming and setup required to execute an action within an Agent. However, the Oracle documentation on the matter is rather good, and the technical integration of this advanced aspect goes beyond the scope of this book:

Agents and Action Framework

At this point we are ready to run the Agent you've been creating thus far. Click the **Save** button icon to save the Agent.

Create a new folder under the **Shared Folders** > **Book** folder structure and name the new folder, **Agents**. Save the Agent as an object named, Chapter 9. The Agent, if scheduled to run on the frequency of once, will begin to execute once the **Save** button is clicked.

If you are ever impatient when creating the Agent and you don't want to wait for the schedule frequency to kick in, you can run the Agent immediately by clicking the Agent icon, a robot with a green arrow, in the Agent form that resides next to the **Save** button. Once you click on the **Execute now** button you should get a message saying that the Agent is running. If the Agent cannot run, for example, to a mail server issue, then you will receive an appropriate message. Otherwise you should receive a successful message:

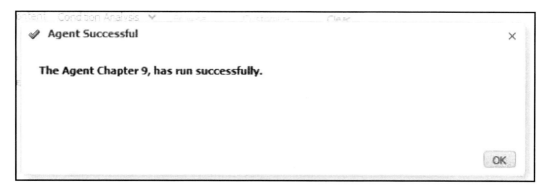

In this example, there should be no errors, so let's look at the result. One could receive errors if the mail server is incorrectly configured. But if not using a mail server and only sending the Agent to the **Homepage** and **Dashboard** option there should be no errors at all.

Because we configured the mail settings for our full example, we can see the analysis has been sent to us in an e-mail (we are checking the e-mail associated with our recipient user list that was created with the previously mentioned mail server):

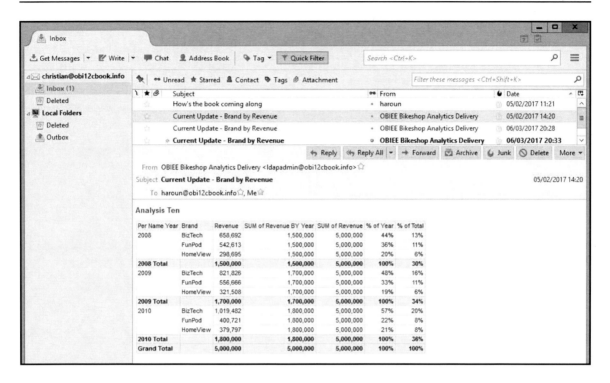

Note that the **From** and **Subject** fields are as we stipulated earlier in the example, and that the analysis is showing in an HTML format within the e-mail as we requested. We did not select the option for having the analysis show as an attachment so there isn't one in the e-mail. The content is embedded in the e-mail itself.

Before we move on, let's see how this looks as a dashboard alert, which was one of the default checkboxes that we kept checked when creating the Agent.

Navigate to the **Home** page screen and observe the global header:

You can see that we have a new **Alerts** section in our home screen that has a link to the results of the Agent, that is, the analysis that was just run via the Agent. We also have a yellow bell icon in our toolbar that we can click on to see all of our current alerts, if more than one, or the content of the existing example alert by clicking the **View** link:

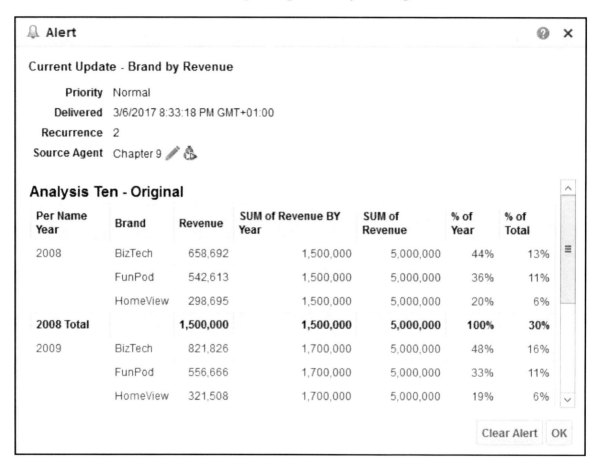

Agents can send notifications to both a device and to the home page screen of OBIEE. These can be useful options for enhancing a user's workflow, especially in conjunction with the conditions that we can add to an Agent as we've shown in the preceding example.

Actions

Actions were introduced in OBIEE 11g. **Actions** are operations or processes initiated within OBIEE that provide extensible functionality to an end-user or the Oracle BI system. They can allow straightforward functionality such as providing a navigation option to other areas or reports in OBIEE or they can, with varying levels of complexity, invoke external systems. Using the most complex of capabilities, one could leverage OBIEE as part of a full business process workflow.

Let's go through a couple of examples for basic navigation using Actions. We will then briefly talk about the possibilities that exist in invoking other system functions.

BI Navigation

The most basic Action is that of navigating from one OBIEE object to another. We have already covered drilling using RPD hierarchies and Master-Detail linking in one of the previous chapters. Navigation Actions can be changed for an analysis column heading or value area via the **Interaction** option on a column's Column Properties in the **Criteria** tab for an analysis.

Let's create an example using the analysis, **Analysis Ten**, created in a previous chapter.

Navigate to the **Catalog** page and locate the **Analysis Ten** analysis object.

Open the **Analysis Ten** analysis and then click the **Save As...** icon button to save the report as a new report called **Analysis Ten - Original**.

Return to the Catalog page and once more locate and open the **Analysis Ten** analysis object that you opened before.

We simply made a backup copy of this file in the previous step and we want this **Analysis Ten** object to be updated as it is already used in the dashboard page layout to avoid having to change the dashboard layout again.

Let's set it up so that an **Action Link** will appear if you click on a particular Brand in that report, allowing for navigation to another analysis that has a different detail or alternate variety of metrics.

Locate the **Brand** column and then access its **Column Properties**. Next, click on the **Interaction** tab:

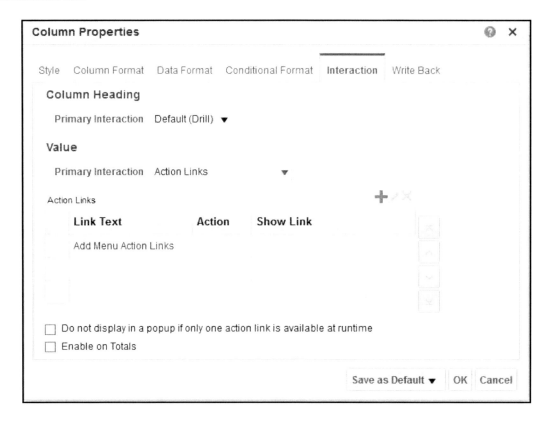

In the **Interaction** settings (for the Brand column), override the choice of interaction for the output **Value** > **Primary Interaction** dropdown by choosing **Action Links**. You are then presented with a table of action links that is currently empty.

Note that **Action Links** is a table where you can add a variety of links if desired. The end-user would then have a menu of **Action Links** to choose from when clicking on a value for the **Brand** column.

In our example, we are only concerned with adding the one navigation action. To add a new Action Link action, click the green + sign, and you are then shown the **New Action Link...** prompt:

We can input the **Link Text**, which acts as a label description that the user sees when picking this action. Enter in the **Link Text** field, `Other Details`.

Click the green gear icon to add a new action. Choose **Navigate to BI Content**.

You are then prompted to choose another analysis from the Presentation Catalog. Let's choose our *Analysis Seven* analysis from the `Shared Folders/Book` folder:

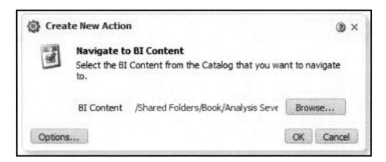

Agents and Action Framework

Once we have chosen the analysis that we want to navigate to, we can click **OK** at the **Create New Action** confirmation prompt shown previously. Click **OK** again to close the **New Action Link...** prompt. And click **OK** once more to close the Column Properties prompt.

Save the **Analysis Ten** analysis that you are currently working on by clicking the Save icon button.

Navigate back to the Oracle BI Catalog page and locate the **Analysis Ten** analysis in the list and click on the **Open** link, which is shown under the analysis title of the object.

Click on BizTech for one of the top years when the report opens and notice what happens:

Analysis Ten						
Per Name Year	Brand	Revenue	SUM of Revenue BY Year	SUM of Revenue	% of Year	% of Total
2008	BizTe	--- ---	1,500,000	5,000,000	44%	13%
	FunP Other Details		1,500,000	5,000,000	36%	11%
	HomeView	298,695	1,500,000	5,000,000	20%	6%
2008 Total		**1,500,000**	**1,500,000**	**5,000,000**	**100%**	**30%**
2009	BizTech	821,826	1,700,000	5,000,000	48%	16%
	FunPod	556,666	1,700,000	5,000,000	33%	11%

You can see an Action Link menu pop up with one option for our **Other Detail** link. If we click on that, we are transported to the **Analysis Seven** report:

Analysis Seven				
Per Name Year	Brand	Product	Revenue	Target Revenue
2008	BizTech	V5x Flip Phone	112,742	95,908
		CompCell RX3	57,256	46,973
		Touch-Screen T5	102,482	98,861
		KeyMax S-Phone	76,029	68,501
		SoundX Nano 4Gb	102,606	91,887
		MicroPod 60Gb	125,403	105,893
		Bluetooth Adaptor	42,077	40,043
		MP3 Speakers System	40,098	32,390
	FunPod	MPEG4 Camcorder	115,434	109,606

You can see that this is a very straightforward process that brings potential business value. You can expound upon this example by adding multiple links in a menu to give a user greater flexibility in navigating to other reports and representations of data.

Web navigation and passing a parameter

Having covered our first basic action link, let's cover another type, specifically navigating to a web page. As our starting analysis, let's build a basic report that contains some details about the company's brands, office locations, and so on. Our users want to be able to link to current information or search the web about the business, and it would help them if they could quickly do it from the report, rather than having to open a browser and type in a web address and search for that data as a separate step.

To modify the analysis we've been working on in this chapter, Analysis Ten, in the **Catalog** page find the analysis and click edit to edit the report. In the **Criteria** tab, expand the `Offices` folder of the **Sample Sales Lite** subject area. Double-click the **Office** column to add it to the **Selected Columns** area.

Next, remove the **Per Name Year** column by clicking on its respective properties menu and selecting the **Delete** option.

Click the **Results** tab to see the results of the change.

Now drag the **Office** column of the table view to the first position column of the table to the left of the **Brand** column.

Also remove the **Brand** column, deleting it from the **Criteria** tab selected columns.

Save the report:

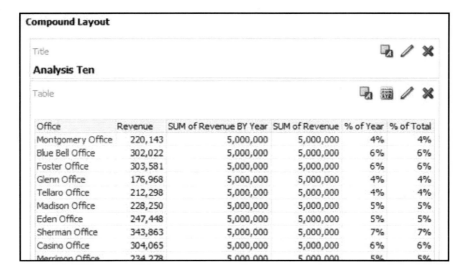

Agents and Action Framework

Now we will edit the **Office** column properties to add a parameterized Action Link. We follow the same process as the previous edit of interaction functionality, but this time we choose the **Navigate to a Web Page** option when doing so.

Click on the **Criteria** tab and then click the **Column Properties** option from the **Office** column's properties menu. Click on the Interaction tab and expand **Value** > **Primary Interaction** to select the **Action Links** option.

Click the green + button to add a new action link. Click the green gear icon button and select **Navigate to a Web Page**. This opens a prompt where we can define the web address and parameters that we may want to pass.

Enter the following web address, in the **URL** field:

`https://www.google.co.uk/search?q=@{1}`

Next click the **Define Parameters** button:

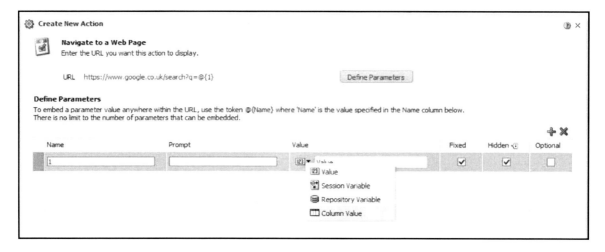

On the **Create New Action** prompt we should review a few elements. Firstly, you specified the **URL**, which defines the web page by which to navigate. Next, we wanted to be able to dynamically pass in the Office name of any item we select from our tabular analysis results so we need to set up a *Parameter*. Luckily, a parameter is automatically defined for you denoted by the `@{1}` characters that were added to the end of the **URL** that you entered after you clicked the **Define Parameters** button.

Check the **Fixed** and **Hidden** checkboxes. Uncheck the **Optional** checkbox for the row.

Remove any values from the **Prompt** column field for the row as we don't want to prompt the user, we simply want this to be a transparent experience when they click on the Office name.

The syntax, `@{1}`, for passing a parameter is straightforward. The numeric (can be alphanumeric) value in this case, **1**, identifies the parameter entry in the **Name** column of the **Define Parameters** area. You can also add more parameters by yourself to identify more dynamic or static parameters as needed.

The `Define Parameters` table is where we define the IDs (**Name** column) and the **Value** that we are passing. Note that we are passing the actual value of the column selected at runtime, but we could pass a static value or a variable.

We could also prompt the user for a value, but we do not need this in our example, so we have left the **Prompt** label column empty and marked the prompt as **Fixed** (the value passed cannot be changed) and **Hidden** (the user does not need to see the value passed as we already have it in the column they are clicking).

Having chosen that we are passing dynamically a column value, let's choose the actual column, **Offices.Office**, which we need to pass in by clicking on the **Column Value** option and then from the little down arrow to the right of the value field column selecting the "**Offices**"."**Office**" option:

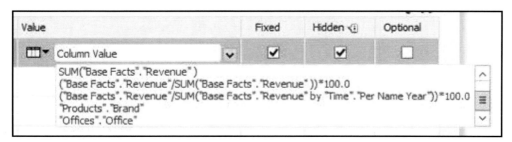

Click the **OK** button.

Now in the **Link Text** field enter the value, `Search Google for Latest News`, so this will be the name of the Action Link that users see when they click on the row value of the column.

Before closing the prompts, let's add some conditionality to the Action Link.

Adding some conditionality

You may have noticed in our first example that we had the option to conditionally show a link. Our current example will use the **Conditionality** option shown in the **New Action Link...** prompt.

Click the **Conditionality** option of the **Show Link** section and then click on the filter icon image and select the **Revenue** item:

Like any filter, we need an operator and a value to provide the scenario, which qualifies to prove true in order to show the desired result. In this case, we will set the value to 250,000 and the operator to **is greater than or equal to**.

Click **OK** to complete the condition:

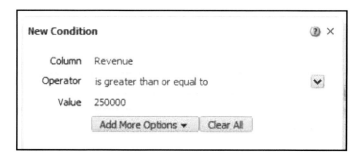

Click the **OK** button to close the **New Action Link** prompt.

 There is a checkbox option on the Column Properties, Interaction tab **Do not display in a popup if only one action link is available at runtime**, which enables a user to click on a link value and immediately trigger the action link if only one action exists, instead of showing the action link description to then be clicked.

Now click **OK** again to close the **Column Properties** prompt.

Save the analysis.

Note that we can also save and store an action in the presentation catalog, just like a filter or Agent. This is useful if we commonly need to use the same action in multiple reports.

Run the report by clicking on the **Results** tab and then clicking on the Preview icon in the results editor toolbar, selecting the Default option:

Analysis Ten

Office	Revenue	SUM of Revenue BY Year	SUM of Revenue	% of Year	% of Total
Montgomery Office	220,143	5,000,000	5,000,000	4%	4%
Blue Bell Office	302,022	5,000,000	5,000,000	6%	6%
Foster Office	303,581	5,000,000	5,000,000	6%	6%
Glenn Office	176,968	5,000,000	5,000,000	4%	4%
Tellaro Office	212,298	5,000,000	5,000,000	4%	4%
Madison Office	228,250	5,000,000	5,000,000	5%	5%
Eden Office	247,448	5,000,000	5,000,000	5%	5%
Sherman Office	343,863	5,000,000	5,000,000	7%	7%
Casino Office	304,065	5,000,000	5,000,000	6%	6%
Merrimon Office	234,278	5,000,000	5,000,000	5%	5%
Perry Office	290,749	5,000,000	5,000,000	6%	6%
Eiffel Office	353,699	5,000,000	5,000,000	7%	7%
Spring Office	369,523	5,000,000	5,000,000	7%	7%
Mills Office	292,520	5,000,000	5,000,000	6%	6%
College Office	172,104	5,000,000	5,000,000	3%	3%
Guadalupe Office	202,370	5,000,000	5,000,000	4%	4%

We have modified the report slightly, but note that the Conditionality works and that only the Office names having revenue of $250,000 or greater have links associated with them.

Let's test the link by clicking on an **Office** name, for example **Spring Office**, and then click the **Search Google for Latest News** option Action Link:

We are sent to the Google search site with the **Spring Office** as the main search criteria. Note in the URL that our column value for the Office name has been passed as a parameter, as we had set up and envisioned.

Note on Invoke Actions

In addition to the **navigate** type of Actions, we can also **Invoke Actions**. Invoked Actions are those that allow you to manipulate functions and processes outside of OBIEE via a variety of methods. You can create Actions that invoke the following:

- Web Service
- Java method
- Browser script
- HTTP request

This is an advanced topic and beyond the scope of this book. But if your organization or client is interested in truly incorporating OBIEE into their workflow with products such as E-Business Suite, Oracle Process Manager, and so on, then you should take some time to look into these options via Oracle documentation `https://docs.oracle.com/middleware/1221/biee/BIEUG/actions.htm#BIEUG644`.

These Actions can be used to simply bring back information from an external system into a dashboard for a user to reference, or even to update an external system directly as a result of an analysis being executed in OBIEE. For example, you may have noticed that when creating an Agent, there is a tab for adding an action. We could create an Agent that periodically runs and if it produces a certain result, feed that into an invoke action to update an external system. We can also create Actions that can be invoked directly from a dashboard. The potential for automating your workflows as a central step inside of an analytics system have increased greatly with this release.

A review - what I should know now!

For self review and recap of the chapter, here are a few questions based on topics covered in this chapter:

- What is an Agent?
- How do I send an analysis by e-mail?
- How do I send an alert to a dashboard?
- What is an action?
- How do I pass a parameter to a web address?
- What types of Actions can I create?

Additional research suggestions

- Help files in the **Presentation** Catalog

Oracle documentation on Actions

- https://docs.oracle.com/middleware/1221/biee/BIEUG/actions.htm#BIEUG644
- Oracle Documentation on Delivering Content:

  https://docs.oracle.com/middleware/1221/biee/BIEUG/delivers.htm#BIEUG280

Summary

This is a very basic introduction to Agents and Actions. We hope that you can see the potential for flexibility that they can bring to your existing IT investments. There are near boundless opportunities for automation, increased navigation, and workflow processing.

As we have mentioned in other chapters, to add this functionality without confusing your users, (with a plethora of unnecessary options), you will need to rely on a good education process with your end-users.

Business intelligence at its best is about managing by exception and creating a call to action. It should be providing insights that require you to explore, amend, or seek further possibilities in your business. With the Action Framework, Oracle has succeeded in putting emphasis on this allowing you to seek out how your Oracle BI system can lead users to actually process and change business.

10
Developing Reports Using BI Publisher

Oracle BI has fully integrated a common Oracle reporting technology that is almost ubiquitously embedded in Oracle Applications-**BI Publisher** (**BIP**). Once known as **XML Publisher** (**XMLP**), BI Publisher has been associated with analytics, reporting, and business intelligence under the ranks of Oracle for a long time.

BI Publisher has the ability to connect to many disparate data sources, which makes it a very powerful tool within any organization's enterprise business intelligence toolbox. But the real power comes in two main forms--the ability to manipulate each report at a very granular level by modifying XML and the ability to print crisp, pixel-perfect reports, referred to as **highly formatted documents**.

Pixel-perfect reporting entails that Oracle BI Publisher has the ability to allow a report template to be developed in one of the BI Publisher's several template development outlets such as Microsoft Word (Template Builder for Word), Microsoft Excel (Analyzer for Excel), Adobe Reader, or a web-based interface, and then print a hard copy of the report to render exactly as it looks when developed on the computer. Several organizations leverage BI Publisher to print shipping labels, checks, invoices, W-2 forms, and utility statements. As an example, in the mail, you may receive a quarterly mutual funds investment statement complete with page headers, footers, page numbers, and charts, and not even know that potentially you are holding a document created dynamically via Oracle BI Publisher.

This chapter covers the main features of BI Publisher in order to get you up to speed in using the tool. We will also mention some of the new features of 12c. Oracle BI Publisher contains a lot of functionality and there are books out there that solely cover this tool. The material in this chapter is aimed at providing a crash course, which should give any reader enough hands-on exercises to get their feet wet and enough of a platform for further research and experimentation.

Don't miss the installation integration checkpoint!

It is important to know that Oracle BI Publisher 12c is provided in the core Oracle BI 12c installation. During the installation process, you are able to choose to install, or not to install, one or all of the three Oracle BI software suites--Oracle BI Enterprise Edition, Oracle BI Publisher, and Oracle Real-Time Decisions. All suites are selected to be installed by default. Toggling one or more of the options will determine the software that gets installed, but it also determines the default integration between these software items. By keeping Oracle BI and Oracle BI Publisher selected, the security integration with Fusion Middleware Security and other integration configurations are set during the installation. You cannot go back at a later time to modify this installation configuration. Any post-install integration would be a manual effort.

With that said, those previously exposed to BI Publisher will appreciate that BI Publisher 12c can still be installed as a standalone software. That is, it would function correctly and contain all of the features inherent with BI Publisher in the absence of the core OBIEE platform component (presentation services, Oracle BI server, and so on) installation. This configuration could be required in some circumstances, such as an organization only purchasing a license for Oracle BI Publisher. This book focuses on the default installation integration option (that is, both Oracle BI Enterprise Edition and Oracle BI Publisher selected during the components installation configuration) and will continue with that as a prerequisite for all subsequent exercises.

As a quick side note, even when Oracle BI and Oracle BI Publisher are installed on the same server, as per the default installation configuration, BI Publisher continues to leverage its legacy standalone application context root, which can be accessed via the following URL, `http://<server_name>:<default_port>/ xmlpublisher`.

The default installation configures BI Publisher with the Fusion Middleware Security options. Users can potentially log in to both the `/xmlpublisher` application path and the `/analytics` application path. BI Publisher is still ultimately administered via the BI Publisher Administration page interface, although a link exists on the Oracle BI Presentation Services Administration page, which merely navigates to the BI Publisher Administration page.

What's all this XML talk?

The original name of BI Publisher was XML Publisher. The original name emphasized the basis of the tool--XML. At its debut, it was one of the only, if not the only tool that leveraged the power of the XML open standard to retain its core metadata. This is still true, even though the name of the tool has changed. XML is ubiquitous throughout the Web. Just about all major report vendors and web technologies can consume, parse, or otherwise leverage XML to produce dynamic information. A good example of this would be the **Portable Document Format** (**PDF**) standard, with which BI Publisher interacts seamlessly.

The basic development functionality of BI Publisher is straightforward and provides excellent results. However, the greatest flexibility of developing with BI Publisher comes when knowledge about advanced XML formatting can be leveraged. In BI Publisher's core all details, datasets, templates, and other data are stored as XML. These XML files can be manipulated manually or via the GUI interface. For basic efforts, manual editing of the XML is likely not required. However, when attempting novel solutions and advanced customizations, manual editing of the XML is preferred. Ramping up on your XML knowledge is a great idea in general and it is highly recommended when engaging with BI Publisher development.

Where does BI Publisher excel?

Yes, BI Publisher is now published reporting.

Reports created in BI Publisher should be called a **published report**. This is to differentiate from ad-hoc reports in the rest of the OBIEE system, which we have discussed, for example, **analyses**. Keep in mind that Oracle BI cannot create an ad-hoc analysis request with the same pixel-perfect perfection that a published report from BI Publisher can. So the distinction in nomenclature is warranted from both a technical and functional perspective.

The act of creating an analysis request, dashboard, dashboard prompt, filter, or condition is referred to as **interactive reporting**. You can see this description, **Analysis and Interactive Reporting**, from the Oracle BI 12c portal **Home** page under the **Create...** section. You can also see a link to **Published Reporting** (what we are concerned with in this chapter) in the same section in the following screenshot:

Ultimately, the gist is that there is some overlap. This is largely due to Oracle integrating multiple standalone products into its reporting suite. The overlap will drive the need to clarify on terms and nomenclature. There is no doubt that nomenclature will become more refined as the Oracle BI roadmap goes forward. For now, it can't be emphasized enough that every organization should ensure that consistent nomenclature and terminology is used, so that confusion is mitigated.

Oracle BI Foundation versus Oracle BI Publisher

When to use Oracle BI instead of Oracle BI Publisher is a common question. The question has become more frequent since the integration of Oracle BI Publisher inside the Oracle BI Enterprise Edition platform. Unfortunately, the answer to the question is itself a question-- *what are the primary reporting requirements?* The reason for the rebuttal question is due to the subtle differences in the tools. Oracle BI and Oracle BI Publisher have their individual strengths and weaknesses. A few follow-up questions like these might follow:

- Will the reports be delivered externally to clients for formal presentation?
- Do these reports need to be printed in a certain format consistently?
- Do reports need to be available in both online and print format?
- Will the documents need to be sent automatically to a printer or fax?
- Will reports get built dynamically or programmatically via code?
- Can the report developers upload their own data sources?
- Do watermarks need to be added to reports?

If the answer is yes to any of these questions, that places a check in the column for Oracle BI Publisher. Clearly more questions along these lines should be asked with the purpose of exposing the pros and cons of each.

Operational reporting is another scenario that gets brought into the conversation when determining which tool to leverage. Both tools can be used for **Operational Data Store (ODS)** type reporting requirements, but with Oracle BI Publisher's Interactive Viewer, another check just may go into the column for BI Publisher. OBIEE can also handle this, but with more of a top-down approach and enterprise deployment cycle.

Ultimately, OBIEE contains analysis and interactive reporting tools for building ad-hoc queries, dashboards, and distributed reporting architecture. Oracle BI Publisher reports can be displayed in Oracle BI portal dashboards and can also be distributed via the Oracle BI platform's distributed reporting and delivery architecture, or via its own standalone tools and configuration. With such flexibility and each having certain unique capabilities, it is not a surprise that these two tools are now seamlessly integrated into the Oracle BI 12c software product suite.

New features and enhancements

Following are the new features and enhancement.

Improved Oracle BI 12c look and feel

The rewrite that took place on the Oracle BI 12c platform also applies to Oracle BI Publisher 12c. The clean Web 2.0 interface makes the **user experience** (**UX**) working with BI Publisher much more intuitive. In addition to new graphics, layout, and features, the biggest enhancement that relates to the look and feel is the improved ability to create the pixel-perfect template and reports within the web-based interface. There are many changes, such as custom fonts, which enable you to present your reports in a more attractive manner. This has built in the massive step forward from the previous 11g version.

Delivering documents to the cloud

Oracle, in line with industry trends, has placed a lot of emphasis on the cloud. In 12c, as well as all of the other normal destinations for a report, you can deliver reports to Oracle's cloud storage, ready for others to access.

Better encryption and security

12c also allows the enabling of encryption so that files uploaded to the cloud are secure. You can also enable the use of PGP keys very easily, so only authorized persons can view your reports.

Report design basics, terminology, and locations

As we have mentioned, the integration between BI Publisher and OBIEE can be confusing. Aside from basic terminology, it is important to note the nuances that exist because of this integration. That is to say, many people assume that basic items such as data sources are one and the same for BI Publisher as they are for Oracle BI, which is false. This section highlights a few basic terms that will be used throughout this chapter when stepping through the development of reports. It will also highlight when to go where for what as it relates to basic management of BI Publisher and the integration with Oracle BI 12c.

Report design components

Several components must be configured before adding a table, dropdown, or otherwise building a report in BI Publisher. Here are the basic items that will comprise most reports that you will develop.

Data model

BI Publisher must use one or more data sources and/or subsets of data datasets that can be used in one or more reports. The structure in which these items are defined is referred to as a **data model**. It also provides the structure and relationship between datasets. Both complex datasets and simple data sets (such as a list of values, parameters, and other metadata) are configured here.

A data model usually has the ability to configure one or more data sets, event triggers, flexfields, list of values, parameters, and bursting property options. A BI Publisher data model is not an RPD. It cannot be leveraged as a source for creating ad-hoc analysis requests in Oracle BI presentation services.

Layout

In order for data to be presented as desired in a report, there first must be a design. A layout consists of a template file and a set of properties for rendering the template file. Legacy template design tools such as MS Word and MS Excel still exist. However, with Oracle BI 12c, the template design can dynamically take place in the BI Publisher GUI for true Web 2.0 functionality.

Properties

Properties allow you to control design formatting, display, and generation of the report.

Translations

BI Publisher allows for both catalog translation and template translation. Both are achieved via an export, translate, and import process, and by leveraging the open standard **XML Localization Interchange File Format** (**XLIFF**) to handle the structuring of this process. The template translation is ultimately a way to translate just the final report presented by metadata. A catalog translation can potentially translate all objects in the BI Publisher catalog. Both translation types can handle multiple local code translations.

Where to administer BI Publisher

Security is always a good starting point when learning a new tool. Without it, you have no control on the application. As mentioned before, BI Publisher could stand alone as its own FMW application. In a standalone BI Publisher deployment, security can be configured using FMW security or several other authentication and authorization types. In either case, the BI Publisher Administration page can be located by accessing the following URL, `http://<server_name>:9704/xmlpserver/ servlet/admin`. During the default Oracle BI installation configuration, BI Publisher is automatically configured to be embedded within OBIEE. This means that the BI Publisher Administration page can also be accessed by clicking on the **Manage BI Publisher** link in the OBIEE Administration page: `http://<server_name>:9704/ analytics/saw.dll?Admin`. Both administration pages require you to log in with user credentials having administration (BI Administrator role) privileges, such as the WebLogic administrator user account.

Default embedded BI Publisher configurations

Based on the default Oracle BI suite installation and configuration, the transparent integration between Oracle BI Foundation and BI Publisher is made. This default setting implies several configurations:

- BI Publisher Security is set to Fusion Middleware Security
- Files such as BI Publisher data sets, templates, and so on, are stored in the Presentation Catalog
- BI Publisher administration can be accessed from the Oracle BI Administration page and the BI Publisher/xmlpserver application
- BI Publisher integration with Oracle BI Presentation services is automatically configured for the default instance of Presentation services that are installed on the same server
- A BI Publisher JDBC data source pointing to the Oracle BI ODBC port `9502` is created by default, so that BI Publisher can use certain Oracle BI objects as data sources

Where to build a data model

A data model defines the data sets that we can use to build one or more reports. The data model can be created via the `/xmlpserver` application URL or the/analytics application URL. The former is primarily used for standalone BI Publisher deployments, although you could also use it when full integration with the Oracle BI 12c suite has been deployed on your server.

> For the exercises in this book, you can use the Oracle BI 12c analytics portal--`http://<server_name>:9704/analytics/`--unless otherwise stated.

Where to add a data source connection

Out-of-the-box, data source connections cannot be created in BI Publisher unless you have administration privileges. More importantly, the only place to create a new data source, which may be used globally in BI Publisher, is within the Oracle BI Publisher **Administration** page. This centralizes data source creation across the application. It also allows an administrator to restrict access to the predefined data sources. As mentioned in the preceding section, the BI Publisher **Administration** page can be accessed via two options. The following screenshots shows the **Data Sources** control section within the BI Publisher **Administration** page:

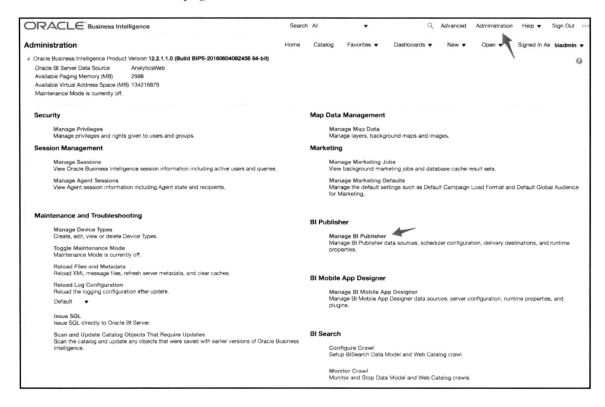

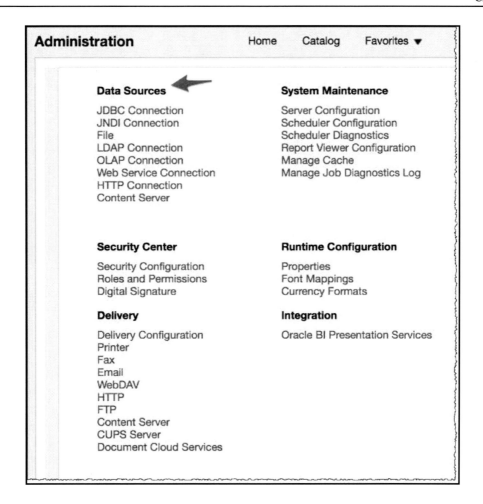

What is a JNDI data source?

From the myriad of data sources that BI Publisher can access, one is simply labeled as a JNDI connection. Most people that have general data warehousing experience know what the other four types of data source connections are. However, as for JNDI, it is somehow elusive.

Java Naming and Directory Interface (JNDI) is a powerful type of connection that resides on the application server (in this case, WebLogic Server) and is especially favorable for using with deployed JEE applications that are related in some way. More importantly it provides a means to connect to a JDBC data source, via a connection pool. Connection pools create certain efficiencies in applications when multiple users are querying the same data source from one or more applications. The JNDI connection must be established on the application server itself and cannot be accomplished from the BI Publisher interface. In this case, you would have to open the WebLogic Server Administration Console and navigate to **Services** | **Data Sources** to create a new JNDI connection. Once the JNDI connection has been created, the JNDI connection name/alias can be entered in the **JNDI Name** field while creating that data source type in BI Publisher.

Let's get publishing

As promised, the rest of this chapter will get you rolling with hands-on exercises for learning BI Publisher. Here, the goal is to step through the critical parts for setting up a BI Publisher 12c environment, creating a report or two, and preparing a report for delivery. Along the way, we will highlight features that you should keep an eye out for, research on your own at a later date, or simply understand to make your development cycles easier.

Let's start with administration. Because without that, there isn't much else you, or any of your users, will be able to do.

Administration management of BI Publisher

This section gets away from the theory and core explanations that you've read so far. You will take a step-by-step journey through a real-world implementation. This includes how to assess the Fusion Middleware Security application roles, create several data sources, and ensure that application roles have access to the desired data sources. All of this effort prepares you for creating an actual BI Publisher--sorry (!)--Published Reporting report.

Accessing the BI Publisher Administration page

Getting to the **Administration** page is the first step in this process. Start by following these steps:

1. Log in to the Oracle BI Analytics portal: `http://<server_name>:<default_port>/analytics/`, with the WebLogic administrator user credentials.
2. Click on the **Administration** link in the global header section that we showed you in a previous screenshot.
3. In the subsection labeled as **BI Publisher**, click on the **Manage BI Publisher** link.

> The first time you click on this link, the page may not seem to render correctly. Wait for 3 minutes or so for the contents of the page to render as this may be the first time that the BI Publisher application /xmlpublisher has been called.

Verifying application roles

From the BI Publisher Administration page, verify the existing application roles available from FMW Security. Again, FMW Security aims to manage all privileges by application roles as a more streamlined way of organizing users from multiple identity providers. It is also an open standard way of authorization:

1. Click on the **Security Configuration** link under the **Security Center** subsection.
2. Scroll down to the bottom of the page and notice that, as per the default installation configuration, BI Publisher security has been set up to use the Oracle Fusion Middleware authorization model:

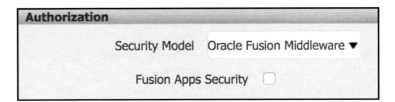

[373]

3. Scroll back to the top of the page and click on the **Roles and Permissions** tab:

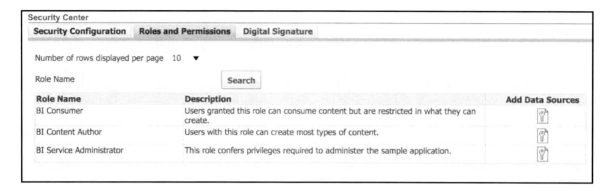

4. Review the application roles available under this tab. These are the same application roles that were created in Chapter 6, *Understanding the Systems Management Tools*.

Notice how an application role, which doesn't show here, is the authenticated user role. This application role has special properties within Fusion Middleware Security. Special consideration should be taken before removing this role from the Enterprise Manager Fusion Middleware Control application roles panel. But if your project's security calls for stringent control and you need to remove this role, please note that this will immediately affect the BI Consumer application role and all other principals related to it.

Creating the data source JDBC connection

As a prerequisite to this chapter, you should have already deployed a database to your relational database management system. This exercise will make reference to the database dump conducted against OBIEE. The JDBC connection information should be similar if you are using a MySQL database, or in our case, an SQl Server DB:

1. Navigate back to the BI Publisher **Administration** page.
2. Click on **JDBC Connection.**
3. On the **JDBC** tab, click on the **Add Data Source** button.
4. Enter your database connection information in the fields available under the **General** section of the **Add Data Source** page.
5. In the **Data Source Name** field, enter `AdventureDB`.

6. Click on the **Test Connection** button to validate that the information entered is accurate and returns a successful test message:

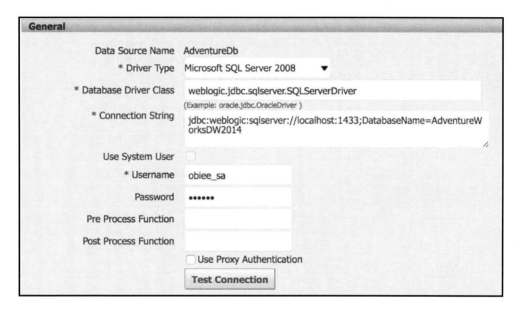

7. Scroll down to the bottom of the page and focus on the **Security** section.
8. Select **BI Content Author** in the **Available Roles** column and use the **Move** button to add this role to the **Allowed Roles** column:

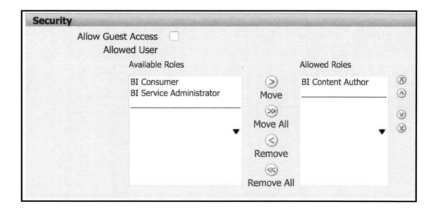

9. Scroll back to the top of the **Add Data Source** page.
10. Click on the **Apply** button located towards the right of the page.

Creating a file (XLS) data source

In order to use any type of file as a data source with BI Publisher, the potential data source filesystem location must be declared as a data source, using the same principle as creating any other connection. The interesting thing about the filesystem data source is that you have to assign a top-level filesystem directory as the source, and not the individual file itself, in the **Administration** page. At a later time, this allows you to either upload the file or leverage a file that exists in the data source directory as a feed for your reports. To keep it simple, let's create a **File** data source in a readily available path on your server:

1. In the BI Publisher Administration page, click on the **File** link under the **Data Sources** subsection.
2. We will use OBIEE sample data that we can see if data source name and file directory:

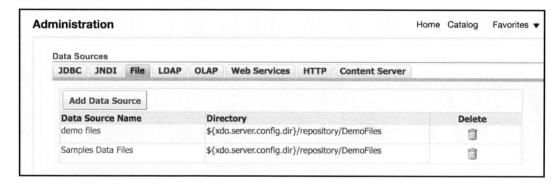

Alternatively, if we had our own file we could click on the **Add Data Source** button and add a name in the **Data Source Name** field. Then in the **Full Path of the Top-level Directory** field, enter the folder that is located on the server where you have installed Oracle BI Publisher. On a Linux system, this may be /home/<user>/, for example.

If you are using an MS Windows OS, it may be necessary to enter the directory path using forward slashes and not the standard back slashes. This is usually due to the Java OS agnostic escaping of special characters of which a Nix system is already compliant when it comes to the handling of a directory path syntax.

3. Click on the **Data Source Name**. In the **Security** subsection, select **BI Content Author** in the **Available Roles** column and use the **Move** button to add this role to the **Allowed Roles** column.
4. Click on the **Apply** button located towards the right of the page.

Verifying application role data source privileges

After creating several data sources, there is a simple way to verify the data source assignment privileges for each application role:

1. On the BI Publisher Administration page, click on the **Roles and Permissions** link under the **Security Centre** subsection.
2. On the **BI Author Role** row, click on the key image under the **Add Data Sources** column:

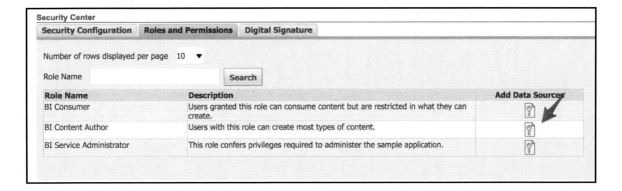

3. The resulting page, **Add Data Sources: BI Author Role**, shows all assigned data source privileges from the data sources created so far:

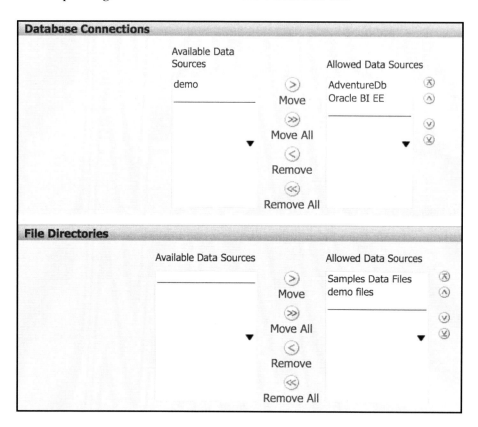

 Please note that this is not the same as row-level security. It merely denotes the data sources that users assigned to the BI Author application role are allowed to access.

4. Scroll back to the top of this page and click on the **Cancel** button towards the top-right of the page.

Be aware that the session timeout settings differ in BI Publisher when compared to Oracle BI Foundation Presentation services. You may be conducting configurations in the BI Publisher **Administration** page via Oracle BI Presentation services and notice that some commands don't function properly. This may be due to your BI Publisher session timing out. If so, click on the **Administration** link in the global header again and navigate to **Manage BI Publisher** once more.

Setting up a data model

Now that the data sources have been created, the **data model** modeling can begin. Th following is a standard initial process:

1. Plan and select the data sources.
2. Create a data model.

A helpful hint for any administrator is to plan out the initial process as diligently as possible to avoid a maintenance burden.

During the creation of data sources, enter proper descriptions, and keep notes as to why the data sources were created. Due to the ease of adding data sources without enterprise top-down guidance, as in the Oracle BI metadata repository RPD, it is easy to have superfluous or nonutilized data sources cluttering the tool. Part of a BI Publisher administrator's duties may be to design a solid security model that restricts the number of users who can build a data model in order to keep the number of data models in the system manageable. On that note, let's get cracking with creating our first simple data model.

This exercise and the remainder of the development exercises will take place in the Oracle BI Presentation Services portal. Although the BI Publisher environment /xmlpserver application can be used for development, our examples follow the principle that the two environments are fully integrated and the most common entry point to the system will be the OBIEE Presentation services.

[379]

Developing Reports Using BI Publisher

Creating a new Presentation Catalog folder

As with **Object Orient Programming** (**OOP**), all Oracle BI artefacts should be organized in a way that common artefacts are grouped together and made able to be easily repurposed whenever possible. Oracle BI Publisher 12c provides this capability to reuse data models across multiple reports. Let's begin by creating the container folder:

1. Log in to the Oracle BI /analytics portal with the WebLogic or BI Admin administrator user credentials.
2. Click on the **Catalog** link in the global header.
3. On the **Catalog** page, click on the **Shared Folders** folder in the **Folders** pane.
4. Click on the **New** icon from the menu bar and click on the new **Folder** icon to create a new folder:

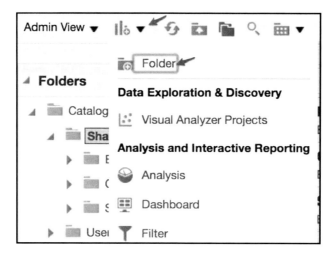

5. Name the folder as `BI Publisher Reports` when the **New Folder** prompt appears.
6. You should now have a folder named `BI Publisher Reports` under the `Shared Folders` catalog directory. In the next step, we will create a data model and add it to this folder.

Creating a new data model

In this section, you will create a single data model for the finance reports that we will create soon:

1. Click on the **New** dropdown from the **Global Header** section and select the **Data Model** option under the **Published Reporting** section:

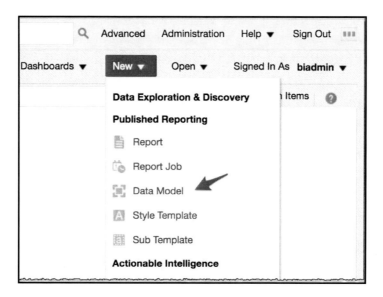

2. On the resulting page (or under **Properties**), several fields are available to begin entering metadata for the data model.
3. In the **Description** field, enter `Finance`.
4. In the **Default Data Source** field, change the drop-down field value to **AdventureDB:**

Developing Reports Using BI Publisher

5. Click on the Save disk icon in the upper-right corner of the web page. It is located underneath the **Sign Out** link area. The **Save As** dialog box will appear.
6. In the **Name** field, change the Untitled value to Finance.
7. Select the BI Publisher Reports folder, which you created in the previous exercise, from the the dialog box on the left-hand side of the page.
8. Click on the **OK** button in the **Save As** dialog box to complete the operation.

A data model can hold one or more related or unrelated data sets. Data sets are the means to which the data we wish to populate reports is organized. The first data set to create is one that allows the data in our AdventureWorks database to be joined logically. Even though a relationship may exist at the physical database via a primary key/foreign key relationship, it must still be logically represented in BI Publisher. This logical representation of the relationships allows the GUI interface to manage and optimize queries, parameterization, and so on. Follow the next steps to create a simple data set for the main report that you will create.

9. Open the **Finance1** data model, created while following the steps mentioned in the preceding section, if it is not already open.
10. Expand the **Data Model** node in the left pane of the **Data Model Editor** and click on the **Data Sets** option:

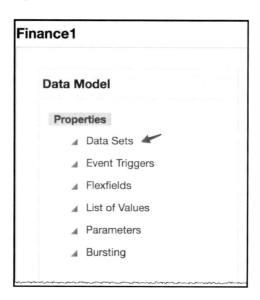

11. The main editor window will show that the **Diagram** tab is selected and the **Global Level Functions** layout node is available.
12. Click on the new data set icon and select the **SQL Query** option:

13. In the New Data Set - SQL Query prompt:
14. Enter `Finance` in the **Name** field.
15. Select the **AdventureDB** option from the **Data Source** drop-down list.
16. Click on the **Query Builder** button in order to select the SQL tables that will comprise the data set.

Creating an SQL query data set

The **Query Builder** window will open and the data source's available objects will be listed on the left pane of the window:

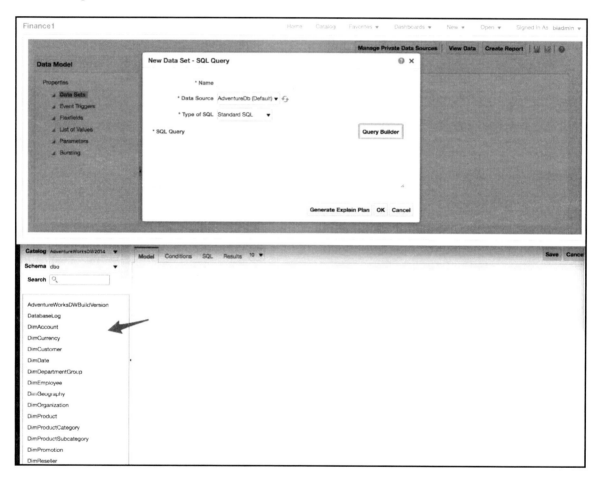

Note that we can see the warehouse physical tables. You can also swap between DB catalogs and schema, and search for objects in the left pane.
Click on the following tables in the left pane of the window to bring them into the main panel of the **Query Builder**: `FactFinance`, `DimOrganization, DimDate, DimScenario, DimDepartmentGroup,` and `DimAccount`.

Join the tables with their respective relationships by clicking on the empty box corresponding to the column of each table where a relationship exists:

1. Click on the empty box besides the **OrganizationKey** column of the `DimOrganization` table.
2. Now click on the empty box besides the **OrganizationKey** column in the `FactFinance` table.
3. This creates the join between the two tables. The join is indicated by a light blue line:

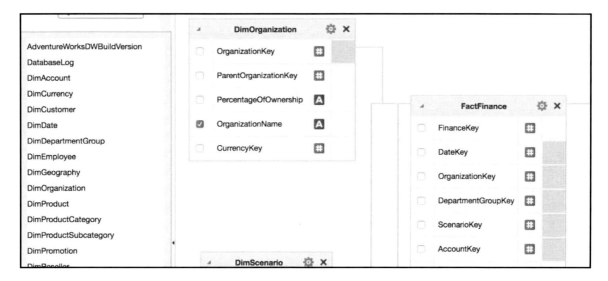

4. Check the checkbox next to **OrganizationName** in the `DimOrganization` table.
5. The join will be successful, but the columns that will be retrieved from that table will not be defined. For defined surface columns in a dataset, the checkbox corresponding to the desired column of each table must be checked.
6. Using the same join routine as mentioned in the preceding step, join the following table (column) references below the respective columns in the `FactFinance` table:
    - **DimDate (DateKey)** to **DateKey**
    - **DimScenario (ScenarioKey)** to **ScenarioKey**
    - **DimDepartmentGroup (DepartmentGroupKey)** to **DepartmentGroupKey**
    - **DimAccount (AccountKey)** to **AccountKey**

7. To surface the correct column fields that we wish to use in a report, click on the checkbox corresponding to the following table (column) references:
    - **DimDate (CalendarYear)**
    - **DimScenario (ScenarioName)**
    - **DimDepartmentGroup (DepartmentGroupName)**
    - **DimAccount (AccountType)**
8. Click on the **Save** button in the **Query Builder** window.
9. This will return you to the **New Data Set - SQL Query** window. This window will show the joins that have been made during your interaction with the Query Builder. However, the generated syntax is not always the best syntactically or the most optimized for your specific database. So when you click **OK**, you may experience an error. Advanced queries should leverage a predefined SQL to save time and ensure accuracy. Create your SQL in a SQL IDE, such as Oracle SQL Developer first, and then copy and paste it into the **SQL Query** field. This is often a best practice. As a shortcut, remove the content from the **SQL Query** field and type or paste in the following more advanced SQL statement. This will give us a simple data set to play with:

```
select  dg.DepartmentGroupName,
        d.CalendarYear,
        sum(f.Amount)
from
        DimDepartmentGroup dg,

        DimDate d,

        FactFinance f
where   ( dg.DepartmentGroupKey = f.DepartmentGroupKey and
          d.DateKey = f.DateKey )
group by dg.DepartmentGroupName, d.CalendarYear
```

We are using SQL Server and our sum function here may result in an unwieldy `float` datatype. We can change this to a double using `sum(cast(f.Amount as decimal(30,4)))`.

[386]

10. Click on the **OK** button to close the **Create Data Set - SQL** window.
11. The resulting data set will be displayed in the main editor pane and also in the left pane with the name that we have defined:

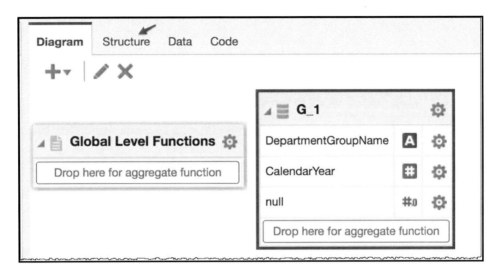

Adjusting data set display names

Each data set has the ability to represent columns with an alias just like in a standard SQL. Using the Query Builder, the names that would ultimately be shown to report developers and report viewers are the physical data source column names. However, they can be changed in the data set, so that these business names are there by default when development starts:

1. In the column under the **Business View** header, the **Display Name** column shows the value displayed for this data set column. Click in the field for each of the **Display Name** columns and change the values to the following business name representations.
2. Make sure the **Table View** option is selected.

3. Click on the **Structure** tab in the main editor window. The tabs are located directly above the option you selected earlier to create a data set:
   - `null` to `Revenue`
   - `DepartmentGroupName` to `Department`
   - `CalendarYear` to `Year`

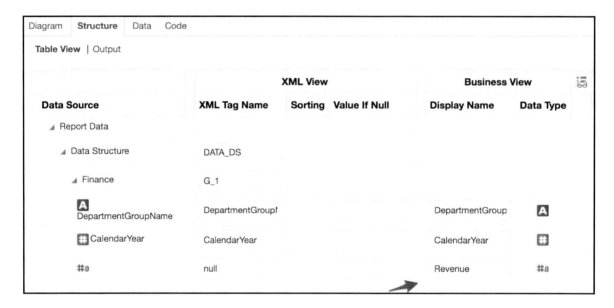

4. Click on the save disk icon to save the data model. The save disk icon is located under the **Sign Out** link in the upper-right corner of the web page.

Creating a parameter

By default, an SQL data set is static. That is to say that the current logic you have coded in your SQL statement will not change or be dynamically filtered. Static reports are too rigid to be effective in today's enterprise. So, parameterization or the ability to change a data set by passing a variable to replace a filtered value within the query creates a dynamic result. One or more parameter variables can be created for a data model. A parameter can be created explicitly just as you created a data set by selecting the option in the left pane and then creating the parameter in the main editor, or it can be done using the Data Set Editor itself. Now we'll conduct an exercise using the latter approach:

1. Return to the **Finance1** dataset.
2. Click on the **Diagram** tab in the Data Model Editor

3. Click on the data set to select it.
4. Click on the pencil icon for editing a data set from the menu under the **Diagram tab**.
5. In the **SQL Query** field, in the SQL statement, find the WHERE clause with the following syntax:

   ```
   where
   d.CalendarYear = 2013
   ```

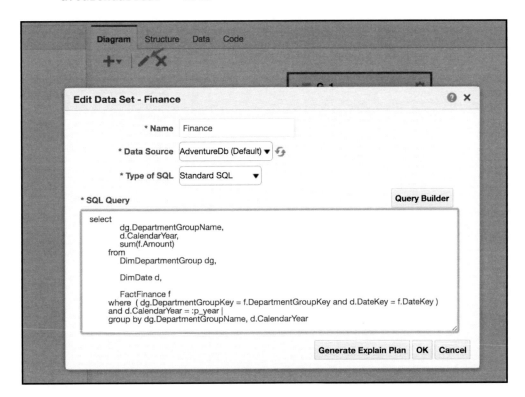

6. Click **OK** to check that your syntax is correct. Now edit the SQL query again and change the SQL syntax to the following by modifying the value 2001 to `:p_year` and `d.CalendarYear = :p_year`.
7. Ensure that the syntax is correct (that is, a colon : before `p_year`) and click on the **OK** button.

Developing Reports Using BI Publisher

8. Notice that after you click on the **OK** button, you are prompted with the following question: **Please select one or more bind variables to create corresponding parameters.**
9. Check the box by **p_year**:

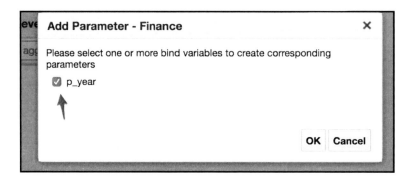

10. Click on the **OK** button to accept and you will be navigated to the **Parameters** tab of the Data Model. Notice that under the **Parameters** option, a new item now exists: p_year:

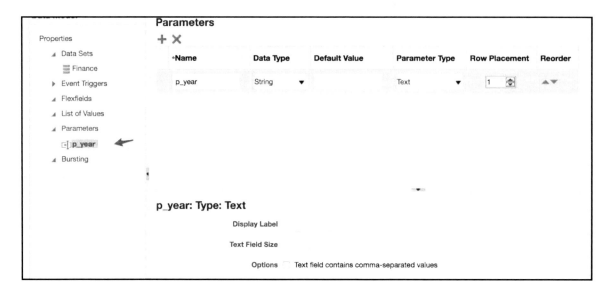

11. Make sure you save your Data Model before moving on.

[390]

Creating a list of values

A parameter is now in place to dynamically adjust the SQL query result set. A good idea is to provide a drop-down list, or similar, to allow for selecting one or more values to manipulate our new dynamic query. In BI Publisher, this is commonly referred to as a **list of values**. A list of values can be a hardcoded static list defined once, or it can stem from a data source query. This example uses the former approach. To create a static list of values follow these instructions:

1. Enter new values in the following column fields.
2. Click on the plus icon to add a new list of values.
3. Click on the **List of Values** option on the left-hand side pane of the data model:
    - Enter LOV_YEAR in the **Name** field.
    - Select **Fixed Data** from the **Type** dropdown.
4. A new sublevel appears after selecting the **Fixed Data** value from the **Type** dropdown.
5. Click on the plus icon in the sublevel table to create the first record of the static data. This will become a value in a drop-down list containing years that will get passed into the dataset.
6. Click on the green plus icon again to confirm the preceding input and create a new record.
7. Repeat steps 5 and 6 to enter values for years 2007 to 2017.

Developing Reports Using BI Publisher

8. Click on the **Save** button icon to save the data model:

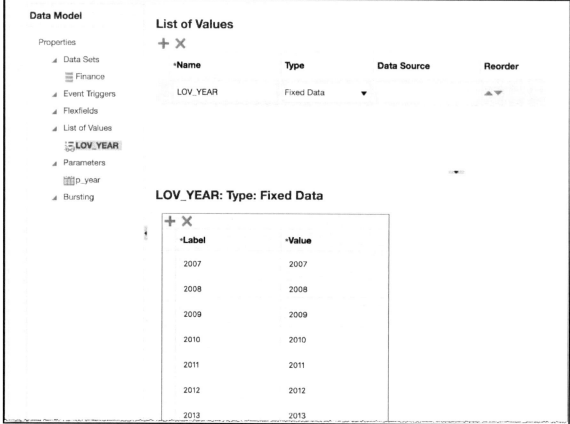

Connecting the parameter to the list of values

1. The p_year parameter is associated with the dataset, but now the list of values, LOV_YEAR, needs to be associated to the parameter. This is fairly straightforward and one of the last steps in wrapping up this data model exercise:
    - Change the **Data Type** column to **Integer**.
    - Enter 2006 in the **Default Value** column field.
    - Select **Menu** from the **Parameter Type** dropdown.

2. Click on the parameter `p_year` on the left pane of the Data Model Editor.
3. On the `p_year` row:
   - Change the **Display Label** value from the default value to `Year`
   - Change the **List of Values** dropdown to **LOV_YEAR**
4. Deselect the **Multiple Selection** and **Can select all** checkbox options.
5. Save the data model:

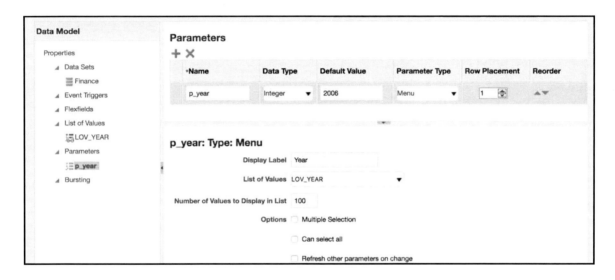

Getting the sample data

Once you are satisfied that the data model is complete for your data requirements (or even during the course of your iterative development), it is always a good idea to look at the data that now stems from your creation. BI Publisher looks at this as sampling your data. This sample data has three purposes. The first allows you to see that your data set has been created correctly and allows you to test your parameterizations and other properties on a small scale. The second allows you to see your data represented in XML format, which is ultimately how BI Publisher data is put together so that it can then leverage open standards for formatting, and so on. The third, is that, a sample data file will be saved in XML format, so that it can then be used to assist you in creating your reports without having to send repetitive queries back to the underlying data source.

Developing Reports Using BI Publisher

 The third point highlights a key distinction from report development with OBIEE's ad-hoc analysis tool versus the production reporting of BI Publisher. With OBIEE's Interactive Reporting, the focus is mostly on the consumption of data. So, even when developing the report, the query attempts to ping the underlying data source each time the analysis request is displayed. BI Publisher has a heavier focus on aesthetics. So, leveraging a sample data file prevents overhead and keeps an emphasis on production report development.

To get at the sample data, follow these instructions:

1. From the Data Model Editor, click on the **View Data** in the upper-right corner of the web page.
2. The resulting page shows the parameter for **Year** at the top of the page and also provides an option to select the number of rows that should be returned:

3. Change the **Year** dropdown to 2013.
4. Change the number of **Rows** to return to **50**.
5. Click on the **View** button.
6. The results are returned in the XML format and this sample set of data is ready to be saved as our sample data.

7. Select the **Save As Sample Data** option:

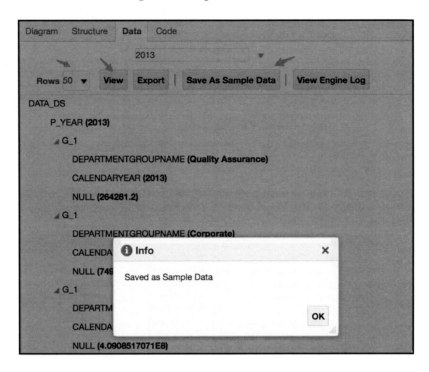

8. Review the Data Model Editor main page. Click on the data model parent level in the left-pane hierarchy, if not taken to this area by default. Under the **Attachment** section, you should see a listing for a `sample.xml` file:

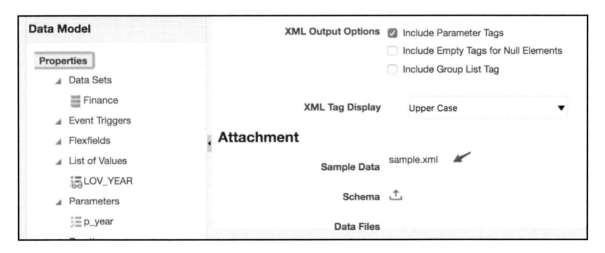

9. Save your data model again. You've successfully created a data model that provides some dynamic functionality. You should now have a good idea of how the baseline data source configurations are put together. Let's wrap up by creating a simple report, using the web-based GUI.

Creating a BI Publisher report using the Layout Editor

Just like the Data Model Editor, which handles the configuration of data sources by using a **Dynamic HyperText Markup Language** (**DHTML**) web-based interface, a complementing report design tool within BI Publisher--**Layout Editor**--also uses DHTML. Historically, BI Publisher users were relegated to using software suite (for example, MS Word) plugins in order to create templates to layout reports and ultimately publish those reports for consumption. Now, the same pixel-perfect layout and design efforts can be achieved in full Web 2.0 glory using the Layout Editor.

Some argue that using the software plugins to develop BI Publisher templates provides more control than what the Layout Editor currently provides. This is debatable.

Each time you attempt to create a published report in Oracle BI 12c, you will be prompted to select an existing data model, create a new one, or upload a spreadsheet to leverage as the data model.

You've created a simple data model in the exercise shown in the preceding section, so that it won't be a problem. After that selection is made, you'll be prompted to select a layout that defines the initial format of your report. You can create a new template, select from a set of very generic starter templates, upload an existing template, or have BI Publisher generate the layout for you based on the structure of the selected data model. You will use the latter option by following these steps:

1. From the global header, select **New** | **Report** under the **Published Reporting** section of the drop-down list:

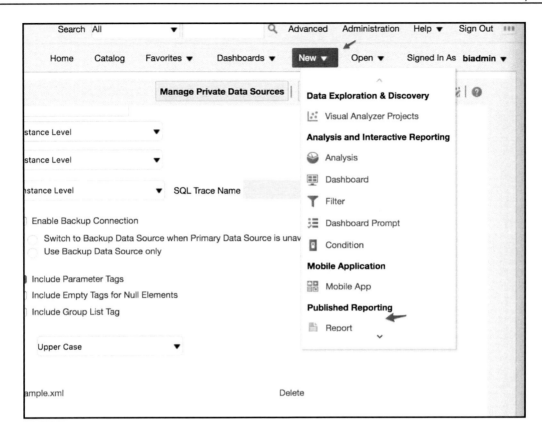

2. Select the **Use Data Model** option from the prompt that appears:

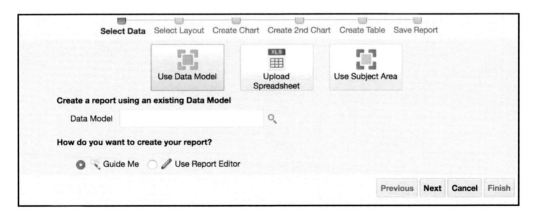

3. In the **Save In** dialog box.
4. Select the **Use Report Editor** option and click on the **Finish** button.
5. Select the `Finance1` file and click on the **OK** button.
6. Click on the magnifying glass and locate the `Finance1` data model file from the `Shared Folders/BI Publisher Reports` folder:
     - Save the file in the `BI Publisher Reports` folder. Of course, you should organize folders in a manner that is logical to your individual project requirements.
     - Enter `Departmental Finance Report` in the **Name** field by replacing any existing default text.
7. Click on the **OK** button to close the dialog box.
8. Click on the **Generate** page image under the **Upload** or **Generate Layout** section:

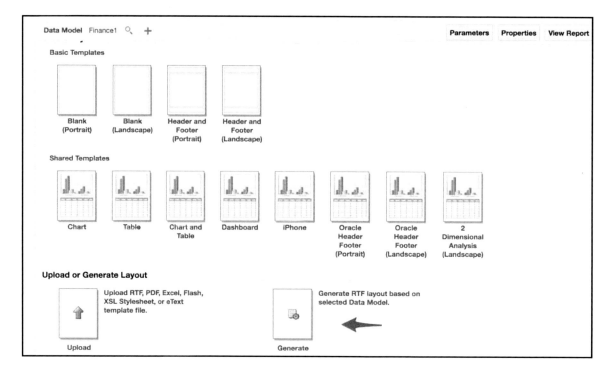

9. The **Auto Generate Layout** prompt will appear.

10. Enter `Revenue per Group` in the **Template Name** field:

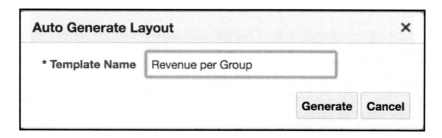

11. Click on the **Generate** button to confirm and initiate the autogenerate layout process. The resulting page shows the report's layout inventory page with a single autogenerated layout.
12. Most of what needs to be done next requires that you now save the report. Click on the save icon in the upper-right corner of the web page. As you may have guessed from the number of prompts in this walkthrough, you should frequently save reports as you develop to prevent loss of work!
13. Click on the **View Report** icon/link next to the save icon to display the autogenerated report:

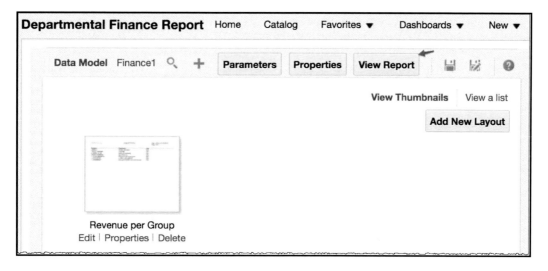

14. The **Revenue per Group** layout of the **Departmental Finance Report** is displayed in all of its very basic data grid glory, along with the parameterized **List of Values** dropdown at the top of the page.

15. Change the value in the **Year** dropdown to **2013** and click on the **Apply** button:

DepartmentGroupName	CalendarYear	Revenue
Quality Assurance	2013	264281.2000
Corporate	2013	7497631.5000
Sales and Marketing	2013	409085170.7100
Manufacturing	2013	548683.9800
Research and Development	2013	74122673.8900
Inventory Management	2013	34623729.3700
Executive General and Administration	2013	15836808.8700

16. Notice that the report changes.

The report is now at a stage where we could start modifying column names and representation to make the report more meaningful. We could also add charts. Using the basic functionality and nice autogenerate feature of the Layout Editor, you saw how easy it is to leverage an existing data model to build a quick report. You can see that a published report can contain one or more layouts. Those layouts can stem from templates designed using the Layout Editor or from an uploaded template from one of the software plugins. The standard data format for a template is a **Rich Text Format** (**RTF**) file noted by the RTF file extension. This published report could now be embedded in an Oracle BI dashboard in the /analytics portal for user consumption or for quick export to MS Excel, if one is only after the data.

We have gone through a basic example in creating and publishing a report. Go ahead and experiment!

Auditing and monitoring BI Publisher

Oracle BI Publisher 12c has the capability to retrieve and analyze data on the way users interact with the tool. As a mainly web- based consumption tool for reporting, users are always logging in to the system, viewing reports, and spending time analyzing data. It's clear that there is a need, from both security compliance and performance improvement perspectives, to collect information regarding how users are using the tool. Since BI Publisher 12c is integrated with Oracle Fusion Middleware, it can leverage the Fusion Middleware Audit Framework.

Spelunking through log files for this information is in the past. The auditing system information can be dumped to a file's system log or a relational database. Clearly with the relational database as the repository, BI Publisher, or some other reporting tool, can easily consume that data feed and put up some quality auditing analytics. This is fairly straightforward to set up and configure. This exercise will walk you through how to achieve this ancillary configuration.

Modifying a few configuration files

This is fairly straightforward. Two files need to be configured so that BI Publisher can recognize the change for capturing and writing the audit information. The following steps should take place on the server where BI Publisher and the Oracle BI server are installed:

1. Locate the `xmlp-server-config.xml` file. This file is located down the long directory path of `$BI_HOMEuser_projectsdomainsbifoundation_domainconfigbipublisherrepositoryAdminConfiguration`.
2. Edit the `xmlp-server-config.xml` file using WordPad or a similar program.
3. Set the following element value properties to true from their default value of false: `MONITORING_ENABLED AUDIT_ENABLED`
4. Add the following element and syntax to the `xmlp-server-config.xml` file directly before the closing `</xmlpConfig>` tag: `<property name="AUDIT_JPS_INTEGTRATION" value="true" />`
5. Save and close the `xmlp-server-config.xml` file.

Developing Reports Using BI Publisher

Your file should look a bit like this:

```xml
<?xml version="1.0" encoding="UTF-8" standalone="no"?>
<xmlpConfigxmlns="http://xmlns.oracle.com/oxp/xmlp">
<property name="SAW_SERVER" value=""/>
<property name="SAW_SESSION_TIMEOUT" value="90"/>
 <property name="DEBUG_LEVEL" value="exception"/>
 <property name="SAW_PORT" value=""/>
 <property name="SAW_PASSWORD" value=""/>
 <property name="SAW_PROTOCOL" value="http"/>
 <property name="SAW_VERSION" value="v4"/>
 <property name="SAW_USERNAME" value=""/>
<property name="MONITORING_ENABLED" value="true"/><property name="AUDIT_ENABLED" value="true"/><property name="AUDIT_JPS_INTEGRATION" value="true"/>
</xmlpConfig>
```

The FMW Audit Framework will now need to have reference to how BI Publisher handles the collection of its auditing information. Copying the existing BI Publisher audit events file to the common directory, where auditing information can be read, is done in a few simple steps:

1. Locate the directory path `$BI_HOMEoracle_commonmodulesoracle.iau_12.2.2components`.
2. N.B. - This path may change depending on your OBIEE version.
3. Create a new directory called `xmlpserver` in this path and using the native OS make a directory command, for example, `mkdir xmlpserver`.
4. If on a Nix OS, be sure to set the read/write permissions according to the same folders existing in this directory.
5. Locate the `component_events.xml` file from `$BI_HOMEuser_projects domainsbifoundation_domainconfigbipublisherrepository AdminAudit`.
6. Copy the `component_events.xml` file to the `xmlpserver` directory created in step 2.

Enabling Audit Policy in the Fusion Middleware Control Enterprise Manager

Using the Fusion Middleware Control Enterprise Manager, the last major configuration to set up auditing can be completed:

1. Log in to Fusion Middleware Control Enterprise Manager.
2. On the left-hand side pane, expand **WebLogic Domain.**
3. Right-click on the **bifoundation_domain** option.
4. Select **Security | Audit Policy.**
5. Click on the row for **BI Publisher Server** to select it.
6. Change the **Audit Level** drop-down value to **Medium.**
7. Notice that the **Enable Audit** column will render several green check marks in place of the **BI Publisher Server.**
8. Click on the **Apply** button in the upper-right corner of the page.
9. As you can see from the Information note at the top of this section, all changes made to this page require a server restart to take effect.
10. Restart the WebLogic Server, which will first entail stopping all Oracle BI system components.

Connecting to the Audit Framework

After Oracle BI 12c restarts, the configuration for auditing will now be in place for Oracle BI Publisher. All login, logout, and report access information will be captured and stored into a physical file on the server. This information could also be stored in a database schema that the RCU utility creates specifically for FMW auditing. To extend the auditing information for storage in a relational database, and not the filesystem, a few additional steps, including running the RCU utility again (remember you ran the RCU once before during the installation of Oracle BI 12c) are required.

Viewing the auditing log file

Confirm that the WebLogic Server has been restarted. Start the Oracle BI system components and confirm that the /analytics application is available. You would normally check it when making the Oracle BI server available. To check if the log file is working properly, follow these steps:

1. Log in to the /analytics server, for example,
   `http://<server_name>:<server_port>/analytics/`.
2. Click on the **Catalog** link from the global header.
3. Expand the folders `Shared Folders` and click on the `BI Publisher Reports` folder.
4. Click on the Open link for the Departmental Finance Report.
5. Clicking on this link will open the report within the Oracle BI Analytics application and will trigger the audit log file to be created and begin retaining entries.
6. On the Oracle BI server, locate the `audit.log` file in `$BI_HOMEuser_projectsdomainsbifoundation_domainserversbi_server1logs auditlogsxmlpserver`.
7. Open the `audit.log` file to view the entries.

Viewing the audit.log file, you can see that one or more entries have been made based on your actions against the BI Publisher report. If you change the report display to HTML or PDF, another audit line will be registered in the file. You cannot delete the file while the WebLogic Server is running as it is locked for writing by the **Java Virtual Machine (JVM)** process that is controlling the auditing functionality. The audit log entries are somewhat cryptic, but still legible. You can clearly see the name of the user accessing the report, the report display type, timestamps, and so on. The next step, which is beyond the scope of this book, would be to configure the auditing and monitoring data to be placed into a database instead of the filesystem. A database audit repository would allow you to frontend some of this information and analyze its data with any other data.

Moving on, a few common questions have arisen with the new BI Publisher and Oracle BI embedded integration of 12c. Though not an exhaustive list, these few items warrant mention here.

Timeout issues

You may have noticed that your session timed out while conducting the exercises in this chapter. If you didn't this time around, you will most likely experience this at some point while developing within Oracle BI Publisher 12c. The session timeout is actually not readily configurable for BI Publisher via any GUI as it is with Oracle BI Presentation services. The timeout for BI Publisher is set to 30 minutes, by default, with a warning around 15 minutes of inactivity. In order to change this, you will need to inflate/decompress the BI Publisher JEE **Enterprise Archive** (**EAR**) file deployed on the WebLogic Server. Then you will need to access the `web.xml` file and modify the session-timeout property to a higher value in order to increase the timeout period. From there you can recompile the inflated files back into the EAR file format and redeploy the application to the application server.

Connecting to Oracle BI server data sources

Yes, Oracle BI server can be used as a data source to create a data set in the BI Publisher. A newcomer to the Oracle BI might think that since the Oracle BI server RPD is accessible via Presentation services and an ODBC connection, then BI Publisher should be able to access the RPD subject areas, just as Oracle BI can. This logic is only partially correct. BI Publisher does not currently have the ability to cherry pick Oracle BI subject area elements as if using the Analysis Ad-Hoc Editor. BI Publisher has two options to reference the Oracle BI server data. The first is to select an analysis request developed in the Analysis Ad-Hoc Editor and save to the Presentation Catalog. Typically, this will be an analysis request created specifically for the purpose of being consumed in a BI Publisher report. That report is usually saved in a folder location close to the BI Publisher report that ultimately leverages the said data. The second option is to create an analysis request, select the **Advanced** tab in the Ad-Hoc Editor, and copy the SQL that is generated for that request. That SQL can then be pasted into a BI Publisher data set. The latter option is the best option.

BI Publisher Application Programming Interface

BI Publisher offers third-party or custom integration functionality via a Java API and a set of web services that communicate with the BI Publisher server. These API methods can interface with just about all areas of BI Publisher including user management, translation deployment, managing portions of the catalog, scheduling artifacts for delivery, and more. In many ways, this API is similar to the Oracle BI API; however, for day-to-day functionality to advanced functionality of communication with an application, the BI Publisher API seems to be better-rounded. Keep in mind that the BI Publisher API does not communicate with the BI server directly or vice-versa.

BI Publisher Scheduler

The Oracle BI development hasn't yet flushed out all of the integration points between BI Publisher and the Oracle BI server as of this release. One of those disconnects has to do with the way the Oracle BI Server's scheduler system delivers, distributes, or bursts its artifacts to the masses. Currently the BI Publisher Scheduler, referred to as the **Quartz Scheduler**, and the Oracle BI Server Scheduler, Delivers, are separate tools. Oracle BI Delivers cannot burst BI Publisher reports, although it may reside in the same Presentation Catalog. However, currently the BI Publisher Quartz Scheduler is much more powerful than the Oracle BI Delivers Scheduler and it has a better API. It has delivery destinations that can be conjured and a more robust failover system that can take advantage of another open standard application--Apache ActiveMQ.

High availability

Determining failover and highly available architectures for Oracle BI Publisher in standalone mode poses no major challenges when compared to the HA topology and configuration for the Oracle BI Enterprise Edition. Luckily, when Oracle BI Publisher 12c is embedded in the Oracle BI Enterprise Edition, the BI Publisher HA architecture follows the core HA topology for the larger Oracle BI Server platform implementation. This makes sense seeing how both applications will be deployed to the same managed application server and, by default, share the same metadata database repository schema created by the RCU.

A review - what I should now know!

For self-review and a recap of the chapter, here are a few questions. There is no answer key. These questions are for your own reflection on this chapter:

- What is a BI Publisher data model?
- What is the relationship of layouts/templates to a BI Publisher report?
- What qualitative information can BI Publisher auditing provide?
- What does the acronym JNDI stand for? What is the difference between using it and a standard JDBC connection?
- Describe the main benefit of developing a report in the BI Publisher versus Oracle BI Analysis/Answers.

Summary

This chapter provided information about Oracle BI Publisher 12c's new features and several of its nuances. It briefly compared Oracle BI and BI Publisher, and discussed some commonalities. You walked through an exercise that allowed you to interact with the new Data Model Editor and Layout Editor for a first-hand experience. This chapter highlighted terminology that is used specifically when working with BI Publisher and other concepts that continue to build your knowledge about Java and the WebLogic Application Server. In the exercises, you continued to use the data source from the AdventureWorks database. Finally, you were able to configure the BI Publisher auditing and monitoring functionality. The auditing configuration currently places metadata into a filesystem location for logging and you saw how that process works and is managed.

11
Usage Tracking

Monitoring what your new Oracle BI system is doing, and how well it does it, is vital for the longterm success of a project. Analysis of the system usage can help to improve performance and user adoption. It is just as useful to know who is not using the system as who is using it.

One of the great features of Oracle BI is that you can use the system, its dashboards and analysis, to monitor the system itself, which means to say that you can use OBIEE analysis to tell you how OBIEE is performing for your users.

In this chapter, we will learn how to activate the usage tracking feature and create useful reports from it. You will also learn how to fine-tune and improve the usage tracking feature.

What is usage tracking?

The idea is simple: save each request that is made to the BI Server in a record in a table, in a database. In that record of the request, state who issued it, what they ran, when it ran, and how well it performed. These are the typical attributes that are stored:

- User runs the request
- Date and time shows when the request was started and ended
- What was requested gives the details of the item that was run
- Time taken breakes down into various parts
- Number of rows
- Error codes
- System setup

Once the information has been captured in the database table we can analyze it. This is best done using OBIEE!

Setting up usage tracking

Let's get the system set up to track usage. For our system, which uses the standard table method, the configuration is in three parts, and they are all linked to each other. The steps are:

1. Setting up the database tables.
2. Setting up the BI Server repository.
3. Updating the BI Server's configuration.

There is an option to store the usage tracking records in a text file, but as this is not as useful as the database method, it will be more difficult and slower to analyze a text file than a database table.

Setting up database tables

Near the beginning of the book, we ran the **repository creation utility** (**RCU**) to set up some schemas in the database for OBIEE to use. This created a database schema called BIPlatform with several tables, some of which are used for storing usage tracking records. Also worth noting is that you can move the usage tracking tables to another database and/or schema, but at this time we recommend you just use the tables provided by the RCU.

Tables created in the BI Platform Schema that relate to usage tracking are:

- S_NQ_ACCT
- S_NQ_DB_ACCT
- S_NQ_INITBLOCK

The S_NQ_ACCT table has been in use since the nQuire days (hence the NQ in the name), but it has been updated in recent releases. It stores records relating to the logical query that is run. The S_NQ_DB_ACCT table supplements the logical record with details of the physical query that was run against the database. The S_NQ_INITBLOCK table is new and is used to log the queries run when a user logs in.

Another table, S_NQ_SUMMARY_ADVISOR, is also installed by the RCU, but it does not relate directly to usage tracking. It is an added feature that helps to identify possible aggregates that would speed up dashboard performance.

Setting up the BI Server repository

The usage tracking record capture process uses a table that is defined in the BI Server repository (RPD file). This is simply a reference to the S_NQ_ACCT table, with a connection pool that has the write ability.

To create the metadata in the repository you can use the import metadata functionality in the BI Administration tool by following these steps:

(Before you start, take a backup of the repository):

1. Open the BI Administration Tool.
2. Open your repository (use a local master copy):

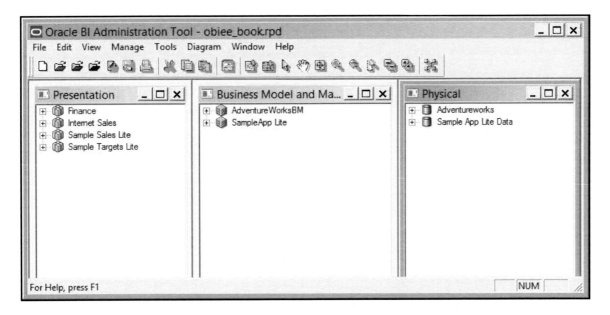

Usage Tracking

3. Navigate to **File | Import Metadata...**:

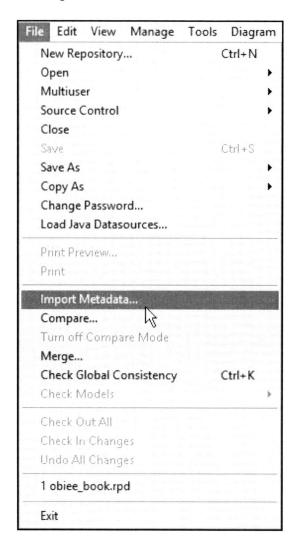

4. Select a connection to the Database Server.

5. Enter the credentials for the BIPLATFORM user:

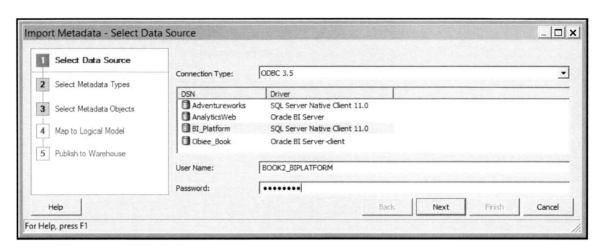

6. Click **Next**.
7. Select **Tables**:

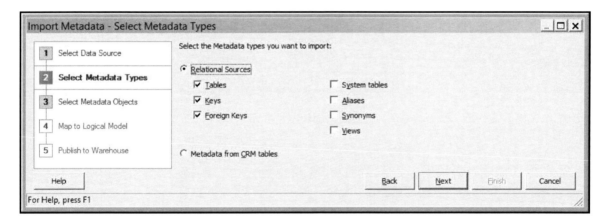

8. Click **Next**.
9. Select the three tables.

Usage Tracking

10. Click **Finish**:

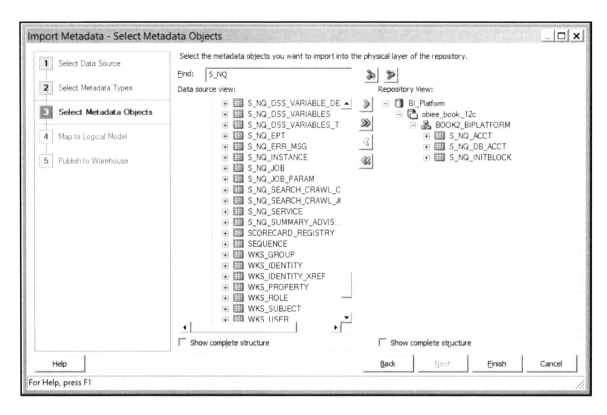

You now have a new database in the **Physical** schema:

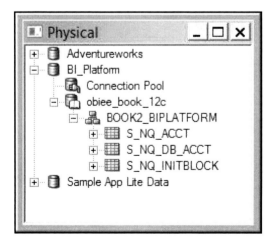

[414]

At this stage we can configure usage tracking to use the preceding tables, but before we do, we will create the business model and presentation layer objects:

1. Right-click on the S_NQ_ACCT table.
2. Select **Properties.**
3. Uncheck the **Cacheable** option.
4. Click **OK**.
5. Repeat the removal of caching for S_NQ_DB_ACCT and S_NQ_INITBLOCK.
6. Right-click on the S_NQ_ACCT table again.
7. Select **New Object** and then **Alias**.
8. Enter the name: Usage Tracking Logical.
9. Right-click on the S_NQ_ACCT table again.
10. Navigate to **New Object | Alias**.
11. Enter the name Fact Usage Tracking.
12. Click **OK**.
13. Using the same technique, create an alias of S_NQ_DB_ACCT and call it Usage Tracing Physical.
14. Create an alias of S_NQ_INITBLOCK and call it Usage Tracking Initblock.
15. Now create a physical join from the fact table to the Logical and Physical aliases.
16. Right-click in the middle pane, and select **New Business Model.**
17. Enter the **Name**: Usage Tracking.
18. In the new business model, create a logical fact table using the **Fact Usage Tracking** alias.
19. Create a logical dimension using the Usage Tracking Logical.
20. Add another logical table source that includes the physical tables: Usage Tracking Logical and Usage Tracking Physical.
21. Rename the columns to more user-friendly names.
22. Create a Presentation catalog.

Usage Tracking

You should end up with a repository looking like this:

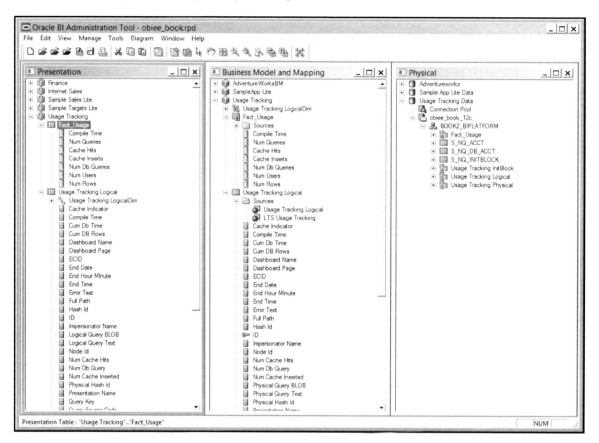

We will provide examples of the RPD on the support book website.

Updating the BI Server configuration

Now that we have the tables set up in the RPD file, we can configure the BI Server to start recording usage:

1. Take a backup copy of the file NQSConfig.ini, which is in the folder Oracle_homeuser_projectsdomainsbiconfigfmwconfigbiconfigOBIS.

2. Open the file NQSConfig.ini in a text editor.

3. Find the section called USAGE_TRACKING and change the enable setting to **Yes**.
4. Change the settings for the tables and connections for the entries:
   - PHYSICAL_TABLE_NAME
   - CONNECTION_POOL
   - INIT_BLOCK_TABLE_NAME
   - INIT_BLOCK_CONNECTION_POOL

   See the following code:

   ```
   PHYSICAL_TABLE_NAME = "Usage Tracking
   Data"."obiee_book_12c"."BOOK2_BIPLATFORM"."S_NQ_ACCT";
   CONNECTION_POOL = "Usage Tracking Data"."Connection Pool";
   INIT_BLOCK_TABLE_NAME = "Usage Tracking
   Data"."obiee_book_12c"."BOOK2_BIPLATFORM"."S_NQ_INITBLOCK;
   INIT_BLOCK_CONNECTION_POOL = "Usage Tracking Data"."Connection
   Pool";
   ```

5. Save the file.
6. Restart the BI Services:

```
[USAGE_TRACKING]
ENABLE = YES;
DIRECT_INSERT = YES;
PHYSICAL_TABLE_NAME = "Usage Tracking Data"."obiee_book_12c"."BOOK2_BIPLATFORM"."S_NQ_ACCT";
CONNECTION_POOL = "Usage Tracking Data"."Connection Pool";
INIT_BLOCK_TABLE_NAME        = "Usage Tracking Data"."obiee_book_12c"."BOOK2_BIPLATFORM"."S_NQ_INITBLOCK";
INIT_BLOCK_CONNECTION_POOL   = "Usage Tracking Data"."Connection Pool";
```

At this point, every request made to the BI Server will be logged in to the S_NQ_ACCT table.

> Usage tracking is not related to the LOGGING LEVEL variable that each user has. Logging level relates to the amount of information that is placed into the NQQuery.log file.

Analyzing usage

Now that we are getting data into the tables and have set up the BI repository to access the data, we can start creating analyses to see what is going on. Typical analyses that I would create are:

- Top 10 slowest dashboards
- Top 10 slowest analyses
- User activity over time
- Non-users
- Dashboard usage analysis
- Error reports

Usage measures

Before using some of the measures, you need to understand what each one does and how they are relevant. The following describes each field in the main usage tracking table:

- `TOTAL_TIME_SEC`: The time (in seconds) that the Oracle BI Server spent working on the query while the client waited for responses to its query requests. This setting is the same as the response time in the `NQQuery.log` file. Usually it is the difference between the start time and the end time. The same results are returned from the following function:

    ```
    ROUND((CAST(END_TS as DATE)-CAST(START_TS as DATE))*86400)
    ```

- `COMPILE_TIME_SEC`: The time (in seconds) required to compile the query.
- `ROW_COUNT`: The number of rows returned to the querying client.
- `CUM_DB_TIME_SEC`: The total amount of time (in seconds) that the Oracle BI Server waited for backend physical databases on behalf of a logical query.
- `CUM_NUM_DB_ROW`: The total number of rows returned by the backend databases.
- `NUM_DB_QUERY`: The number of queries submitted to backend databases in order to satisfy the logical query request. For successful queries (`SuccessFlag = 0`), this number will be 1 or greater.
- `NUM_CACHE_HITS`: Indicates the number of times the existing cache was returned.
- `NUM_CACHE_INSERTED`: Indicates the number of times the query-generated cache was returned.

- `QUERY_TEXT`: The SQL submitted for the query.
- `QUERY_BLOB`: The data type is `ntext` when using SQL Server, and CLOB when using Oracle, DB2, or Terradata databases. It contains the entire logical SQL statement without any truncation.
- `QUERY_KEY`: An MD5 hash key that is generated by Oracle Business Intelligence from the logical SQL statement.
- `SUBJECT_AREA_NAME`: The name of the business model being accessed.
- `REPOSITORY_NAME`: The name of the repository the query accesses.
- `IMPERSONATOR_USER_NAME`: User ID of an impersonated user. If the request is not run as an impersonated user, the value will be `NULL`.
- `USER_NAME`: The name of the user who submitted the query, from the `USER` variable.
- `PRESENTATION_NAME`: The name of the Presentation Catalog in Oracle BI Presentation Services.
- `QUERY_SRC_CD`: The source of the request; for example, Drill or Report.
- `SAW_DASHBOARD` The path of the dashboard. If the query was not submitted through an Interactive Dashboard, the value will be `NULL`.
- `SAW_DASHBOARD_PG`: The page's name in the Interactive Dashboard. If the request is not a dashboard request, the value will be `NULL`.
- `SAW_SRC_PATH`: The path name in the Oracle BI Presentation Catalog for the request.
- `START_DT`: The date the logical query was submitted.
- `START_HOUR_MIN`: The hour and minute the logical query was submitted.
- `START_TS`: The date and time the logical query was submitted.
- `END_DT`: The date the logical query was completed.
- `END_HOUR_MIN`: The hour and minute the logical query was completed.
- `END_TS`: The date and time the logical query finished. The start and end timestamps also reflect the time that the query spent waiting for resources to become available.
- `ERROR_TEXT`: The error message from the backend database. This column is only applicable if `SUCCESS_FLG` is set to a value other than `0` (zero). Multiple messages will concatenate and will not be parsed by Oracle BI Server.
- `CACHE_IND_FLG`: The default value is `N`. `Y` indicates a cache hit for the query and `N` indicates a cache miss.

- **SUCCESS_FLG**: This indicates the completion status of the query:
    - 0: The query completed successfully with no errors
    - 1: The query timed out
    - 2: The query failed because row limits were exceeded
    - 3: The query failed due to some other reason

The following describes each field in the extra usage tracking table used to store physical SQL sent to the database:

- **QUERY_TEXT**: The first 1024 characters of the SQL query
- **QUERY_BLOB**: The whole SQL query sent to the database
- **TIME_SEC**: The time taken to return data from the database
- **ROW_COUNT**: The number of rows returned from the database
- **START_TS**: Start time
- **START_DT**: Start date
- **START_HOUR_MIN**: The time (in hours and minutes) that the query was sent to the database
- **END_TS**: The time the results were returned to the BI Server
- **END_DT**: The date the results were returned to the BI Server
- **END_HOUR_MIN**: The hours and minutes in the HHMM format that the data returned

Customizing your setup

This section is optional. The preceding instructions are suitable for a small implementation, but will not cope well in a system with a very large number of users.

In a standard setup that we have demonstrated previously, the usage records are captured (that is, inserts) in standard tables held in the BIPlatform schema and this table is also used in the analysis (that is, reads).

This is not the most efficient way for either process, the insert or the read:

- The insert record process ideally does not want to be slowed down by indexes, column constraints, and read contention
- The analysis process ideally wants indexes, summaries, foreign keys, and so on, to speed up the reports

The standard out-of-the-box setup makes a compromise and puts some indexes on the table. An alternative method is to separate the two processes completely! The benefit is faster insertions of usage tracking records and faster analysis of the results. The downside is that you have to wait until the ETL process has moved your usage tracking data into the analysis tables.

In our preferred setup, we keep the `S_NQ_ACCT` table in the RCU created schema, and drop any indexes that are created. This is the Capture Table. Then we create another table, say, `W_USAGE_TRACKING`, and use this one to report against. This is the `Analysis` table.

Each night, or more regularly if required, transfer the records from the `Capture` table to the `Analysis` Table. Then make sure that the analysis table is optimized for reporting by ensuring that indexes are on the columns we need to report against and the appropriate stats are in place. Then, create summaries of this table to speed up the reports. These summaries can be materialized views or static tables.

Additional data

The preceding tables are all you need to store the usage, but to create effective dashboards of the actually usage, you will need additional data, for example, a date table, a table of time, a table of dashboards, pages, and of users.

The `W_USAGE_TRACKING` table is nearly identical to the capture table, except that we add extra fields. One of these fields is `DATE_WID`. This is so that the table can be linked to our standard `W_DATE_D` table. We add indexes to the table, on the `date_wid` field, and on the fields that will be filtered, such as `USER_NAME` and `SAW_DASHBOARD`. An additional task could be to create a day-level summary table that calculates performance measures for the day and will be joined to the `W_DATE_D` table, therefore enabling fast trend analysis.

The extra data tables listed previously are not installed into the Oracle BI schemas; you have to add them to your warehouse.

Oracle has provided a calendar table script and a time script that you have to run yourself. If you want to add more details about the dashboard and users, you will need to add these yourself manually.

Usage Tracking

To add the Oracle-provided tables and data in an MS SQL Server database, undertake the following steps:

1. Navigate to the folder `oracle_homebibifoundationsamplesusagetracking`.
2. Unzip the `.zip` files that contain the tables and data scripts called `UsageTracking-datafiles.zip`.
3. Open a connection in SQL Server Management Studio, and connect to your warehouse schema.
4. Execute the file `SQLServer_create_nQ_Calendar.sql` (from the `samplesusagetracking` folder).
5. Execute the file `SQLServer_create_nQ_Clock.sql`.

    This means the tables are now created so we now need to add some data to them.

6. Execute the file `SQLServer_nQ_Calendar.sql`.
7. Execute the file `SQLServer_nQ_Clock.sql`.

You will now need to model your date and user tables together with the new warehouse-based usage tables in the repository.

A review - what I should now know!

For self-review and to recap the chapter, here are a few questions based on the topics covered:

- What is usage tracking?
- What three areas are configured to get usage tracking working?
- What is `TOTAL_TIME_SEC`?
- Should I use a warehouse table to report against or should I use the RCU table?
- What types of report should I build to improve usage?

Summary

In this chapter, we showed how to set up the system to track user activity impacting the BI Server.

Usage tracking plays an important role in managing the overall health of the OBIEE system. It should be used regularly to identify heavy users and heavy usage times, along with bottlenecks. Use the stats over time to ensure that users are not turning off due to poor performance. User adoption can also be improved by identifying people that are not using the system. It can also be used to check that cache seeding is effective.

12
Improving Performance

So far in this book, you have installed your system, set up your database sources, created dashboards, and have monitored the usage. This is not the time to sit back and relax! You have installed OBIEE on a machine with the suitable levels of CPU, disk speed, and RAM, but is your system actually performing well?

In this chapter, we will learn some common techniques to reduce common bottlenecks that can exist in the process of delivering dashboards and reports to the users. We will look across the whole system, defining poor performance and where required, take steps to improve the performance.

What is poor performance?

If a dashboard loads in 20 seconds, is that good or bad performance? We tend to answer this question in terms of user expectations and technical capability. User expectations are what we manage every day on a project and sometimes these are really easy to meet, other times totally impossible! We recently had a client who was switching from a very slow reporting system (which will remain nameless) where a report would take 45 minutes to run. When we replaced the report with a dashboard that took 20 seconds, they were delighted. A similar dashboard, at another recent investment-banking client, was deemed to be far too slow at 20 seconds, as they required information in less than 3 seconds per dashboard page. Because the first client was happy with a 20-second wait, there was no further performance work undertaken, even though I knew that we could get the report down to less than 3 seconds. The banking client demanded better performance so we spent hundreds of man hours reducing the dashboard time down to a 1 second response.

To calculate potential efficiency savings, add up the total number of hours per year that your users wait for information and set a reasonable target that they should be waiting. That target should even go as low as 1 second per query!

One recent client has 100,000 users. If each user logged in once per week and ran a dashboard that took 1 minute more than necessary, then the client could be wasting 40 MAN YEARS per year.

If your client is happy with the response times, but your current system is technically capable of reduced dashboard delivery times, then should you spend time delivering these improved times? The simple answer is "yes". As your system grows, with more users and more dashboards, there will certainly be a hit to performance overall. Improving the performance of every dashboard, request, and report will help to increase total capacity and keep your project being funded and expanded. There will probably be a need to prioritize the order in which to improve performance of dashboards, and for this I suggest a combination of client priorities and picking on the slowest ones first. In practice, this means that the estimated total time to develop a dashboard should always include an element at the end to review performance and to make suitable changes.

Where can I improve the performance?

As we have seen in the previous chapters, there are several components in your OBIEE system. Each one of these can be tuned to help improve performance, along with some other factors. The areas to look for the most gains are:

- Hardware
- Database design
- BI Server
- Web Server
- Domain settings
- Network

We will look at each of these to see the techniques that could be employed. For each of the preceding areas there are three main ways to improve performance:

- **Do less work**: It means making parts of the system work with smaller datasets, such as using aggregate fact tables
- **Do the same work, but faster**: It means getting better equipment that can cope with the volumes of data and with the system components
- **Cheating**: It means getting the results ready before the user needs them

Hardware

There are no silver bullets when it comes to improving performance, but there are some recent developments in hardware that come pretty close. Massive gains can be had in request response times by buying some impressive new hardware. The first piece of hardware that has been available for a few years is the Oracle Exadat machine. This **Oracle Exadata Storage and Database machine** has transformed the ability of Oracle databases by bringing together several technology advances into the one box.

The statistics for a full system are very impressive:

- 576 CPU cores
- 24 TB RAM for database processing
- 280 CPU cores dedicated to SQL processing
- Eight database servers
- 14 storage servers
- 360 TB of flash cache
- 40 Gbit/sec InfiniBand
- Up to 224 TB space per rack
- Up to 18 racks can be connected

The preceding stats can transform even the most stubborn client demands into reality. For example, a recent proof of concept that we undertook reduced a dashboard response from over 3 minutes to 8 seconds. Another recent client uses an Exadata box and has over 2 terabytes of live data that is regularly used in dashboards. So far, the performance has been so good that no tuning has been required by the end users (although we will still tune for expansion).

At the same time that OBIEE 11g was released, Oracle also released the Exalytics in-memory machine. Another super-fast machine from the Sun part of Oracle, but this time aimed directly at OBIEE users (Exadata is for any database use). The Exalytics machine contains a huge amount of memory and lots of processing power, along with some in-memory software that will optimize the way the data is extracted for OBIEE to use. Also included in the machine is the OBIEE software itself, thereby reducing the need for another set of application servers.

Its impressive stats include:

- 3 terabyte of RAM
- 72 CPU cores on 10 quad-core chips
- InfiniBand networking

The use of OBIEE on an Exalytics machine enables a special Admin tool feature called **Summary Advisor**. This tool uses the usage tracking statistics to provide advice on which summary tables will improve performance, and then helps to generate in-memory TimesTen database tables that are then integrated into the BI Server Repository. These tables are normally aggregated data that will respond quicker than going to your database source. The result is instant response times on dashboards that previously could take minutes and, therefore, will allow for more concurrent users, and more advanced features, such as the new graphical tools and master detail instant reports.

Full speed ahead

If you combine the power of the Exadata Storage and Database machine with the clever power of the Exalytics machine, you will have a superb platform to delight end users. The Exadata Database machine is used for the warehouse and it is the source for a large detailed analysis, with the Exalytics machine providing the summary aggregated data and Essbase cubes.

More servers please

Another way to use hardware to help with performance is to spread the load. If your budget does not allow for Exadata machines then you could try adding more commodity machines and use a larger cluster of OBIEE servers. Remember that the OBIEE server software is designed for a certain number of users, and that 1,000 users is normally the limit, but feel free to add more servers to lower the average number of users per server.

You can also split the database over several servers using a cluster or even split some data out to a separate database.

Do not rule out any option, even if you have a limited budget.

The investment in the machines described previously is not insignificant, but the benefit to end users is huge. Take our large user base example and you can see that even a few seconds can add up to a big reduction in efficiency for an organization. You will also save a large amount of developers' and DBA time, which for external consultancy, or even internal teams, can be relatively expensive.

Database

The database is crucial to the reporting performance and it can be improved in two ways:

- Database configuration
- Database design

The first way is with the configuration of the database in terms of the parameters used and the structure of the data files/tablespaces. There are a large number of options, on many types of database and, therefore, too many to go through them in this book (we recommend that you read *Oracle Database 11gR2 Performance Tuning Cookbook* by *Ciro Fiorillo*), but what we can say is that there will certainly be some parameters that will make a big difference!

Setting STAR_TRANSFORMATION_ENABLED in an Oracle database can make a huge difference when reporting on your Star schema-based data.

Work closely with the database administrators to tune the settings that meet your needs. The settings that normally have a large impact on an Oracle database are those relating to memory and those relating to the storage such as block sizes and tablespace structures. Testing of the database performance should be done in isolation of OBIEE, by use of an SQL development tool, such as the Oracle SQL Developer, but use the SQL generated by the OBIEE server as a basis for tuning.

The second area for a database to be tuned is with the object structures. Using a smaller set of data or the smart use of indexes, stats, joins, and views can make a huge difference to speed. An example of design is to take a table with a large number of rows, say 10 million records, and create a materialized view that aggregates the data into a result set of say, 10,000 rows. When a user runs an analysis that only displays the aggregate result then they will hit the smaller table. This can be achieved either by adding the aggregate into the OBIEE repository (see the next section), or by making the materialized view available to rewrite queries.

In Oracle Automatic Query, rewrite can be a feature of materialized views. When you create a materialized view with this option set, then queries that run in the database will automatically be rewritten when they match the data requirements with the materialized view contents.

For full details on designing a database for performance, please see Chapter 15, *Reporting Databases*, techniques for creating a reporting database.

BI Server

Once you have created a smaller dataset, as shown earlier, you need to use it when it matches the scope of the dimensions in your analysis. There are two ways you could do this:

- Separate fact tables
- Aggregate logical table sources

Using a separate logical fact table for aggregate facts is not a commonly used option. The only time it is suitable is where the aggregate facts are not simple sums (or simple averages). Aggregate logical table sources is my favorite feature of the OBIEE Server. We can create an aggregate table (or materialized view) and use this directly in the BI Server Repository, alongside the detailed fact tables. The BI Server then chooses which table. Let's walk through a working example.

The steps are:

1. Create an aggregate materialized view.
2. Import the new object into the physical layer in OBIEE.

Remember that it is best practice to create an alias for your physical layer objects. See the chapter on developing the BI Repository for the import metadata step:

1. Add the new physical table as an additional **logical table source** (**LTS**).
2. Map the fields as appropriate. You can map the same column to both the logical table sources.
3. Set the content level so that the BI Server knows how to use the new LTS. The logical table source content level needs to be set to detail for the matching level, but not set for the other dimensions.

Now we have created a summary set of data and added it to the BI Server Repository.

The BI Server will now use the smaller table to answer requests if it is suitable, which will normally speed up the response times.

More performance tips

Follow these tips to improve performance:

- Try to avoid using normal (opaque) views unless they are the only way to introduce hints and an SQL that performs well
- Make sure you leverage the features of the database, and understand what they mean to performance
- Try not to overload the BI Server and database with lots of queries by keeping to the general rule of 10 or less requests per dashboard page

The use of cache

When a user request is made, the result of the request can be stored in a local file on the BI Server. This is called a cached result. The BI Server normally works by sending a query code to a database, file, or Excel, and processing the results it gets. The slow part of the process is usually the waiting for the data source system to get the answer together. Passing the call to the data source, and having the result already, is a great way to cheat the system into being faster. Luckily, it is possible to get the results before the user runs their dashboard, and then store these results in a cache. Cache entries are results that are stored in a file on the BI Server machine and the BI Server knows when it can use these pre-prepared results, instead of going to the database to get the answer. If the same request is made again, by the same user or even a different user, then the result cache is used instead of issuing an SQL against the database.

Cache is not the only answer to all your performance issues. In fact, it should be treated as a last resort and only as a temporary solution, until you get the hardware/database performance that you need. There are limitations as to how much you can store in the cache, in terms of both individual result sets and the total overall size of the cache. There are also issues relating to how you refresh the cache, removing old stale data, and populating new data. Without a pre-populated cache, the first user to run the dashboard will still experience a slower performance.

Improving Performance

Setting up the cache

The global cache is shared by all BI Servers participating in your cluster. In addition, each BI Server maintains its own local query cache for regular queries. The global cache needs to be stored in a shared filesystem. Shared files requirements for the global cache are as follows:

- All BI Servers in the cluster must have read and write access to the global cache directory
- The global cache parameters are configured in the `NQSConfig.INI` file for each BI Server node participating in the cluster. The global cache is controlled centrally
- The BI Servers maintain a query cache, which is a local cache of the query results

To enable the cache, carry out the following steps in Fusion Middleware Control:

1. Log in to Fusion Middleware Control, Enterprise Manager.
2. Expand the Business Intelligence node in the `Farm_domain_name` window.
3. Click on **biinstance**.
4. Click on **Configuration**, and then click on **Performance**.
5. Click on **Lock and Edit Configuration**.
6. Check the box for **Cache Enabled**.
7. Set the amount of cache size to 20 MB.
8. In a clustered environment, set the **Global Cache** section, specify the shared location for the Oracle BI Server Global Cache, and specify 250 MB for the global cache size. In a Windows environment, Enterprise Manager Fusion Middleware Control requires that a UNC path be used to define the shared location of the Oracle BI Server Global Cache.
9. Click on **Apply**.
10. Click on **Activate Changes**.

The cache entries that are made will become stale when new data arrives in the warehouse. It is, therefore, possible to set a length of time that a cache entry is still usable. This can be minutes, hours, days, or unlimited. There is also a method called event polling, which is a way to tell the BI Server that one of the tables in the cache has been updated. For more details about event polling, see the *Gerardnico* wiki at http://gerardnico.com/wiki/dat/o biee/event_table or the Oracle documentation on *Cache Event Processing with an Event Polling Table*. Also, see the documentation of the shared folders used in OBIEE.

Web servers on top

There are configurations available for an OBIEE system, which include the use of a pure web server on top of the installed application. The use of a web server layer will enable load balancing and high availability. The web servers will also be able to serve up objects such as images quicker than the Weblogic server can. In `Chapter 14`, *Ancillary Installation Options*, we demonstrated how to install the proxy plugin, which enables the separate web layer. Go back and give it a try!

Domain setup

The usual suspect when it comes to slow performance is the database, and hopefully you have tuned this as much as possible. If you are expecting very high numbers of users then, in addition to adding web servers (as previously), you will need to deploy more application servers. This will spread the load across different machines and will provide high availability cover.

For an enterprise setup, this will mean installing separate machines with a full application installation, including an admin server and managed servers. This is outside the scope of this book, but you can find information in the Oracle documentation that explains the steps. Find the OBIEE high availability section of the documentation, currently at:

https://docs.oracle.com/middleware/12212/lcm/BIEIG/GUID-16C01B4A-5054-473E-8C99-FB56E091D2E9.htm#INSOA433

A review - what I should now know!

For self-review and recap of the chapter, here are a few questions based on the topics covered in this chapter:

- Where can I improve performance?
- What is performance data?
- How do I implement a web server into the OBIEE system?
- What are the cache settings?

Summary

In this chapter, we introduced the idea of improving overall performance by working on the individual components that make up an OBIEE system.

We showed how the new hardware can accelerate the performance to a near real-time point, making performance good enough even for the most demanding of customers (including investment bankers!). Monitoring performance is vital to ensure that the system is delivering what the users want in a timely manner, and with 12c it is easy, thanks to the storage of the logical and physical SQL. Use this information to tune your system, and keep tuning never stop tuning.

13
Using the BI Admin Change Management Utilities

We have covered the fundamental techniques of OBIEE development, and through that process we have also studied the fundamental tools needed for OBIEE development. With this knowledge in hand, we can go over some of the other utilities in the Administration tool. These facilities are less utilized, but they can aid and smooth the development process.

Previously, we have carried out all of the tutorials and development examples as a lone developer, but in larger projects we may have a group of developers accessing and modifying the same RPD. To this end, the OBIEE Administration tool provides the ability to merge multiple versions of an RPD as well as functionality for groups to manage development on a sole repository (*multiuser development*).

Problems with multiple developers

As in any IT project, source and version control are points of concern. In OBIEE, there are a couple of issues specifically associated with multiple developers working on an RPD.

Unlike other forms of development, all of our metadata is contained in a single file, that is, the RPD. If we are using a form of revision control, such as CVS software, we are restricted to saving a version of the whole RPD file, even if it contains many projects/business areas. This does not help us if we want to work independently on subsets of the RPD. It also makes it difficult to record what changes individual developers are making and on what objects. All of these challenges increase the difficulty of having developers work on multiple development paths with an aim to consolidate them into one RPD at the end, as would commonly be the case in large projects.

As we cannot use third-party tools for version control, Oracle has provided us with tools for merging separate RPD development paths and recording changes. In previous versions, these tools have been buggy and cumbersome to set up, but there have been improvements in these areas, so it is worth taking a look at the possibilities.

Outside of these inbuilt tools, we can also consider how to manage multiuser developments by ourselves.

Merges

During the initial development, for example, for a proof of concept, it is common to have one developer working on the system with a full release of an RPD from development to production. At that moment, change control is simple as the whole updated RPD is kept with versioning via a third-party tool, such as **Visual SourceSafe** (**VSS**) or **Subversion** (**SVN**).

However, as a project matures in a live environment, you may have minor changes that are made online or quick point releases made directly to production in order to support urgent user requests. In parallel, we would commonly be developing a major DEV to PROD release as a part of the next stage for the project.

This means that you need to merge changes from both the amended PROD RPD and the new DEV release candidate. If the PROD changes are minor, developers may keep a log of changes and manually add them to the DEV RPD. For more involved or for a larger amount of changes, it would be best to utilize a tool that will help to merge the process. As we previously mentioned, the RPD is one encapsulated file, so tools used for programming are not useful. One way around this is to try and utilize the Administration tool's inherent merger facility. Let's take a look at the types of methods of merging processes that are possible.

Three-way merge

A three-way merge is widely seen as the most robust method for revision control in the IT industry, and it is recommended by Oracle. It is especially important to have a robust process when you are merging repositories with the same base and, possibly, conflicting objects. In our example, we will have three RPDs:

- **Current repository**: This is the RPD where we merge our changes. In our example, the latest DEV version
- **Original**: This is the original and base PROD release from which the other two RPDs are branched off
- **Modified**: This is the Current PROD version with live changes

So let's begin. Firstly, open the current repository (in offline mode) and navigate to **File | Merge...**:

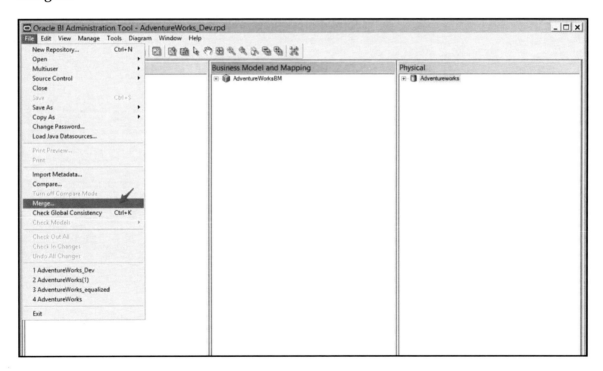

Using the BI Admin Change Management Utilities

You can see the **Merge Repository Wizard - Select Input Files** screen in the following screenshot:

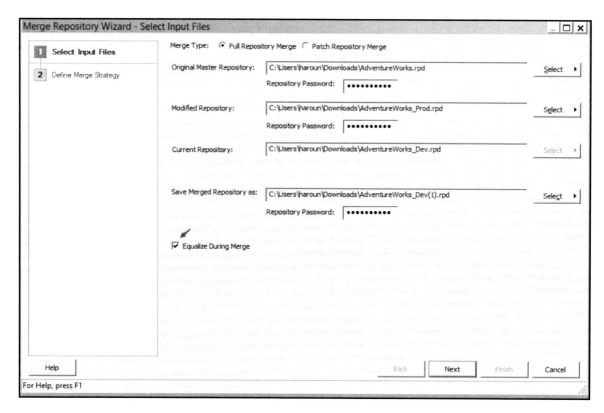

Then select the **Original Master Repository** and **Modified Repository**, and input their passwords too. Also select the **Full Repository Merge** radio button at the top of the **Merge Repository Wizard - Select Input Files** screen, as we are dealing with whole repositories.

Note that we have checked the **Equalize During Merge** box. This solves a potential issue where the same object in both changed RPDs have different object IDs. This can happen if we needed to recreate the object from scratch in one of the RPDs.

Once this has been done, click on **Next**. At this point, you will get the option to check the global consistency of all the RPDs that we have referred to. In preparation for this process, we should have already verified this and been happy with the results, so click on **No**.

The merge tool will now check for conflicts between the RPDs. If there are any conflicts, those will be displayed in the **Merge Repository Wizard - Define Merge Strategy** screen. Here we will be able to choose how to rectify the conflict:

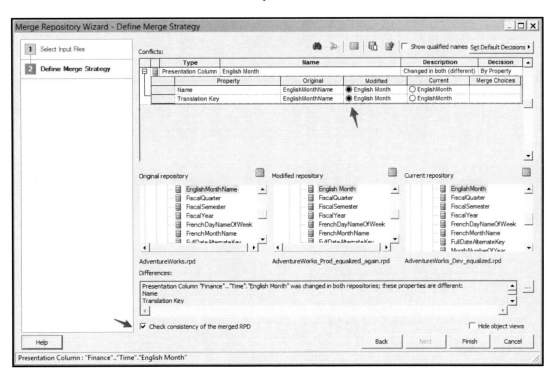

In the preceding screenshot, you can see that we only have one conflict and they all stem from differing names for the **EnglishMonth** column in the three RPDs: **EnglishMonthName**, **English Month**, and **EnglishMonth**. Via a radio button, we can choose whether to go with the **Modified** (Current PROD) or the **Current** (DEV) version. Let's go with the DEV version, as our users wanted that updated.

Once we have resolved all conflicts to our satisfaction, check the **Check consistency of the merged RPD** box. This is good practice, as it ensures that the consistency of the newly merged RPD is ascertained straight away.

Note that if we want a file record of all of the conflict resolution decisions that we have made, we can generate that using the floppy disk icon on the top right of the screen:

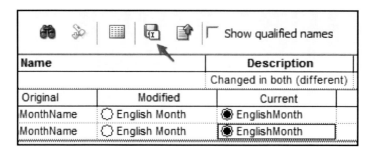

Once we are happy, we can click on **Next** and the merge process takes place. This may take some time depending on how big your RPDs are, and how many merge conflicts need to be resolved.

Once the process has finished, we are left with the Current RPD file, but with the newly merged changes within it.

> Remember to perform a regression test for all of your Current PROD reports with this newly merged RPD. You will also need to test any development reports to ensure that the merge has not affected those pieces of development as well.

Two-way merger

This is commonly carried out when you have two separate RPDs that need to be merged, but they have no common parent. This happens when, for example, you are combining two entirely separate streams of work. An example of this would be the AdventureWorks core model and a separate usage tracking model. If the two RPDs contain completely different subject areas, business models, and data sources, you can easily cut and paste these objects entirely from one RPD to another. However, this is sometimes far from ideal and requires an experienced and knowledgeable developer who has implicit knowledge of both RPD developments.

Best practice in this case is to carry out a two-way merge using the previously discussed merge tool. This time when you are prompted for an original RPD, as we do not have an original trunk parent, you can provide a dummy RPD. This is known as a **parentless three-way merge**.

Multiuser development

Now consider a scenario where you need to merge multiple RPDs, and the possibility that your project and RPD have become so large that you will need multiple developers. In small proven teams, access to the RPD for development can easily be maintained through open communication, such as verbal means or even e-mail/messaging in conjunction with a change log where developers record their amendments. However, in larger teams where there is the possibility of development conflicts over shared objects and the need for more robust version control, we will need to look at other options.

Online development

One option is to have the RPD accessed via a centrally running OBIEE environment. This means that all developers will access the RPD in an online mode via the Administration tool. When working on objects, developers will have to check them in and out on the server itself.

Therefore, from the Administration tool, we can open the online repository by navigating to **File** | **Open Online** or by choosing the blue folder icon in the toolbar:

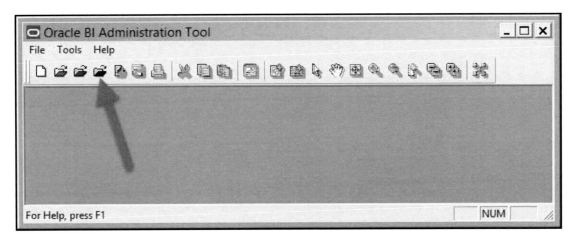

Using the BI Admin Change Management Utilities

We are then prompted for the online RPD details:

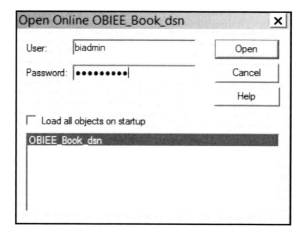

Once we are within the online RPD, we can amend the objects that we want to change. So let's change the name of the **Month** logical column. Double-click on the **EnglishMonthName** logical column. At this point, you will see the **Check Out Objects** screen:

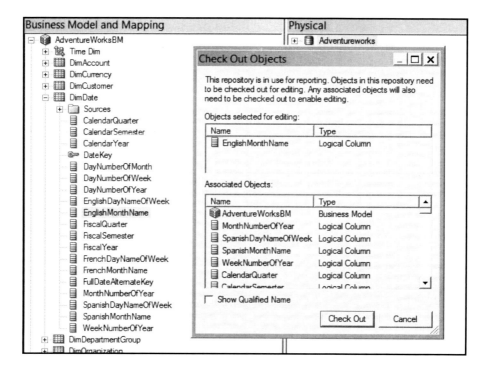

Note that all associated objects up to the business model level have also been checked out, even when such a simple amendment is made. Once we click on **Check Out**, we are then returned to the RPD. However, note that the icons have changed for the objects that we have checked out. This shows that they are locked for the amendment:

Using the BI Admin Change Management Utilities

Once we have made our change, we can check in the objects by choosing the check-in icon in the toolbar, as shown in the following screenshot. As a general tip, note how you can see that we are in online mode due to the **Online** title heading of the Administration tool:

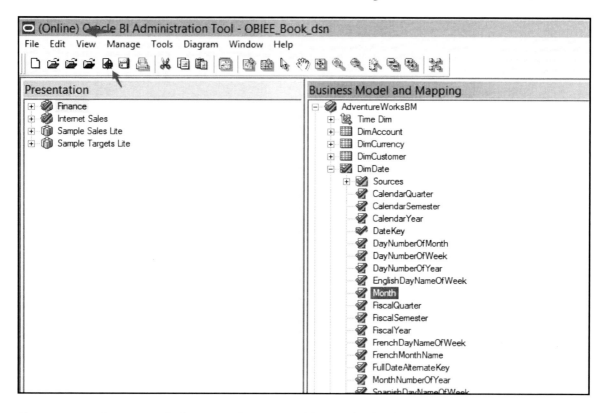

Once you are happy with the amendments and have checked in your objects, you will be asked to confirm whether you want to run another global consistency check.

We are also reminded that if we are in a clustered environment, we will need to restart these nodes. This is done through the Enterprise Manager.

Advantages and disadvantages

There are multiple drawbacks to this method:

- There is a known bug in 12c that corrupts the repository when you try to save an online version locally.
- Low-level objects cannot be checked out without checking out their parents. For example, if you want to change a logical column name, the whole logical table gets checked out. If you want to change a logical table, the whole business model is checked and locked for other users.
- There is no recommended limit to the number of developers that should use this process at the same time. The upper limit depends on having an adequate server architecture in place. However, in the experience of the authors, not all DEV environments are specified correctly due to budget/resource constraints. In this case, the constant checking in and out, running of consistency checks, and saving online RPDs can result in corruption. This is common when you have large RPDs on low memory machines.
- There is no version control. You cannot check which developer changed which object.
- You still have to manually restart non-master nodes in a cluster environment. Bear this in mind if you ever need to make a change in online mode on a production environment.
- If you have a very large RPD such as in *Oracle Business Intelligence Applications*, the checking in/out and saving process can take a very long time. This can possibly lead to corruption of the RPD.

The advantages are as follows:

- Developers only need a local Administration tool
- All other components, for example, BI and web server are shared
- Testing is done on that shared environment
- No set up is needed outside of a normal OBIEE install
- You do not need to deploy the RPD to the server for report/dashboard developers to see the changes

Multiuser Development Environment

Another alternative is to implement the **Multiuser Development Environment** (**MUDE**). This enables us to split the RPD into self-contained areas or projects. The master RPD is put in a shared area, and then projects are worked on by an individual developer and merged back into the master.

This is slightly more complex and convoluted compared to online development. Rather than accessing one central environment, developers must have their own full development environment. They will need a local BI and web server in order to test changes locally, in addition to a local Administration tool. However, due to the possibility of proper segmentation of the RPD, it is arguably safer.

So let's step through an example. Firstly, create the project subsets. Navigate through **Manage** | **Projects...** within our master RPD that has been opened in the Administration tool:

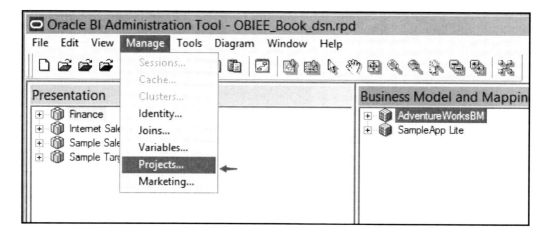

Chapter 13

Then you will enter the **Project Manager** screen where you can define your subsets. Navigate to **Action | New Project...**:

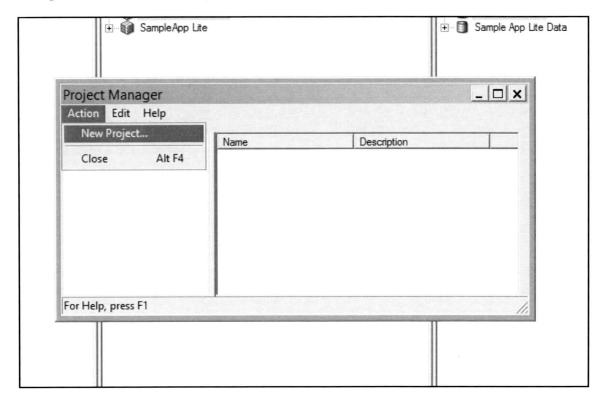

[447]

Using the BI Admin Change Management Utilities

Now you can choose the objects that our project will contain. You can choose whole business models or subject areas down to tables. You can also choose other objects, such as initialization blocks:

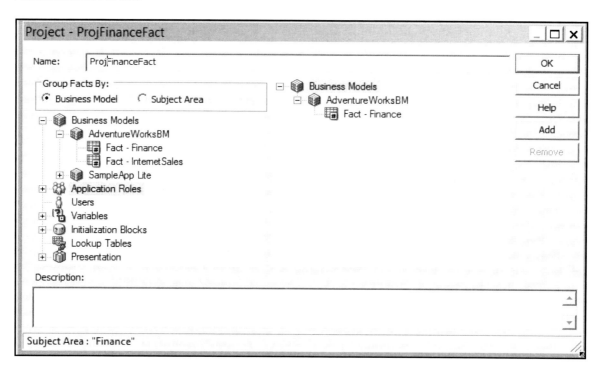

Let's create two projects: one for the main AdventureWorks Finance fact and another for the Internet Sales fact model. Once this is done, we can place the master RPD in a shared location of our choosing.

The master RPD has now been set, so we will now access it as one of the developers on the project in their local environment. Firstly, open a new local OBIEE Administration tool instance, without opening an RPD. Now we want to define where our master RPD is, so that our local Administration tool will know where it can access the master. We do this by navigating to **Tools** | **Options**:

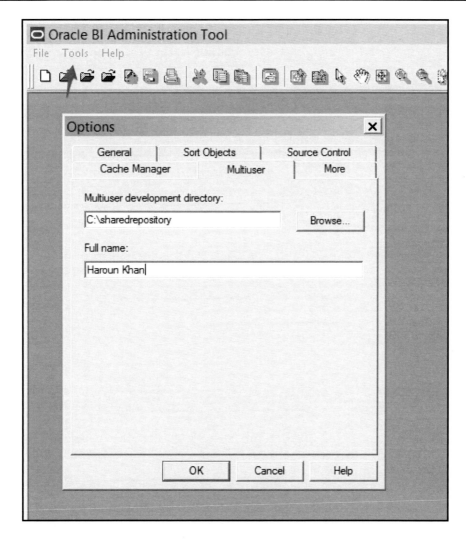

Under the **Multiuser** tab, stipulate the location of the master RPD and your (the developer's) name. This would normally be on a network share that is easily accessible by all users.

The **Full name:** field is used for recording change control, as any changes and comments will be recorded with this name attached to them. Once this has been done, we are ready to locally access one of the projects that we have previously set up in the master RPD.

Using the BI Admin Change Management Utilities

Click on **OK**. Then navigate to **File** | **Multiuser** | **Checkout...**:

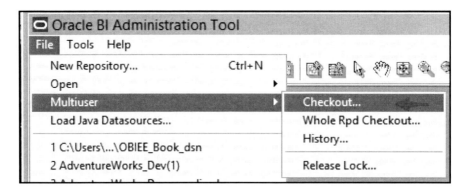

We are then prompted to choose an RPD in that directory and its password:

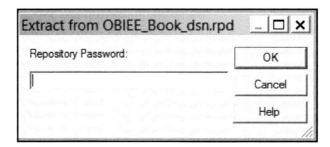

We are then prompted to choose one or more of the projects in the master RPD. Let's go ahead and choose the one that covers the main finance fact:

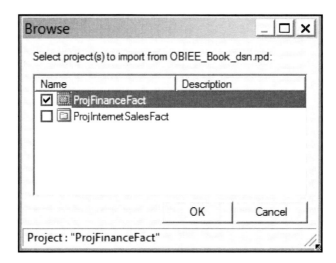

[450]

Once we have chosen the project and clicked on **OK**, a subset RPD containing only this project will be copied to our local development machine. Then we are prompted to name this new subset RPD and save it in our local repository directory:

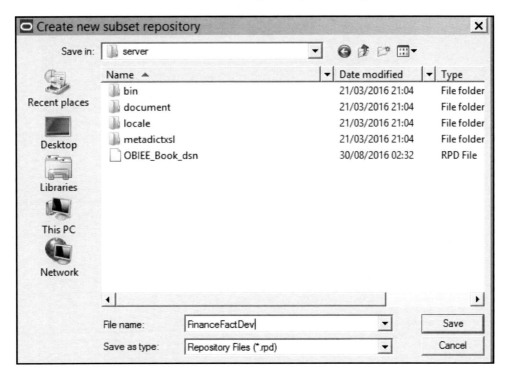

Once this is completed, we are now ready to make changes in our local environment. As a simple example, let's change the logical column `Month` by renaming it to `Months`.

Using the BI Admin Change Management Utilities

After our changes have been made, and before we merge them with the master, we can compare our subset RPD with the original. We do this by navigating to **File | Multiuser | Compare with Original...** (by the way, don't confuse this with **File | Compare...**, which you can use to compare one RPD to any other):

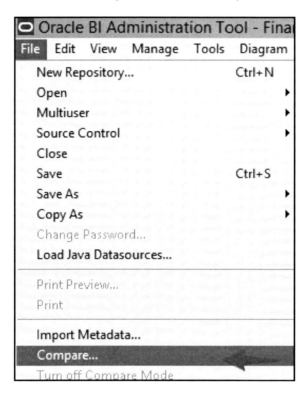

Chapter 13

You select the original RPD and at this point, you will be presented with a screen showing the summary of all the changes that we have made. If you do not recognize a change or a difference, and wish to investigate it further, you can mark an individual change. Let's do that now by choosing the change and clicking on the **Mark** button:

Using the BI Admin Change Management Utilities

Once you have done this and have returned to the main repository, you can see that the change has been highlighted. Note the subtle icon in the following screenshot that highlights our change:

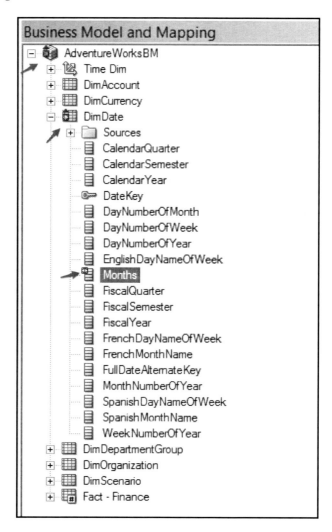

If you are happy with the change, let's go ahead and merge our local changes back with the master. After doing the normal sanity check, such as checking the global consistency, we can merge our local changes with the master by choosing **File** |**Multiuser** | **Publish to Network...**:

Chapter 13

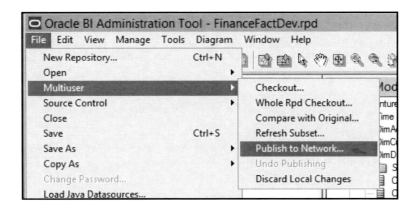

At this point, the master RPD needs to be saved and locked by the system to ensure that no one else is making changes to the RPD at the same time.

The records on the **Lock Information** screen show the following:

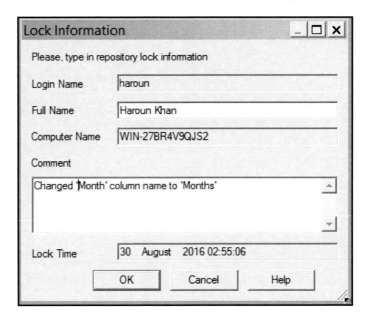

- **Login Name**: This field should be filled in with the username that we logged into the RPD
- **Full Name**: This contains the name that we input when we set up our local Administration tool for multiuser development

Using the BI Admin Change Management Utilities

- **Computer Name**: This field should be completed with your local development environment computer name
- **Lock Time**: This field contains the time at which the lock and change will be recorded
- **Comment**: This contains the reason why we are locking the RPD. This will be stored in a history that is accessible by all developers. So it is worth spending a bit of time to make salient and descriptive comments about the set of changes that have been made. Once we click on **OK**, the three-way merge process (that we have described at the beginning of this chapter) takes place on your local machine. Once you have stepped through the process, and dealt with any conflicts, the merged master is copied back to the central server

At anytime, we can access the master to look at the development history. This is done from the **Multiuser** menu, as shown in the following screenshot:

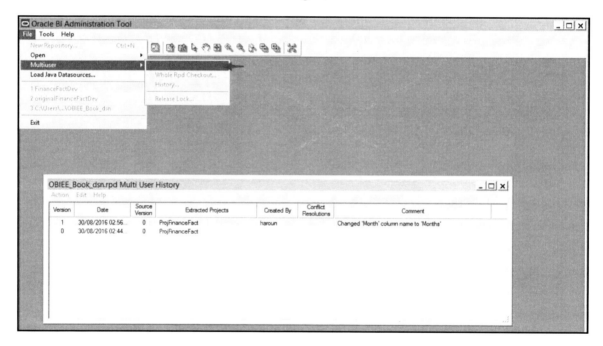

If we do this now, we can see that our change has been recorded in the history list. Through the **Action** option on this screen, we can also view or rollback the last set of changes and revert to the previous RPD version:

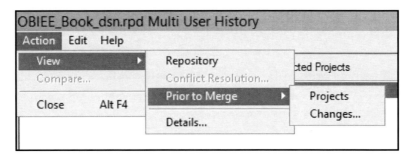

Advantages and disadvantages

The main disadvantages are:

- The definition of projects can be cumbersome and very time consuming to set up correctly
- Each developer needs their own complete development environment including licensing
- The overhead of the previous two points can make the development process slow
- Regression and whole system testing needs to be carried out on the whole master RPD after merging is completed. This is in addition to developers unit testing in their own environments

The main advantages are:

- There is version and change control of objects within the RPD
- The developer who made a change is recorded, and they can make comments
- Rollback of changes is theoretically possible

A review - what I should now know!

For a self-review and a recap of the chapter, here are a few questions based on important topics covered in this chapter:

1. How do you merge multiple RPDs?
2. What are the options in instituting a multiuser development environment?
3. What are the pros and cons of multiuser online development?
4. How do you set up a local environment ready for MUDE?
5. What is a project in MUDE?
6. Can you manage change outside of these tools?

Additional research suggestions

Help files in the Presentation Catalog Oracle documentation can be found at: `http://www.oracle.com/technetwork/middleware/bi-enterprise-edition/documentation/bi-ee-087853.html`

Summary

We have demonstrated the methods of merging. We have also highlighted the two main Administration tool assisted ways of conducting multiuser development. Any well-run project must have a well-managed and formal change process in place. Ideally, your project should choose the methods appropriate to the size of both the project and development team, and whether the team is co-located or scattered across multiple sites. Whatever you choose should be documented and adhered to rigidly by developers, so it is well worth consulting them to develop a consensus on what is suitable.

Sharing an online RPD is very simple, but it lacks the full tracking that is provided by implementation of the full MUDE system. MUDE is great in providing a non-circumventable system of recording change. However, a MUDE system does require far more overhead in licensing, equipment, and setup time. This is because developers need a full local OBIEE development environment in place, in addition to the central system, rather than merely needing a locally installed Administration tool. Also, as we briefly mentioned at the beginning, do not be afraid to use traditional/basic methods such as organizing time-shares on an RPD, creating a change log on a spreadsheet, and periodically making RPD backups. Especially when the development team is co-located and experienced, such a simple approach may suffice and has proven to be successful on the majority of projects.

Whatever you choose, ultimately the goal is that changes are made in a systematic and controlled manner so that they are introduced in a way that precludes and ameliorates the risk of faults being introduced. This requires a system that encourages coordination between developers, but at the same time remember we do not want to make the process so onerous that we hinder the rapid development that OBIEE supports!

14
Ancillary Installation Options

In Chapter 3, *Installing on Windows Server 2012* the steps for installing Oracle BI 12c on a Windows Server operating system were highlighted. Unlike previous versions of Oracle BI, there is only one enterprise installation process, which helps to simplify getting up-and-running with the software. The installation has given you a fully functioning Oracle BI 12c foundation from which to work and develop. The install conducted earlier in the book is for a sandbox or development environment. It would also work in a simplified production environment. Several other advanced installation and post-installation configuration options are considered for production environment architecture. Several of these additional installation and environment configuration options are what we will cover in this chapter. You'll learn how to configure these options, step-by-step, while some of the more advanced options will be discussed at a high-level. Ultimately, the idea in this chapter is for you to be well informed about the capabilities of setting up a production-ready Oracle BI 12c environment.

The nature of this chapter requires additional components and configuration, which may be advanced for someone just getting started with Oracle BI or server infrastructure to conduct. So feel free to read through this chapter without applying the steps explained if you're looking to avoid making changes to the environment in which you've currently been working.

Oracle BI 12c on its own server

For most implementations, Oracle Business Intelligence will run on its own physical or virtual server. This is often the case so that no other enterprise application suite run on the same machine, thus competing for the server's resources. Often the terms BI Server or BI Box is used when talking about the Oracle BI application server. In a **high availability** (**HA**) or failover architecture, the number of servers is increased in order to handle additional consumption of the server's resources or concurrent usage that is anticipated. Each server is then a node in a cluster of servers. Each node gets classified as an instance of Oracle BI. Typically, each Oracle BI instance will run on a physical server in production (plausibly in test or **quality assurance** (**QA**) environments as well), but usually on a virtual machine in a development or sandbox environment. This mindset for using physical machines to run enterprise applications is quickly changing and IT groups are beginning to use virtual machines even in production environments due to the reduction costs and maintenance efforts. In a high availability environment, the application tier, which is where Oracle BI server and its many Java-based components run, are on one server and the web (HTTP) tier is on a separate server for each environment (that is, test, production, and so on).

Before installing Oracle BI, it works best if you understand the architectural needs of the implementation. If you only require a single Oracle BI instance per each environment then there isn't much to worry about in the way of the install and the instructions provided in earlier chapters will suit you well. However, if failover, high availability (horizontal scaling), or vertical scaling (increasing the nodes on a single machine) are needed, you will need to make several environment architecture decisions as part of an installation planning process.

High availability and failover planning

Making any enterprise environment **high availability** (**HA**) is an advanced process. It usually requires several technical components involving both hardware and software. The hardware components are classified under: server hardware, load balancers, and firewall. The software components are classified as: database, application tier, web tier, identity store (LDAP), and storage (that is, SAN/NAS).

The most important part, which is most commonly missed when setting up an Oracle BI HA environment, is the pre-configuration process. This is where a network administrator is required to set up shared storage locations on a NAS/SAN and also to configure the web tier and load balancer (that is, virtual servers, virtual IPs, and DNS). The network administrator during this process should also set up the selected shared storage locations with mapped paths/mounts. These shared storage locations are critical for installing the Oracle BI system into a HA environment; if they are not conducted correctly, the failover effect being sought may not function properly.

Oracle provides the Oracle BI **Enterprise Deployment Guide** (**EDG**), which illustrates a diagram of a basic HA environment as well as installation and configuration processes to ensure your organization can leverage the best practices and recommended setup for Oracle BI HA. Attempting to create an HA environment for Oracle BI without following these instructions is not recommended. Links to the specific documentation can be found here, `https://docs.oracle.com/middleware/1221/core/BIEDG/toc.htm` and further `https://docs.oracle.com/middleware/1221/biee/BIESG/highavail.htm#BIESG1584`.

Oracle even provides a specific Planning Workbook spreadsheet for the Oracle BI 12c configuration planning process, which can be found here `http://www.oracle.com/pls/topic/lookup?ctx=fmw122100&id=biedg_workbook`.

Silent installation

Just like the RCU installation, there is a silent installation component that can be used in Oracle BI 12c for a quicker approach to installing the system. This option is great for streamlining installations or when attempting to simplify a production control change management process where you are required to hand-off an installation process and/or document it for a change management team, who would then commence the installation without your involvement on other servers. This idea of a silent install may seem difficult and unfamiliar at first. The easiest way to create a silent installation script is to start the Oracle BI 12c installation wizard as you did in `Chapter 3`, *Installing on Windows Server 2012*. If you recall in the **Summary** step of the install there was a **Save Response File** button at the bottom of that step in the wizard. You can repeat the process as a mock configuration within the intention of not conducting another full installation, but rather to set and store the necessary configuration options and preferences as if conducting the installation for real. Then on the last **Summary** step in the installation wizard click the **Save** button to create a response file:

Ancillary Installation Options

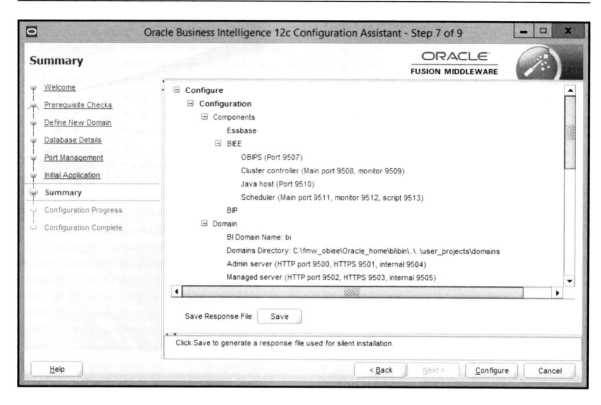

Once the response file is saved to a location that can be accessed at a later time, with a name that marks the occasion (for example, `obi12c_book_install.rsp`), you can exit the installation wizard without actually completing the installation. This response file can then be used against the installation wizard command line (CLI) executable and scripted into a batch file. The same process can be used for the Oracle BI 12c configuration, which is the bulk of the configuration if comparing those two setup wizards. Executing the response file is fairly straightforward, for example:

```
../bi/bin/config.bat -silent -response C:tmpobi12c_book_install.rsp
```

The `deinstall` process can be conducted in a similar fashion using the `silent` method with the `deinstall` command.

Although the silent installation option exists, we find that installation of the Oracle BI 12c platform is often an intimate affair and best conducted manually using the GUI installation wizards. For more information on the silent install method, please see the Oracle documentation, https://docs.oracle.com/middleware/1221/core/BIEIG/GUID-4F0BD89A-C8BE-4851-8D0C-422779D5BC1D.htm#INSOA375.

Custom ports and port management

Fusion Middleware products are riddled with configuration preference options and perhaps that is what makes these tools so great. Another option that is available to you during the Oracle BI installation process is the ability to modify default ports that are assigned to Oracle BI and Fusion Middleware for accessing their applications. For example, if you wanted to change the default port for Oracle BI Presentation Services, 9500 to 8000, you could do that at the **Port Management** step in the installation wizard. This is shown in the following screenshot, which you saw in Chapter 3, *Installing on Windows Server 2012* during the installation by changing the **Port Range Starting Port** to 8000 instead of 9500 as you did during the installation. Please note that desires of modifying ports as a means to an end after the Oracle install completes should be redirected to an HTTP tier configuration instead of Oracle BI or WebLogic configurations:

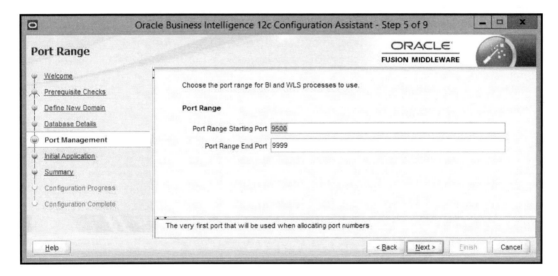

Post-installation modifications of ports for Oracle BI are only important in two situations: when running multiple instances of Oracle BI or another application on the same server or when you plan to have no multi-tier server architecture as part of your Oracle BI architecture design. Otherwise, you would always have a web tier HTTP server sitting above your Oracle BI and Fusion middleware servers from which you are in a much better management position and have greater flexibility in assigning ports, virtual IP addresses, and DNS names to access your Oracle BI applications from.
Previous versions of Oracle BI 11g had the concept of static ports configuration, but this option is not available in Oracle BI 12c.

Keeping with the default options should be rather easy as most Oracle BI implementations should be a single Oracle BI tenant on the server on which it is installed. Therefore there should be no port conflicts. If you wanted to change the port for the Oracle BI /analytics application to port `80`, (which is the default web port that requires no port number to be entered for the URL) in the browser address bar, then you shouldn't use this option, but rather a web tier server to handle that proxy for you. Compatible Web Tier servers for Oracle BI are IIS, Apache, or Oracle HTTP servers, to name a few.

Installing Oracle BI 12c on *Nix

One of the obvious options for installing Oracle BI 12c is the choice of operating system. `Chapter 3`, *Installing on Web Server 2012* did a nice job of showing the Oracle BI 12c installation on Microsoft Windows Server 2012. However, on a *Nix (that is,: Unix or Linux) operating system there are few, if any, differences mainly because the same GUI is available for all operating systems. As the person conducting the installation on a *Nix environment, you may or may not have the option to directly remote or log on to the server allocated for the Oracle BI environment. In which case the *Nix administrator must provide **Secure Shell (SSH)** access with display/xhosts options or VNCServer access. This will enable one to use a tool such as Putty or TightVNC to access the GUI Oracle BI 12c installation wizard.

A Linux-based **virtual machine** (**VM**) image was produced by the Oracle BI Product Management Development team with the release of Oracle BI 12c. It is referred to as the Oracle BI Sample Application. This VirtualBox-based VM image comes complete with Oracle BI 12c sample data, dashboards, and reports and it contains all of the necessary environment variables, and so on, as a set of examples for a basic Oracle BI 12c Linux implementation. The Sample Application is crucial for anyone wishing to see best practices on reports, dashboards, and the RPD; however, it is not a step-by-step learning resource like this book. In other words, keep reading and learn from real-world experts like us.

Information about the Oracle BI 12c Sample Application is found here, `http://www.oracle.com/technetwork/middleware/bi-foundation/obiee-samples-167534.html`.

Listening on port 80

Briefly in the preceding section, *Custom ports and port management*, you read about the potential for users to access the Oracle BI application by entering a URL into the address bar without a port number. So instead of `http://myserver.com:9500/analytics` they can use `http://myserver.com/analytics`. This configuration is achievable by incorporating what is known as a web (HTTP) tier proxy. In most architectures, the web tier that handles all of the HTTP traffic and the application tier that handles all of the dynamic rendering, database connection, and so on, are separated. Although usually this is done by means of separate physical servers, the configuration can be achieved on the same physical server as long as the server is robust enough to handle the added resource needs of the web tier server. The web/HTTP servers that are compatible with Oracle BI 12c are Microsoft **Internet Information Services (IIS)**, **Oracle HTTP Server** (**OHS**, and Apache Web Server. OHS is merely a more robust implementation of the open source Apache Web Server solution. Each of these web tier servers can integrate on a Windows operating system, but only OHS and Apache can be integrated on a Unix/Linux operating system. Another very robust HTTP web server is called NGINX (pronounced Engine-X).

We already discussed how Oracle WebLogic Server is a robust application server and how although it can definitely handle incoming HTTP traffic like a champ it does not have all of the features of a pure HTTP server such as IIS or Apache. One of the nicest features about a web server is that it can compress and cache both static files and dynamic requests from the application server in order to speed up response times when a user requests information from the server. For Oracle BI, this means that a user's dashboards will render faster in their browser as well as any queries they may submit.

Not all client web browsers are created equally. Specifically **Microsoft Internet Explorer (MSIE)** versions 7 and 8 have a hiccup that causes pages to render slower on them when benchmarked against other web browsers such as Mozilla Firefox or Google Chrome. This issue potentially affects your Oracle BI implementation, especially if an organization uses MSIE as the corporate web browser standard. There are also other organizations that have seen where a version of their web browser client standard is not directly supported by Oracle BI, instead of trying to force users into configurations such as IE's Enterprise Mode, there is a more global, safer solution. One can fix these browser compatibility issues by putting a web tier in front of our application tier. It will not only increase the speed of Oracle BI in Internet Explorer, but other browsers and consumption devices such as mobile tablets as well. Because we are using a Microsoft Windows Server in this book as our core operating system for the exercise, you will learn how to set up this web tier compression configuration using NGINX.

You do not need to conduct this web tier exercise right now in order to complete any of the other exercises in this book. It is merely here as a reference and considered an advanced implementation configuration that should actually take place after your Oracle BI installation.

Configuring a HTTP proxy with the NGINX web server

Let's take a HTTP web server, NGINX, well known in the industry for performance and flexibility, and add it to our server to enable URL access to OBIEE without requiring port numbers. You'll first download the NGINX web server, begin the quick configuration, and then test the results:

1. Download NGINX for the Windows OS (or your *Nix OS) at http://nginx.org/en/download.html.
2. Select the latest Mainline version for NGINX/Windows.
3. Before installing NGINX, make sure that your IIS services are stopped and that it, and no other service, is listening on the default port 80. You can do this by clicking on **Server Manager** accessing **Roles | Web Server (IIS)**, and then double-clicking on **Internet Information Services**. In the **IIS Manager**, right-click on the server name and select the **Stop** option.
4. Create a folder on the Windows OS in the C: drive called **NGINX**.
5. Copy the downloaded NGINX .zip file into this directory and then extract the file to this location so that you have the path and file, C:NGINXnginx-<version>nginx.exe available.
6. Open a command prompt as an Administrator.
7. In the command prompt:
    1. Change the directory to the NGINX file location, cd C:NGINXnginx-<version>
    2. Execute the following command:

    `start nginx`

8. Open the Windows task manager and verify that one or two nginx.exe... services are running.
9. Open a web browser and navigate to the URL, http://localhost, and you should receive a message stating, **Welcome to nginx!**

In order to now configure the proxy reference to the /analytics portal for Oracle BI, you need to update a configuration file in the path where you have installed/copied the NGINX downloaded application:

1. Access the path where you copied NGINX.exe, for example, C:NGINXnginx-<version>.
2. Open the directory, conf, which is a child directory of the main nginx-<version> directory.
3. Open the nginx.conf file for editing so that a few straightforward changes can be made.
4. Edit the file by locating the first reference to a line with server { in the line.
5. Directly above the server { line make some space by creating a few line breaks and then enter the following code:

```
#obiee 12c book example proxy
    server {  # simple reverse-proxy
    listen       80;
    server_name  localhost;

    # pass requests for dynamic content to app server
    location / {
      proxy_pass      http://localhost:9502;
    }
    }
```

6. The preceding code (don't forget the starting and ending brackets) provides a very simple configuration for a server reference, listening on port 80 for the server name of localhost where any location URL path entered (/) will proxy to the URL http://localhost on port 9500. Also, not that the pound (#) represents commenting out any characters on the same line that come after it.
7. Save the nginx.conf file.
8. Return to the command prompt you have open where you started the NGINX server using the start nginx command.
9. In the command prompt enter the following command:

    nginx.exe -s reload

    This will reload the configuration file with your changes into the server to take effect.

10. Open a web browser and now enter the URL, http://localhost/analytics.

Ancillary Installation Options

 Note how you are now taken to the OBIEE server portal page and can log in without any problem. When you log in, the URL remains without the port number, just as you desired.

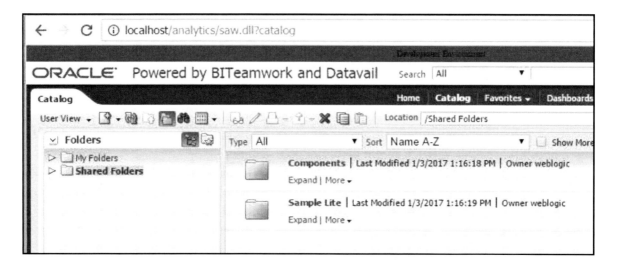

There is so much more to learn about HTTP servers and how they relate to load balancing and other capabilities to modify the entry point URL or DNS seen by users. We've found that not all network administrators, from company to company, are created equally. So be sure to solicit time or advice from a professional services group when you have some unique requirements or special connectivity needs around accessing your analytics portal across the network, or if you think your system access could be more fluid within the organization.

Enabling compression on web servers

Enabling compression at the web/HTTP server tier comes at the highest recommendation of Oracle. Particularly, this configuration solves a problem inherent in Internet Explorer browsers. This compression configuration exponentially optimizes response times from requests sent to the Oracle BI server and should be conducted in every environment in which you wish to install Oracle BI 12c, but especially in Oracle BI 11g if you still need to use that legacy environment.

All major HTTP servers have the ability to cache static files and compress files and data traffic over the network to expedite responses to user requests flowing through the Oracle BI system.

Setting up compression for the NGINX HTTP server

Compression reduces the size of transmitted data. Nginx does not compress data that has already been compressed. And the compression happens at runtime, which increases potentially the processing overhead on the server. But with a beefy server with plenty of processor capacity, compression will be the icing on the cake for your BI users:

1. Open the `nginx.conf` once more and prepare to edit the file in the next steps.
2. Add the following two lines of code inside the `server {` section you added in the previous section directly after the line, `server_name localhost`:

   ```
   gzip on;
   gunzip on;
   ```

3. Save the file: the content excerpt you've been updating should now look similar to the following screenshot:

   ```
   36      #obiee 12c book example proxy
   37          server {  # simple reverse-proxy
   38              listen        80;
   39              server_name   localhost;
   40
   41              gzip on;
   42              gunzip on;
   43
   44              # pass requests for dynamic content to app server on main port
   45              location / {
   46                proxy_pass      http://localhost:9502;
   47              }
   48          }
   ```

4. Execute again from the command line the reload command for `nginx`:

   ```
   nginx.exe -s reload
   ```

5. Refresh the browser page you previously accessed for the /analytics portal and you will most likely notice no material difference in speed right away. But just know it is there and ready to help your Oracle BI system handle more concurrent user requests than it did before.

Ancillary Installation Options

If you are really curious about the compression modification, we suggest you look at a couple of different things. First, read more about the use and recommendation of compression via HTTP servers (IIS, Apache, NGINX, and so on) in Oracle Support ID `1333049.1` and how compression solves an issue that still exists with Internet Explorer 8/9 browsers. Second, if prior to configuring the **gzip** and **gunzip** option, you were to use any of the web traffic analyzer tools such as **Firebug** for Firefox or **Developer Tools** for Chrome browsers, you would see that prior to the setting the following screenshot under **Response Headers** states the server is `nginx/1.11.10`, but there is no **Content-Encoding** attribute:

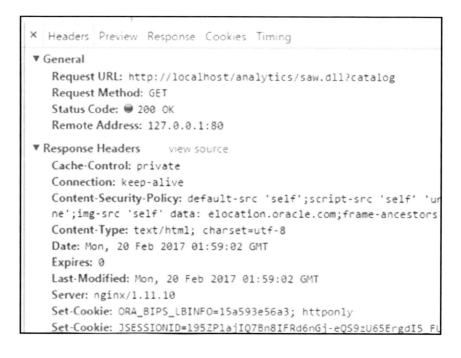

After the compression setting, you can see that, under **Response Headers**, the **Content-Encoding** is now set to **gzip**, showing that compression is turned on:

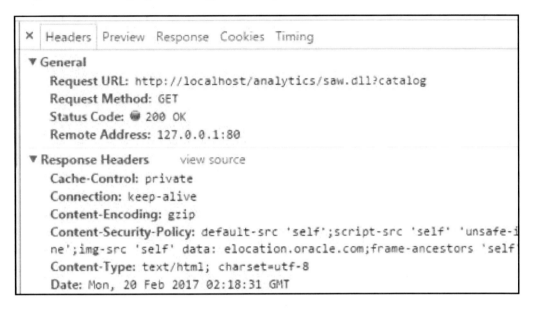

Automating starting and stopping

A very common question among enterprise deployments of an Oracle BI solution is, How can I have Oracle BI start up when the server boots? Or, especially with a Windows OS, How can I log off the server where Oracle BI resides and still keep the Oracle BI server application running? The solution or answer to this question is ancillary when compared to the overall architecture, security, and metadata modeling efforts behind the main BI effort. Nonetheless, once this keep-alive solution is implemented you'll wonder how you did without it.

On a Windows OS we can take advantage of Windows Services. On a *Nix server we can take advantage of the `rc.local` or `init.d` and `chkconfig` system start up and shutdown functions. Either approach involves writing a few short batch (or shell on *Nix) scripts, saving them to the appropriate location on the server and assigning the scripts to the correct start-up and shutdown function delegate for the operating system.

Ancillary Installation Options

Regardless of OS, Oracle BI 12c has simplified this process by allowing bitools command-line files that are part of the Oracle BI 12c LCM to control this process in a very straightforward manner. By executing the `bitools` start command, the process runs by starting the WebLogic Server NodeManager and calling the start of the WebLogic Admin Server, the BI Managed Server, and the BI Components. The bitools stop command calls the same process in reverse to properly shutdown the system. So as an administrator, one only needs be concerned about automating the start and stop commands for a basic Oracle BI implementation such as what is covered in this book.

Again, since we are using a Windows Server operating system, this exercise will highlight that operating system and take advantage of **Windows Services**.

Scripting Windows Services

On a Windows OS, the automation of programs on startup or shutdown typically involves using the Windows Services. This could also be done using the task scheduler or other popular methods. The following steps will focus on using the Windows Services `SC.EXE` command to create a windows service:

1. Navigate to the Windows Services panel by clicking on the Start menu and then searching for Windows Services.
2. Click on the option and then scan the resulting services list for an entry that starts with Oracle.
3. Open a command prompt and ensure that you are logged in as an Administrator or running the command prompt as an Administrator.
4. Enter the following command to create the start service, adjusting the path to the `bitools` folder to reflect your environment:

```
SC CREATE OracleBI12cStartup binPath=
"C:fmw_obieeOracle_homeuser_projectsdomainsbibitoolsbinstart.cmd"
    DisplayName= "Oracle BI 12c Startup Service"
```

5. View the resulting output and ensure the result was successful by checking the Windows Services list. Click **Refresh** on the list to see your new service listed:

6. Enter the following command to create the stop service, again adjusting the path to the `bitools` folder to reflect your environment and the correct command name:

    SC CREATE OracleBI12cShutdown binPath=

"C:fmw_obieeOracle_homeuser_projectsdomainsbibitoolsbinstop.cmd"
    DisplayName= "Oracle BI 12c Shutdown Service"

7. Again, refresh the Windows Services list to see the new service.
8. Right-click the startup service, change the necessary option to run at start up and click the **OK** button to close the prompt:

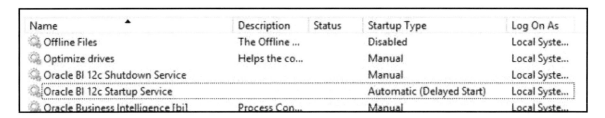

You should now, upon startup of your Windows Server, feel fairly confident that your Oracle BI system starts up fully when the machine is rebooted.

To delete a windows service, a Windows OS administrator can run the `SC DELETE` command followed by the service name, for example: `SC DELETEOracleBI12cShutdown`, to remove the windows service completely.

The shortcut that you created after the installation from Chapter 3, *Installing on Windows Server 2012* can still be used from the desktop and, since it points to the same startup script that the Windows Service you created does, you can have confidence in your testing of either approach to starting Oracle BI.

Another crowd favorite for creating Windows services is using a tool such as the **Non-Sucking Service Manager** (**NSSM**), which is open source and very reminiscent of the OPMN tool most will remember from the predecessor Oracle BI 11g system. NSSM helps to provide error logs and event logs from failed processes and ensures that programs are actually started or stopped with a high-level of confidence. Read more about NSSM at http://nssm.cc/usage.

Ancillary application integration awareness

Oracle BI is marketed as a product that can connect and be configured with several cutting-edge productions such as Oracle **Enterprise Performance Management** (**EPM**) to view financial reporting and also Oracle MapViewer to incorporate visual spatial analytic views into reports and dashboards. Although these are great concepts and ideal for many organizations, they are not set up by default. They are considered native extensions, but they do involve additional efforts through configuration in order to introduce them into your Oracle BI implementation. Some of these integration points such as EPM require configuration with the Oracle BI Action Framework, which requires additional modification to a physical configuration file on the server and a credential key configuration via the WebLogic Server Administration Console. Others require a separate server configuration as with incorporating MapViewer to develop custom maps, tiles, and layers, or to leverage existing or default ones.

We mention this here not to pass judgment on Oracle BI as a tool, but so that you are aware of some additional efforts required to hook in all the bells and whistles of Oracle BI. This also gives you a sense of how straightforward or how complex you can make your Oracle BI implementation. From a project management perspective, milestones are crucial when laying out your Oracle BI project. From a technical perspective, there's a lot of amazing stuff you can do with this tool; expanding your skillset or getting some outside assistance will be key for meeting those milestones on time, managing expectations, and understanding the art of the possible.

Recommendations for further learning

This chapter looked at additional installation and configuration options for Oracle BI 12c. You've read brief discussions on a few topics that we would have loved to include at depth, but perhaps those topics were either too advanced to explain in a mixed-topic chapter or outside the scope of this book. However, here are a few recommended topics for you to investigate further on your own in order to continue your learning:

- Oracle BI Enterprise Deployment Guide Shared Storage Pre-Configuration: `https://docs.oracle.com/middleware/1221/core/BIEDG/toc.htm`
- NSSM Windows Services: `http://nssm.cc/usage`
- NGINX Beginners Guide: `http://nginx.org/en/docs/beginners_guide.html`
- Oracle BI 12c Sample Application (SampleApp) Virtual Machine Image: `http://www.oracle.com/technetwork/middleware/bi-foundation/obiee-samples-167534.html`
- Oracle Fusion Middleware Install, Patch, and Upgrade Documentation Launch Page: `https://docs.oracle.com/middleware/1221/cross/installtasks.htm`
- NGINX Proxy Configuration: `https://www.nginx.com/resources/wiki/start/topics/examples/full`

A review - what should I know now?

For self-review and to recap the chapter, here are a few questions based on important topics covered in this chapter:

- Is high availability (HA) an option available in the Oracle BI 12c installation wizard or an architectural configuration?
- How can the Oracle BI application portal, /analytics, listen on port `80` to be accessible from the network using a URL such as `http://<server_name>/analytics`?
- When should the listen ports of any Oracle BI or WebLogic component be changed from its default?

Summary

In this chapter, we highlighted some of the most common post-configuration installation options and discussions seen in many real-world implementations that we've experienced. The sections in this chapter aimed to provide both a step-by-step explanation and a bit of food for thought on how to strategically approach hurdles confronted by most organizations implementing Oracle BI. An attempt was made to focus on items surrounding the installation planning process itself and to illustrate that the means to control the Oracle BI application in a more complex architecture is possible. Although most of the discussions and exercises in this chapter do not have any bearing on the immediate success of the other hands-on exercises that you conduct in this book, they will act as a reference for any future Oracle BI 12c installation planning.

15
Reporting Databases

"It's all about the database" - Anonymous.

No book on Oracle BI would be complete without introducing the concepts of a reporting database.

Just to be clear, **Oracle Business Intelligence Enterprise Edition** (**OBIEE**) is neither a database nor a storage system for data. OBIEE grabs data from a source (which is normally a database), and sends it to your screen (or e-mail, PDF, and so on) in a presentable format.

As discussed in previous chapters, the source data can be held in a variety of formats including, but not limited to, spreadsheets, tables, and XML. However, for most large implementations, a database is the only suitable source. If there are millions or even billions of data items, then a database is crucial. Moreover, a well-structured and well-maintained database is essential for the very survival of an OBIEE project. Size matters when it comes to design: the bigger the database, the better the design needs to be; otherwise it will be impossible for your clients to run the reports.

The new big data paradigm challenges our assumption that it is all about the database. This is because of the huge amount of data capture that is taking place in non-structured form. Databases give us nice **structured** data, but data is now held in **semi-structured** form, for example in XML documents, or XML streaming of data. Data is also held in **unstructured** form, such as simple text files, PDF, MS Word documents, and so on. These new formats add to the reporting complexity and may seem exciting now, but do not take away the fundamental fact that structured data in a database is still the easiest to use for reporting.

This chapter can only introduce the main concepts of a reporting database, because the process of creating an efficient database is the subject of dozens of books and blogs (see the recommended reading list). However, the following details should provide enough information to create a database that is fit for use in an Oracle Business Intelligence system.

This chapter is split into three parts:

- A brief introduction to the theory
- Guidelines for creating a warehouse
- Creating a warehouse example

Theories and models

It is said that creating a database is more about art than it is about science. I tend to agree with this. However, a number of theories and rules have evolved over the last 40 years that are worth understanding before attempting to build a database for an Oracle Business Intelligence system.

From an overall design perspective, there are two scientific types of database:

- Transactional databases
- Reporting databases

A **transactional** database is designed for the input and update of data, usually in small, high volume changes to the data; whereas a **reporting** database is designed for fast access to data, which can be transformed into useful information for decision-making. The common name for a reporting database is the data warehouse (a phrase originally coined by Bill Inmon, the inventor of data warehousing).

The following diagram shows how tables in a transactional model are laid out. It shows a small extract of the system that will be used throughout this book, and is based on a Microsoft AdventureWorks system:

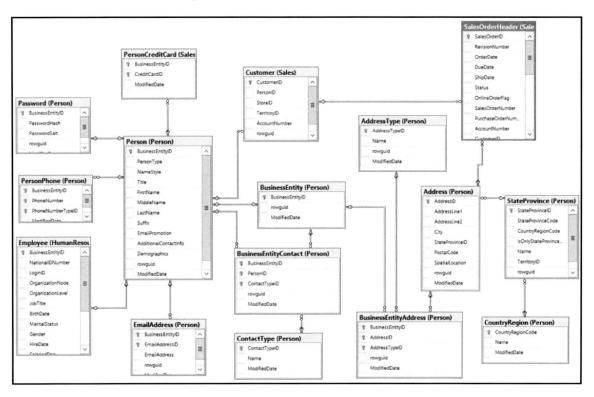

Reporting Databases

The following diagram shows an example of the structure of a reporting database. You can see how it contrasts in the way the tables are joined together. There are fewer tables, all joined via a single table (known as the Fact table), in this example the **FactFinance** table:

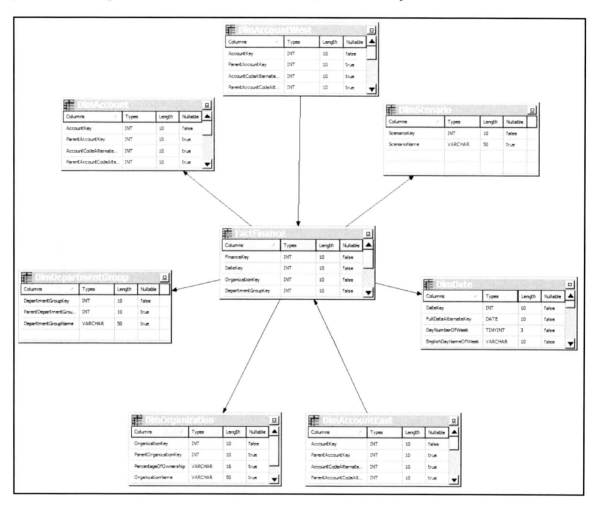

Reporting databases

There are two main theories for the design of a reporting database:

- Relational modeling
- Dimensional modeling

Relational modeling

The layout of data in relational modeling is similar to that of a transactional system, that is, third normal form. These types of warehouse are normally intended to populate smaller databases for operational reporting, or **Operational Data Store** (**ODS**). An Operational Data Store is a type of database that is usually used as an interim storage area prior to loading a corporate warehouse or for processing data and then loading data back into a source system. They are often multi-departmental level and typically data is checked against a set of rules, and updated in batches. They do not contain history and are not designed for large scale reporting.

A note on normalization:
The early development of theories of database design is dominated by E. Codd, whose works in the 1970s inspired a generation of new databases, including Oracle. In 1969, Codd proposed a relational model, which essentially ensured that tables in the database contain specialist data, such as customer names or sale orders, and that these tables relate to each other using a key field. In 1970 he expanded the theory to include normalization. The process of normalizing a database consists of reducing tables down to their smallest size, both in columns and rows, by breaking them down into smaller tables. The objective is to remove data replication. Codd's theories on normalization and the 12 rules of database construction that he created in the 1980s still apply today. I recommend that anyone serious about building large scale Oracle BI systems read his work; or at least the summaries! Sources:
http://en.wikipedia.org/wiki/E.F._Codd
http://en.wikipedia.org/wiki/Database_normalization
http://www.dbnormalization.com/difinitions-of-the-normal-forms
http://en.wikipedia.org/wiki/Relational_model

Dimensional modeling

Dimensional modeling was proposed by Ralph Kimball in the mid-1990s as a method of speeding up report production and simplifying the database layer. The model is a response to the large complex relational databases (also known as **Entity Relational** or ER databases).

Kimball published papers that showed why ER databases are not suitable for reporting:

> "In our zeal to make transaction processing efficient, we have lost sight of our original, most important goal. We have created databases that cannot be queried! Even a simple order-taking system creates a database of dozens of tables that are linked together by a bewildering spider web of joins."

Kimball, 'A Dimensional Modeling Manifesto,'Kimball Group - `http://www.kimballgroup.com/1997/08/a-dimensional-modeling-manifesto/`

The main advantage of Kimball's dimensional modeling is that it reduces the number of tables and joins, which in theory, results in a faster query run-time, and a much simpler model for report developers to work with.

Dimensional modeling actually consists of tables of **dimensions** and a table of **facts**:

- Dimension tables hold information that is largely non-numeric, that is, descriptive text, dates, references, and so on. The records are related to an entity, such as a tennis player and usually represent an aspect of the data stored in the Fact table.
- The table of facts holds data that can be aggregated, for example, counted, summed, averaged, or some other calculation. The facts records are normally transaction or activity-related, such as person's holiday record.

The Date table is an example of a table of the dimension type. It contains a list of dates, each of which is defined by a number of descriptive fields, or **attributes**, which could include Month Name and Year, for example.

Dimension tables can also contain columns that are structured to represent a **hierarchy**, that is, the relationship between different attributes within the dimension. For example, one possible hierarchy in the Date table is represented by the fields Year Number, Quarter Number, Month Name, and Date. This hierarchy has four levels, with Year at the top and Date at the bottom (most detailed) level.

An example of a Fact table is a table recording Daily Sales by Store. In this example, the Fact table might contain three columns recording the Date, Store Name, and Sales Amount.

Tables in a dimensional database are normally joined together by linking the dimensions to the facts. This is known as a **star schema** model, and is shown in the following diagram. The joins between the tables are using key fields. The key field on the dimension will be the primary key for that table, and the key fields on the facts are foreign keys.

As you can see, dimensional modeling enables a much less complicated layout than the relational modeling system, and has fewer joins. The Dimension tables (labeled with the prefix **Dim**) only join to the Fact table, which sits centrally:

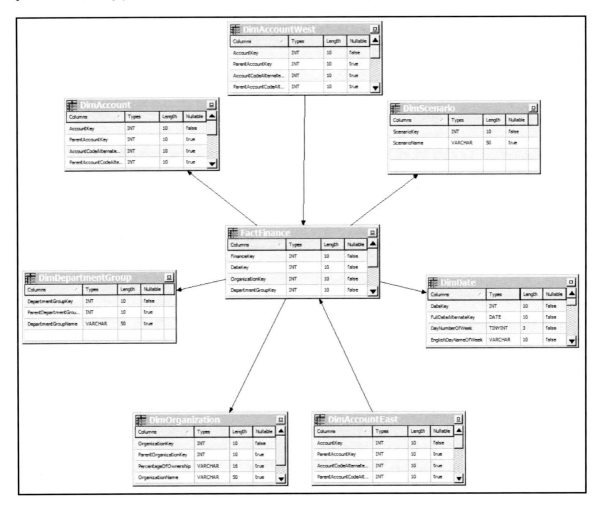

Why is database theory important?

The introduction to the theories behind the relational database may seem a little dry, and you may be wondering why we are looking at the theories of databases in an OBIEE book. But for every single project you undertake, it is essential that you have a good understanding of the data structures that you will be using, particularly when designing the OBI repository. If you want your project to succeed, then speed is crucial; but this is only achievable with the correct design. Choosing the correct design is therefore crucial, which means understanding the theory.

In this book, you are using dimensional modeling in the OBIEE configuration. It is also worth mentioning that there are other models that can help certain types of reporting. This includes OLAP cube models and column-based databases, both of which are worth reading up on, but are not covered in this book.

Designing your database - objectives, rules, and goals

Whenever you create a data warehouse for reporting, you have to consider that there are finite resources. There is never enough space to store data, never enough time to populate the database, and never enough processing power to use a fully normalized source. Even with the latest super-fast technologies, such as Oracle exadata, there is a limit to the amount of data that can be stored or processed in a given time period.

The primary objective should always be to speed up report production, which means using a dimensional model, particularly when storing a large amount of data. As discussed in the theories section, using an Entity Relational database would reduce the redundancy of data, and therefore reduce the amount of data stored and the time taken to load it; however, report production times would increase.

It is always necessary to make a trade-off between **Data Volume** (to increase the speed of reporting), **Load Speed** (to minimize the amount of time loading a database), and **Read Speed** (minimize to keep the project going!). Each of these factors affects the other, as indicated in the following diagram. If the amount of data stored is increased, Read Speed will be minimized (good), but Load Speed will be increased (bad):

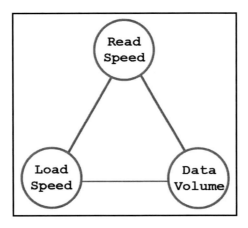

In order to ensure a good balance between Data Volume, Load Speed, and Read Speed, you should use a set of objectives, rules, and goals in your designs.

Objectives

My objectives when building a warehouse, in no particular order of importance, are:

- Objective 1: Fast reporting
- Objective 2: Fast data loading
- Objective 3: Minimize data volume
- Objective 4: Accurate reporting

We believe that fast reporting is better than fast loading. A delay in the availability of the system (while it uploads new data) is acceptable for a time, but if it takes an inordinate amount of time to run reports, the users will soon switch off. However, this does not mean that the system can be offline for the update process when the users requires access on an ongoing, daily basis. If this happens, your users will decide to look elsewhere for their reports.

Note that if loading times are an issue then you could explore the use of a Dual warehouse solution - load one while you use the other, then switch warehouses.

Rules

In order to achieve the database objectives listed previously, there are a number of rules that must be adhered to:

- Rule 1: Complete dimensions
- Rule 2: Build generic tables
- Rule 3: Partition large tables
- Rule 4: Prudent indexing
- Rule 5: Aggregate everything
- Rule 6: Constant analysis of usage and accuracy
- Rule 7: Manage statistics
- Rule 8: Understand the granularity

These rules emphasize the use of **Performance Data**.

> **Performance Data:**
> Performance Data is the data created in a warehouse that makes reports run faster. This includes not only the data to make queries use less data, but also data that reduces the number of joins in queries. **Types of Performance Data include:**
>
> - Roll up data (aggregated data)
> - Subsets
> - Star fields
> - Mini dimensions
> - Flat tables
> - Indexes
> - Materialized views (for pre-joined or pre-calculated tables)
> - Calculated data

Rule 1 - complete dimensions

A complete dimension has two aspects:

- Complete in terms of number of rows
- Complete in terms of number of attributes (fields)

If you have a Fact table that has a field related to a dimension (for example, the Sales Order Fact contains the Order Taken Date, which links to the Date table), then the Dimension table must contain a row which corresponds to every date within the fact. The ultimate way to enforce this is to add a referential integrity rule to your tables. However, this should *not* generally be done as it impacts on load speed and will result in failed loads.

Similarly, any attributes assigned to a dimension must be complete. For example, you may have a Shops table which lists shops and includes contact details. Each shop will have a location (city, town, village, and so on) which must be included in the Shop Dimension table.

With this kind of scenario, there is a choice to be made: you can either apply a relational model, or add the relevant data to the Shops table's attributes. If you choose to follow a relational model, the Location Table can be joined to the Shops table for reporting purposes, which is a very simple process. However, my preference is to bring the relevant data into the Shops table's attributes (fields). These might include Location Name, Address, Country, and Postal Code.

Rule 1 fulfills Objectives 1 and 4, but at the cost of Objectives 2 and 3. Using a relational join for the location attributes helps with Objectives 2 and 3 but undermines Objective 1.

Rule 2 - build generic tables

It is vital to ensure that your model can cope with reporting requirements, both now and in the future. Building a table just to suit a particular report might be great in terms of getting the job done quickly; however, you will inevitably end up having to re-write large amounts of the **Database, Extract, and Load** (ETL) and reporting system whenever any changes to requirements occur.

Take the example of a Contracts table that has been built specifically to handle monthly salaried shop and head office employees. If the client later requires reports on sales achieved by temporary Saturday morning staff on weekly contracts, what do you do? You could build another dimension for these contracts or re-write the Contracts table to accommodate both sets of staff. But then what about the sales team who were acquired this month, carrying their own contracts?

As you can see, it is much better to build generic tables in the first place that will be better able to satisfy a wide range of data types and user requirements.

Rule 3 - partition large tables

Partitioning is a way of breaking down large tables into smaller sets of records. Large tables can be partitioned by a single field value, such as an organizational unit. This should really be an obvious thing to do, even if your database does not have the option to partition tables automatically. If using Oracle's partitioning capability, you will require an extra license, but it is worth investing in as it overcomes the need to create and maintain a manual partitioning system.

My own working method is to apply a partitioning solution as soon as the number of records in a table exceeds 10 million, but you can partition smaller tables too. I once encountered a project which had a table with 1.6 billion rows and no partition. I doubt that any report would ever run on that table, however long you waited; and it was certainly not good at updates and indexing!

Rule 4 - prudent indexing

Prudent indexing ensures that Objectives 2 and 3 are not undermined. Indexes should help with joins and data filters, and can be the difference between a working database and one that has no value whatsoever. Unfortunately, there is often a tendency to over-index. When building a database, in the first instance, you should only add indexes to fields that are used in the joins. Over time, you can analyze usage patterns and then decide whether or not more indexes are required to improve reporting performance.

Removing unnecessary indexes will save time in the loading process and may even improve reporting performance. The Oracle database system now includes an option to monitor index usage, which can be very revealing (to implement, add MONITOR USAGE to the index definition).

Rule 5 - aggregate everything

My motto is that if it can be aggregated, then aggregate it! If you have a Daily Sales Fact then why not create a Monthly Sales Fact? And how about Annual and Weekly Facts? Provided the aggregate is used in the analysis, the report performance will usually be significantly better when accessing smaller datasets. Aggregating is therefore great for Objective 1. The downside is that all the aggregates need to be populated and stored, which is contrary to Objectives 2 (Loading time) and 3 (Amount stored). Again, a balance needs to be struck.

Aggregations need not apply only to facts; they can also be applied to dimensions. If you take the Date table, which may have tens of thousands of rows, and aggregate this to Year level, this could result in only a couple of hundred records. This table can then be used to join to the Year Aggregate Sales Fact. The two combined will have a huge performance benefit over the Date Table joining to the Daily Sales and grouping by Year.

Rule 6 - constant analysis of usage and accuracy

You should analyze usage and accuracy constantly, because no matter how quickly your database is loaded, if the reporting system is slow to produce reports, your customers will soon lose interest and your project will collapse. It is crucial to know if a report is slow, and preferably before your customers know! Make sure that you have excellent feedback from your reporting system about the speed of reports; and also the speed of loading and, as far as possible, the accuracy of data in the warehouse.

My personal favorite way to do this is to create a dashboard showing usage, performance, and data items. Monitoring systems are often forgotten during the development stage and can be difficult to acquire funding for at a later stage. Make sure you factor them in from the start. If there is only one thing that you take from this chapter, remember that monitoring will make things so much easier; monitoring and Performance Data.

Rule 7 - manage statistics

Managing statistics is not just about gathering statistics each night; it's about ensuring that your queries are tuned for the tables that they run against. When building queries, you will use Oracle's **Explain Plans** feature to let you know what it plans to do. Automatically creating new stats on your table each night can interfere with Explain Plans, which is the last thing you will want when you have found one that really suits your purposes. The best way I have found to avoid this is to save the stats for a table and then import them to the table after each load. This ensures that the Explain Plan you want to use will be used. It is also possible to work with managing Explain Plans in a similar way. The stats will still need to be reviewed regularly when the table size changes significantly; but the monitoring tools you have put in place will tell you when a table has changed size, or when a query is slowing down over time.

Rule 8 - understand the granularity

Last but certainly not least, don't compromise data granularity. In order to create reports that use non-related information, it can be tempting to break the natural granularity of the data. Take, for example, an employee database recording sickness absence. The granularity here is the employee and the time (measured in days). An employee could be working on more than one project. If you were requested to produce a report showing absence by project, how could this be done? The tempting thing would be to break the granularity of the data by creating more than one record in the Absence Fact table; one for each employee, date, and project. Don't do this. Keep the data stored at its natural granularity and join an Employee/Projects table to the Absence Fact table (using the Employee key).

I have seen various methods which show how to break a single record down into multiple records, allocating the facts across those records. However, I find it best to ignore these theories, and stick to the natural granularity of the original fact.

Goals

Along with rules that should be followed, I have goals that I aim for in the design and ongoing upgrade of a warehouse. In an ideal world, we would only work with simple data, have unlimited resources, and have access to **Online Transaction Processing** (**OLTP**) source systems. In the real world, we have awkward datasets (for example, many to many to many relationships), no way of putting triggers in the source system, and we never have enough computing power. Compromises therefore have to be made. But never compromise your objectives, try not to compromise your rules, and keep these goals in mind when responding to difficult design choices:

- Goal 1: Keep it simple
- Goal 2: Minimize the use of Type 2 Slowly Changing Dimensions
- Goal 3: Use data, not functions
- Goal 4: Minimize joins
- Goal 5: Reduce snowflaking
- Goal 6: Make it flexible

Goal 1 - keep it simple

This should be self-explanatory, but the goal is to be able to come back to your design (either you or the next consultant who will be editing your code) and understand what it is doing quickly. This entails making fewer objects, and keeping code to a minimum. It also includes choosing your platform code carefully. Try to avoid mixing SQL code in the database, with SQL code run in the ETL layer, with SQL run in OBIEE. Decide where you will execute SQL and stick to it.

Goal 2 - minimize Type 2 Slowly Changing Dimensions

Slowly changing dimensions are tables where the dimension attributes change over time. For example, a staff member may get married and then change their last name. Your choice in the warehouse is how to record the change. A dimension that includes the current staff member details and a record for their previous details is called a **Type 2 Slowly Changing Dimension (SCD)**.

I tend to avoid these SCD tables wherever possible. If you cannot avoid them, due to the need for reporting dimension changes over time, then try to keep the history of a dimension record in separate table. The dimension history table can still be used in reporting where required, but does not impact every report.

Also, if you do need to use a dimension history table, be careful about the keys you implement. Make sure that your facts are able to link to each relevant record of the dimension, not just to the dimension record in force when the fact was created.

Goal 3 - use data, not functions

The use of database functions in reporting can have a hugely detrimental effect on the speed of reports. Wherever possible, get the results of the functions into the table as extra fields. This can be done during the data loading process.

Goal 4 - minimize joins

Joins are normally bad for performance. If data can be held in one table, then hold it in one rather than two. Try to follow the Kimball star schema methodology where practicable. This can mean the same piece of information is held in two tables, but you will benefit from faster reporting.

Goal 5 - reduce snowflaking

Snowflakes are where the dimensional model is mixed with the relational model. A central fact is joined to the dimension, but that dimension then joins to another dimension (which does not join to the fact).

Snowflakes in a warehouse are not ideal. Snowflaking is normally slower due to increasing the number of joins, but can also indicate that the dimension has not been built completely.

Goal 6 - make it flexible

Try to ensure that you have not created objects and data that are only fit for the reporting requirements you already have.

Take for example, an initial requirement to report games won by year for a player. The table storing tennis games won by player could be at year level, but what if you then want to drill into by month? Store the data at month level in the first instance and you can satisfy both requirements.

Design summary

Try to gain a good level of understanding regarding star schema database design, because it will speed up your report performance. However, be aware of the speed and data triangle, and therefore the need to compromise.

Each data warehouse needs to weigh up the outcomes required against the technical objectives in order to determine which rules and goals are to be observed. This will then lead to a suitable warehouse design.

Whenever you have a design choice to make, score the possible methods against your Rules and Goals. This usually results in an obvious best approach.

Creating a warehouse

This section of the chapter will lead you through the design and build process for the small warehouse (often referred to as a data mart) used for the reporting examples in the following chapters of this book.

For this book, we have taken the Microsoft AdventureWorks sample system, which already includes a warehouse schema for reporting.

Therefore, in this next section I will use a theoretical tennis statistic reporting system to show you the steps involved in designing a data warehouse.

The first step is to assess each source system table for its type of data in order to determine if it fits into a Dimension table, a Fact table, or another table type. Based upon our assessment of the source tables, we can then design and build the warehouse tables. This is followed by the creation of a process to copy the data from the source to the warehouse. Finally, we review and tune the database in order to ensure that we can meet the goals we have set.

Source system assessment

We will start with the list of source tables. For each one, we will note which data type they are, examine the contents, determine if they are required in the warehouse, and consider any other factors that might be significant.

Reporting Databases

The standard approach is to look at the table from three angles:

- Physical attributes:
    - What are the columns and their data types?
    - What restrictions are there?
    - And most importantly, what keys are there?
- Data content:
    - Try to get as big a sample of the data as possible
    - Bring it into a system you understand, such as Excel, Access, or a database
    - Finally, try to understand the field contents and numbers involved
- Business use:
    - Find out how the table is used in the source system
    - If the table is used in an existing reporting system, what reports use the table (and how!)?

The tables in the Tennis Statistics source system are split into Men's Tour and Ladies' Tour tables, along with some joint lookup tables, for example Tennis Court Types. A section of the database showing Men's Tennis is shown in the following diagram:

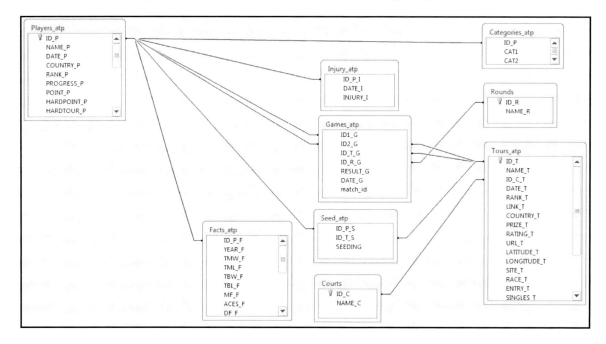

Using the approach shown previously, we create the following table:

Source Table Name	Content	Rows	Potential Warehouse Target	Warehouse Notes
PLAYER_ATP	List of Male Players	23,535	Player Dimension	The ATP and WTA source tables will be combined into one warehouse table.
PLAYER_WTA	List of Female Players	11,769		
ROUNDS	List of Tournament Rounds	17	Round Dimension	
COURTS	List of Court Types	6	Court Type Dimension	
TOURS_ATP	List of Tournaments for Male Players	8,381	Tournament Dimension and Stadium Dimension	The ATP and WTA source tables will be combined into one warehouse table.
TOURS_WTA	List of Tournaments for Female Players	4,500		
GAMES_ATP	Each game played at a tournament, with the result	335,563	Match Dimension, and Match Fact	Create two records in the MatchFact, one for each player in a singles match, or four records for a doubles match.
GAMES_WTA	Each game played at a tournament, along with the result	170,844		
CATEGORIES_ATP	Extra information on a male player		Player Dimension	Consider keeping in a separate table if the Player Table becomes too wide (that is, too many columns).
CATEGORIES_WTA	Extra information on a female player			
FACTS_ATP	Annual statistics for each male player	1,530	Player Year Facts	Player yearly summary can also include stats not in the FACTS_ATP table.
FACTS_WTA	Annual statistics for each female player	0	n/a	

Warehouse design

We can now draw up a design for the warehouse, with a star schema in mind. Our goals are to reduce joins and therefore reduce snowflake designs, and make the design flexible enough for any reporting that we would like to think of. We will also keep in mind the rules laid out in the first section of this chapter.

Warehouse tables

The initial result of our analysis has resulted in six Dimension tables and two Fact tables. This is not set in stone; we need to be flexible enough to add more tables later if the report requirements dictate. There are no aggregate tables yet in place, because at this stage we do not know where, if any, there are performance issues. Given that we have designed a star then initial performance for a two million record table should be good:

Warehouse Table Name	Content	Type	Granularity
W_PLAYER_D	List of Players	Dimension	Player
W_ROUND_D	List of Rounds	Dimension	Round
W_DATE_D	List of Dates	Dimension	Day
W_COURT_TYPE_D	List of Court Types	Dimension	Court Type
W_STADIUM_D	List of Stadium	Dimension	Stadium
W_TOURNAMENT_D	List of Tournaments	Dimension	Tournament
W_MATCH_F	Matches at a tournament	Fact	Match, Player
W_TOURNAMENT_F	Players at a tournament	Fact	Tournament, Player

These tables can be arranged into the two following star schema layouts, with joins between the tables using the primary keys for the dimensions.

The match star schema

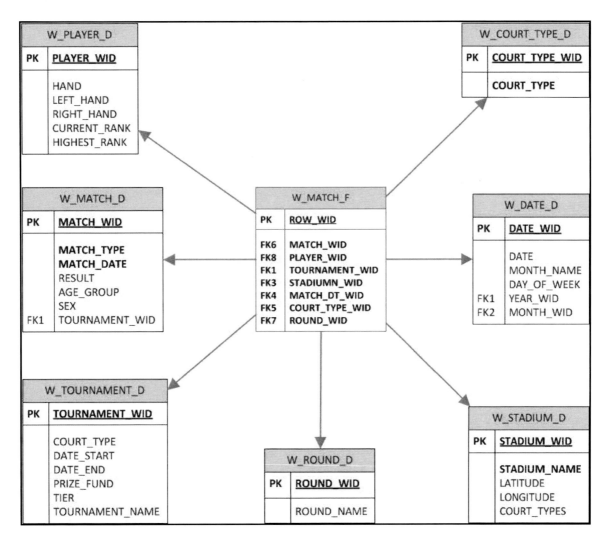

Note the direct connection from the Tournament Dimension table (`W_TOURNAMENT_D`) to the Match Fact table (`W_MATCH_F`). If we modeled the Tournament table to connect to the Match table (`W_MATCH_D`) and did not have a Tournament `WID` field in the Match fact, then we would have a snowflake design.

Reporting Databases

 WID is a column name suffix that was introduced to us in the Siebel days. It stands for Warehouse ID, and is used to name the field which is normally part of the key for a table. For example, DATE_WID would be used on the date table and would contain a warehouse derived ID. In the Oracle BI Applications databases, you often see ROW_WID as the primary key on the Dimension tables.

The tournament star schema

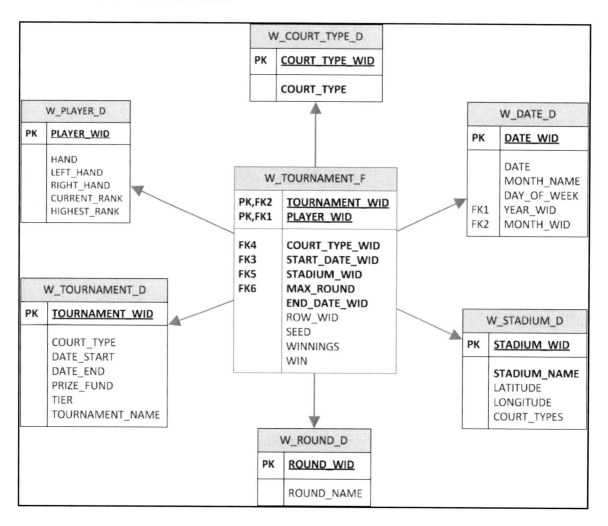

With the previous two star designs, we are now able to respond to a whole range of analyses, such as how many matches do left-handed players win in the Southern Hemisphere each year on hard courts!

Populating and tuning

Having designed your warehouse, it's now time to create the objects.

Creating the tables is straightforward and can be achieved using free tools such as SQL Developer.

You are now faced with choices over the use of indexes and partitions. The general rule of thumb is to only create what you need. If an index is not going to be assisting in reports then do not create it. If a table has more than 10 million records then it becomes a good candidate for partitioning. The latest versions of Oracle have a useful feature for auto incrementing partitions which can make the whole process much easier to implement (make sure you have the right license though!).

Primary keys should be added where suitable, certainly on the Dimension tables, but also on the Fact tables provided they do not slow down the loading process too much. If you are not able to use a unique key in the fact due to massive amounts of data, then it is prudent to check that the dimensions rule is not broken, that is, make sure there are no references in the fact to dimension records that do not exist.

Monitoring and maintaining

Having created and populated our warehouse the hard work begins! Once the Oracle BI tool starts to throw requests at our database we will learn where the bottlenecks are. Monitoring the **ETL** and database statistics each day are vital to ensure that potential breakages are avoided. This includes understanding how the tables are growing each day, and what the impact is on our allocated disk space.

The latest version of Oracle Enterprise Manager (11g) has a substantial set of monitoring processes that makes it an invaluable tool in your armory.

Implement **Usage Tracking** in Oracle BI to understand where your customers are experiencing slow performance, and act on the information gathered. This could be adding indexes, Performance Data or even changing the way that OBI accesses the star.

Usage tracking will be explained in detail later in this book.

Some definitions

Acronyms	Definitions
ETL	**Extract, Transform, and Load**: The process of taking data from a source system into a warehouse.
SQL	**Structured Query Language**: The basic language that databases such as Oracle and SQL Server understand. SQL is used to create data, create database objects such as tables, and to query data.
Performance Data	I use this term to describe any data which helps to speed up reporting performance. This includes creating aggregate tables, for example the Tournament Fact table. It also includes the use of subsets of data, partitioning of tables, and indexing.
Star Transformation	A special feature of Oracle databases is their ability to maximize the performance of a query that uses a star design table layout. Oracle can build a more efficient query than usual due to the fact that it knows all Dimensions join to the Fact table.
Hints	Hints are used to help an Oracle database to query the tables in the most efficient manner. This could include telling Oracle to use particular join methods or indexes.
Exadata	An Oracle machine that increases performance of the Oracle database by bringing together the storage, processing, and database operating system into one box.
Cubes	A cube is a special way of organizing data so that it can be queried extremely quickly. Data is often aggregated in cubes so that numbers are available to the user without the database having to do any calculations.
Slowly Changing Dimensions	A dimension record, for example a player, does not normally change once it has been created. However, if a player married and then changed their last name, the warehouse designer needs to decide how this is reflected in the Dimension table. If you create a new record based upon the player's new details then you have created a Slowly Changing Dimension table.
Indexes	Indexes are used to help a database access data more quickly than simply by looking at the data itself.

Hierarchies	Records in a table can often have a parent:child relationship which develop into a hierarchy of levels. For example, in the Date table, we have Date, which has a parent of Month, which has a parent of Year. The hierarchy is then: Year | Month | Date

A review - what you should know now!

- How a reporting database needs to be structured
- You need to set objectives when you create a warehouse (for example, the ETL should run in 3 hours)
- What the rules are for creating efficient warehouses
- The goals you can use when designing a warehouse
- The steps involved in creating a warehouse from a source database

Summary

In this chapter, we introduced the basic concepts of database design, and which ones are more suited to reporting. We have also seen how a balance between report speed and data loading needs to be struck, given limited resources.

To ensure that your database is useful to its customers, it should achieve certain objectives which are met using rules and goals that you lay down in the initial design phase and follow up in each design choice.

Implementing a database does not stop when the objects are created, but should be followed up with a continuous monitoring and maintenance process.

In the production of this book, we have created a small warehouse for reporting on Tennis Statistics. All the database objects and data are available for download from the book's website.

16
Customizing the Style of Dashboards

Oracle Business Intelligence 12c comes with built-in styles which create a specific look for your users. The default style includes an Oracle logo in the top-left, a gray border, black words, blue page titles, and a white page background. This style is called Alta. There are several styles you can choose from, each with their own set of colors, spacing, and region shapes. Each dashboard can use a different style which you can set yourself at any time.

If none of the available styles suit your company or project, then the good news is that you can create your own styles and load them into the BI Server. You can also change the default styles for all dashboards if you need to.

This chapter shows you how to change styles, and how to create and implement a new style.

Throughout the Oracle BI system, users are presented with words and messages that guide them. An example would be the *sign out* message, which is fairly obvious what it does! But other messages may need further explanation, such as the *No results* default message. The good news is that messages can be in the default language of your users, so English speakers see English messages, but your Spanish users see Spanish messages.

This chapter will also cover how to change messages throughout the system.

What's the idea?

Let's first qualify what it means to customize the style of the Oracle BI dashboard. There are several approaches to modifying the look, feel, and overall integration associated with the Oracle BI dashboard. This could include anything from adding a custom button or link, appending a third-party widget, changing the logo, or changing the color scheme present in the out-of-the-box Oracle BI product. Now that the definition is out of the way, the question is: what do the customization requirements seek to accomplish? Do the customizations seek to modify form, function, or both?

The most common directive of customizing a dashboard has to do with modifying the color scheme seen in the Oracle BI portal. This is referred to as branding. Branding is really a marketing term but it is used ubiquitously for this scenario as it applies to web-based applications. One of the main ideas behind branding the Oracle BI portal is to increase user adoption among the user base. Internally, users are much more likely to begin using Oracle BI and stay within the tool if it doesn't seem foreign to their current corporate tools. Think about it this way; if Sally Joe, in finance, navigated from her company's Intranet, which clearly displays the company logo, colors, and so on, using a hyperlink on the main page, to an Oracle BI dashboard in order to view a profit and loss report, the segue could potentially appear seamless. That is, Sally Joe would see the requested data in the dashboard and still appear to be within her company Intranet instead of a bland (although kind of good looking), out-of-the-box application that looks like some new tool she has to learn.

This chapter focuses mainly on that branding of Oracle BI 12c dashboards using styles.

Multiple skins and styles in one environment

Oracle BI can house several customized looks or branding profiles. This can be dynamically set by associating a particular style with a particular user, group, or application role. Let's say Sally Joe in the Finance department logs in to the Oracle BI portal. Sally may be presented with a blue and white color scheme with the corporate logo showing in the portal whereas her constituent, Erich in the European office, may log in to the Oracle BI portal and be presented with a brown and gold color scheme showing the flag of Germany as the logo. This dynamic shifting of branding to specific end users can be achieved by relating a specific style to a specific user, group, or application role. It could also be established by setting a default style for all users and having only specified users, groups, and roles associated with a different perspective.

Another nuance is that several aspects of branding can be localized. That is to say that depending on the locale or location from which an end user has associated themselves (usually determined by the browser and language settings of the workstation being used), a different appearance or branding may be applied and rendered during their interaction within the Oracle BI portal. This can be seen ubiquitously in the exercise steps in the *Custom messages* section in this chapter.

Hands-on - go time!

The remainder of this chapter provides a systematic guide on implementing what is referred to as basic branding. The goal of the exercise is to take an out-of-the-box Oracle BI dashboard and transform the default style to contain the logo and colors of Company XYZ. Each step builds upon the one before it, so following the steps in order will be crucial to the end result. It is recommended to leverage the operating system's default text editor when making changes to base files provided by the Oracle BI platform filesystem; in our case, we are using Notepad++.

In the first exercise, we will look at how we can change a dashboard to use one of the existing styles that Oracle provides out-of-the-box.

Changing styles

Before we create our style, lets investigate the existing available styles:

1. Log into OBIEE 12c.
2. Open our **Dashboard One**.
3. Select the **Edit Dashboard** icon.

Customizing the Style of Dashboards

4. Select **Dashboard Properties...**:

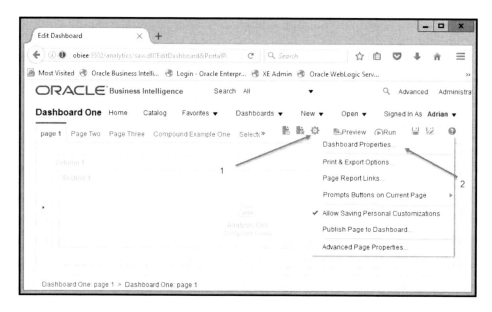

5. Change the **Style** to **blafp** (stands for BI look and feel):

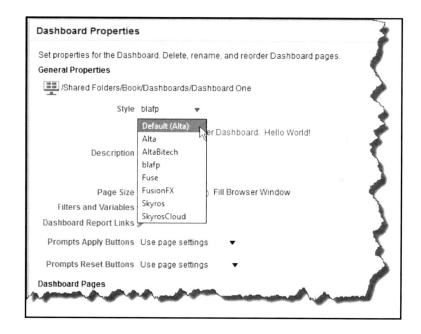

6. Click on **OK**.
7. Save the dashboard.
8. Click on **Run**.

You now see a significantly different looking dashboard page than when you started:

 Note the different style of page tab, the blue background, and the little icons on the menu items.

Creating your own look and feel - overview

The steps in the following section take advantage of the Oracle BI 12c skinning and styling customization options. Modifying these options is predominantly manual in nature. The idea of look and feel as it relates to Oracle BI translates into skins, styles, and messages.

Messages are usually the textual elements that are shown in the Oracle BI portal (presentation services) and can be anything from the header logo and text, to the name of each link shown above the dashboard tabs. An example of the latter would be changing the sign out link on the portal dashboard to render `Get out of here!` instead.

Styles and skins relate to both the color scheme shown in the Oracle BI portal and the visible nature of Oracle BI Analysis Views. An example of modifying a style would be to change the background color of a dashboard from the default white color to a light gray. An example of skinning would be to modify the bar chart's color scheme from its default to a custom color palette.

Customizing the Style of Dashboards

Creating new styles and skins means creating the files and folders which contain your custom code, and deploying these files into the BI Server.

Two deployment methods:

The deployment of a new style can use either a **full application** method, or it can be using a **shared folder**. We will examine both methods.

Examples of the files and folder structures required for your custom code can be found in the analytics **Enterprise Application aRchive (EAR)** file. The analytics EAR file can be found in the `<Oracle_home>bibifoundationjee`.

You can open EAR and WAR files using the 7-zip utility. See http://www.7-zip.org/

Inside the EAR file is a **Web Application Archive (WAR)** file, which contains the `res` folder; for example, see `<Oracle_home>bibifoundationjeeanalytics.earanalytics.warres`. Here you will see the styles which are already available to your users, such as Skyros, Alta, blafp, Fusion, and FusionFX.

The folders that should be used as templates are prefixed with `s_` and `sk_`, which specifies the style and skin folders respectively. As an example, one of the default sets of style and skin folders provided out-of-the-box are `s_blafp` and `sk_blafp`. If modifying both the skin and styles, both of these folders will be leveraged.

In addition to styles and skins, custom messages can be used to modify the Oracle BI dashboards. There are hundreds of messages within the Oracle BI 12c environment that are dynamically accessed and generated at runtime. The core messages can be located in XML files contained within the following folder:
`<Oracle_Home>bibifoundationwebmsgdbmessages`.

Each XML file acts as a grouping container, as suggested by the name, containing one or more message objects that are referenced by Oracle BI at runtime. These messages can be overridden, and a few will be in this exercise. This dynamic messaging system also allows flexibility for localization (that is, translation into other languages or specific text to other languages). In order to either create custom templates or modify a template to another language, a separate custom messages folder and XML file will be established away from the default message folder referenced in the preceding section. The message that is desired to be overridden, is usually first assessed from the default messages folder location. Attributes about the message are noted and the overriding message is then created in a new arbitrarily named XML file. The XML file is placed in a `filesystem` folder, and is ultimately moved into a web application (or folder) that gets deployed to the WebLogic Application Server.

> You should never modify the original default skin, styles, or messages folders and/or files directly. A copy of the base files should be made and then modified.

Creating your style

Before we can deploy the style code, we need to create it! We could do this from scratch, or by copying an existing style's folders, or you may prefer to take a shortcut and start with an existing pre-built structure. Luckily, Oracle have provided a simple EAR file to start with, called `bicustom-template.ear`. The bicustom EAR file is based upon the Skyros style. You can find this file in `<Oracle_home>bibifoundationjee`.

The first stage is to extract the files:

1. Create a working folder, for example `C:fmw_bookobiee_dev`.
2. Create a subfolder called `ear`.
3. Create another subfolder called `war`.
4. Copy the `bicustom-template.ear` into the `ear` folder.
5. Extract the `bicustom-template.ear` file into `c:obiee_devear` using 7-zip, or use the Java command:

    ```
    cd c:fmw_bookobiee_devear
    jar xvf bicustom-template.ear
    ```

6. Check that you now have a folder call META-INF and a WAR file in the `ear` folder.

Customizing the Style of Dashboards

7. Delete the `bicustom-template.ear` file.
8. Extract the file `bicustom.war` into `c:obiee_devwar`, use 7-zip or a `Jar` command:

   ```
   copy bicustom.war c:fmw_bookobiee_devwar
   cd c:fmw_bookobiee_devwar
   Jar xvf bicustom.war
   ```

9. Delete the file `C:obiee_devearbicustom.war` (we will generate our own war file).

If the `Jar` command is not recognized, either add the java JDK folder to the path environment or call JAR using the full pathname.

10. You now have the files you need to make a style for your project:

Code management:

In this example, we have put our code into the folder, `C:obiee_dev`, which we have added to our code management system. We use GitHub, but you can use any form of SVN -- just make sure you are using one!

In this exercise, we will modify the Oracle BI 12c dashboard for a fictional organization, Company XYZ. Their standard company color palette is made up of the following:

- **Color #1**: Light Steel Blue
- **Color #2**: Gray
- **Color #3**: Black

Modifying the code

We are now going to create our new style by renaming the component parts and mapping them to a style:

1. Rename the folder s_Custom to s_BookStyleOne.
2. Create a folder called sk_BookStyleOne in the same folder as s_BookStyleOne.
3. Edit the file, filemap.xml, changing s_Custom to s_BookStyleOne, and sk_Cusom to sk_BookStyleOne.

   The code should now read as follows:

   ```
   <FileMap>
      <Styles Default="s_blafp">
         <Hierarchy>s_Skyros / s_BookStyleOne</Hierarchy>
      </Styles>
      <Skins Default="sk_blafp">
         <Hierarchy>sk_Skyros / sk_BookStyleOne</Hierarchy>
      </Skins>
   </FileMap>
   ```

4. Save the file.

   You will now have two folders in the res folder:

5. Edit the file `master.css` (in the `ress_BookStyleOnemaster` folder).
6. Find the entry for `masterBrandingArea`, and change the values to:

```
.masterBrandingArea {
    background-color: lightsteelblue;
    color: black;
    padding: 5px;
}
```

7. Find the entry for `masterMenuButtonGlobal`, and change the values to:

```
.masterMenuButtonGlobal {
    color: black;
}
```

8. Save the file.
9. Edit the file `custom.css` (in the `ress_BookStyleOnemaster` folder).
10. Add an entry for a dashed line at the top:

```
.HeaderBarSeparator
{
    border-top: 1px dashed magenta;
}
```

11. Save the file.

OK, that's enough to demonstrate what changes can be made, lets now test this code in OBIEE.

In the first example, we will use method one; Create and deploy an **Enterprise Application aRchive** (**EAR**) file. We will use the Java JAR command in a cmd window to create our files.

Chapter 16

 Creating an EAR file which contains all of your custom code makes it easier to deploy and re-deploy into different environments and into a clustered environment.

12. Using Java, zip up the contents of the `war` folder, into a WAR file called `bicustom.war`:

    ```
    cd c:fmw_obieeobiee_devwar
    Jar -cvf bicustom.war *
    ```

13. Copy the `bicustom.war` file into the `ear` folder:

    ```
    copy bicustom.war ..ear
    ```

14. Use Java to zip up the contents of the `ear` folder, creating a file called `bicustom.ear`:

    ```
    cd c:fmw_obieeobiee_devear
    Jar -cvf bicustom.ear *
    ```

15. Now copy the file to the components folder, which in our case is located at: `<ORACLE_HOME>user_proctsdomainsbibidatacomponentsOBIPS`:

    ```
    copy c:fmw_obieeobiee_devearbicustom.ear c:fmw_obieeoracle_home
    user_proctsdomainsbibidatacomponentsOBIPSbicustom.ear
    ```

You now have a file ready to deploy, so we will now use the WebLogic screens to deploy the file:

1. Log into the OBIEE Administration Console at `http://localhost:9500/console`.
2. Click on the **Deployments** link.
3. Click on the **Lock & Edit** button.

[515]

Customizing the Style of Dashboards

4. Click on the **Install** button:

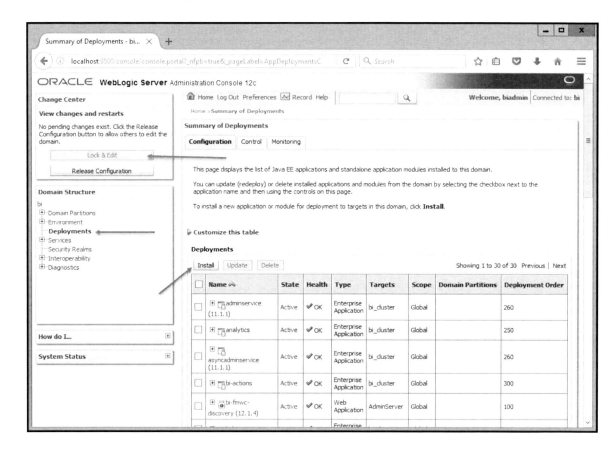

Chapter 16

5. Navigate to the path where the `bicustom.ear` file is:
   `c:fmw_obieeoracle_home user_proctsdomainsbibidatacomponentsOBIPSbicustom.ear`:

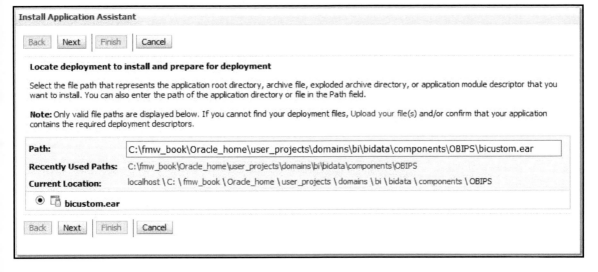

6. Click on **Next**.
7. Select **Install this deployment as an application**:

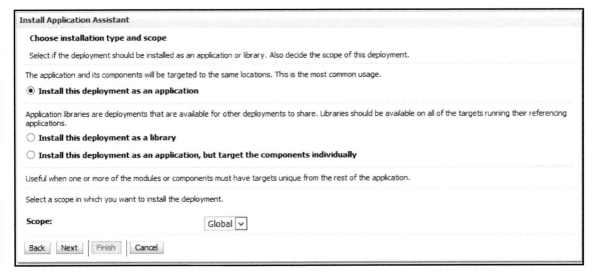

[517]

8. Click on **Next**:

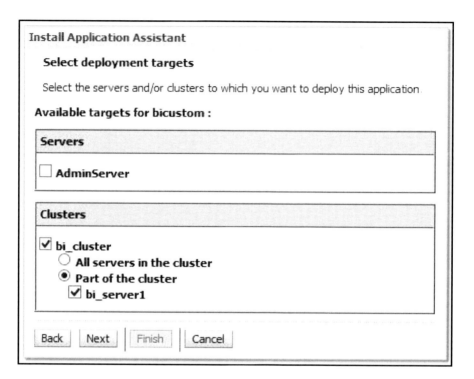

9. Select the **bi_server1** option.
10. Click on **Next**.
11. Select the option **I will make the deployment accessible from the following location**.
12. Click on **Next**.

13. Click on **Finish**:

Install Application Assistant

Review your choices and click Finish
Click Finish to complete the deployment. This may take a few moments to complete.

Additional Configuration
In order to work successfully, this application may require additional configuration. Do you want to review this application's configuration after completing this assistant?

○ Yes, take me to the deployment's configuration screen.
◉ No, I will review the configuration later.

Summary

Deployment:	C:\fmw_book\Oracle_home\user_projects\domains\bi\bidata\components\OBIPS\bicustom.ear
Name:	bicustom
Staging Mode:	I will make the deployment accessible at C:\fmw_book\Oracle_home\user_projects\domains\bi\bidata\components\OBIPS\bicustom.ear
Plan Staging Mode:	Use the same accessibilty as the application
Security Model:	DDOnly: Use only roles and policies that are defined in the deployment descriptors.
Scope:	Global

Target Summary

Components	Targets
bicustom.ear	bi_server1

[Back] [Next] [Finish] [Cancel]

14. Click on the **Activate Changes** button.

The application is now installed on the BI Server, but is not yet running, and is not yet being used by OBIEE. First, we will set it to be running, then we will restart the service so that OBIEE picks up the new code:

1. Click on the **Control** tab.
2. Select the **bicustom** application.
3. Click on Start.

Customizing the Style of Dashboards

4. Click on **Servicing all requests**:

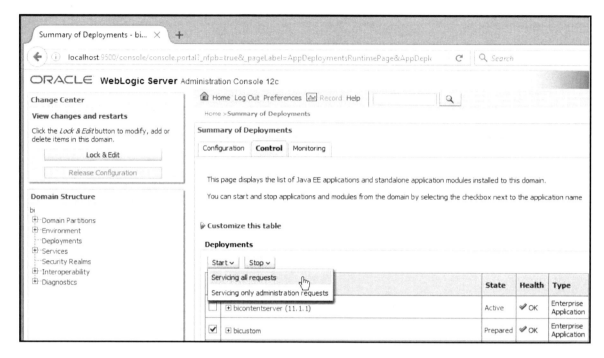

5. Click **Yes** to start servicing requests:

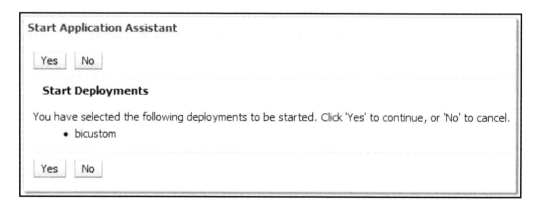

Chapter 16

So, the application is now running, but OBIEE still doesn't know about it. In theory, we could restart the OBIEE Presentation Service now and the new style would be available. In practice, we usually find that a full restart is best for a new deployment:

1. Stop and start your OBIEE system.
2. Log into OBIEE.
3. Edit **Dashboard One**.
4. Click on the tools icon.
5. Click on the **Dashboard Properties...** link:

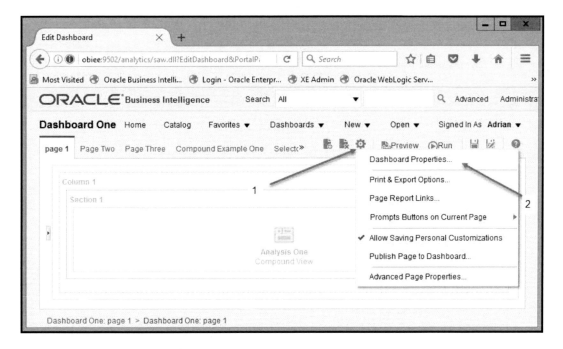

6. Click on the **Style** list.
7. Change the style to **BookStyleOne**.
8. Click on **OK**.
9. Save and run the dashboard.

You will now see your dashboard in our new corporate colors. Notice the dashed line and the Steel Blue header background.

Congratulations, you have implemented a new style.

Updating your style

Editing your new style can be easily achieved using the following steps:

1. Update the style ear file with your changes.
2. Update the deployed application.
3. Restart the presentation service.

Let's give it a try:

1. Update the CSS and image files in your style. For example, change the dashed line to solid (in `custom.css`):

   ```
   .HeaderBarSeparator
   {
       border-top: 1px solid magenta;
   }
   ```

2. Create a new `bicustom.ear` file which includes your updated code.
3. Copy into the OBIPS folder, that is, `c:fmw_obieeoracle_home user_projectsdomainsbibidatacomponentsOBIPS`.
4. Log into OBIEE Console.
5. Click on the **Deployments** link.
6. Click on the **Lock & Edit** button.
7. Select the **bicustom** application.
8. Click on the **Update** button.
9. Click **Finish** (you can skip all steps).
10. Click on **Activate Changes** button.

There is no need to restart the presentation service, but you will have to reload the files and metadata in the OBIEE Administration screen:

1. Click on **Administration**.
2. Click on **Reload Files and Metadata**:

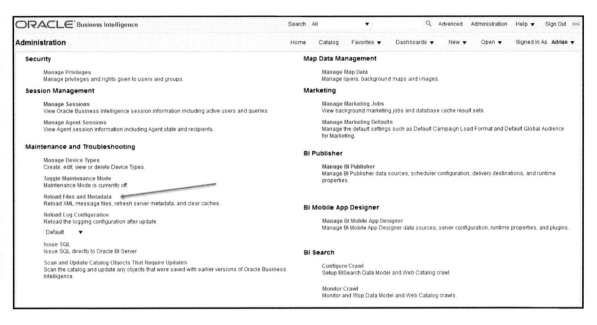

At this point, you may have to clear your cache in your browser.

When you view **Dashboard One**, you should now see the solid magenta line.

Alternative deployment method

We mentioned earlier that there are two ways of implementing your custom code. Previously, we have shown how to implement using a deployed application in the WebLogic server.

We will now look at the alternative method, which is to deploy a folder instead of an application.

In the first part, we will create a new style in a `custom` folder.

Customizing the Style of Dashboards

This time we will start with a copy of the Skyros code, which we will get from the `analytics.ear` file:

1. Extract the folder, `s_skyros` and `sk_skyros` from the folder `C:\fmw_book\Oracle_home\bi\bifoundation\jee\analytics.ear\analytics.war\res`, into a temporary folder.
2. Create a folder for the custom code. Create `C:\fmw_book\BookCustomCode`.
3. Extract the `bicustom.war` file into `C:\fmw_book\BookCustomCode`.
4. Delete the folder `C:\fmw_book\BookCustomCode\res\bicustom`.
5. Copy `s_skyros` from the temporary folder into `BookCustomCode\res`.
6. Copy `sk_skyros` from the temporary folder into `BookCustomCode\res`.
7. Rename the `s_skyros` folder (in the `res` folder) to `s_BookStyleTwo`.
8. Rename the `sk_skyros` folder (in the `res` folder) to `sk_BookStyleTwo`.

You should now have the current folders in place, ready for creating a new style:

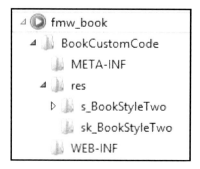

9. Edit the `filemap.xml` file (`C:\fmw_book\BookCustomCode\filemap.xml`):

```
<Styles Default="s_blafp">
  <Hierarchy>s_Skyros / s_BookStyleTwo</Hierarchy>
</Styles>

<Skins Default="sk_blafp">
  <Hierarchy>sk_Skyros / sk_BookStyleTwo</Hierarchy>
</Skins>
```

10. Edit the CSS file `master.css` (found in the `master` folder):

    ```
    .masterBrandingArea
    {
        background-color: burlywood;
        color: black;
        padding: 5px;
    }
    ```

11. Edit the CSS file `custom.css` (also found in the `master` folder):

    ```
    .HeaderBarSeparator
    {
        border-top: 5px solid blanchedalmond;
    }
    ```

Now we will deploy the new custom folder into OBIEE:

1. Log in to Oracle WebLogic Server Administration Console.
2. Click **Lock & Edit**.
3. Click on the **Deployments** link.
4. Click on the **Install** button.
5. Select the folder containing the new custom style:

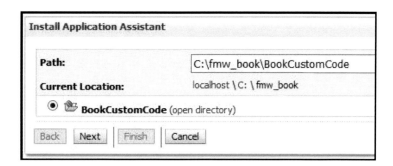

6. Click **Next**.
7. Select **Install this deployment as an application**.
8. Click **Next**.
9. Select **bi_cluster** as the deployment target.
10. Click **Next**.

Customizing the Style of Dashboards

11. Set the name to `AnalyticsRes`.
12. Select **I will make the deployment accessible from the following location**.
13. Click **Next**.
14. Select **Yes**, take me to the deployment's configuration screen.
15. Click **Finish**.
16. Click the **Configuration** tab.
17. Enter `/analyticsRes` in the **Context Root** box.
18. Click **Save**.
19. Click **OK**.
20. Click **Activate Changes**.

Now we will start the new application:

1. Click on the **Deployments** link.
2. Select the **Control** tab.
3. Select the **analyticsRes** checkbox.
4. Click **Start**, and then select **Servicing all requests**.

In order for OBIEE to use the new folder, we need to update the configuration file, `instanceconfig.xml`.

This file is located in `<BI DOMAIN>configfmwconfigbiconfigOBIPS`.

Please take a backup of the file before editing it:

1. Edit `instanceconfig.xml`.
2. Add the following code:

    ```
    <!-- Customisation added -->
    <URL>
    <CustomerResourcePhysicalPath>C:fmw_bookBookCustomCoderes
    </CustomerResourcePhysicalPath>
    <CustomerResourceVirtualPath>/analyticsRes/res
    </CustomerResourceVirtualPath>
    </URL>
    ```

3. Stop and restart the OBIEE system.

We will now check that **BookStyleTwo** is available:

1. Log into OBIEE.
2. Edit **Dashboard One**.
3. Click on the tools icon.
4. Click on the **Dashboard Properties....** link.
5. Click on the **Style** list.
6. Change the style to **BookStyleTwo**:

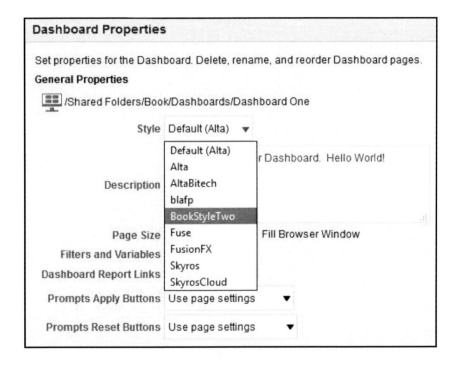

7. Click **OK**.
8. Save and run the dashboard.

You can now change the CSS directly in the **BookStyleTwo** CSS files, and the changes can be instantly viewed in OBIEE.

This method lends itself very well to dynamic implementations, where changes are required quicker.

Customizing the Style of Dashboards

Custom messages

The words that you see on the screen can be changed to suit your company.

Let's do a simple example, where we change the title from Business Intelligence to OBIEE 12c Book:

1. Create a file called `custommessages.xml`.
2. Add the following entry:

   ```
   <?xml version="1.0" encoding="utf-8"?>
   <WebMessageTables
   xmlns:sawm="com.siebel.analytics.web/message/v1">
   <WebMessageTable system="Custom Messages" table="Messages">
   <WebMessage name="kmsgHeaderBIBrandName"><TEXT>OBIEE 12c</TEXT>
   </WebMessage>
   </WebMessageTable>
   </WebMessageTables>
   ```

3. Create a folder called `customMessages` in the `OBIPS` folder, that is, `C:fmw_bookOracle_homeuser_projectsdomainsbibidatacomponentsOBIPScustomMessages`.
4. Copy the `custommessages.xml` file into the new folder.
5. Reload the files and metadata in the Administration screen:

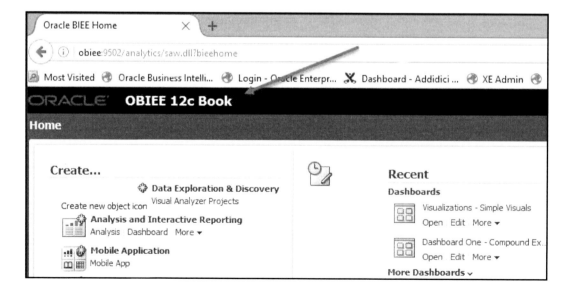

[528]

Chapter 16

A review - what I should now know!

- How to change the style of the dashboard
- Using existing styles
- How to create your own look and style
- How to create custom messages

Summary

In this chapter, we showed how to make your system match the style of your company. We showed two methods of deploying custom styling; the deployed application and the deployed folder method. Which method you choose will depend on your standard company policy.

We also showed how to change the words displayed on the screens using a custom message table.

The changes shown were minor, but you now have the framework to implement your customizations, including CSS and images.

When you create your own style, follow a few simple rules:

- Don't boil the ocean - make small incremental changes
- Involve marketing - try to follow corporate color schemes
- Consider your users' screens. We often work with customers who have smaller screens than the developer!

17
Upgrading to 12c

Phew! So, we are at the end of the book, having taken you through all the areas you need to be confident in using, administering, and developing in OBIEE. It's a lot to take in, but also remember that this is a starting point. Many of the previous chapters could be expanded to become books in their own right!

We are aware that many people reading this will have already used a previous version of OBIEE, so for our final chapter, let's look at the upgrade process for the most fundamental parts of the system, from a version-11g implementation to 12c, that is, the Repository and Presentation Catalog.

The upgrade process for this is extremely straightforward as Oracle has provided an easy-to-use upgrade tool that we will step through in this chapter. We are helped in that user-interface and infrastructure changes are not as big from 11g to 12c as they were from older versions to 10g.

If you are upgrading a current live implementation, the wider implications of the upgrade must be considered, especially the possible effects on current functionality. Therefore, in this chapter, we will also touch upon the thinking and planning that is needed prior to a full upgrade for a current live implementation.

It is also advisable to review the install we did in `Chapter 3`, *Installing the Windows Server 2012*, as there is some crossover depending on the import method you choose.

Checking the 11g system and files

Before attempting an upgrade, ensure that you have the necessary files and the correct administrator details for the following:

- 11g RPD
- 11g Presentation Catalog

You should also be running at least the following OBIEE versions and have filesystem permissions on both:

- **1.1.7 OBIEE**: Your current running version must be at least this version. Any version below this cannot be upgraded to 12c
- Your new 12c system

You should also consider the following before the upgrade:

- Check that the new 12c system has the correct database connectivity setup for the newly upgraded 11g RPD. For example, on an Oracle database, this would mean configuring the `TNSNames.ora` file on the new system. Remember that 12c utilizes its own `TNSnames.ora` file rather than requiring a separate Oracle client installation.
- If you have other customizations on your current 11g implementation, you may need to reapply these. This may include CSS files to change the look and feel of the frontend, or enhanced functionality via JavaScript. Also, rather than reapplying, you may actually need to redevelop customized styles and skins. You can ascertain this by testing your old customization during the regression cycle that we will go through at the end of this chapter.

Before embarking on the upgrade of these components, also check that you have started up all of the relevant 12c services. These services are as follows:

- BI services
- WebLogic Server
- Enterprise Manager

You can test this by logging in to the following links (the port numbers will be different if you have changed these in your initial installation):

- **Enterprise Manager**: `http://localhost:7001/em`
- **Weblogic Server Console**: `http://localhost:7001/console`

Also, ensure that Weblogic authentication has been configured so that 11g users can sign into the 12c domain. This is not the part of upgrade so will need to be done as a separate exercise.

- **OBIEE Answers**: `http://localhost:9704/analytics`

The upgrade process has changed from previous versions and is now a bit more command-line driven. However, it is more comprehensive in that it requires less reconfiguration after running the process.

Oracle provides a simple and straightforward script for this called the **BI Migration Script** (`migrationtool.sh`). This is used to export both 11g OBIEE and BI Publisher objects into an export bundle that can be imported into the new 12c instance.

Generation

First we need to generate that export bundle. The BI Migration Script is used to create a single, self-executing jar file that we can use to create the 11g export bundle. You can find the script at `ORACLE_HOME/user_projects/domains/bi/bitools/bin/migrationtool.sh`.

This will be on your new 12c system, so `ORACLE_HOME` should be replaced with the path to Oracle 12c that your installation set.

Now we can generate the `.jar` file by running the following:

> `ORACLE_HOME/user_projects/domains/bi/bitools/bin/migrationtool.sh package bi-migration-tool.jar`

Or we can do this by instigating the command from the directory where the script is:

> `migrationtool.sh package bi-migration-tool.jar`

This command will create the `bi-migration-tool.jar`. This jar file now needs to be moved to the old 11g system.

[533]

Export bundle

Once we have the .jar file on our 11g system, we can run it to create the export bundle that contains all of our OBIEE and Publisher objects. The command is as follows:

```
$JDK_HOME/bin/java -jar bi-migration-tool.jar out $ORACLE_HOME $DOMAIN_HOME ./12import.jar
```

Remember to change the direction of the slash marks for Windows.

The following is a breakdown of this command:

- The out tells the tool to run in Export mode
- ORACLE_HOME is the Oracle_BI directory inside Middleware
- DOMAIN_HOME is normally the user_projects/domains/bi directory inside Middleware
- ./12import.jar is the name and location of the .jar file that holds our 11g objects. In our example, we have placed the .jar file in our current directory, but we could replace that command with another file location

Once run, you will see output at the command line as the tool logs into the 11g system and performs the export. At the end of this process, you should see the following messages:

- Export succeeded
- Migration action succeeded

And the bundle will be ready for copying into the new 12c system.

Bundle contents

It may be of interest to you as to what the bundle contains. Most files in the .jar are unreadable system-specific binaries, but if you opened the file, you would see the following:

- NQSConfig.ini (11g version)
- NQSConfig.ini (12c version)

Also, you will find something called the **Business Intelligence Archive (BAR)** file. This is a new 12c object, which gathers together three of the main OBIEE objects, and enables such an easy transfer process:

- `live.cat`: This is our 11g Presentation Catalog in an archive format
- `live.rpd`: This is our 11g RPD that has been upgraded to 12c
- `system-jazn-data.xml`: This contains our security metadata, that is, our 11g Application Roles and Policies

Importing the bundle

There are two options for importing the `.jar` file into our new 12c system:

- Configuration Assistant
- BI Migration Script

Let's take these in turn.

Import via the Configuration Assistant

This is the Oracle-recommended method and is suitable if you are configuring the new 12c system for the first time. This is an important point, so if you have already configured the 12c system, skip this section and move onto importing via the migration script. Remember, we used the assistant in `Chapter 3`, *Installing on Windows Server 2012*. So please refer back to that chapter for a refresher if needs be (or if you run into issues), as we will not cover the process in the same detail again here:

1. Proceeding with the Configuration Assistant, from your command line, go to `ORACLE_HOME/bi/bin folder`:

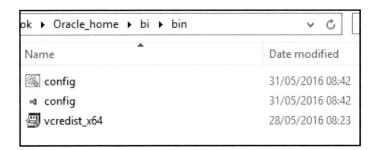

Upgrading to 12c

2. Start the assistant using `./config.sh` for Unix or `config.cmd` for Windows.
3. Select the components you wish to install, for example, BI Publisher, as shown in `Chapter 3`, *Installing on Windows Server 2012*.
4. Click **Next** on the **Prerequisite Checks** screen, ensuring that there are no errors.
5. You will now see the **Define New Domain** screen. As per `Chapter 3`, *Installing on Windows Server 2012*, input the **Domain Directory**, **Domain Name**, **Domain Home**, **Username**, and **Password**:

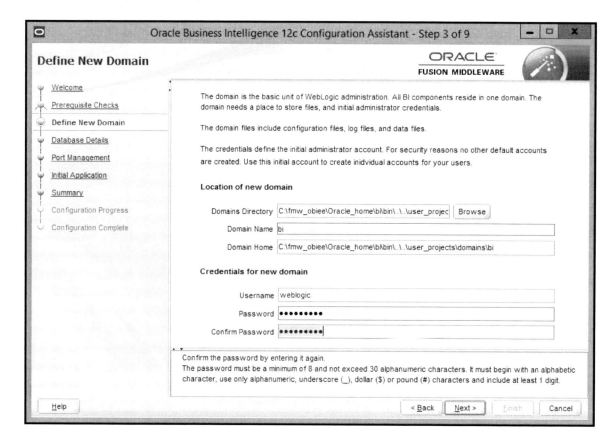

6. On the next page (**Database Details**), choose to create a new schema or an existing one, again, as per `Chapter 3`, *Installing on Windows Server 2012*.
7. On the next **Port Management** screen, specify the appropriate port selection and click **Next**.

Chapter 17

8. We will finally arrive at the **Initial Application** screen. This is where we finally differ from the clean install process:

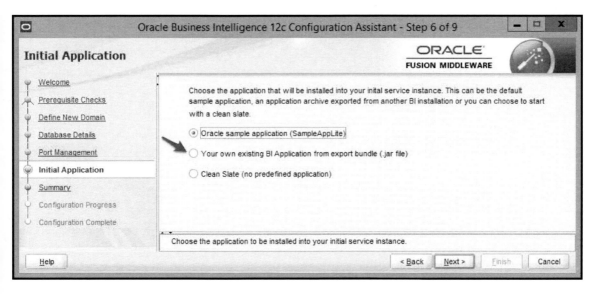

9. Ensure that you choose the **Your own existing BI Application from export bundle (.jar file)** option rather than a **Clean Slate (no predefined application)** or sample app. Click **Next**.
10. Choose the `12import.jar` file from the directory that you have placed it in. This is the jar that contains our 11g objects. Click **Next**.
11. Now you will see the summary screen. Verify the details, and if they are correct, click **Configure** to start the upgrade process (note that you can also save a response file at this point, for a silent installation).
12. On the **Configuration Complete** screen, review the summary, which you can save if you wish. Once you click **Finish**, OBIEE will open in a browser, whereupon you can log in and check your upgraded reports and dashboards.

 Remember to start up any 12c services at this point.

Import via the BI Migration Script

As we previously noted, if you have already configured OBIEE 12c, you need to use the **BI Migration Script** (`migration-tool.sh` or `.cmd` for Windows). This is a quicker process in terms of steps (as the 12c system is already set up!):

1. The script exists on `user_projects/domains/bi/bitools/bin/`, so change to that directory.
2. Execute the script and import by running the following script:

   ```
   user_projects/domains/bi/bitools/bin/migration-tool.sh in
   /temp/12import.jar ssi
   ```

We can break down the parameters for this command as follows:

- `in`: This argument tells the tool that we are importing objects.
- `/temp/12import.jar`: This, as you know, is the export bundle that contains our 11g objects. If the `.jar` file is in a different folder, you will have to provide the full directory path for this argument.
- `ssi`: This is the default server instance name for OBIEE. If your server instance is different, this argument will have to be changed appropriately.

> If you are not sure of your instance name, go to `Oracle_Home/user_projects/domains/bi/bidata/`.

The folder here will tell you your instance name that you set on the initial install:

1. Once you have executed this command, you will be prompted for the 11g RPD password. Once the migration has succeeded, you will get both Import succeeded and Migration succeeded messages.
2. Start the 12c services and you are ready to validate the upgrade.

Connectivity

Before testing the system, there are some manual steps that you need to look at when migrating. These should form part of any larger migration plan and are extremely important.

Firstly, you must ensure the Oracle BI 12c system has proper connectivity. This is a manual process; there are no migration tools, and you must check the following:

- NQSConfig.ini
- odbc.ini (non-Oracle DSNs)
- tnsnames.ora
- instanceconfig.xml (for the Presentation Server)
- userpref_currencies.xml (if you are muti-currency)
- bridgeconfig.properties (for Presentation Server plug-in information)

These details can be manually copied from the 11g instance or manually inserted in the appropriate format and location for the 12c instance.

Consistency check

At this stage, a consistency check of the RPD should also be run. During each iteration of OBIEE, the consistency check has become rather more strict, and more comprehensive in its validation rules. This means that any modeling in the 11g RPD that was incorrect/not in line with best practice may be highlighted. This may be flagged as a show-stopping error, which must be solved before the RPD can go live. For example, in 12c, the validation rules are rather more stringent about correct logical-column mappings. The naming rules are also stricter, so there cannot be leading or trailing spaces. Both of these issues will ag errors that will stop validation of a whole section of an RPD.

Other issues may produce warnings. These will not hinder deployment, but should ideally be resolved. An example of this is that the consistency check will now ag up a connection pool that is being used both for report queries and as an initialization block for variables. This is because it can create a potential problem with resource contention.

The key message is that an RPD upgrade should be run well in advance of a go-live date, to give a developer enough time to sort through any unforeseen issues.

Security and manual migration

- Before going live, you should perform a sanity check for all security settings in WebLogic and make sure that application roles are set up as required. This will form part of the regression-test cycle that we will discuss in a moment. Note that BI System User is removed in 12c.
- In the upgraded Web Catalog, 11g Catalog Groups have been replaced by 12c Application Roles. You will still need to migrate catalog groups from the 11g version manually.
- You will also need to manually migrate the following from 11g to 12c:
    - Weblogic Security Configuration
    - Fusion Middleware Configuration
    - Fusion Middleware Control, that is, the General, Presentation, Performance, and Mail sections.
    - Fusion Middleware Control Log Settings
- Also note, and plan into your activities, migration for those optional components that you currently use:
    - BI Publisher
    - Usage Tracking
    - Scheduler
    - Essbase

These upgrades are outside the scope of this chapter as they are also quite involved, so please refer to the Oracle documentation at: http://docs.oracle.com/middleware/1221/core/BIMIG/

Regression testing

Unlike other IT systems, which tend to have very daily procedural or coded steps, business intelligence systems have an inherent complexity due to the query engines that form a large part of the system. OBIEE is no different, and with an upgrade like this, it is vital that we should test the system before releasing it live to our business users. In addition to the extra validation rules in the consistency check, there are changes to the query engine that can subtly alter queries that have been modeled identically in both 11g and 12c. Also, due to the upgrade and changed functionality in the Web Catalog, upgraded reports may show changed behavior. This can range from missing labels to reporting aggregates, producing results different from those previously expected.

The basic stages of a full regression test are described in the following sections.

Unit testing

Once the upgrade has been completed as mentioned, a global consistency check should be run on the RPD and, if any errors occur, they should be noted and solved. Individual reports should be sanity checked by the technical team to ensure that results are being presented and that there are no other errors, such as, database connectivity or server errors, discrepancies in results, and visualization errors.

The behavior of customizations, such as the performance of any custom JavaScript, should also be checked. This will enable you to decide if any report actually needs to be completely rebuilt.

If you have updated the scheduler, then **agents** should be run to check for errors.

Full regression testing

A test team should be used to see whether the datasets being generated by reports are the same as before the upgrade.

As mentioned, the security model has changed in 12c. Tests should also check security rules and visibility. This will involve logging into dashboards/reports with different users and checking if the appropriate object and/or data is being displayed for that user and user group. This is even more important if you have decided to make radical changes to your security model in order to better utilize the changes to security functionality and capability that arrive with 12c.

User acceptance testing

The final stage of testing will be User Acceptance testing by the end business users, to ensure that they are happy that the system is fit for purpose and in line with the requirements for the previous implementation. This will also include the testing of agents and ad hoc answers' requests.

If the project is well run, the scripts for all of these tests should be available from the last iterative implementation in the project's life cycle. If not, we cannot stress enough how important it is to create a robust set of scripts that have been created in conjunction with the business and end users.

At each stage of testing, errors should be tracked and dealt with by a developer.

To aid a robust test cycle, you may wish to do further research into third-party test-automation tools such as HP LoadRunner or the open-source Selenium.

A review - what I should now know!

In addition to understanding how to utilize the Upgrade Assistant in order to migrate some of the core components to 12c, you should also have an understanding of the following issues before you embark on an upgrade of your current implementation:

- Understand the original 11g architecture and plan how you will migrate across. This is especially important if the current implementation is in a clustered environment or has a lot of customization.
- Understand and plan for the new skillsets required when implementing and supporting 12c. For example, WebLogic is a new middleware component in 12c that was not previously part of the product set.
- It may be necessary to create a proof of concept, and/or, at the very least, carry out a dry run. This will give you an opportunity to perform a consistency check for the upgraded RPD. If this highlights new issues in the RPD and Web Catalog, a better understanding of how much time/resources is needed to x these will be reached.
- Agree acceptance criteria with the business and with management.
- Document the full upgrade with a list and instructions on migrating customizations.

- Document and implement a comprehensive testing strategy. This will incorporate everything, from testing individual reports to checking security rules and privileges.
- Provide training and manage expectations for end users. Both the look and feel, and functionality, are radically different in 12c. Users, especially power users, will need training on the new features.
- Work out a pathway on how to utilize the new features and capabilities of 12c.

Summary

As we have demonstrated in this chapter, the actual upgrade process using the Oracle-provided Migration Tool is very simple. However, around this, there are many other issues that we have touched upon, and these issues need to be looked at if an upgrade is to be successful. These include regression testing and exploring changes to the overall system, such as in security.

Ultimately, the message is, *Plan, Plan, Plan!* The added value that a competent developer can add to this process is a comprehensive understanding of the scope of the upgrade process and the need for business involvement, as well as an implicit comfort with the technical detail.

Index

*

*Nix
  Oracle BI 12c, installing 466

7

7-zip
  URL 39, 510

A

Action Framework 15, 335
Action Link 349
Actionable Intelligence 84
Actions
  about 349
  conditionality, adding 356, 357
  Invoke Actions 358
  navigation 349, 350, 351, 352
  parameter, passing 353, 354, 355
  reference link 359
  web, navigation 353, 354, 355
administration area
  about 86
  briefing books 86
  Visual Analyzer 87
Administration Server 23
Administration
  about 92, 93, 94, 95
  Catalog 98
  catalog objects, securing 103
  catalog, deploying 103
  file management 101
  hidden items 100, 101
  Issue SQL 97
  maintenance 97
  multiple personal dashboards 104, 105
  object, copying 102, 103

permission, inheriting 105
  Session Management 96
  troubleshooting 97
  XML files 101
AdminServer 136
Adventureworks 186
Agents
  about 336
  creating 338, 342, 344, 345, 346, 348
  mail server, setting up 336, 338
answers 83
Apache Directory Service 336
Apache Directory Studio
  URL 169
Application Administration Tools 122
Application Development Framework (ADF) 27
Application Integration Architecture (AIA) 12
Application Programming Interface (API) 28, 122
Application Roles
  about 25, 156
  assigning 159, 160, 161, 162
  creating 159, 160, 161, 162
  managing by 25
  verifying 373, 374
  verifying, for data source privileges 377
associations 155, 156
Audit Framework
  connecting to 403
audit log file
  viewing 404
Audit Policy
  Audit Framework, connecting to 403
  audit log file, viewing 404
  enabling, in Fusion Middleware Control Enterprise Manager 403
  timeout issues 405

B

balanced scorecard 85
BI Cloud Service (BICS) 142
BI Foundation
  versus BI Publisher 365, 366
BI Migration Script
  about 533
  bundle, importing via 538
BI Publisher (BIP)
  about 361
  administration 368, 372
  administration management 372
  Administration page, accessing 373
  API 406
  application role, verifying for data source privileges 377
  application roles, verifying 373, 374
  auditing 401
  benefits 363, 364, 365
  configuration files, modifying 401, 402
  configuration, for default setting 369
  data model, creating 381
  data model, setting up 379
  data set display names, adjusting 387, 388
  data source JDBC connection, creating 374, 375
  enhancements 366
  features 366
  file (XLS) data source, creating 376, 377, 378, 379
  list of values, creating 391, 392
  monitoring 401
  parameter, connecting to list of values 392, 393
  parameter, creating 388, 390
  Presentation Catalog folder, creating 380
  report, creating Layout Editor used 396, 398, 399, 400
  sample data, obtaining 393, 394, 395
  Scheduler 406
  SQL query data set, creating 384, 385, 386, 387
  versus BI Foundation 365, 366
  XML Publisher 363
BI server data sources
  BI Publisher, API 406
  BI Publisher, scheduler 406
  connecting to 405
  high availability 406
BI Server Repository
  configuration, updating 416
  reference link 254
  setting up 411
BI Tools 36, 141
branding 506
bundle
  contents 534, 535
  export bundle, creating 534
  export bundle, generating 533
  importing 535
  importing, via BI Migration Script 538
  importing, via Configuration Assistant 535, 537
Business Intelligence Application Archive (BAR) file
  about 142, 535
  default files, searching 143
  importing 146, 147, 148
  RPD, downloading 148, 149
  RPD, importing 148
  RPD, uploading 149, 150
  Snapshot Service Instance artifacts, exporting 143, 144
business layer
  about 198
  business model, creating 199, 200
  dimension hierarchies 211, 212, 213
  elements 214, 215, 216
  logical columns 203, 204, 206
  logical joins 207, 208, 210
  logical tables sources 203
  logical tables, creating 200, 201, 202
business model
  about 199
  creating 199, 200
Business Process Execution Language (BPEL) 15

C

call interface 183
catalog
  about 89, 98
  Presentation Catalog 99, 100
certifications matrix
  about 30
  references 30

client software
  installing 108, 109
  testing 115, 117, 118
closed-loop 335
cluster 125, 126
clustering
  about 32
  Oracle BI Server Cluster Controller 33
  vertical, versus horizontal 33
Command Line Interfaces (CLI) 141, 151
Compound Layout 308
compression
  enabling, on web servers 470
  setting up, for NGINX HTTP server 471, 472, 473
Configuration Assistant
  bundle, importing via 535, 537
configuration files
  modifying 401, 402
Configuration tab, Enterprise Manager Fusion Middleware Control
  General tab 139
  Mail tab 139
  Performance tab 139
  Presentation tab 139
Consistency Check Manager 194
Credential Store Framework 16, 26
cubes 502
custom analysis
  creating 258, 260, 262, 263, 265, 266, 267
custom Dashboard
  creating 269, 270
custom database
  design summary 494
  designing 486
  goals 492, 493, 494
  objectives 487
  rules 488
custom look and feel
  alternative method, for deploying 523, 524, 525
  code, modifying 513, 514, 515, 516, 517, 518, 519, 520, 521
  creating 509, 510, 511
  custom messages 528
  custom style, creating 511

style, updating 522, 523
custom ports 465
custom style
  creating 511
  updating 522, 523

D

dashboards 84
data federation
  about 239
  horizontal federation 240
  vertical federation 240
data fragmentation
  about 239, 240
  content-based fragmentation, scenario 241, 242, 243, 244, 245, 246
data model
  about 367
  building 369
  creating 381
  data source connection, adding 370
  JNDI data source 371, 372
  setting up 379
data set
  display names, adjusting 387, 388
data source connection
  adding 370
Data Source Name (DSN) 111
Data Sources
  about 127, 128, 129, 180
  JDBC connection, creating 374, 375
Data Volume 486
Database Administrator (DBA) 65
database
  connection, configuring 114
DefaultAuthenticator 130
Delivering Content
  URL 360
Delivery Content tab, attributes
  content 342
  delivery 343
  false condition 343
  format 343
  subject 342
Diagnostics tab, Enterprise Manager Fusion

    Middleware Control
        Log Configuration 140
        Log Messages 140
dimensional modeling 484
directory folder structure
    about 35
    BI_CONFIG_HOME directory 36
    configuration files 37, 38
    DOMAIN_HOME (BI_DOMAIN) directory 36
    log files/diagnostics 37
    ORACLE_BASE directory 36
    ORACLE_HOME directory 36
Domain Structure 123
Dynamic HyperText Markup Language (DHTML) 396

E

Enterprise Application aRchive (EAR) file 405, 510, 514
Enterprise Deployment Guide (EDG)
    about 34, 463
    URL 463
Enterprise Java Beans (EJB) 21
Enterprise Management (EM) 70
Enterprise Manager (EM) 23, 122, 151
Enterprise Manager Fusion Middleware Control
    about 23, 136
    Availability tab 138
    BI Foundation Domain Dashboard 137, 138
    Configuration tab 139
    Diagnostics tab 140
    Overview tab 138
    security 140
Enterprise Performance Management (EPM) 476
Entity Relational (ER) database 484
event polling
    URL 432
Exadata 502
Exadata Database machine
    Exadata Storage, using 428
Execution Context ID (ECID) 154
Explain Plans 491
Expression Builder 229, 230
Extract, Transform, and Load (ETL) 489, 502

F

failover
    about 34
    planning 462
features, BI Publisher (BIP)
    BI 12c, user interface improved 366
    data model 367
    documents, delivering to cloud 366
    encryption 366
    layout 367
    location 367
    properties 368
    report design 367
    report design, components 367
    security 366
    terminology 367
    translations 368
file (XLS) data source
    creating 377, 378, 379
Filter, on RCOUNT(1)
    calculated rows 329
    NTile 329
    TopN 329
filters 282
FMW Security Import/Export utility 165
FMW Security
    migrating, to other environment 163
folder structure, OBIEE
    bi 77
    bifoundation 77
    reference variables 78
    user_projects 77
full application method 510
Fusion Control 23
Fusion Middleware Control (Fusion Control) 136
Fusion Middleware Control Enterprise Manager
    Audit Policy, enabling 403

G

Global Level Functions 383
Graphical User Interface (GUI) 21, 122
Gross Product Profit 228

H

help 87
hierarchies 503
high availability (HA)
  about 34, 406, 462
  URL 433, 463
highly formatted documents 361
hints 502
hMailServer 336
home screen 88
HTTP proxy
  configuring, with NGINX web server 468
Hyperion Financial Management (HFM) 17

I

iBot 336
Identity Store 16, 26
Implicit Fact 224, 226
indexes 502
initialization block 246, 247, 248, 249, 250, 253
installation media
  about 60, 77
  BI application, configuring 69, 70, 72, 73, 74, 76
  BI Server schema database, configuring 65, 67, 68, 69
  BI Server software, installing 60, 61, 63
  folder structure 77
interactive reporting 364
Internet Explorer (IE) 41
Internet Information Services (IIS) 467
InternetSales fact 236
Invoke Actions 358
IP address
  using 126, 127

J

Java components
  Action Service 15
  Administrative Components 15
  Oracle BI Office 15
  Oracle BI Presentation Service plugin 16
  Oracle BI Publisher 16
  Security Services 16
  SOA Web Service 15

Visual Analyzer 15
Java Development Kit (JDK)
  about 41
  installing 46
Java Management Extensions Managed Beans (JMX MBeans) 15
Java Naming and Directory Interface (JNDI) 372
Java Platform Enterprise Edition (Java EE) 19
Java Virtual Machine (JVM) 404
JavaHost processes 17
JDBC connections 127, 128, 129
JNDI data source 371, 372
JXplorer
  about 132
  URL 169

K

Key Performance Indicators (KPIs) 85
Kimball's dimensional modeling
  URL 484

L

Layout Editor
  about 396
  used, for creating BI Publisher report 396, 398, 399, 400
LDAP Configuration
  URL 169
Lifecycle Management (LCM)
  about 141, 142
  artifacts, deploying 143
  artifacts, migrating 143
  backing up 143
  BAR file 142
  logs, checking 154, 155
  Oracle BI 12c, patching 153
  Oracle BI 12c, upgrading 153
  System Components, starting 151
  System Components, stopping 151
Lightweight Directory Access Protocol (LDAP)
  server 24
list of values
  about 391
  creating 391, 392
  parameter, connecting to 392, 393

Load Speed 486
Log Viewer 140
logical columns
  about 203, 204, 206
  calculations 226, 227, 228
logical join 208
logical table source (LTS) 203, 231, 430
logical table
  about 200
  creating 200, 201, 202
Loopback Adapter
  URL 45

M

machines
  using 126, 127
Managed Servers 20, 23
management tools 122
Map mview 86
MapViewer 86
merges
  about 436
  advantages 445
  disadvantages 445
  multiuser development 441
  online development 441, 442, 443, 444
  three-way merge 437, 438, 439, 440
  two-way merger 440, 441
messages 509
metadata layer 107
metadata schemas
  database, creating 51, 52
  installing 51
  schemas, installing 53, 55, 56
  user, creating 51, 52
Metadata Services (MDS) 13
Microsoft Active Directory (MSAD) 24, 130
Microsoft Internet Explorer (MSIE) 467
multiple developers
  issues 435, 436
multiple skins
  creating, in environment 506
  in environment 507
multiple styles
  in environment 506, 507

modifying 507, 508
Multiuser Development Environment (MUDE)
  about 28, 29, 30, 446, 447, 448, 450, 452, 453, 454, 456, 457
  advantages 457
  disadvantages 457

N

navigate type 358
New
  about 89, 90
  Help 91
  Recent 90
NGINX Beginners Guide
  URL 477
NGINX HTTP server
  compression, setting up 471, 472, 473
NGINX Proxy Configuration
  URL 477
NGINX web server
  HTTP proxy, configuring 468
Node Manager 22, 23, 152
Non-Sucking Service Manager (NSSM) 476
normalization
  references 483
NSSM Windows Services
  URL 477

O

Object Orient Programming (OOP) 380
office integration 87
Online Transaction Processing (OLTP) 492
Operating System (OS) 151
Operational Data Store (ODS) 365, 483
options, analysis building
  about 272, 276, 278, 279, 280, 281, 282, 283, 284, 316
  Catalog 273
  column properties 275
  Columns 273
  columns, displaying 314, 315
  columns, hiding 314, 315
  conditional display 315, 317, 318, 319, 320, 321, 322, 323
  Dashboards, using 324

data, calculating 324, 325, 326, 327, 328, 329, 331, 332
edit formula 274
Filters 273
Graphs 290, 292, 293
Master Detail, linking 321
Menu Bar 272
Narratives 295, 296
Performance Tiles 296, 297, 300
Pivot Tables 293, 294
Prompt, examining 301, 302, 303, 304, 305, 306, 307
Prompts 301
Recap 300, 301, 321
results 308, 309, 310, 311, 312, 314
saved columns 331
Sort 274
Subject Areas 273
Tables 285, 286, 288, 290
Views 284, 285

Oracle BI 11g
  .jar file, generating 533
  bundle contents 534, 535
  bundles, importing 535
  catalog groups, migrating manually 540
  export bundle, creating 534
  files, checking 532
  Oracle BI 12c architecture, terminology differences 11
  system, checking 532

Oracle BI 12c architecture
  about 9, 10, 11
  BI System Components 10
  components 14
  connectivity, ensuring 539
  database repository 13
  installation 362, 363
  Java components 10, 15
  Oracle BI Domain 10
  Oracle BI filesystem 10
  Oracle BI relational repository 10
  reference link 42
  references 38
  Service Instance 10
  System Components 16

  terminology differences, from Oracle BI 11g 11
  WebLogic Server 10

Oracle BI Delivers 139

Oracle BI Metadata Repository (RPD)
  about 13
  business layer 172, 173
  consistency check 539
  physical layer 172
  prerequisites 172
  presentation layer 173

Oracle BI Office 15

Oracle BI Publisher system management 167

Oracle BI SampleApp (OBIEE 12c)
  URL 169

Oracle BI Scheduler 17

Oracle BI Security
  URL 169

Oracle BI, automating
  about 473, 474
  ancillary application integration awareness 476
  Windows Services, scripting 474, 475

Oracle Business Intelligence (Oracle BI)
  about 9
  URL 540

Oracle Business Intelligence Enterprise Edition (OBIEE)
  about 41, 479
  installation media 42, 43, 44
  issues 57
  reference link 458
  system requisites 45

Oracle Client (OCI) 115

Oracle Enterprise Management (EPM) 26

Oracle Exadata Storage and Database machine 427

Oracle Fusion Middleware (FMW) 9, 12

ORACLE HOME 11

Oracle HTTP Server (OHS) 467

Oracle Internet Directory (OID) 24

Oracle Platform Security Services (OPSS) 24, 163, 165

Oracle Process Management and Notification Server (OPMN) 11

Oracle Real-Time Decisions (RTD) 15

Oracle Technology Network (OTN)

URL 38

P

parameter
  connecting, to list of values 392, 393
  creating 388, 390
parentless three-way merge 441
patching
  about 153
  URL 153
Performance Data 488, 502
Performance Management 85
Physical catalog 186
physical column
  calculation 231, 232, 233
Physical Diagram 191
physical join 208
physical layer, objects
  Connection Pools 183, 184, 185
  consistency check 195, 196
  database object 180, 181, 182
  naming conventions 196, 197
  physical catalog 186
  physical join 191, 192, 193, 194
  physical tables 186, 187
  schemas 186
  table aliases 196, 197
physical layer
  creating 173, 174, 175, 176, 177, 178, 179
  metadata, importing 174, 175, 176, 177, 178, 179
  objects 180
physical server
  failover, planning 462, 463
  high availability 462, 463
  silent installation 463
  used, for Oracle BI 12c execution 462
physical tables 186
Policy Store 27
poor performance, improving
  BI Server, using 430
  cache, setting up 432
  cache, using 431
  database design 429
  database, configuration 429
  domain, setting up 433
  Exadata Storage, using with Exadata Database machine 428
  hardware 427
  performance tips 431
  servers, adding 428
  web server, using 433
poor performance
  about 425, 426
  improving 426
port 80
  listening on 467
port management 465
Portable Document Format (PDF) 363
pre-configuration run-down
  shared storage 31, 32
Presentation Catalog
  about 81, 136
  folder, creating 380
presentation layer
  about 217, 218
  aliases 223, 224
  best practices 220, 222
  calculated measures 226
  Expression Builder 229, 230
  Implicit Fact 224, 226
  level-based measure 237, 238, 239
  logical column, calculations 226, 227, 228
  physical column, calculation 231, 232, 233
  time series, measures 233, 234, 235, 236
published report 363
Published Reporting 84

Q

quality assurance (QA) 462

R

rapid application development (RAD) 29
Read Access Memory (RAM) 27
Read Speed 486
regression testing
  about 541
  full regression testing 541
  unit testing 541
  user acceptance testing 542

relational model
  URL 483
reporting databases
  about 480, 481, 482, 483
  dimensional modeling 484, 485
  relational modeling 483
  theories 486
Repository Creation Utility (RCU) 13, 51, 53, 65, 80, 410
Representational State Transfer (REST) 122
Rich Text Format (RTF) 400
roles
  creating 155, 156
rules, custom database
  accuracy, analyzing 491
  aggregate 490, 491
  complete dimensions 488
  generic tables, building 489
  granularity 492
  large tables, partitioning 490
  prudent indexing 490
  statistics, managing 491
  usage, analyzing 491

S

Sample Application
  URL 466, 477
sample data
  obtaining 393, 394, 395
scaling out
  about 31
  clustering 32
  failover 34
  high-availability 34
  pre-configuration run-down 31
search tool 87
Secure Shell (SSH) 466
Security Assertion Markup Language (SAML) 2.0 24
Security Realm
  about 130, 131
  migration utility, using 165, 166, 167
Security Services 16
semi-structured form 479
server
  about 124, 125
  connection, configuring 111, 112, 113, 114
Service Instances in Oracle BI 12c
  URL 170
service-oriented architecture (SOA) 19
setup
  customizing 420
shortcuts
  creating 115
Siebel Email Marketing 85
Siebel Enterprise Marketing Suite 85
silent installation
  about 463
  URL 464
Simple Mail Transfer Protocol (SMTP) 139, 336
Single Enterprise 59
Single Sign-On (SSO) 140
Singleton Data Directory (SDD) 32, 36
Slowly Changing Dimensions 502
Snapshot Service Instance artifacts
  exporting, to BAR file 143, 144
SOA Web Service 15
Solid State Drive (SSD)
  about 45, 47
  URL, for system requisites 45
SQL query data set
  creating 384, 385, 386, 387
star schema model 485
Star Transformation 502
start command
  used, for configuring links 78, 79
stop command
  used, for configuring links 78, 79
Structured Query Language 502
styles and skins 509
subject areas 218, 219, 220
Subversion (SVN) 436
System Components
  about 16
  BI JavaHost 17
  BI Presentation Server 17
  BI Scheduler 17
  BI Server 16
  BI Server Cluster Controller 17
  Essbase 18

Oracle BI 12c, starting 152
Oracle BI 12c, stopping 151, 152
System Management API
  URL 169
system performance
  monitoring 167, 168
system requisites
  about 27
  certifications matrix 30
  client tools 28
  Multi-User Development Environment 28, 29, 30
  references 39

T

three-way merge 437, 438, 439, 440
time series
  AGO function 233
  measures 233, 234, 235, 236
  PERIODROLLING function 233
timeout issues 405
transactional database 480, 481, 482
two-way merger 440, 441
Type 2 Slowly Changing Dimension (SCD) 493

U

unstructured form 479
usage tracking
  about 409, 501
  additional data 421
  analyzing 418
  BI Server repository, setting up 411
  CACHE_IND_FLG 419
  COMPILE_TIME_SEC 418
  CUM_DB_TIME_SEC 418
  CUM_NUM_DB_ROW 418
  database tables, setting up 410
  END_DT 419
  END_HOUR_MIN 419
  END_TS 419
  ERROR_TEXT 419
  IMPERSONATOR_USER_NAME 419
  measures 418
  NUM_CACHE_HITS 418
  NUM_CACHE_INSERTED 418
  NUM_DB_QUERY 418

  PRESENTATION_NAME 419
  QUERY_BLOB 419
  QUERY_KEY 419
  QUERY_SRC_CD 419
  QUERY_TEXT 419
  REPOSITORY_NAME 419
  ROW_COUNT 418
  SAW_DASHBOARD 419
  SAW_DASHBOARD_PG 419
  SAW_SRC_PATH 419
  setting up 410
  START_DT 419
  START_HOUR_MIN 419
  START_TS 419
  SUBJECT_AREA_NAME 419
  SUCCESS_FLG 420
  TOTAL_TIME_SEC 418
  USER_NAME 419
user experience 366
users
  creating 155, 156

V

variables
  about 246, 247, 248, 249, 250, 253
  repository 246
  session 246
virtual machine (VM) 29, 41, 466
virtual server 462
Visual Analyzer (VA) 15
Visual SourceSafe (VSS) 436

W

warehouse
  creating 495
  designing 498
  maintaining 501
  match star schema 499
  monitoring 501
  populating 501
  source system assessment 495, 496, 497
  tables 498
  tournament star schema 499, 501
  tuning 501
Web Application Archive (WAR) file 510

Web Catalog 98, 136
WebLogic Administration Server 19
WebLogic Management Framework (WMF) 14, 151
WebLogic Management Framework
  URL 40
WebLogic Manager Server(s) 19
WebLogic Node Manager 19
WebLogic Scripting Tool (WLST)
  about 14, 21, 122
  reference link 135
  using 133, 134, 135
WebLogic Scripting Tool
  URL 169
WebLogic Server (WLS)
  about 19, 122
  Administration Server 21
  custom applications 132
  domain 20
  groups, creating 156, 157, 158
  installing 47, 50
  limitations 19, 20
  Managed Server 21, 22
  Node Manager 22, 23
  security 24, 25
  security, checking 540
  system tools, controlling 23, 24
  users, assigning to groups 158, 159
  users, creating 156, 157, 158
WebLogic Server Administration Control
  about 122
  accessing 123, 124
  checkpoint 123, 124
Windows Services
  about 474
  scripting 474, 475

X

XML Localization Interchange File Format (XLIFF) 368
XML Publisher (XMLP) 361

Printed by BoD˙in Norderstedt, Germany